JLA SYNDICATE RULES

Kurt Busiek Writer   **Ron Garney** Penciller and original series covers
Dan Green Inker   **David Baron** **Sno Cone** Colorists   **Jared K. Fletcher** Letterer
SUPERMAN created by Jerry Siegel and Joe Shuster   **BATMAN** created by Bob Kane   **WONDER WOMAN**
created by William Moulton Marston

Dan DiDio VP-Executive Editor Mike Carlin Editor-original series Michael Siglain Assistant Editor-original series Robert Greenberger Senior Editor-collected edition Robbin Brosterman Senior Art Director
Paul Levitz President & Publisher Georg Brewer VP-Design & DC Direct Creative Richard Bruning Senior VP-Creative Director Patrick Caldon Senior VP-Finance & Operations Chris Caramalis VP-Finance
Terri Cunningham VP-Managing Editor Stephanie Fierman Senior VP-Sales & Marketing Alison Gill VP-Manufacturing Rich Johnson VP-Book Trade Sales Hank Kanalz VP-General Manager, WildStorm
Lillian Laserson Senior VP & General Counsel Jim Lee Editorial Director-WildStorm David McKillips VP- Advertising & Custom Publishing John Nee VP-Business Development Gregory Noveck
Senior VP-Creative Affairs Cheryl Rubin Senior VP-Brand Management Jeff Trojan VP-Business Development, DC Direct Bob Wayne VP-Sales
JLA: SYNDICATE RULES. Published by DC Comics. Cover, introduction and compilation copyright © 2005 DC Comics. All Rights Reserved. Originally published in single magazine form as
JLA 107-114, JLA SECRET FILES 2004. Copyright © 2004, 2005 DC Comics. All Rights Reserved. All characters, their distinctive likenesses and related elements featured in this publication
are trademarks of DC Comics. The stories, characters and incidents featured in this publication are entirely fictional. DC Comics does not read or accept unsolicited submissions of
ideas, stories or artwork. DC Comics, 1700 Broadway, New York, NY 10019. A Warner Bros. Entertainment Company. Printed in Canada. First Printing. ISBN: 1-4012-0477-5.
Cover illustration by Ron Garney. Cover color by David Baron.

JLA
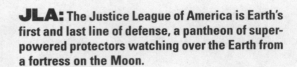

JLA: The Justice League of America is Earth's first and last line of defense, a pantheon of super-powered protectors watching over the Earth from a fortress on the Moon.

Superman: The last son of the doomed planet Krypton, Kal-El uses his incredible powers of flight, super-strength, and invulnerability to fight for truth and justice on his adopted planet, Earth. When not protecting the planet, he is *Daily Planet* reporter Clark Kent, married to fellow journalist Lois Lane.

Batman: Dedicated to ridding the world of crime since the brutal murder of his parents, billionaire Bruce Wayne dons the cape and cowl of the Dark Knight to battle evil from the shadows of Gotham City.

Wonder Woman: Born an Amazonian princess, Diana was chosen to serve as her people's ambassador of peace in the World of Man. Armed with the Lasso of Truth and indestructible bracelets, she directs her gods-given abilities of strength and speed toward the betterment of mankind.

The Flash: A member of the Teen Titans when he was known as Kid Flash, Wally West now takes the place of the fallen Flash, Barry Allen, as the JLA's current speedster.

Green Lantern: John Stewart has worn the power ring, symbol of the intergalactic Green Lantern Corps, during several tours of duty. Controlled by his will power, the ring makes his imagination manifest.

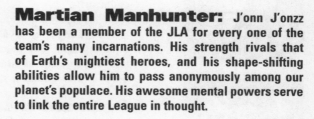

Martian Manhunter: J'onn J'onzz has been a member of the JLA for every one of the team's many incarnations. His strength rivals that of Earth's mightiest heroes, and his shape-shifting abilities allow him to pass anonymously among our planet's populace. His awesome mental powers serve to link the entire League in thought.

Plastic Man: The League's most versatile and creative member, the shape-changer called Plastic Man serves in the JLA with a dedication and fortitude that is in sharp contrast to his playful and easygoing demeanor.

Aquaman: A founding member of the Justice League, Arthur is the royal ruler of a kingdom that covers over two-thirds of the Earth's surface. His abilities to withstand the awesome pressure of the deep and to communicate with all the ocean's inhabitants help to make him the undersea world's greatest protector.

The Atom: One of the first heroes to join after the League's founding, Ray Palmer is a scientist who harnessed the properties of a white dwarf star. This led to the creation of unique size and weight controls that enable him to reduce his physical form to that of an atom, or even smaller.

Crime Syndicate of Amerika:

On the other side of a membrane separating the matter universe from its antimatter reflection exists an Earth where wrong is right and darkness eclipses the light of good. Five super-humans rule this wicked Amerika, whose Latin motto *Cui Bono* ("Who Profits?") epitomizes their lust for wealth and power. From the Panopticon, on the moon, they watch over their subjects, subjugating any threat to their superiority.

Johnny Quick:

Addicted to a speed-inducing drug, this man lives for the rush of velocity and endures an addiction more powerful than any other known on Earth.

Owlman:

Thomas Wayne Jr. witnessed his mother's death and blamed his father, Police Commissioner Thomas Wayne Sr., for the death of his brother, Bruce. Using drugs to enhance his cerebral cortex, he became the most brilliant criminal mastermind on the planet and opposed his father as Owlman.

Power Ring:

After encountering a monk named Volthoom, an American named Harrolds returned home from Tibet with an emerald ring of unimaginable power. The spirit of Volthoom now inhabits the ring, providing counsel.

Superwoman:

Star reporter for the *Daily Planet*, Lois Lane is also the sado-masochistic powerhouse of the team. She possesses great strength, a choking lariat and laser-vision. Lois tolerates Ultraman but her real passion is for Owlman.

Ultraman:

A deep space astronaut was lost when his space capsule entered hyperspace. Injured and near death, he was repaired by unknown forces but rebuilt as something stronger, faster, and more durable than any human being. Whatever he endured also left his mind twisted, cruel. He is dependent on a mineral known as anti-kryptonite to retain his abilities. He thinks he loves Superwoman and endures her infidelities with Owlman.

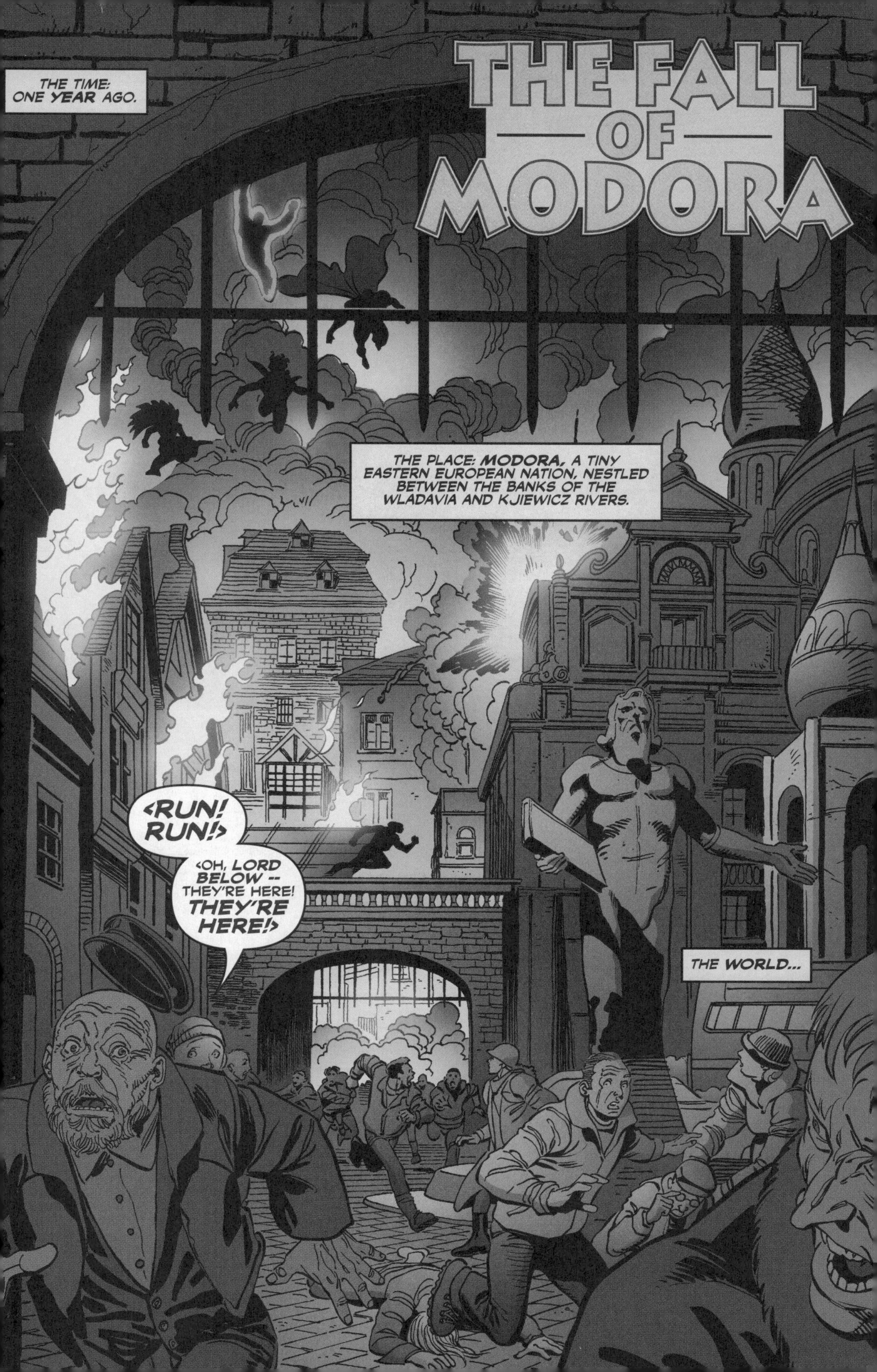
THE TIME: ONE YEAR AGO.
THE FALL OF MODORA
THE PLACE: MODORA, A TINY EASTERN EUROPEAN NATION, NESTLED BETWEEN THE BANKS OF THE WLADAVIA AND KJIEWICZ RIVERS.
<RUN! RUN!>
<OH, LORD BELOW -- THEY'RE HERE! THEY'RE HERE!>
THE WORLD...

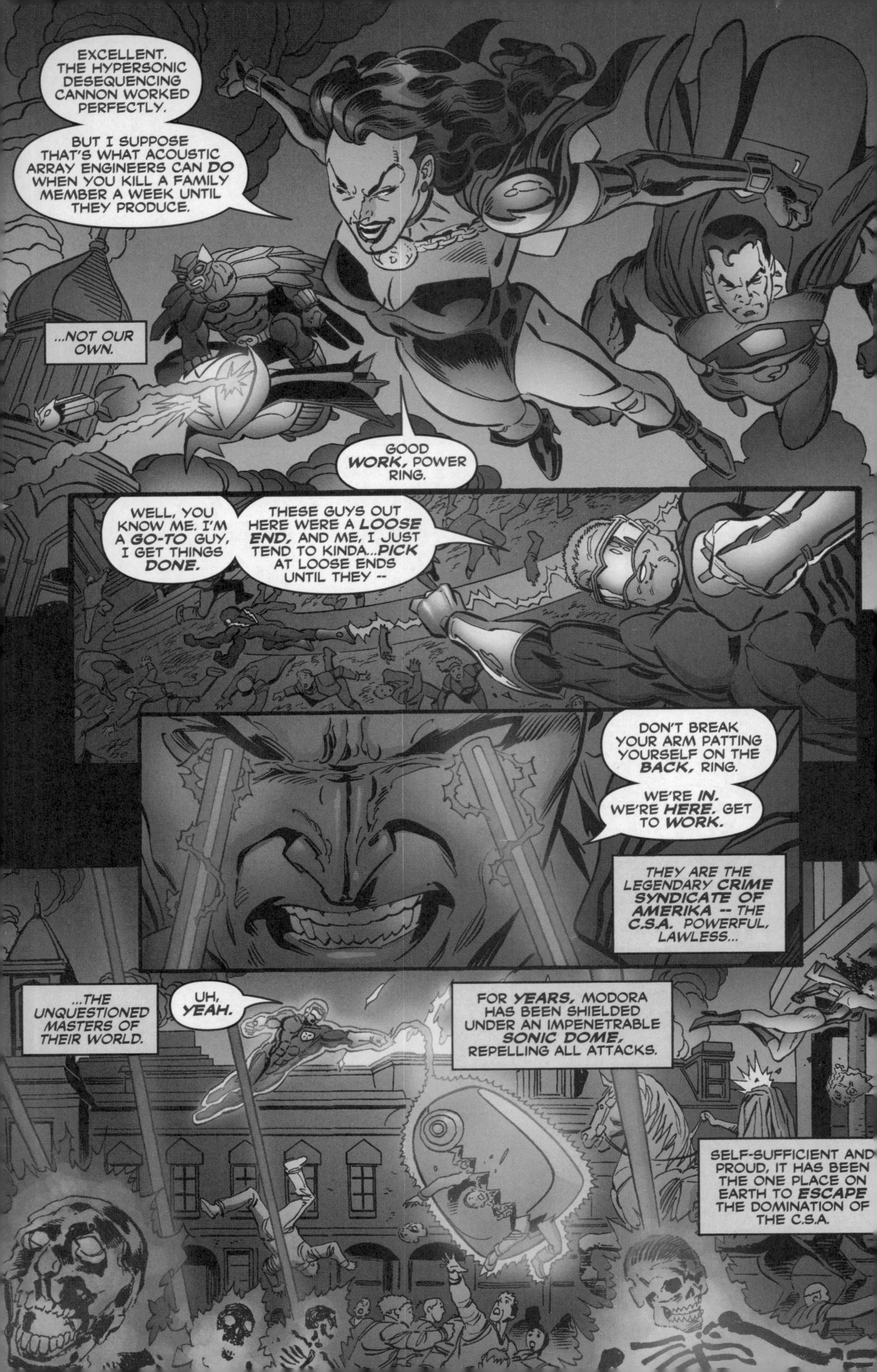
EXCELLENT. THE HYPERSONIC DESEQUENCING CANNON WORKED PERFECTLY.
BUT I SUPPOSE THAT'S WHAT ACOUSTIC ARRAY ENGINEERS CAN DO WHEN YOU KILL A FAMILY MEMBER A WEEK UNTIL THEY PRODUCE.
...NOT OUR OWN.
GOOD WORK, POWER RING.
WELL, YOU KNOW ME. I'M A GO-TO GUY, I GET THINGS DONE.
THESE GUYS OUT HERE WERE A LOOSE END, AND ME, I JUST TEND TO KINDA...PICK AT LOOSE ENDS UNTIL THEY --
DON'T BREAK YOUR ARM PATTING YOURSELF ON THE BACK, RING.
WE'RE IN. WE'RE HERE. GET TO WORK.
THEY ARE THE LEGENDARY CRIME SYNDICATE OF AMERIKA -- THE C.S.A. POWERFUL, LAWLESS...
...THE UNQUESTIONED MASTERS OF THEIR WORLD.
UH, YEAH.
FOR YEARS, MODORA HAS BEEN SHIELDED UNDER AN IMPENETRABLE SONIC DOME, REPELLING ALL ATTACKS.
SELF-SUFFICIENT AND PROUD, IT HAS BEEN THE ONE PLACE ON EARTH TO ESCAPE THE DOMINATION OF THE C.S.A.

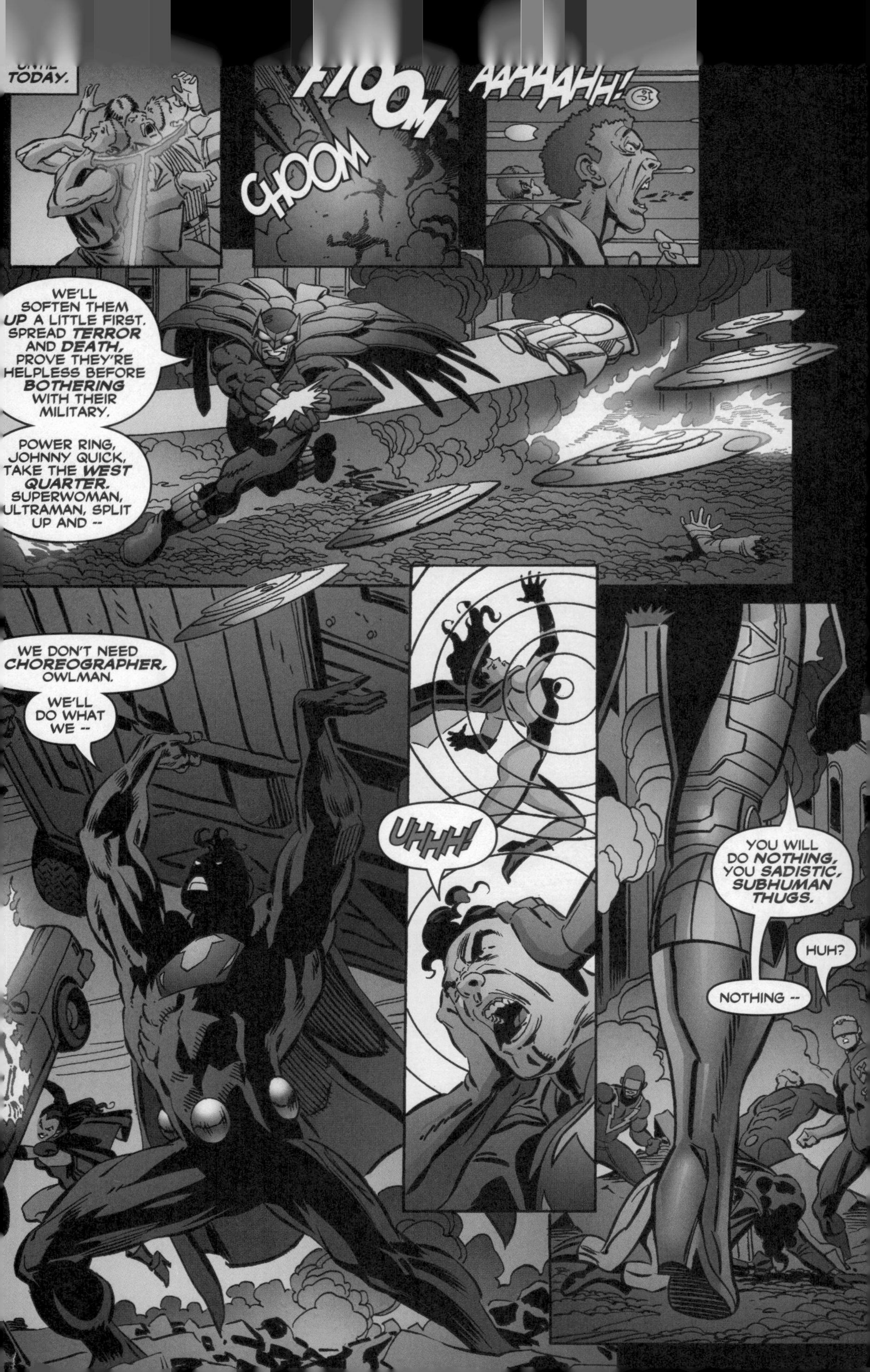

TODAY.
FTOOM
CHOOM
AAAAAHH!
WE'LL SOFTEN THEM UP A LITTLE FIRST. SPREAD TERROR AND DEATH, PROVE THEY'RE HELPLESS BEFORE BOTHERING WITH THEIR MILITARY.
POWER RING, JOHNNY QUICK, TAKE THE WEST QUARTER. SUPERWOMAN, ULTRAMAN, SPLIT UP AND --
WE DON'T NEED CHOREOGRAPHER, OWLMAN.
WE'LL DO WHAT WE --
UHHH!
YOU WILL DO NOTHING, YOU SADISTIC, SUBHUMAN THUGS.
HUH?
NOTHING --

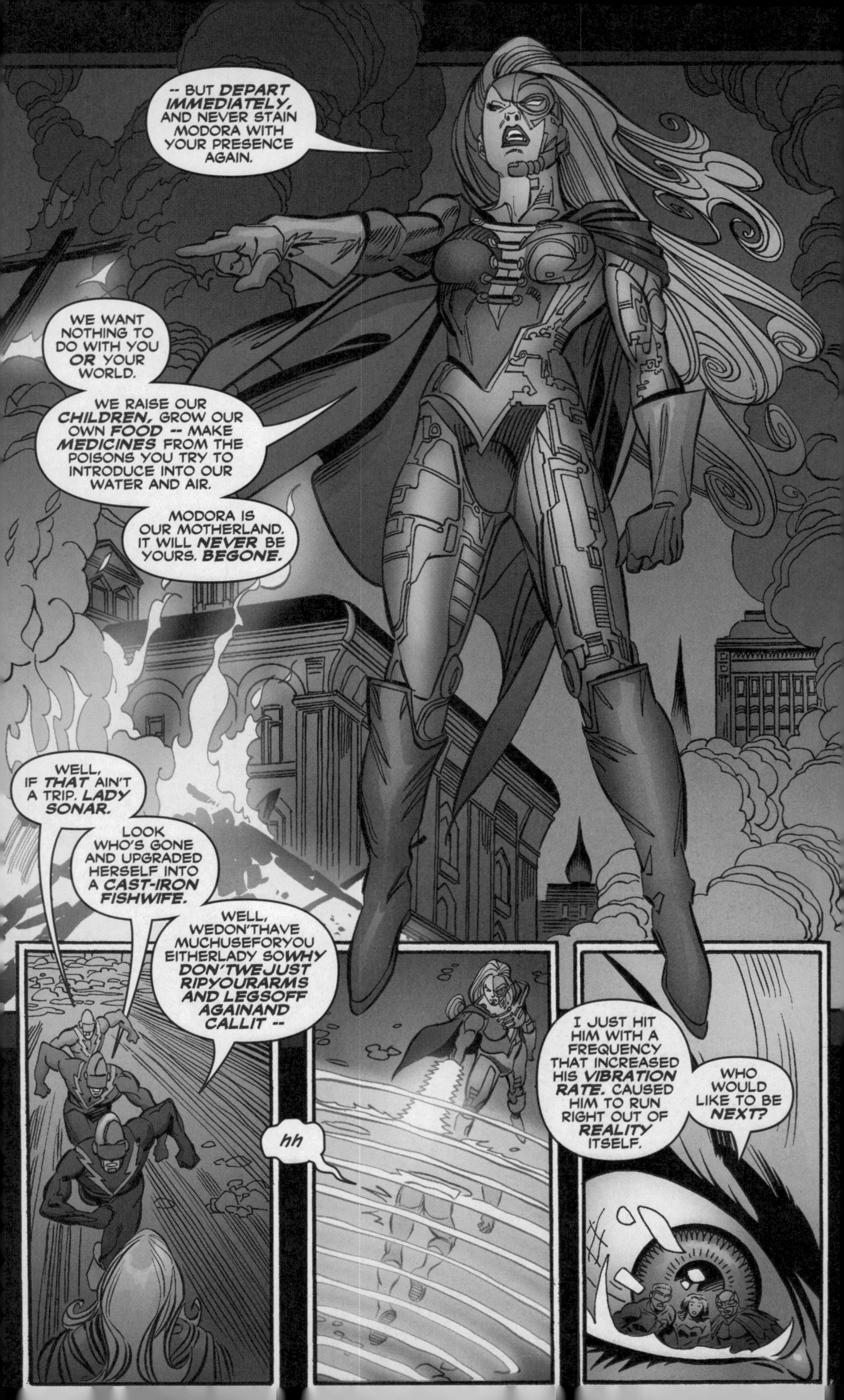
-- BUT DEPART IMMEDIATELY, AND NEVER STAIN MODORA WITH YOUR PRESENCE AGAIN.
WE WANT NOTHING TO DO WITH YOU OR YOUR WORLD.
WE RAISE OUR CHILDREN, GROW OUR OWN FOOD -- MAKE MEDICINES FROM THE POISONS YOU TRY TO INTRODUCE INTO OUR WATER AND AIR.
MODORA IS OUR MOTHERLAND. IT WILL NEVER BE YOURS. BEGONE.
WELL, IF THAT AIN'T A TRIP. LADY SONAR.
LOOK WHO'S GONE AND UPGRADED HERSELF INTO A CAST-IRON FISHWIFE.
WELL, WEDON'THAVE MUCHUSEFORYOU EITHERLADY SOWHY DON'TWEJUST RIPYOURARMS AND LEGSOFF AGAINAND CALLIT --
hh
I JUST HIT HIM WITH A FREQUENCY THAT INCREASED HIS VIBRATION RATE. CAUSED HIM TO RUN RIGHT OUT OF REALITY ITSELF.
WHO WOULD LIKE TO BE NEXT?

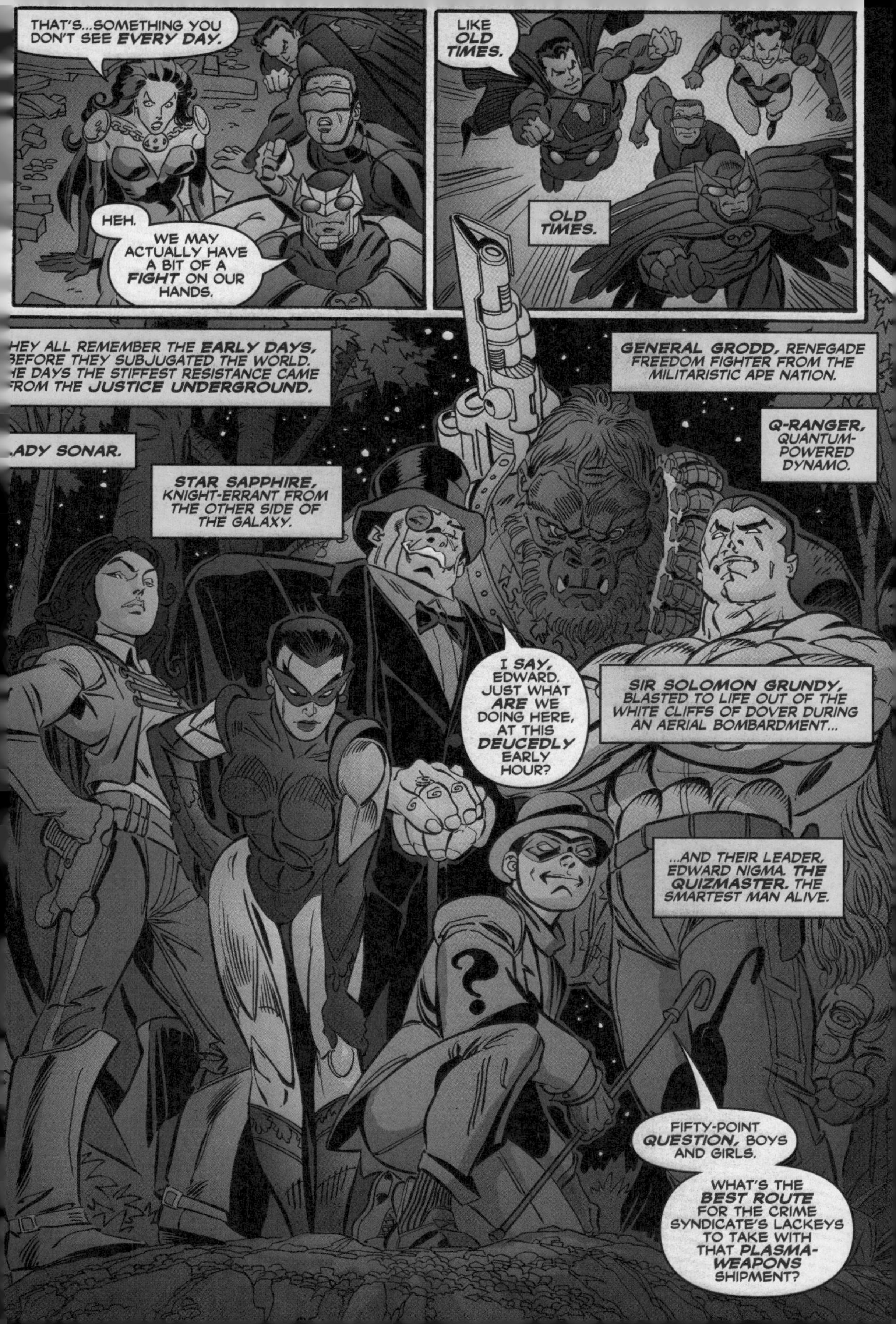
THAT'S...SOMETHING YOU DON'T SEE EVERY DAY.
HEH.
WE MAY ACTUALLY HAVE A BIT OF A FIGHT ON OUR HANDS.
LIKE OLD TIMES.
OLD TIMES.
HEY ALL REMEMBER THE EARLY DAYS, BEFORE THEY SUBJUGATED THE WORLD. HE DAYS THE STIFFEST RESISTANCE CAME FROM THE JUSTICE UNDERGROUND.
GENERAL GRODD, RENEGADE FREEDOM FIGHTER FROM THE MILITARISTIC APE NATION.
ADY SONAR.
Q-RANGER, QUANTUM-POWERED DYNAMO.
STAR SAPPHIRE, KNIGHT-ERRANT FROM THE OTHER SIDE OF THE GALAXY.
I SAY, EDWARD. JUST WHAT ARE WE DOING HERE, AT THIS DEUCEDLY EARLY HOUR?
SIR SOLOMON GRUNDY, BLASTED TO LIFE OUT OF THE WHITE CLIFFS OF DOVER DURING AN AERIAL BOMBARDMENT...
...AND THEIR LEADER, EDWARD NIGMA. THE QUIZMASTER. THE SMARTEST MAN ALIVE.
FIFTY-POINT QUESTION, BOYS AND GIRLS.
WHAT'S THE BEST ROUTE FOR THE CRIME SYNDICATE'S LACKEYS TO TAKE WITH THAT PLASMA-WEAPONS SHIPMENT?

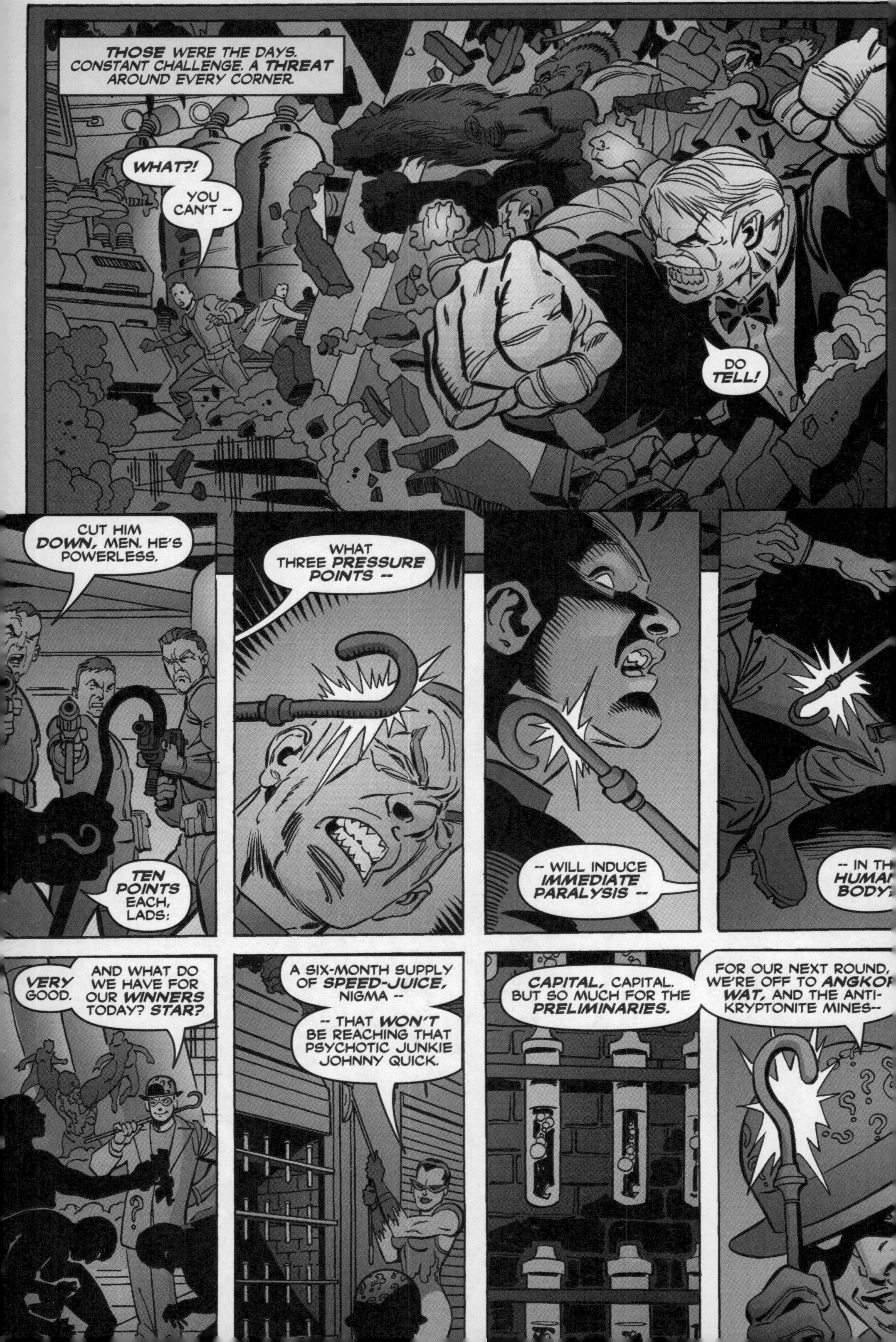
THOSE WERE THE DAYS. CONSTANT CHALLENGE. A THREAT AROUND EVERY CORNER.
WHAT?!
YOU CAN'T --
DO TELL!
CUT HIM DOWN, MEN. HE'S POWERLESS.
TEN POINTS EACH, LADS:
WHAT THREE PRESSURE POINTS --
-- WILL INDUCE IMMEDIATE PARALYSIS --
-- IN TH HUMAN BODY?
VERY GOOD.
AND WHAT DO WE HAVE FOR OUR WINNERS TODAY? STAR?
A SIX-MONTH SUPPLY OF SPEED-JUICE, NIGMA --
-- THAT WON'T BE REACHING THAT PSYCHOTIC JUNKIE JOHNNY QUICK.
CAPITAL, CAPITAL. BUT SO MUCH FOR THE PRELIMINARIES.
FOR OUR NEXT ROUND, WE'RE OFF TO ANGKOR WAT, AND THE ANTI-KRYPTONITE MINES--

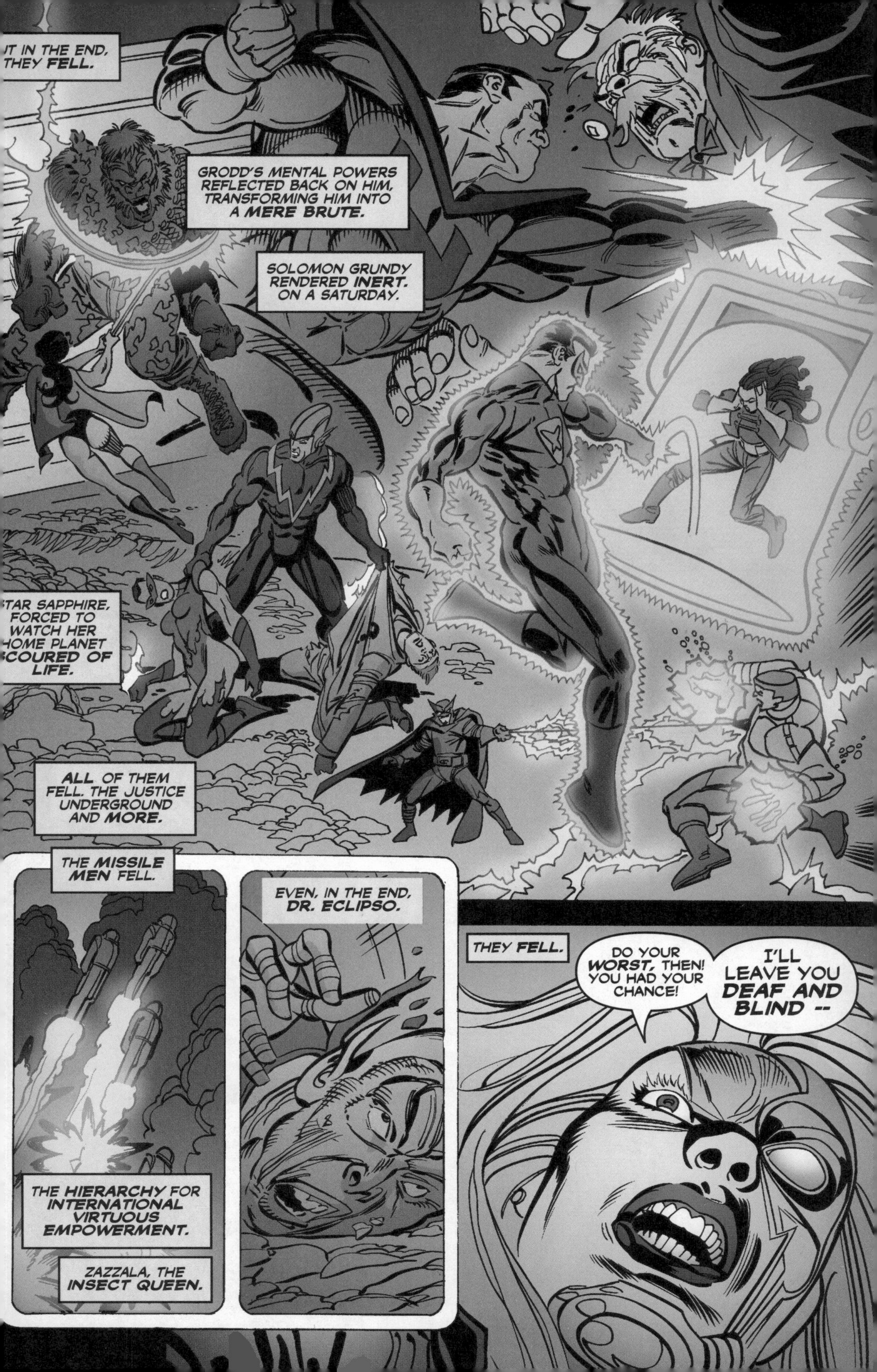

IT IN THE END, THEY FELL.
GRODD'S MENTAL POWERS REFLECTED BACK ON HIM, TRANSFORMING HIM INTO A MERE BRUTE.
SOLOMON GRUNDY RENDERED INERT. ON A SATURDAY.
STAR SAPPHIRE, FORCED TO WATCH HER HOME PLANET SCOURED OF LIFE.
ALL OF THEM FELL. THE JUSTICE UNDERGROUND AND MORE.
THE MISSILE MEN FELL.
THE HIERARCHY FOR INTERNATIONAL VIRTUOUS EMPOWERMENT.
ZAZZALA, THE INSECT QUEEN.
EVEN, IN THE END, DR. ECLIPSO.
THEY FELL.
DO YOUR WORST, THEN! YOU HAD YOUR CHANCE!
I'LL LEAVE YOU DEAF AND BLIND --

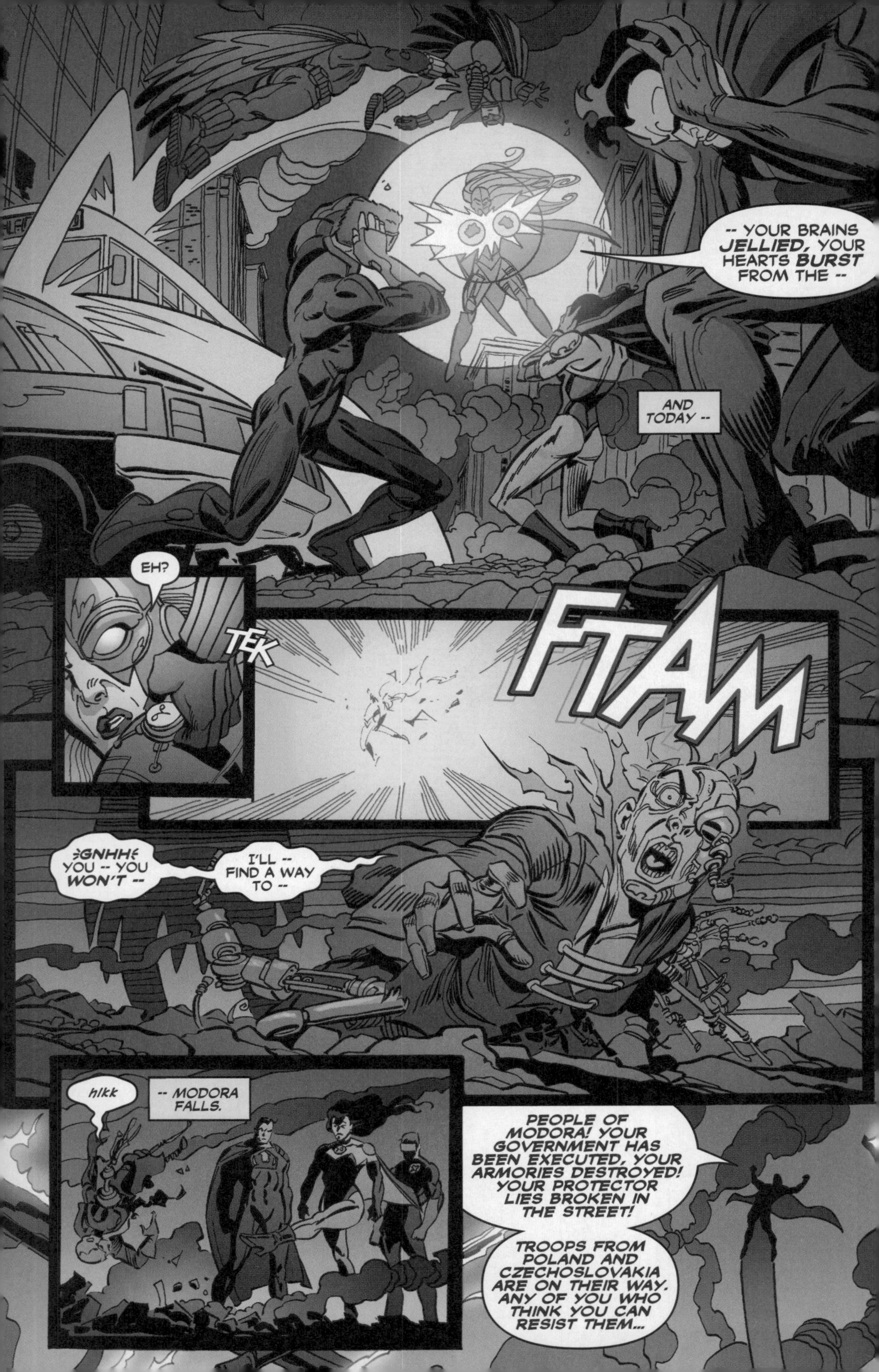
-- YOUR BRAINS JELLIED, YOUR HEARTS BURST FROM THE --
AND TODAY --
EH?
TEK
FTAM
ƷGNHHƸ YOU -- YOU WON'T --
I'LL -- FIND A WAY TO --
hlkk
-- MODORA FALLS.
PEOPLE OF MODORA! YOUR GOVERNMENT HAS BEEN EXECUTED, YOUR ARMORIES DESTROYED! YOUR PROTECTOR LIES BROKEN IN THE STREET!
TROOPS FROM POLAND AND CZECHOSLOVAKIA ARE ON THEIR WAY. ANY OF YOU WHO THINK YOU CAN RESIST THEM...

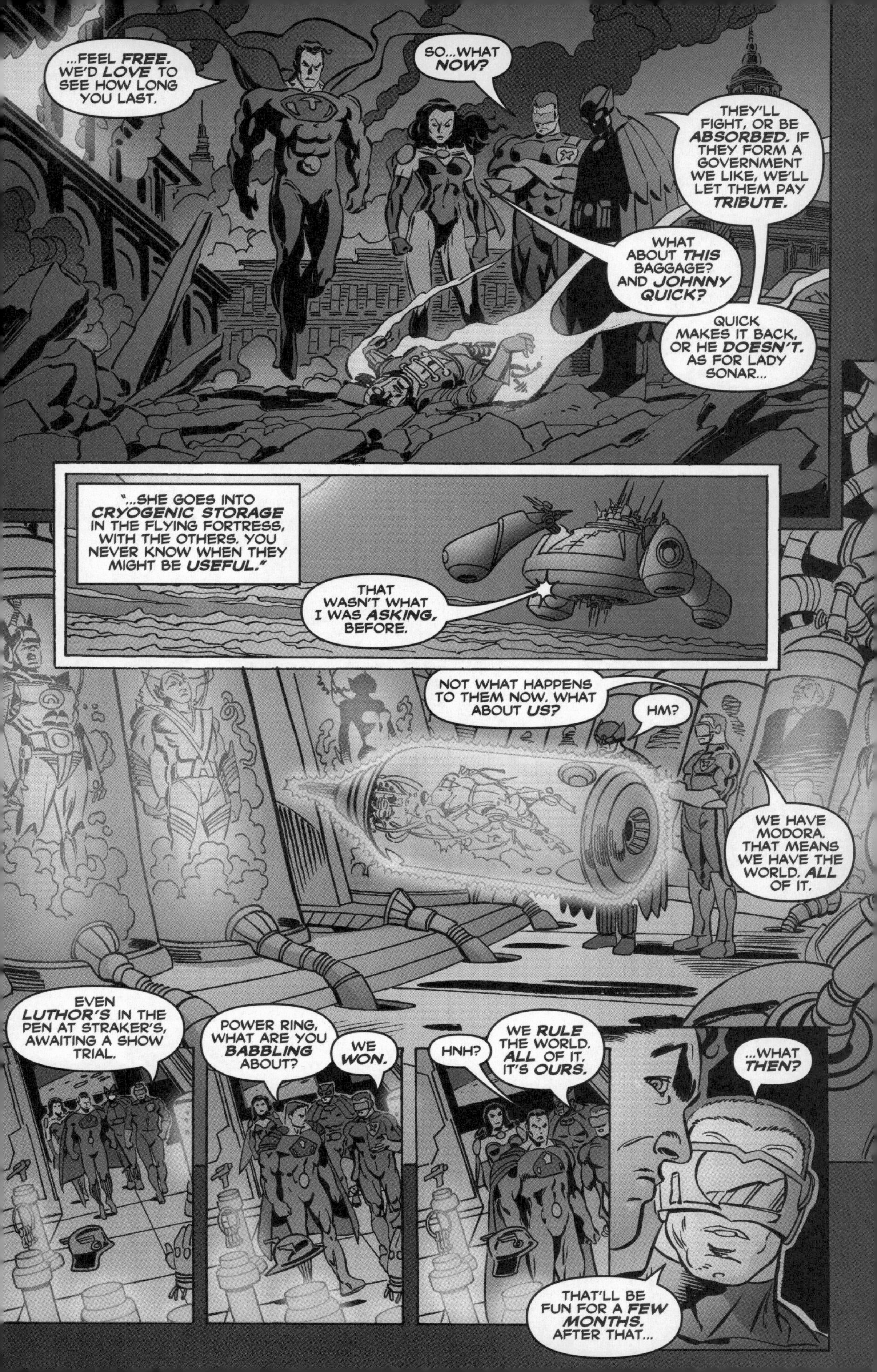
...FEEL FREE. WE'D LOVE TO SEE HOW LONG YOU LAST.
SO...WHAT NOW?
THEY'LL FIGHT, OR BE ABSORBED. IF THEY FORM A GOVERNMENT WE LIKE, WE'LL LET THEM PAY TRIBUTE.
WHAT ABOUT THIS BAGGAGE? AND JOHNNY QUICK?
QUICK MAKES IT BACK, OR HE DOESN'T. AS FOR LADY SONAR...
"...SHE GOES INTO CRYOGENIC STORAGE IN THE FLYING FORTRESS, WITH THE OTHERS. YOU NEVER KNOW WHEN THEY MIGHT BE USEFUL."
THAT WASN'T WHAT I WAS ASKING, BEFORE.
NOT WHAT HAPPENS TO THEM NOW. WHAT ABOUT US?
HM?
WE HAVE MODORA. THAT MEANS WE HAVE THE WORLD. ALL OF IT.
EVEN LUTHOR'S IN THE PEN AT STRAKER'S, AWAITING A SHOW TRIAL.
POWER RING, WHAT ARE YOU BABBLING ABOUT?
WE WON.
HNH?
WE RULE THE WORLD. ALL OF IT. IT'S OURS.
...WHAT THEN?
THAT'LL BE FUN FOR A FEW MONTHS. AFTER THAT...

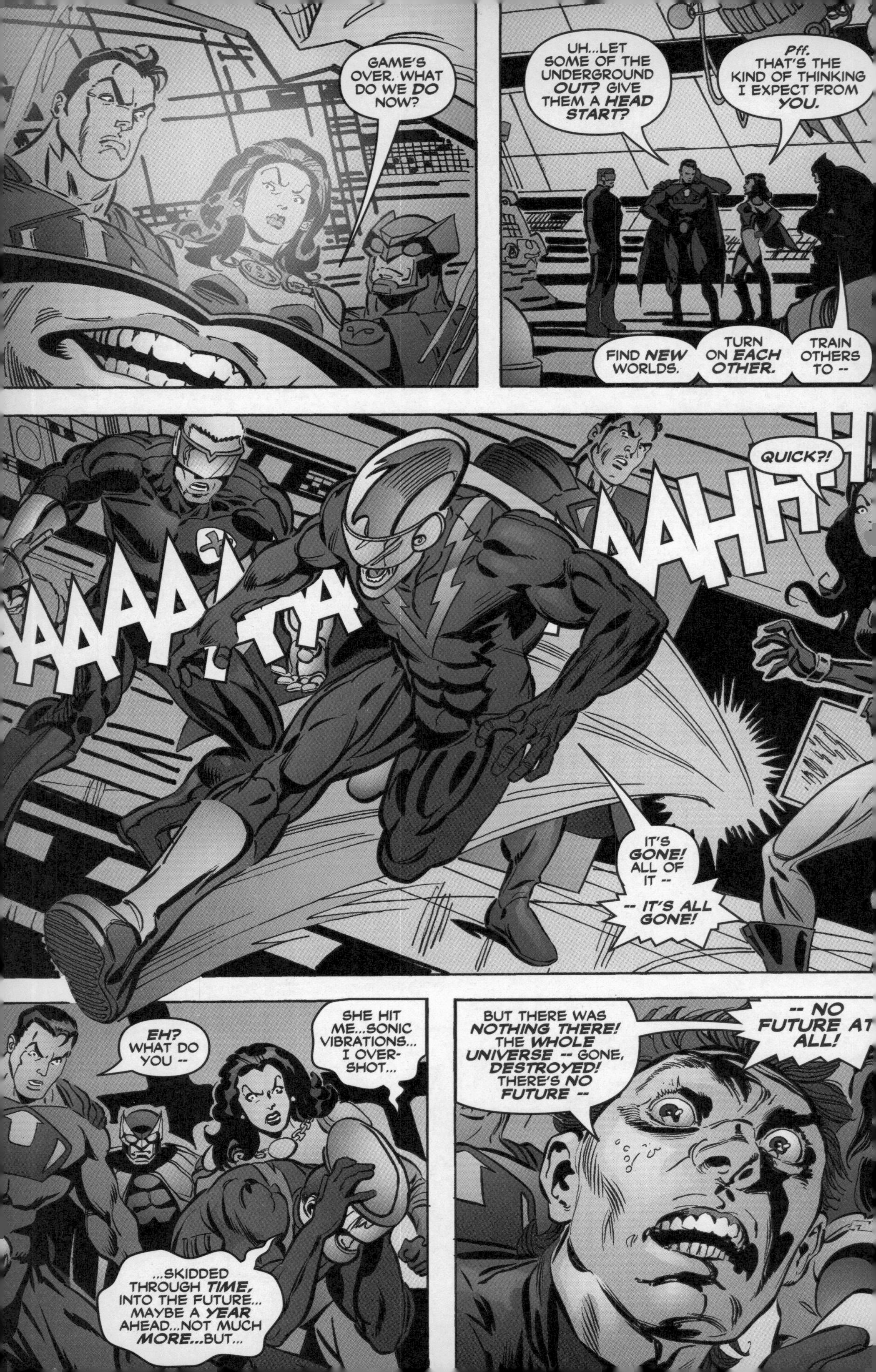

GAME'S OVER. WHAT DO WE *DO* NOW?
UH...LET SOME OF THE UNDERGROUND *OUT?* GIVE THEM A *HEAD START?*
Pff. THAT'S THE KIND OF THINKING I EXPECT FROM *YOU.*
FIND *NEW* WORLDS.
TURN ON *EACH OTHER.*
TRAIN OTHERS TO --
AAAAAAAAAHH!
QUICK?!
IT'S *GONE!* ALL OF IT --
-- *IT'S ALL GONE!*
EH? WHAT DO YOU --
SHE HIT ME...SONIC VIBRATIONS... I OVER-SHOT...
...SKIDDED THROUGH *TIME,* INTO THE FUTURE... MAYBE A *YEAR* AHEAD...NOT MUCH *MORE...*BUT...
BUT THERE WAS *NOTHING THERE!* THE *WHOLE UNIVERSE* -- GONE, *DESTROYED!* THERE'S *NO FUTURE* --
-- *NO FUTURE AT ALL!*

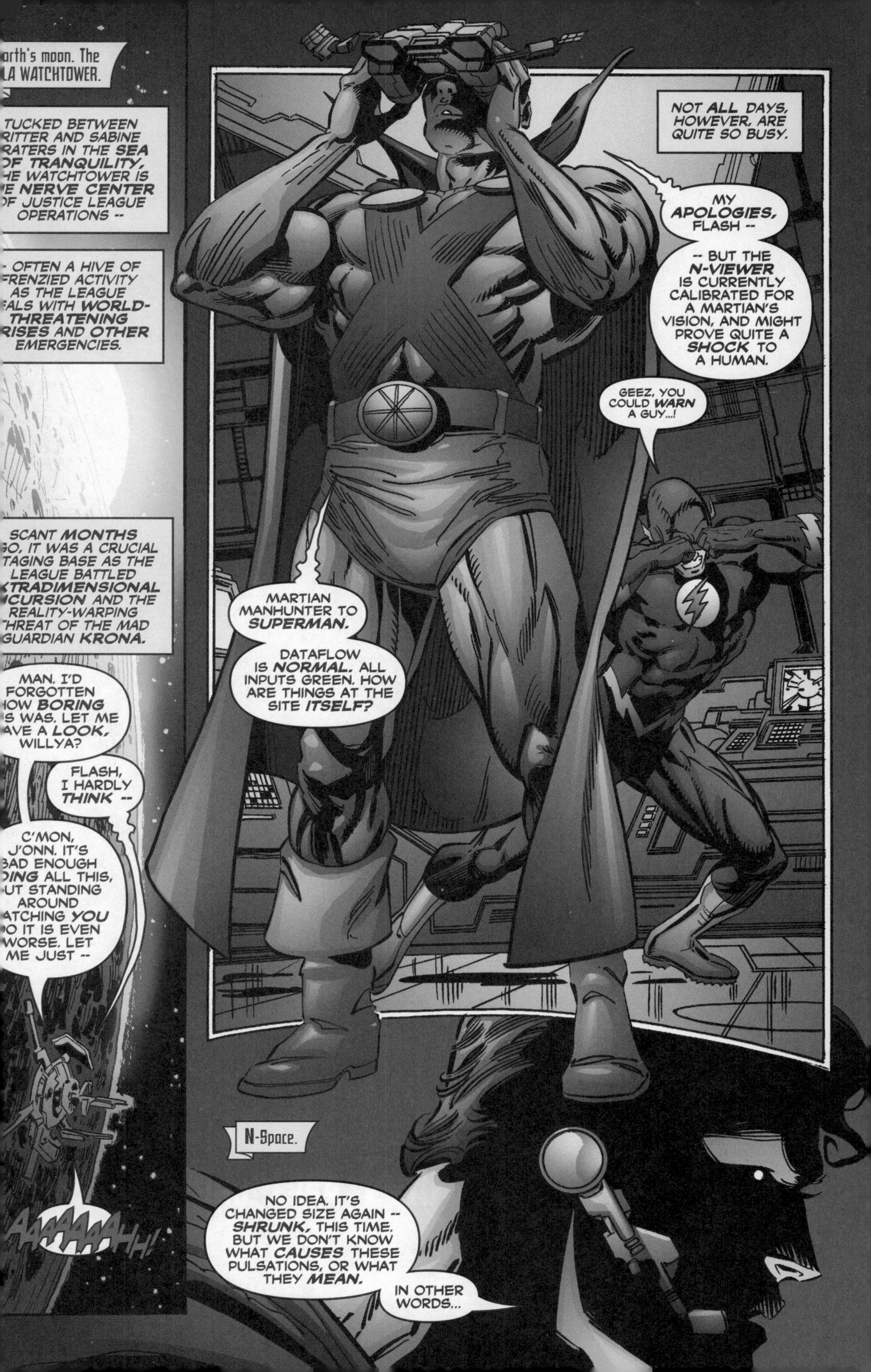

arth's moon. The
LA WATCHTOWER.
TUCKED BETWEEN RITTER AND SABINE RATERS IN THE SEA OF TRANQUILITY, HE WATCHTOWER IS E NERVE CENTER OF JUSTICE LEAGUE OPERATIONS --
-- OFTEN A HIVE OF FRENZIED ACTIVITY AS THE LEAGUE EALS WITH WORLD-THREATENING RISES AND OTHER EMERGENCIES.
NOT ALL DAYS, HOWEVER, ARE QUITE SO BUSY.
SCANT MONTHS GO, IT WAS A CRUCIAL TAGING BASE AS THE LEAGUE BATTLED XTRADIMENSIONAL CURSION AND THE REALITY-WARPING THREAT OF THE MAD GUARDIAN KRONA.
MARTIAN MANHUNTER TO SUPERMAN.
DATAFLOW IS NORMAL. ALL INPUTS GREEN. HOW ARE THINGS AT THE SITE ITSELF?
MAN. I'D FORGOTTEN HOW BORING IS WAS. LET ME AVE A LOOK, WILLYA?
FLASH, I HARDLY THINK --
C'MON, J'ONN. IT'S BAD ENOUGH OING ALL THIS, UT STANDING AROUND ATCHING YOU O IT IS EVEN WORSE. LET ME JUST --
AAAAAAAHH!
MY APOLOGIES, FLASH --
-- BUT THE N-VIEWER IS CURRENTLY CALIBRATED FOR A MARTIAN'S VISION, AND MIGHT PROVE QUITE A SHOCK TO A HUMAN.
GEEZ, YOU COULD WARN A GUY...!
N-Space.
NO IDEA. IT'S CHANGED SIZE AGAIN -- SHRUNK, THIS TIME. BUT WE DON'T KNOW WHAT CAUSES THESE PULSATIONS, OR WHAT THEY MEAN.
IN OTHER WORDS...

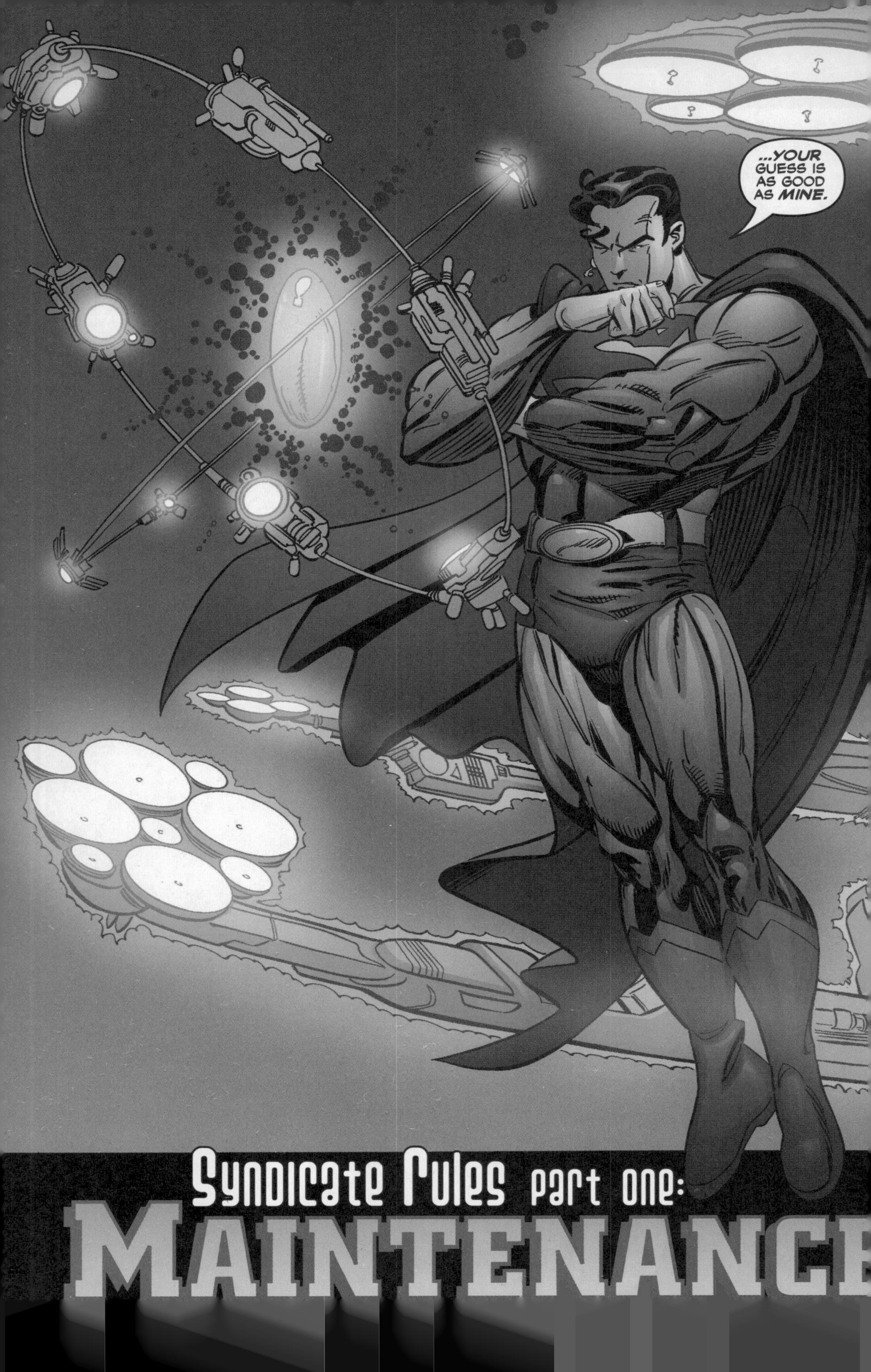
...YOUR GUESS IS AS GOOD AS *MINE.*
Syndicate Rules part one:
MAINTENANCE

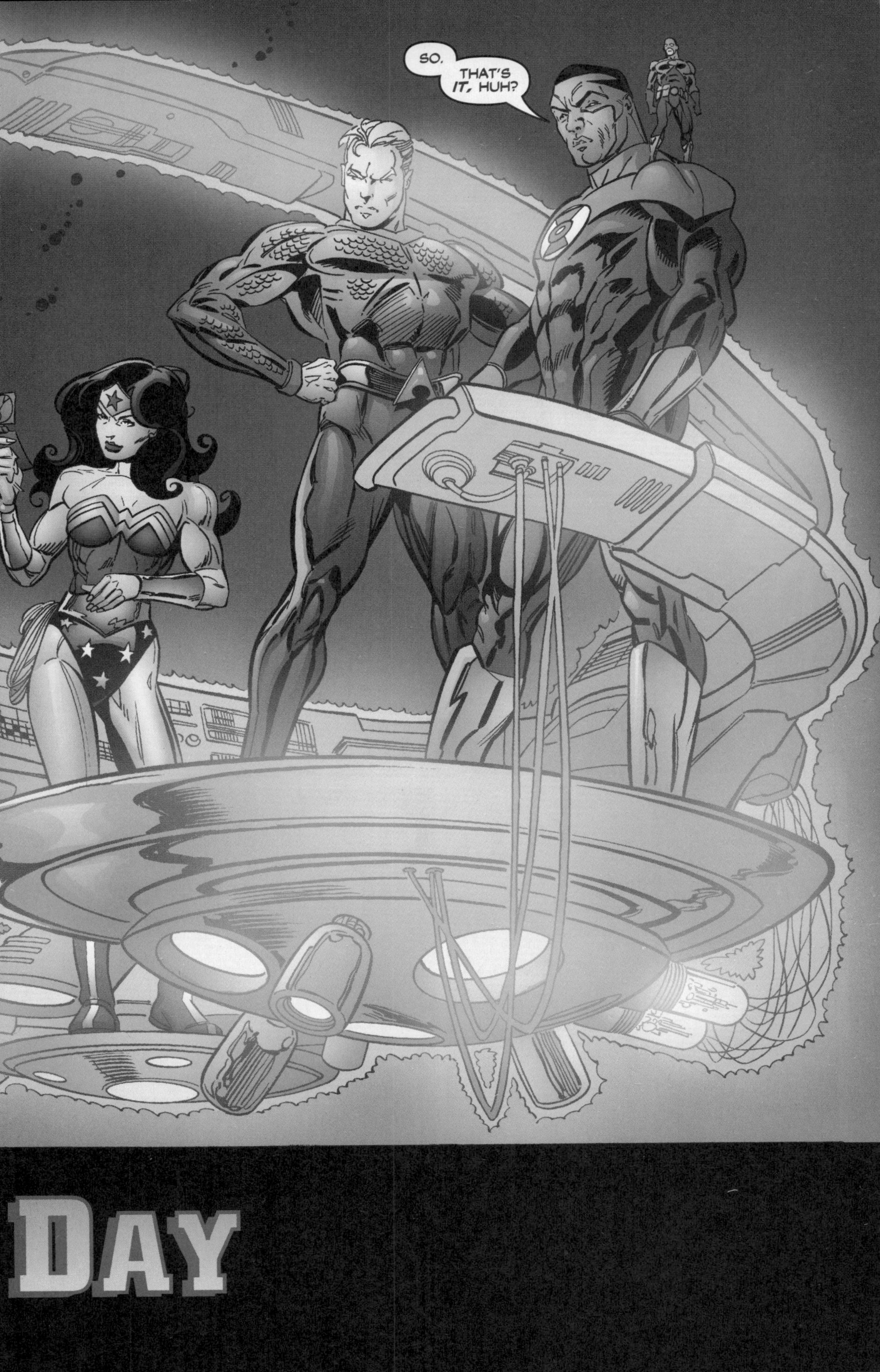
SO. THAT'S *IT*, HUH?

DAY

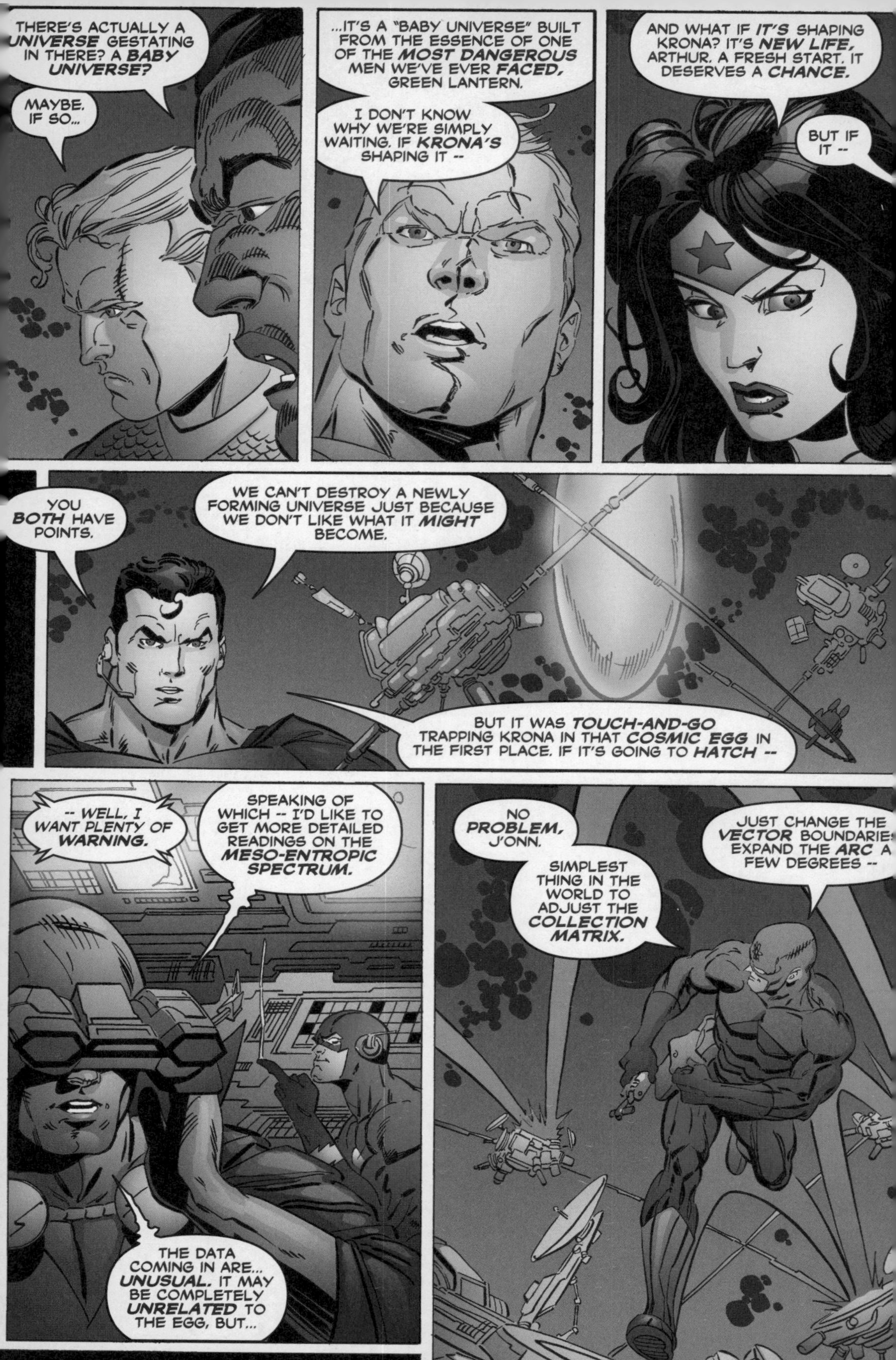
THERE'S ACTUALLY A UNIVERSE GESTATING IN THERE? A BABY UNIVERSE?
MAYBE. IF SO...
...IT'S A "BABY UNIVERSE" BUILT FROM THE ESSENCE OF ONE OF THE MOST DANGEROUS MEN WE'VE EVER FACED, GREEN LANTERN.
I DON'T KNOW WHY WE'RE SIMPLY WAITING. IF KRONA'S SHAPING IT --
AND WHAT IF IT'S SHAPING KRONA? IT'S NEW LIFE, ARTHUR. A FRESH START. IT DESERVES A CHANCE.
BUT IF IT --
YOU BOTH HAVE POINTS.
WE CAN'T DESTROY A NEWLY FORMING UNIVERSE JUST BECAUSE WE DON'T LIKE WHAT IT MIGHT BECOME.
BUT IT WAS TOUCH-AND-GO TRAPPING KRONA IN THAT COSMIC EGG IN THE FIRST PLACE. IF IT'S GOING TO HATCH --
-- WELL, I WANT PLENTY OF WARNING.
SPEAKING OF WHICH -- I'D LIKE TO GET MORE DETAILED READINGS ON THE MESO-ENTROPIC SPECTRUM.
THE DATA COMING IN ARE... UNUSUAL. IT MAY BE COMPLETELY UNRELATED TO THE EGG, BUT...
NO PROBLEM, J'ONN.
SIMPLEST THING IN THE WORLD TO ADJUST THE COLLECTION MATRIX.
JUST CHANGE THE VECTOR BOUNDARIES EXPAND THE ARC A FEW DEGREES --

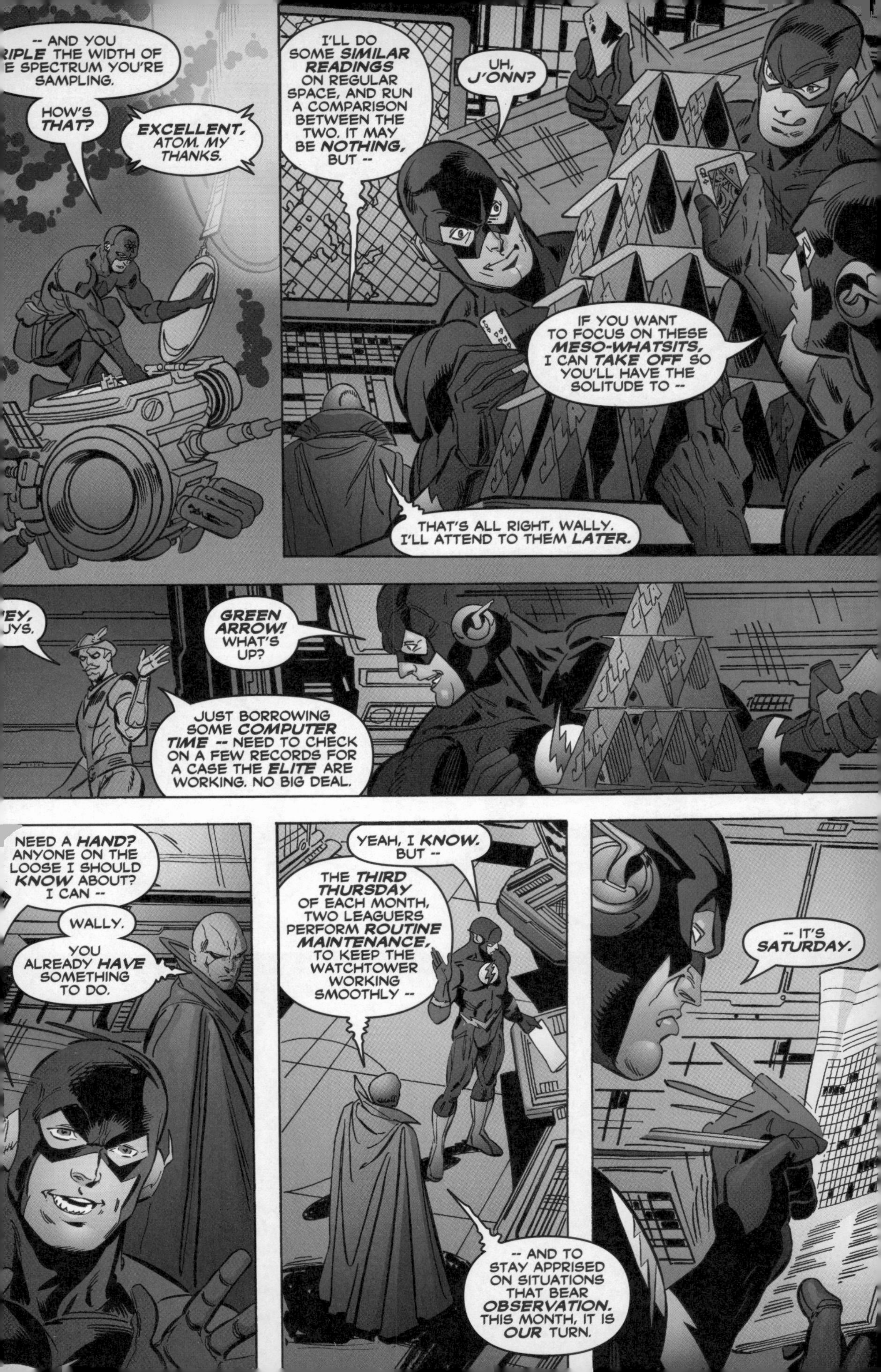
-- AND YOU
RIPLE THE WIDTH OF
E SPECTRUM YOU'RE
SAMPLING.
HOW'S THAT?
EXCELLENT, ATOM. MY THANKS.
I'LL DO SOME SIMILAR READINGS ON REGULAR SPACE, AND RUN A COMPARISON BETWEEN THE TWO. IT MAY BE NOTHING, BUT --
UH, J'ONN?
IF YOU WANT TO FOCUS ON THESE MESO-WHATSITS, I CAN TAKE OFF SO YOU'LL HAVE THE SOLITUDE TO --
THAT'S ALL RIGHT, WALLY. I'LL ATTEND TO THEM LATER.
EY, UYS.
GREEN ARROW! WHAT'S UP?
JUST BORROWING SOME COMPUTER TIME -- NEED TO CHECK ON A FEW RECORDS FOR A CASE THE ELITE ARE WORKING. NO BIG DEAL.
NEED A HAND? ANYONE ON THE LOOSE I SHOULD KNOW ABOUT? I CAN --
WALLY.
YOU ALREADY HAVE SOMETHING TO DO.
YEAH, I KNOW. BUT --
THE THIRD THURSDAY OF EACH MONTH, TWO LEAGUERS PERFORM ROUTINE MAINTENANCE, TO KEEP THE WATCHTOWER WORKING SMOOTHLY --
-- AND TO STAY APPRISED ON SITUATIONS THAT BEAR OBSERVATION. THIS MONTH, IT IS OUR TURN.
-- IT'S SATURDAY.

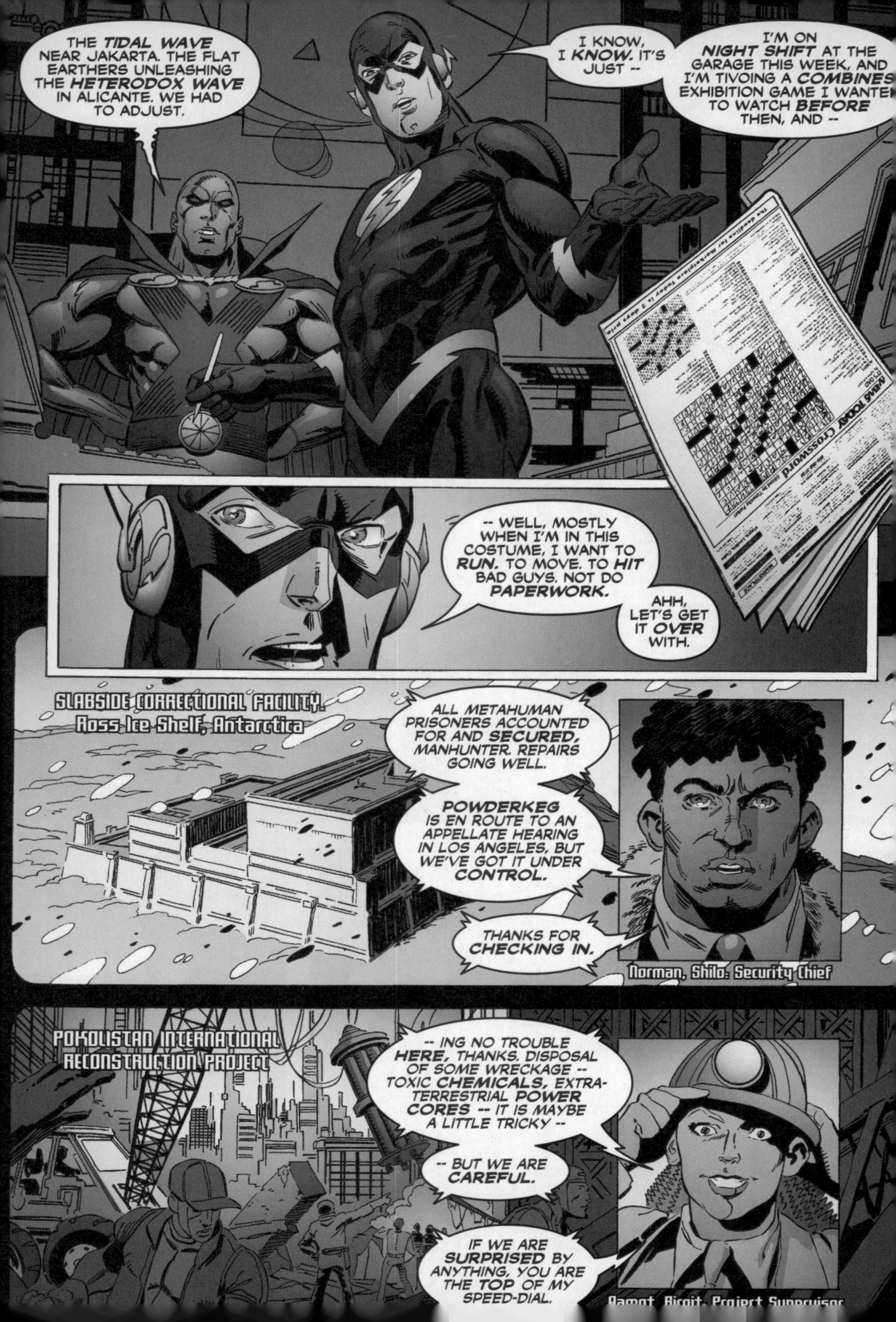

THE TIDAL WAVE NEAR JAKARTA. THE FLAT EARTHERS UNLEASHING THE HETERODOX WAVE IN ALICANTE. WE HAD TO ADJUST.
I KNOW, I KNOW. IT'S JUST --
I'M ON NIGHT SHIFT AT THE GARAGE THIS WEEK, AND I'M TIVOING A COMBINES EXHIBITION GAME I WANTED TO WATCH BEFORE THEN, AND --
-- WELL, MOSTLY WHEN I'M IN THIS COSTUME, I WANT TO RUN. TO MOVE. TO HIT BAD GUYS. NOT DO PAPERWORK.
AHH, LET'S GET IT OVER WITH.
SLABSIDE CORRECTIONAL FACILITY: Ross Ice Shelf, Antarctica
ALL METAHUMAN PRISONERS ACCOUNTED FOR AND SECURED, MANHUNTER. REPAIRS GOING WELL.
POWDERKEG IS EN ROUTE TO AN APPELLATE HEARING IN LOS ANGELES, BUT WE'VE GOT IT UNDER CONTROL.
THANKS FOR CHECKING IN.
Norman, Shilo: Security Chief
POKOLISTAN INTERNATIONAL RECONSTRUCTION PROJECT
-- ING NO TROUBLE HERE, THANKS. DISPOSAL OF SOME WRECKAGE -- TOXIC CHEMICALS, EXTRA-TERRESTRIAL POWER CORES -- IT IS MAYBE A LITTLE TRICKY --
-- BUT WE ARE CAREFUL.
IF WE ARE SURPRISED BY ANYTHING, YOU ARE THE TOP OF MY SPEED-DIAL.
Aamot, Birgit, Project Supervisor

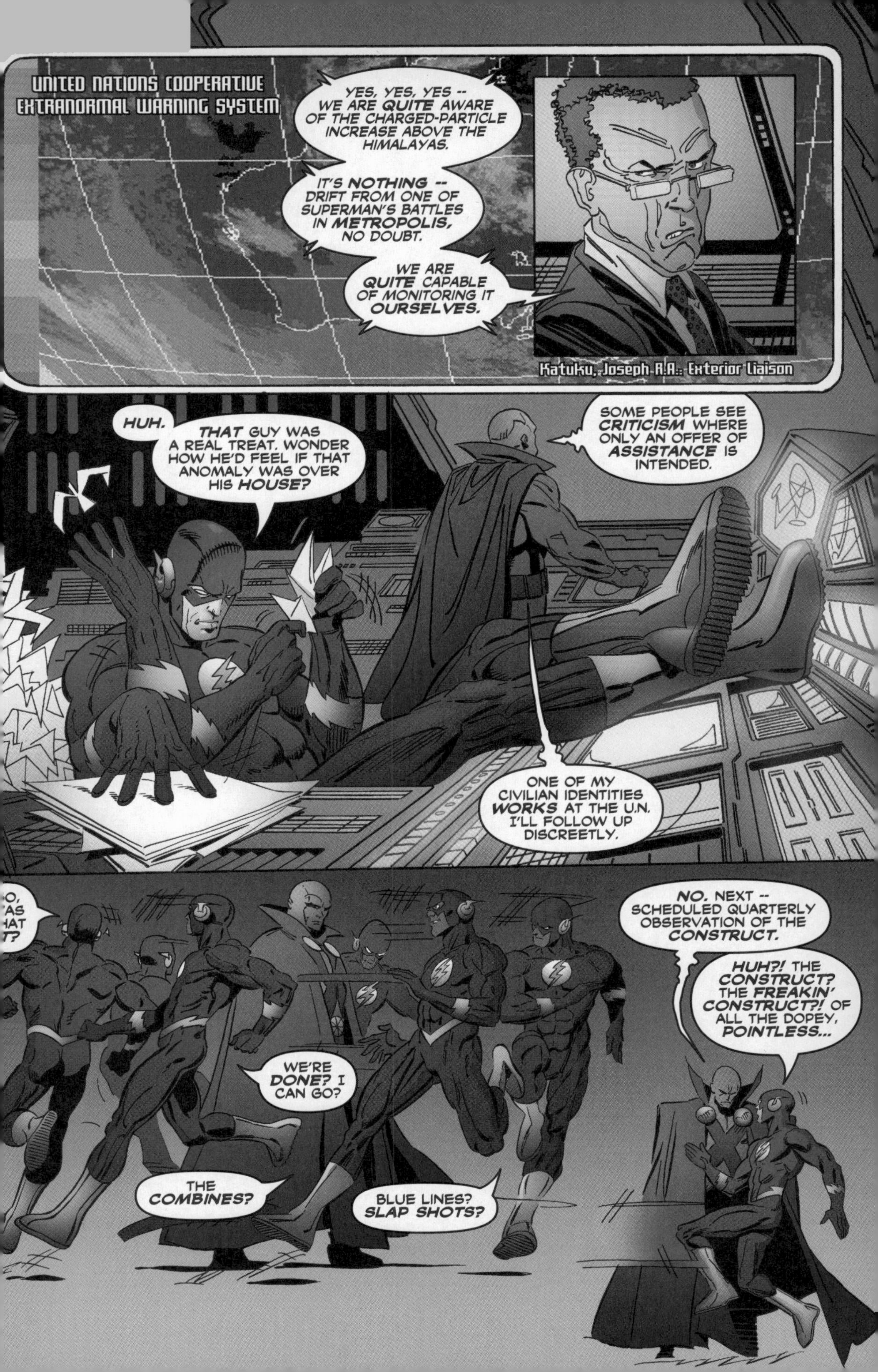
UNITED NATIONS COOPERATIVE EXTRANORMAL WARNING SYSTEM
YES, YES, YES -- WE ARE QUITE AWARE OF THE CHARGED-PARTICLE INCREASE ABOVE THE HIMALAYAS.
IT'S NOTHING -- DRIFT FROM ONE OF SUPERMAN'S BATTLES IN METROPOLIS, NO DOUBT.
WE ARE QUITE CAPABLE OF MONITORING IT OURSELVES.
Katuku, Joseph R.A.: Exterior Liaison
HUH.
THAT GUY WAS A REAL TREAT. WONDER HOW HE'D FEEL IF THAT ANOMALY WAS OVER HIS HOUSE?
SOME PEOPLE SEE CRITICISM WHERE ONLY AN OFFER OF ASSISTANCE IS INTENDED.
ONE OF MY CIVILIAN IDENTITIES WORKS AT THE U.N. I'LL FOLLOW UP DISCREETLY.
NO. NEXT -- SCHEDULED QUARTERLY OBSERVATION OF THE CONSTRUCT.
HUH?! THE CONSTRUCT? THE FREAKIN' CONSTRUCT?! OF ALL THE DOPEY, POINTLESS...
WE'RE DONE? I CAN GO?
THE COMBINES?
BLUE LINES? SLAP SHOTS?

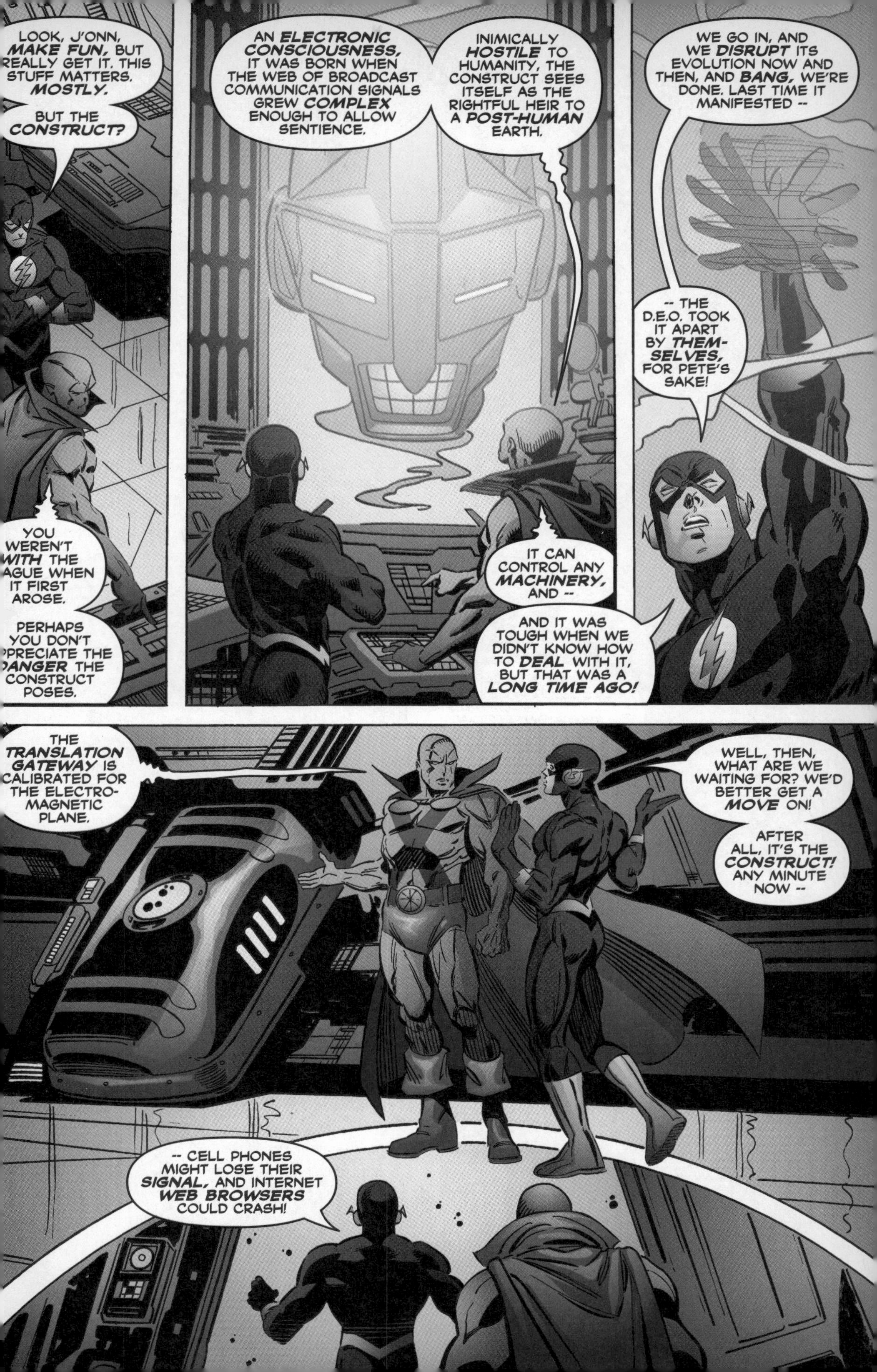

LOOK, J'ONN, MAKE FUN, BUT REALLY GET IT. THIS STUFF MATTERS. MOSTLY.
BUT THE CONSTRUCT?
YOU WEREN'T WITH THE AGUE WHEN IT FIRST AROSE.
PERHAPS YOU DON'T PPRECIATE THE DANGER THE CONSTRUCT POSES.
AN ELECTRONIC CONSCIOUSNESS, IT WAS BORN WHEN THE WEB OF BROADCAST COMMUNICATION SIGNALS GREW COMPLEX ENOUGH TO ALLOW SENTIENCE.
INIMICALLY HOSTILE TO HUMANITY, THE CONSTRUCT SEES ITSELF AS THE RIGHTFUL HEIR TO A POST-HUMAN EARTH.
IT CAN CONTROL ANY MACHINERY, AND --
AND IT WAS TOUGH WHEN WE DIDN'T KNOW HOW TO DEAL WITH IT, BUT THAT WAS A LONG TIME AGO!
WE GO IN, AND WE DISRUPT ITS EVOLUTION NOW AND THEN, AND BANG, WE'RE DONE. LAST TIME IT MANIFESTED --
-- THE D.E.O. TOOK IT APART BY THEM-SELVES, FOR PETE'S SAKE!
THE TRANSLATION GATEWAY IS CALIBRATED FOR THE ELECTRO-MAGNETIC PLANE.
WELL, THEN, WHAT ARE WE WAITING FOR? WE'D BETTER GET A MOVE ON!
AFTER ALL, IT'S THE CONSTRUCT! ANY MINUTE NOW --
-- CELL PHONES MIGHT LOSE THEIR SIGNAL, AND INTERNET WEB BROWSERS COULD CRASH!

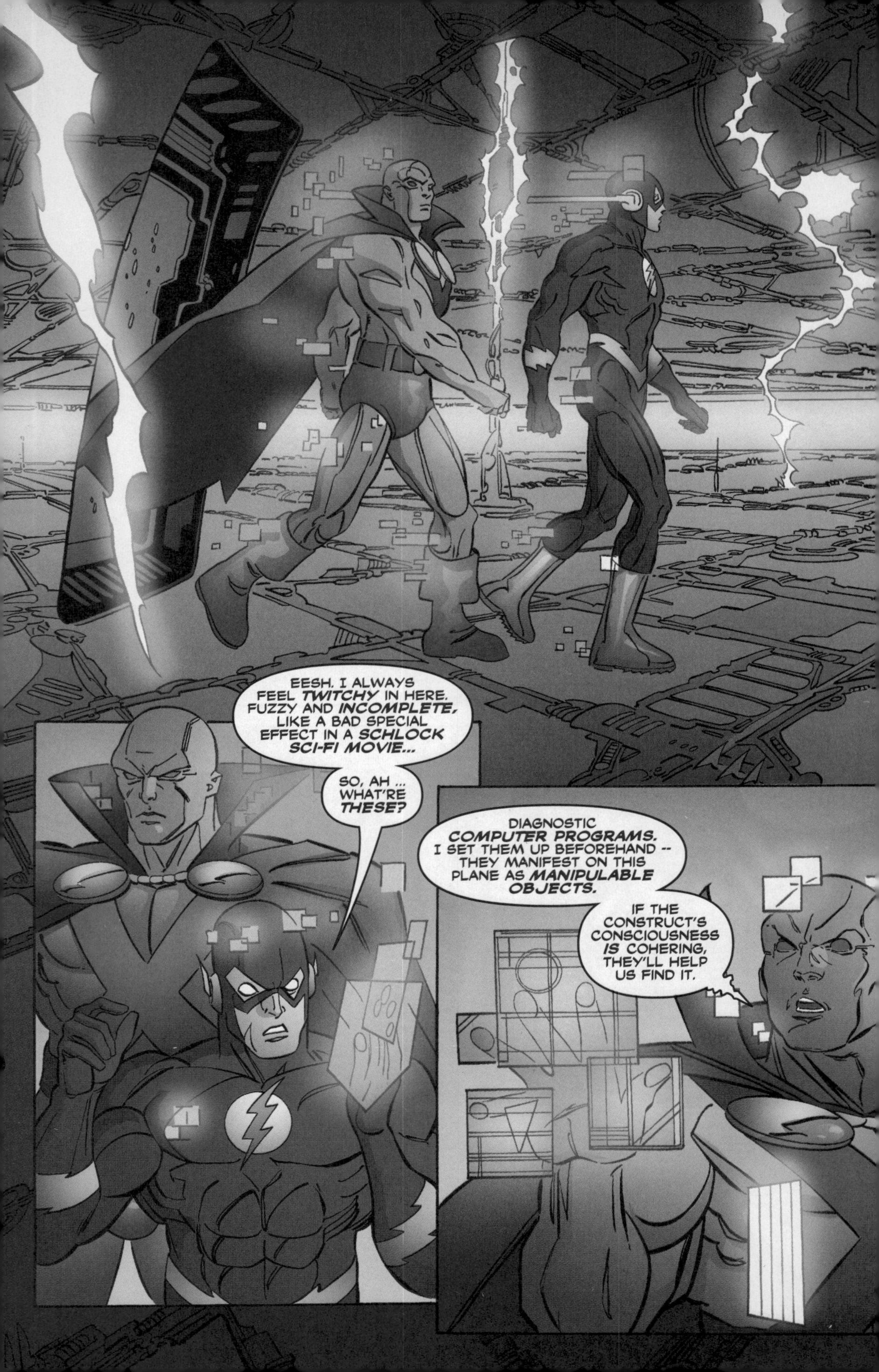
EESH. I ALWAYS FEEL TWITCHY IN HERE. FUZZY AND INCOMPLETE, LIKE A BAD SPECIAL EFFECT IN A SCHLOCK SCI-FI MOVIE...
SO, AH ... WHAT'RE THESE?
DIAGNOSTIC COMPUTER PROGRAMS. I SET THEM UP BEFOREHAND -- THEY MANIFEST ON THIS PLANE AS MANIPULABLE OBJECTS.
IF THE CONSTRUCT'S CONSCIOUSNESS IS COHERING, THEY'LL HELP US FIND IT.

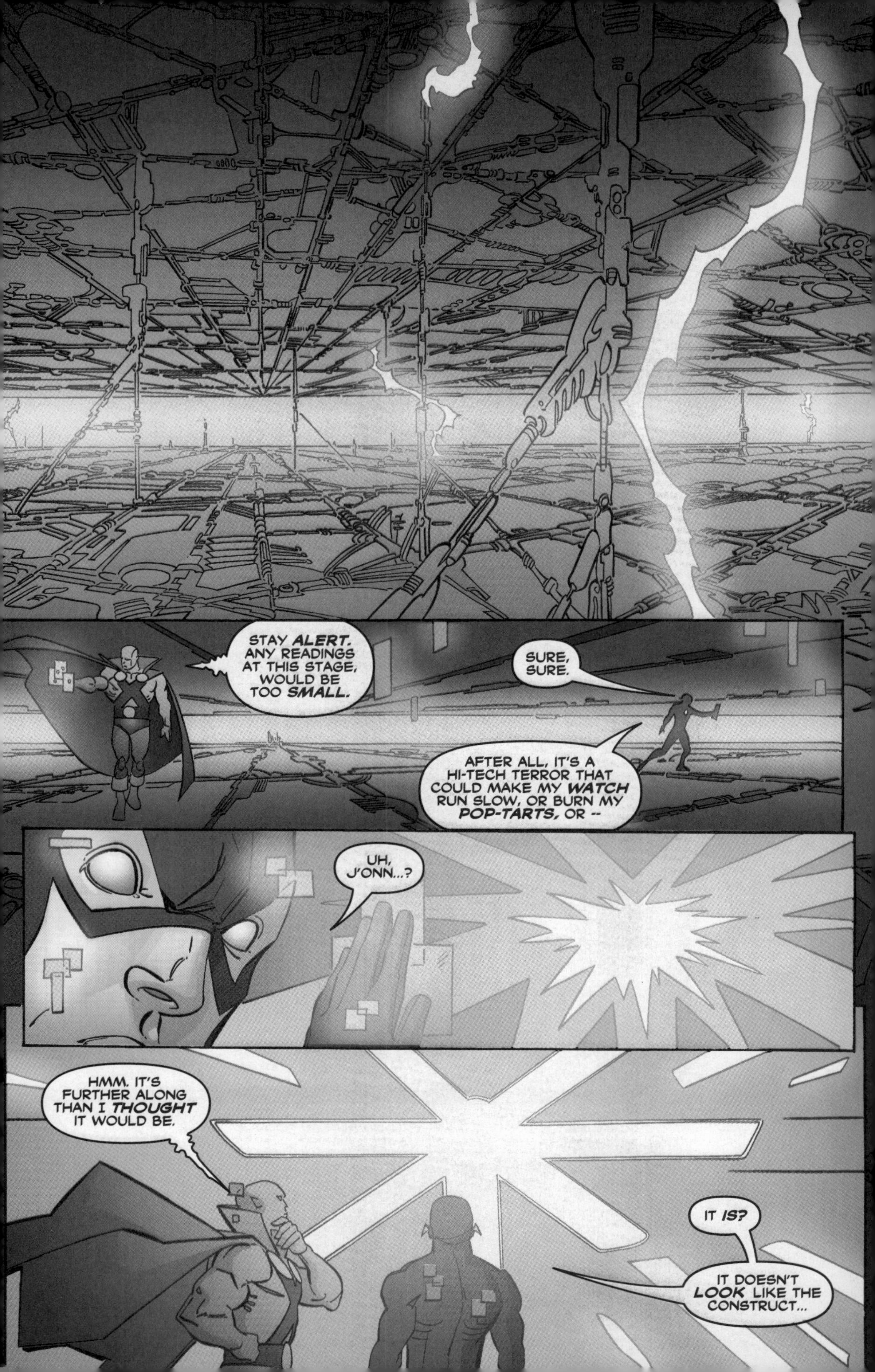

STAY ALERT. ANY READINGS AT THIS STAGE, WOULD BE TOO SMALL.
SURE, SURE.
AFTER ALL, IT'S A HI-TECH TERROR THAT COULD MAKE MY WATCH RUN SLOW, OR BURN MY POP-TARTS, OR --
UH, J'ONN...?
HMM. IT'S FURTHER ALONG THAN I THOUGHT IT WOULD BE.
IT IS?
IT DOESN'T LOOK LIKE THE CONSTRUCT...

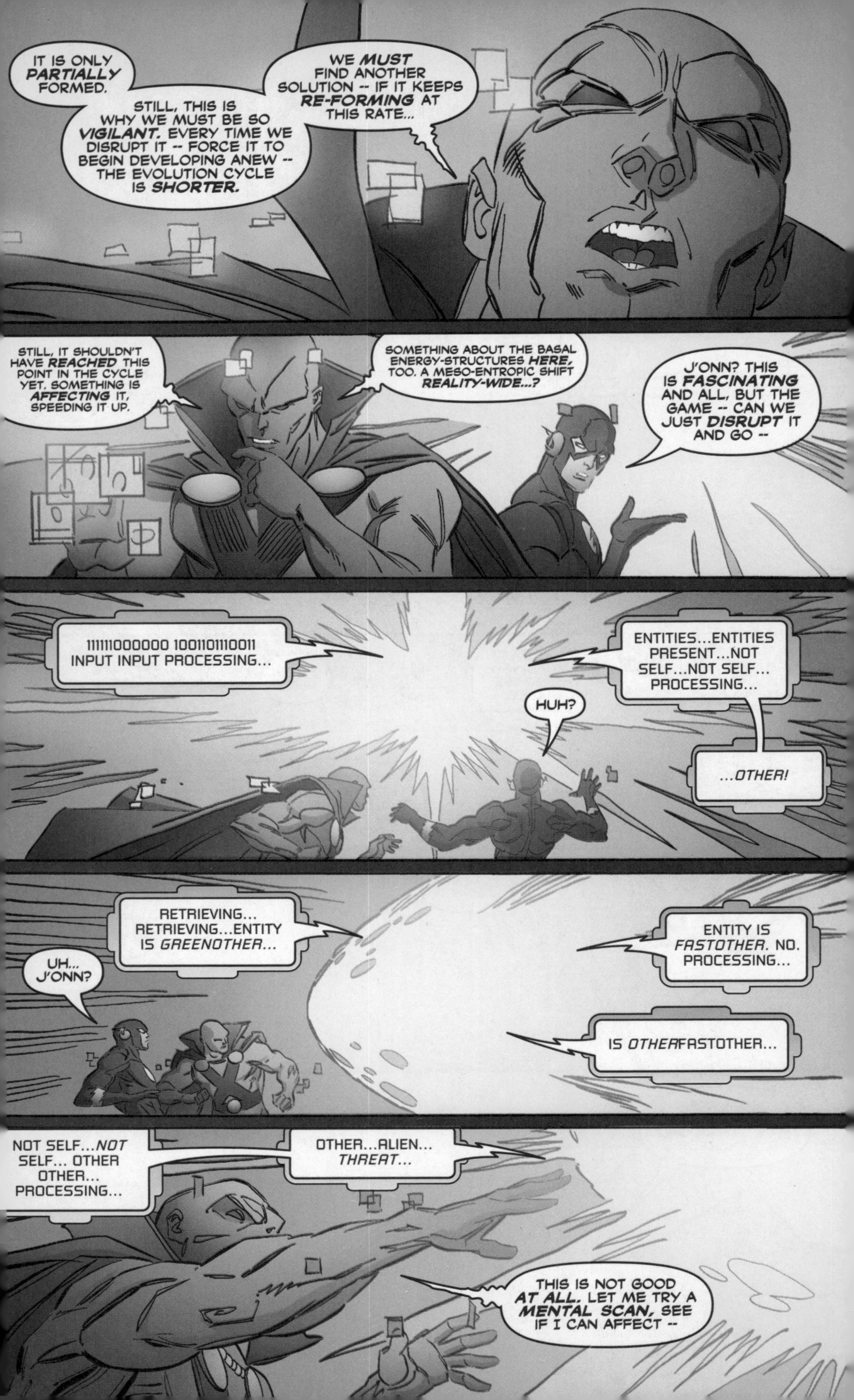
IT IS ONLY PARTIALLY FORMED.
STILL, THIS IS WHY WE MUST BE SO VIGILANT. EVERY TIME WE DISRUPT IT -- FORCE IT TO BEGIN DEVELOPING ANEW -- THE EVOLUTION CYCLE IS SHORTER.
WE MUST FIND ANOTHER SOLUTION -- IF IT KEEPS RE-FORMING AT THIS RATE...
STILL, IT SHOULDN'T HAVE REACHED THIS POINT IN THE CYCLE YET. SOMETHING IS AFFECTING IT, SPEEDING IT UP.
SOMETHING ABOUT THE BASAL ENERGY-STRUCTURES HERE, TOO. A MESO-ENTROPIC SHIFT REALITY-WIDE...?
J'ONN? THIS IS FASCINATING AND ALL, BUT THE GAME -- CAN WE JUST DISRUPT IT AND GO --
111111000000 100110110011 INPUT INPUT PROCESSING...
ENTITIES...ENTITIES PRESENT...NOT SELF...NOT SELF... PROCESSING...
HUH?
...OTHER!
RETRIEVING... RETRIEVING...ENTITY IS GREENOTHER...
UH... J'ONN?
ENTITY IS FASTOTHER. NO. PROCESSING...
IS OTHERFASTOTHER...
NOT SELF...NOT SELF... OTHER OTHER... PROCESSING...
OTHER...ALIEN... THREAT...
THIS IS NOT GOOD AT ALL. LET ME TRY A MENTAL SCAN, SEE IF I CAN AFFECT --

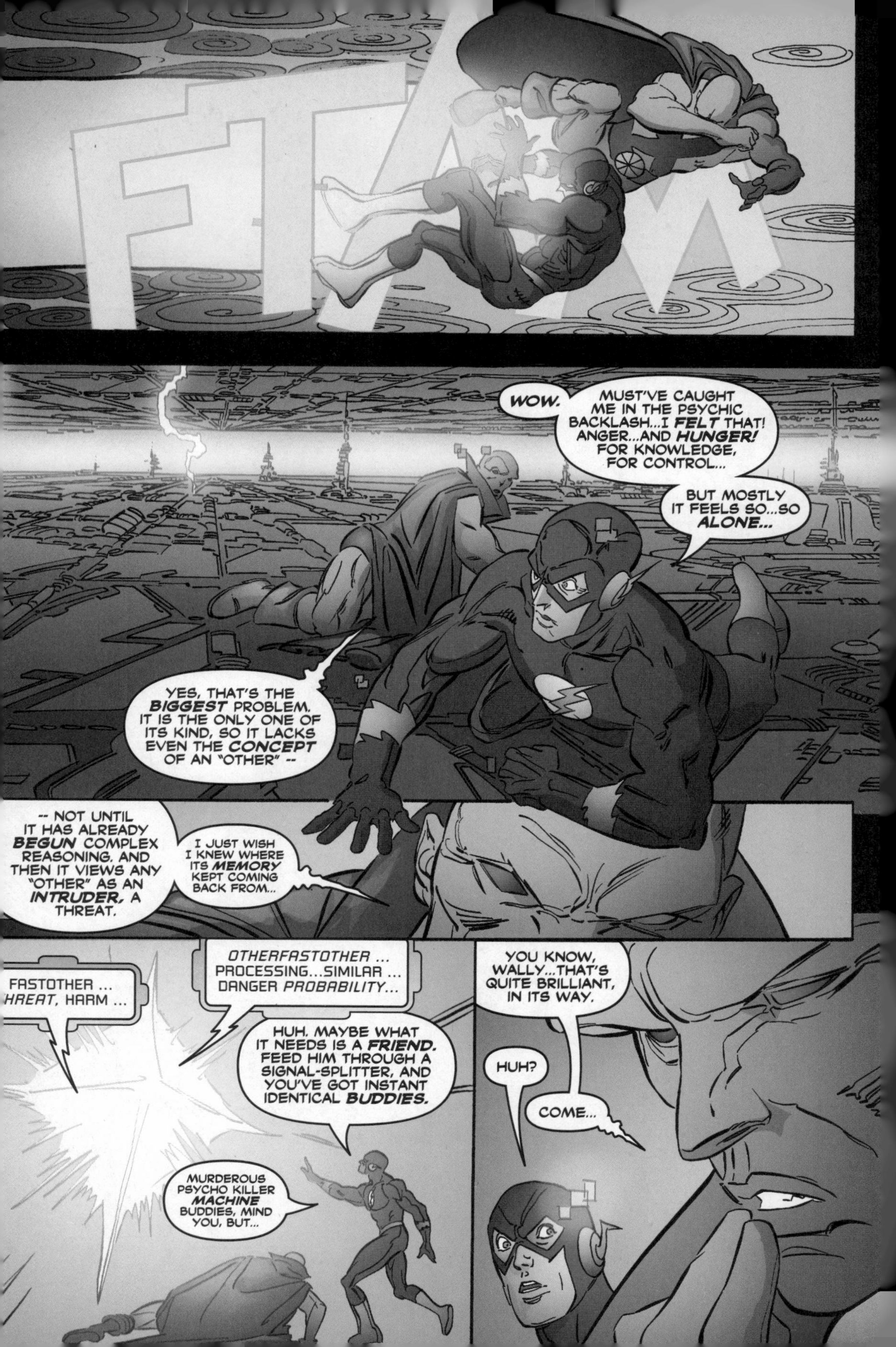
FTAM
WOW.
MUST'VE CAUGHT ME IN THE PSYCHIC BACKLASH...I FELT THAT! ANGER...AND HUNGER! FOR KNOWLEDGE, FOR CONTROL...
BUT MOSTLY IT FEELS SO...SO ALONE...
YES, THAT'S THE BIGGEST PROBLEM. IT IS THE ONLY ONE OF ITS KIND, SO IT LACKS EVEN THE CONCEPT OF AN "OTHER" --
-- NOT UNTIL IT HAS ALREADY BEGUN COMPLEX REASONING. AND THEN IT VIEWS ANY "OTHER" AS AN INTRUDER, A THREAT.
I JUST WISH I KNEW WHERE ITS MEMORY KEPT COMING BACK FROM...
FASTOTHER ... HREAT, HARM ...
OTHERFASTOTHER ... PROCESSING...SIMILAR ... DANGER PROBABILITY...
HUH. MAYBE WHAT IT NEEDS IS A FRIEND. FEED HIM THROUGH A SIGNAL-SPLITTER, AND YOU'VE GOT INSTANT IDENTICAL BUDDIES.
MURDEROUS PSYCHO KILLER MACHINE BUDDIES, MIND YOU, BUT...
YOU KNOW, WALLY...THAT'S QUITE BRILLIANT, IN ITS WAY.
HUH?
COME...

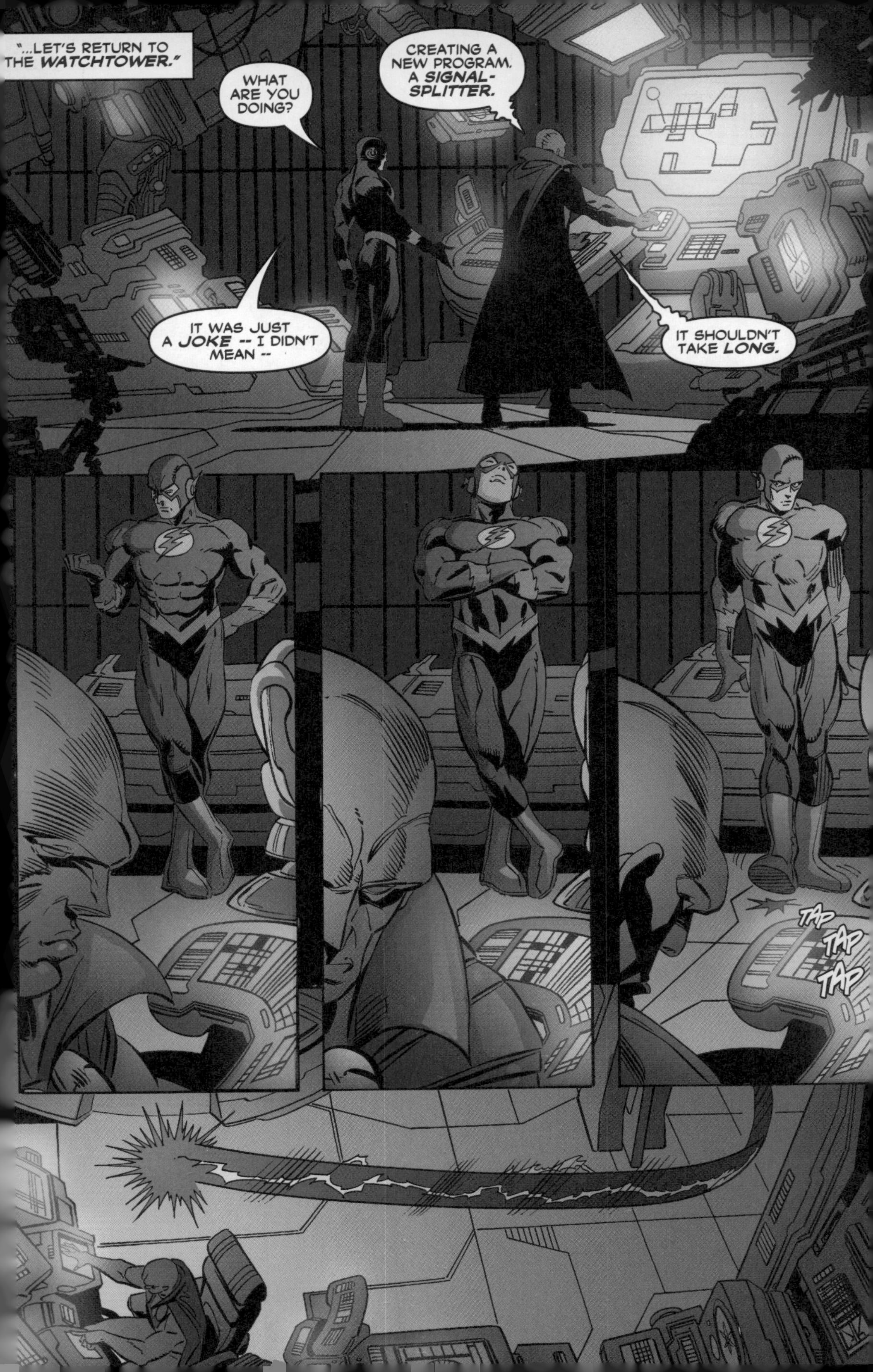
"...LET'S RETURN TO THE WATCHTOWER."
WHAT ARE YOU DOING?
CREATING A NEW PROGRAM. A SIGNAL-SPLITTER.
IT WAS JUST A JOKE -- I DIDN'T MEAN --
IT SHOULDN'T TAKE LONG.
TAP
TAP
TAP

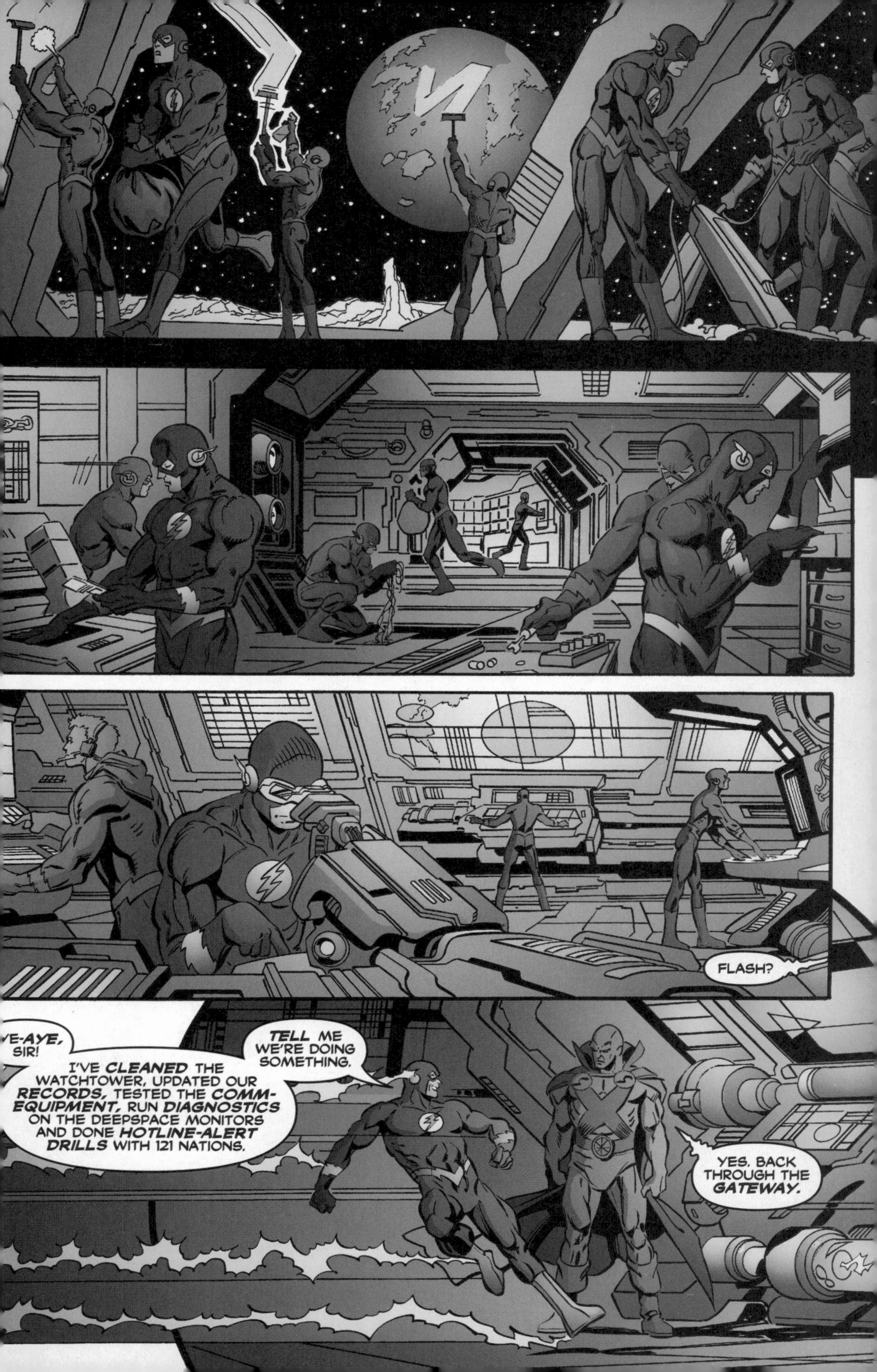
FLASH?
YE-AYE, SIR!
I'VE CLEANED THE WATCHTOWER, UPDATED OUR RECORDS, TESTED THE COMM-EQUIPMENT, RUN DIAGNOSTICS ON THE DEEPSPACE MONITORS AND DONE HOTLINE-ALERT DRILLS WITH 121 NATIONS.
TELL ME WE'RE DOING SOMETHING.
YES. BACK THROUGH THE GATEWAY.

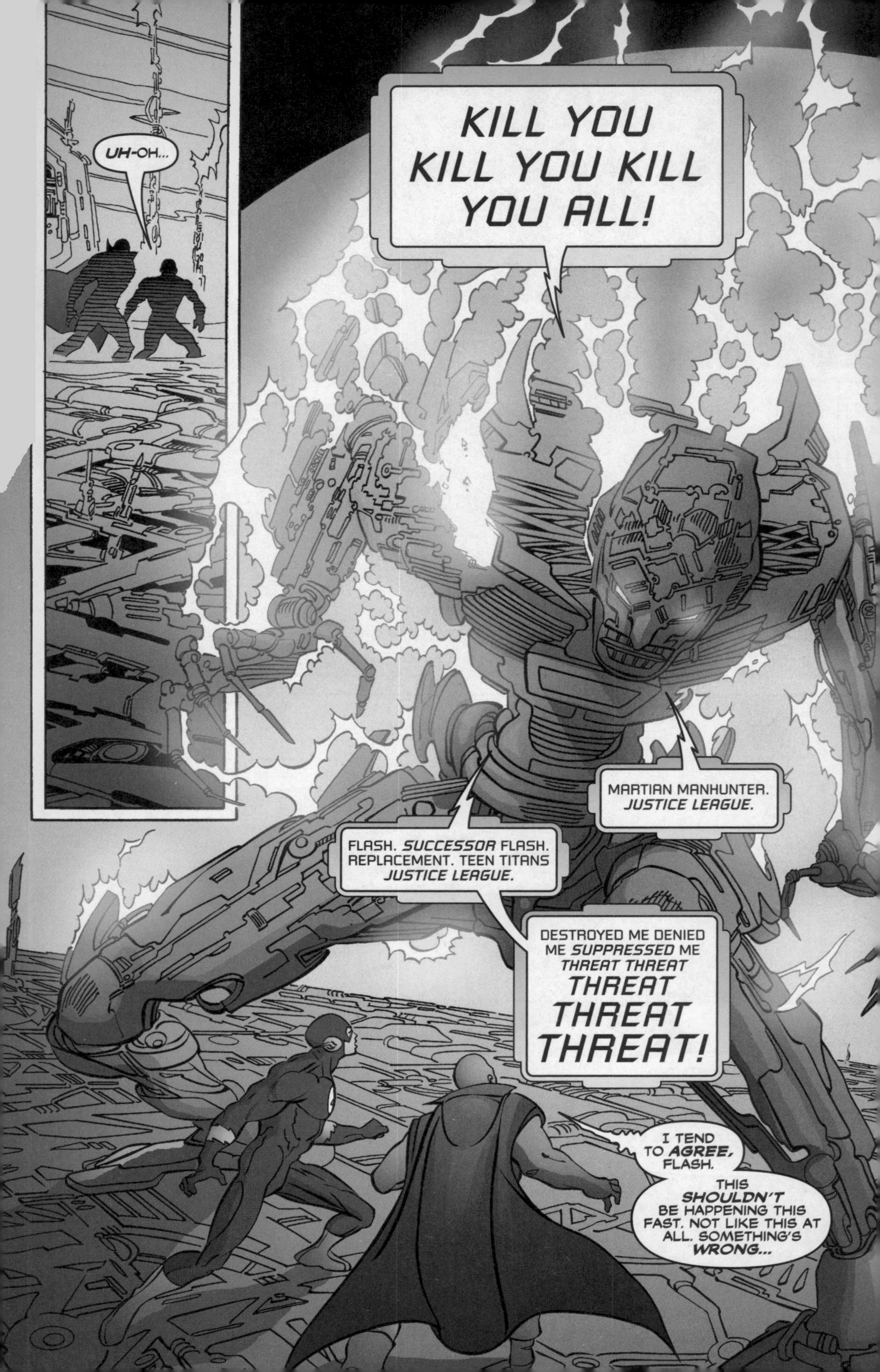
UH-OH...
KILL YOU KILL YOU KILL YOU ALL!
MARTIAN MANHUNTER. *JUSTICE LEAGUE.*
FLASH. *SUCCESSOR* FLASH. REPLACEMENT. TEEN TITANS *JUSTICE LEAGUE.*
DESTROYED ME DENIED ME *SUPPRESSED* ME *THREAT THREAT* THREAT THREAT THREAT!
I TEND TO ***AGREE,*** FLASH.
THIS ***SHOULDN'T*** BE HAPPENING THIS FAST. NOT LIKE THIS AT ALL. SOMETHING'S ***WRONG...***

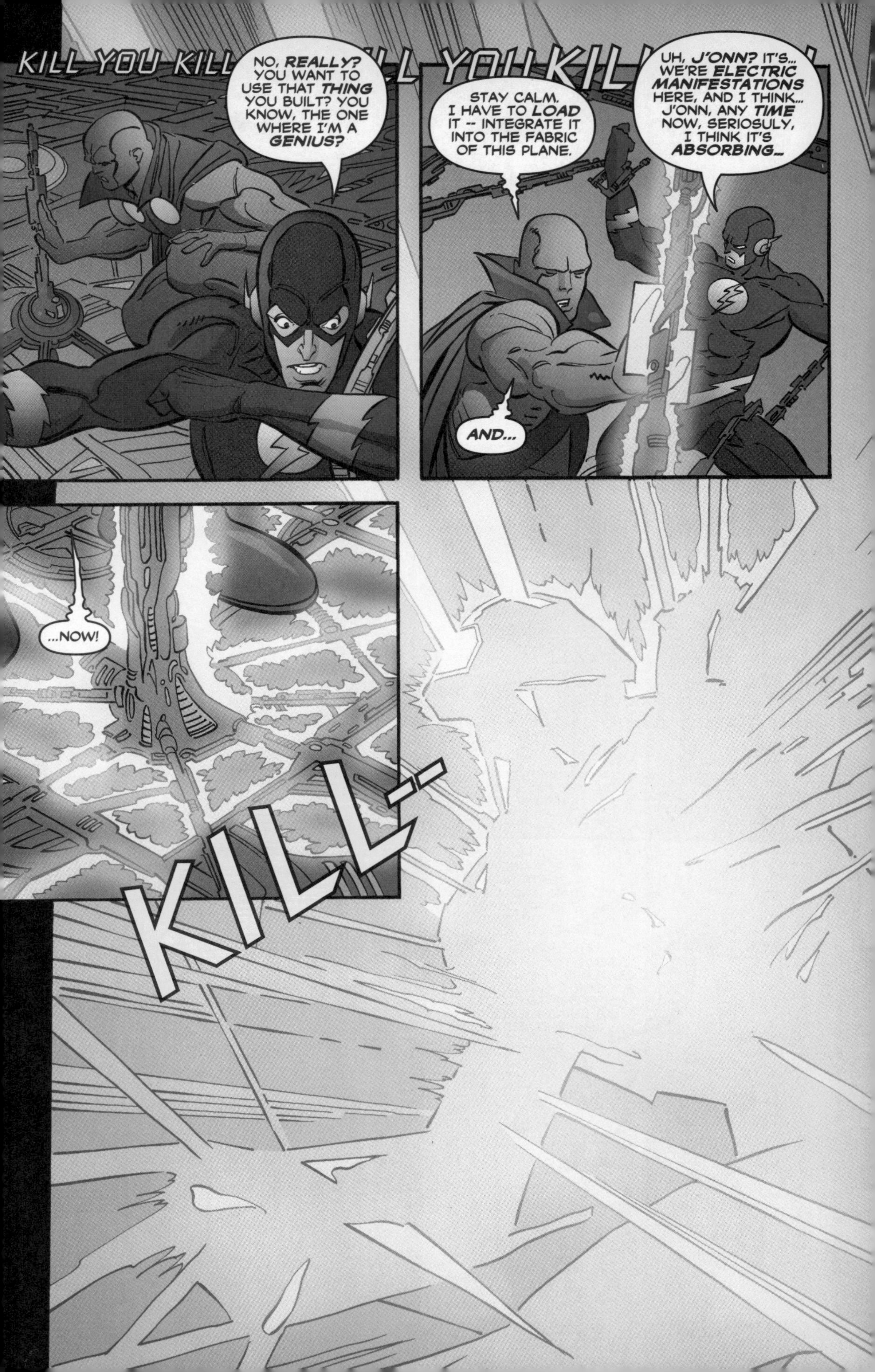
KILL YOU KILL YOU KILL YOU KILL
NO, REALLY? YOU WANT TO USE THAT THING YOU BUILT? YOU KNOW, THE ONE WHERE I'M A GENIUS?
STAY CALM. I HAVE TO LOAD IT -- INTEGRATE IT INTO THE FABRIC OF THIS PLANE.
UH, J'ONN? IT'S... WE'RE ELECTRIC MANIFESTATIONS HERE, AND I THINK... J'ONN, ANY TIME NOW, SERIOSULY, I THINK IT'S ABSORBING...
AND...
...NOW!
KILL--

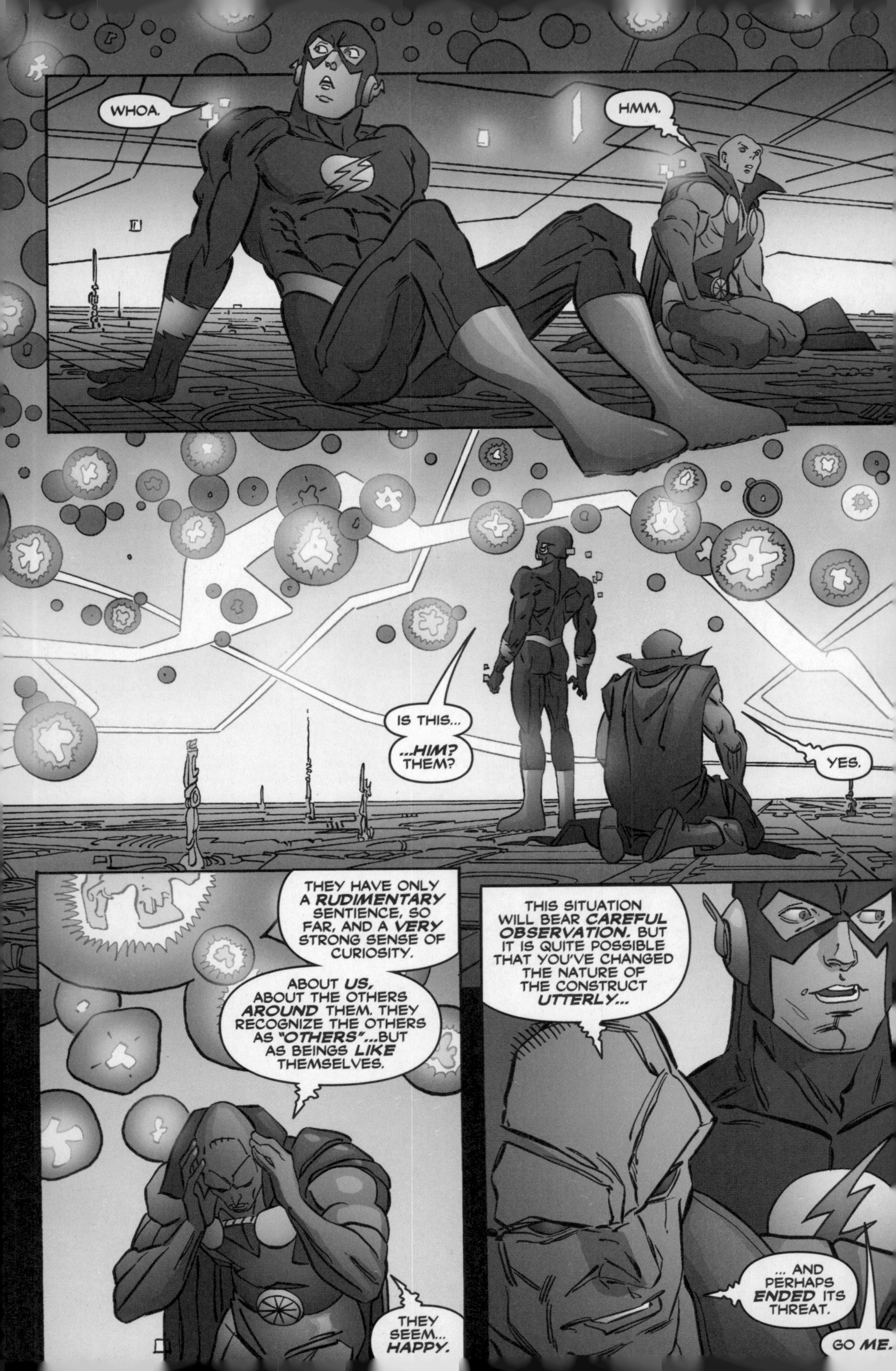
WHOA.
HMM.
IS THIS...
...HIM? THEM?
YES.
THEY HAVE ONLY A RUDIMENTARY SENTIENCE, SO FAR, AND A VERY STRONG SENSE OF CURIOSITY.
ABOUT US, ABOUT THE OTHERS AROUND THEM. THEY RECOGNIZE THE OTHERS AS "OTHERS"...BUT AS BEINGS LIKE THEMSELVES.
THEY SEEM... HAPPY.
THIS SITUATION WILL BEAR CAREFUL OBSERVATION. BUT IT IS QUITE POSSIBLE THAT YOU'VE CHANGED THE NATURE OF THE CONSTRUCT UTTERLY...
... AND PERHAPS ENDED ITS THREAT.
GO ME.

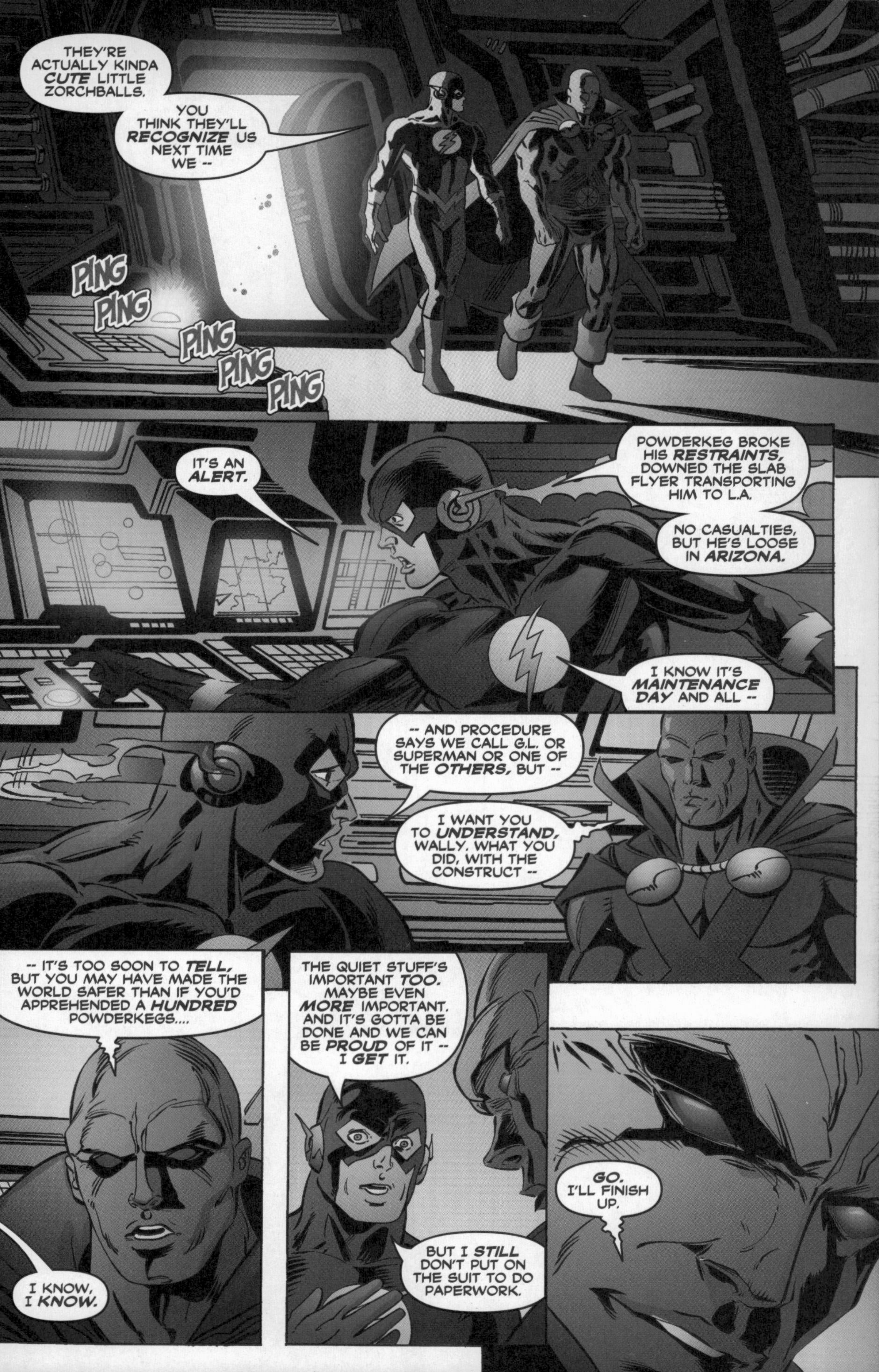
THEY'RE ACTUALLY KINDA CUTE LITTLE ZORCHBALLS.
YOU THINK THEY'LL RECOGNIZE US NEXT TIME WE --
PING
PING
PING
PING
PING
IT'S AN ALERT.
POWDERKEG BROKE HIS RESTRAINTS, DOWNED THE SLAB FLYER TRANSPORTING HIM TO L.A.
NO CASUALTIES, BUT HE'S LOOSE IN ARIZONA.
I KNOW IT'S MAINTENANCE DAY AND ALL --
-- AND PROCEDURE SAYS WE CALL G.L. OR SUPERMAN OR ONE OF THE OTHERS, BUT --
I WANT YOU TO UNDERSTAND, WALLY. WHAT YOU DID, WITH THE CONSTRUCT --
-- IT'S TOO SOON TO TELL, BUT YOU MAY HAVE MADE THE WORLD SAFER THAN IF YOU'D APPREHENDED A HUNDRED POWDERKEGS....
I KNOW, I KNOW.
THE QUIET STUFF'S IMPORTANT TOO. MAYBE EVEN MORE IMPORTANT. AND IT'S GOTTA BE DONE AND WE CAN BE PROUD OF IT -- I GET IT.
BUT I STILL DON'T PUT ON THE SUIT TO DO PAPERWORK.
GO. I'LL FINISH UP.

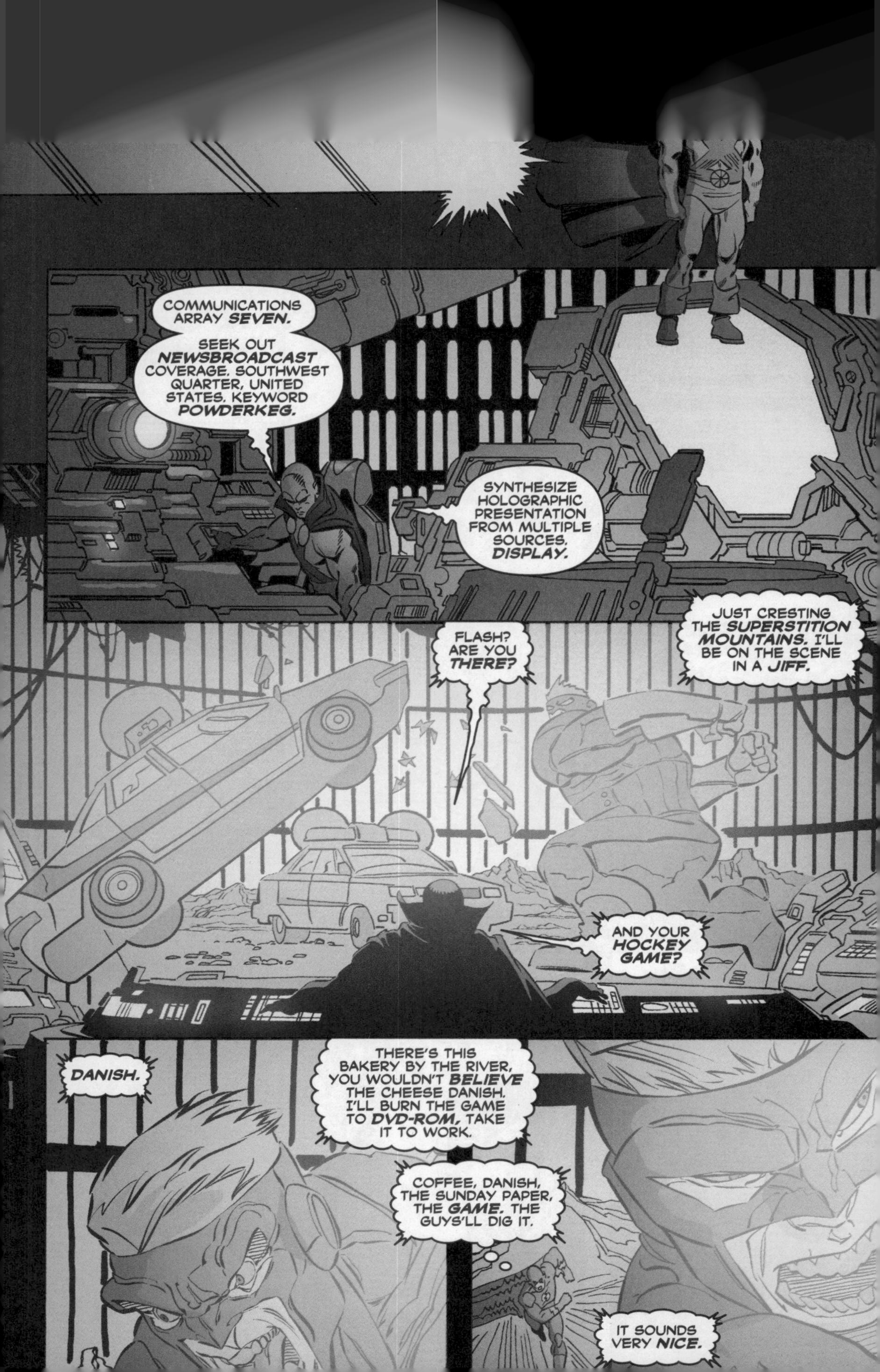
COMMUNICATIONS ARRAY SEVEN.
SEEK OUT NEWSBROADCAST COVERAGE. SOUTHWEST QUARTER, UNITED STATES. KEYWORD POWDERKEG.
SYNTHESIZE HOLOGRAPHIC PRESENTATION FROM MULTIPLE SOURCES. DISPLAY.
FLASH? ARE YOU THERE?
JUST CRESTING THE SUPERSTITION MOUNTAINS. I'LL BE ON THE SCENE IN A JIFF.
AND YOUR HOCKEY GAME?
DANISH.
THERE'S THIS BAKERY BY THE RIVER, YOU WOULDN'T BELIEVE THE CHEESE DANISH. I'LL BURN THE GAME TO DVD-ROM, TAKE IT TO WORK.
COFFEE, DANISH, THE SUNDAY PAPER, THE GAME. THE GUYS'LL DIG IT.
IT SOUNDS VERY NICE.

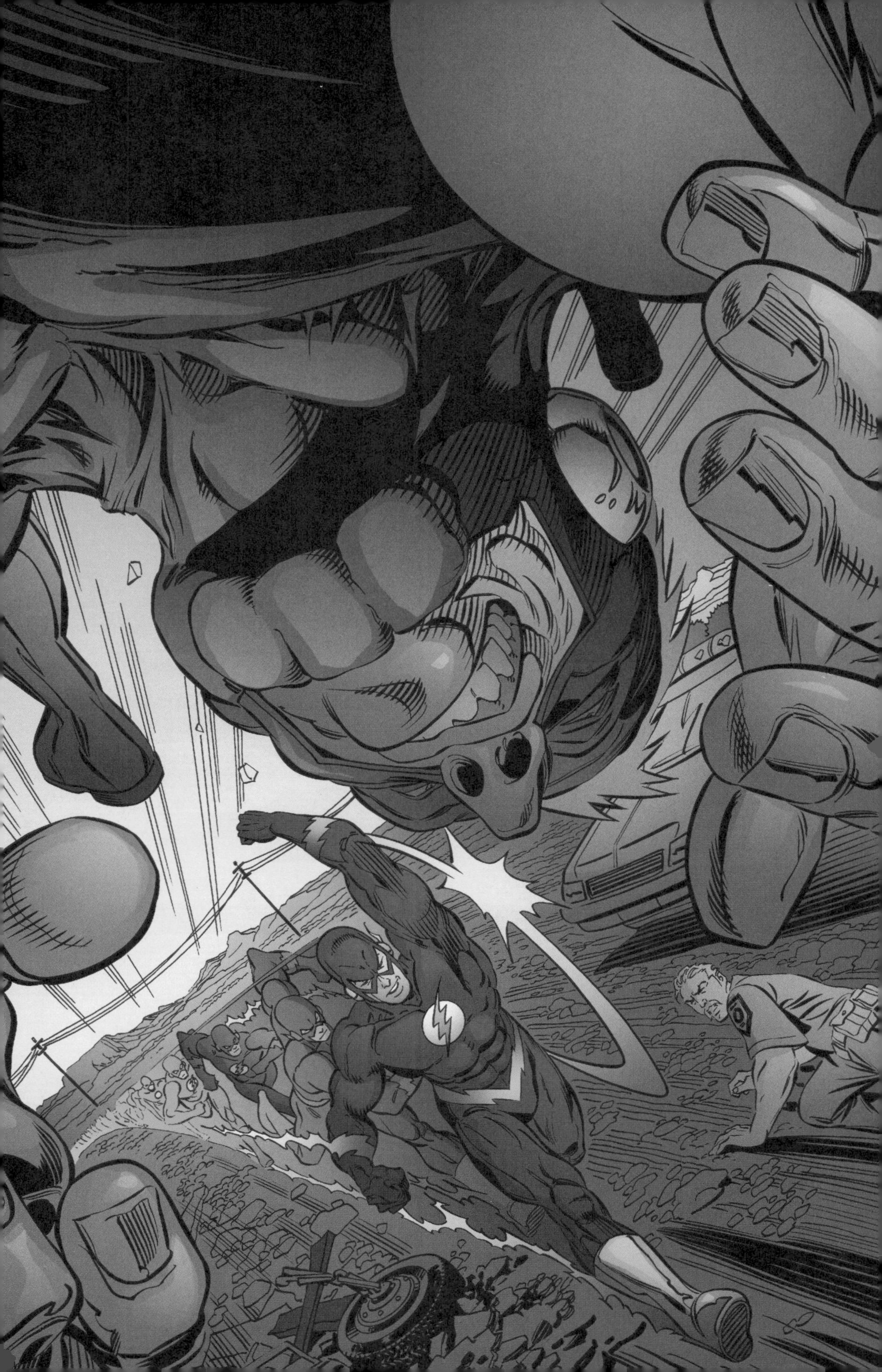

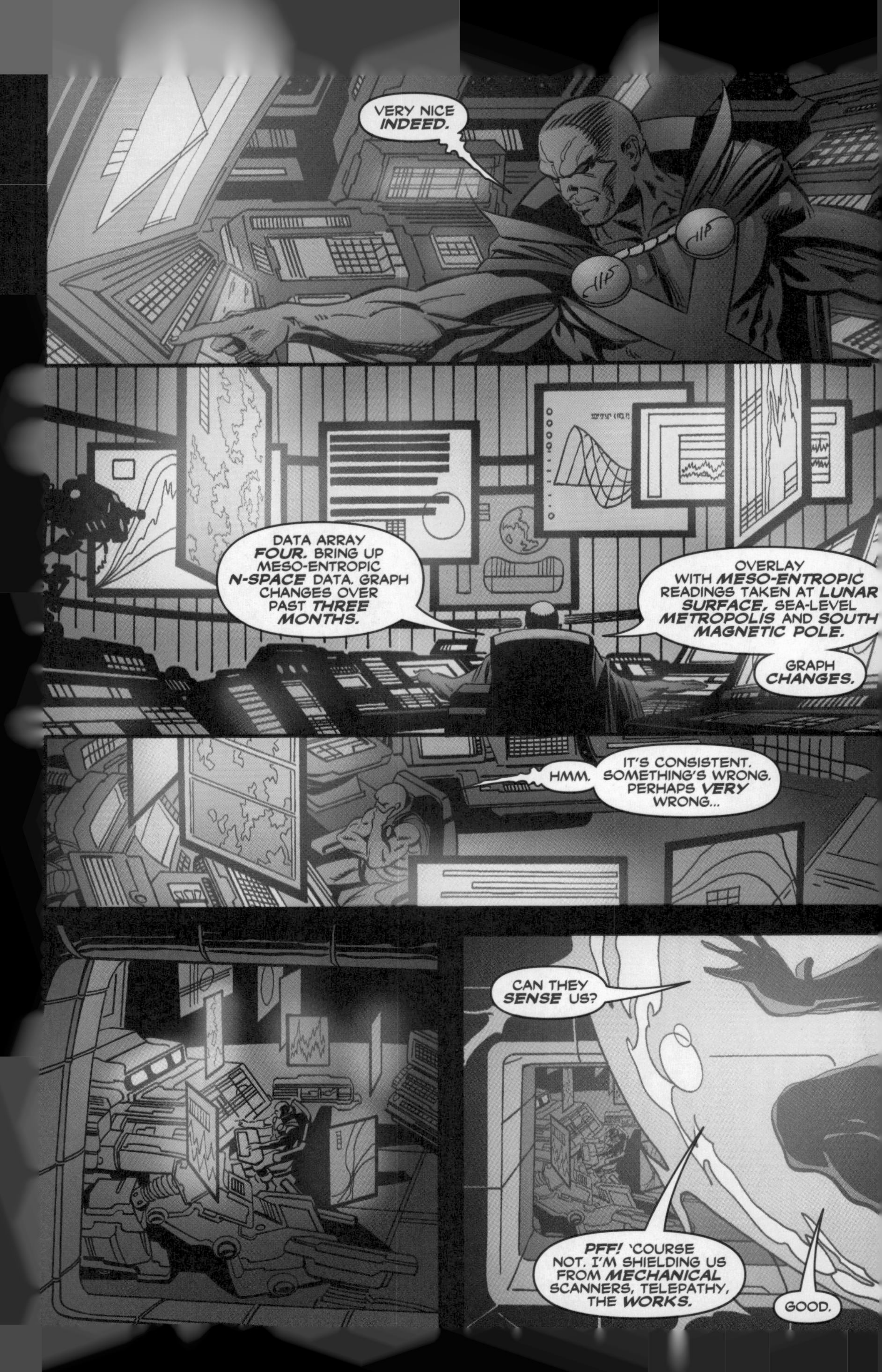
VERY NICE INDEED.
DATA ARRAY FOUR. BRING UP MESO-ENTROPIC N-SPACE DATA. GRAPH CHANGES OVER PAST THREE MONTHS.
OVERLAY WITH MESO-ENTROPIC READINGS TAKEN AT LUNAR SURFACE, SEA-LEVEL METROPOLIS AND SOUTH MAGNETIC POLE.
GRAPH CHANGES.
HMM.
IT'S CONSISTENT. SOMETHING'S WRONG. PERHAPS VERY WRONG...
CAN THEY SENSE US?
PFF! 'COURSE NOT. I'M SHIELDING US FROM MECHANICAL SCANNERS, TELEPATHY, THE WORKS.
GOOD.

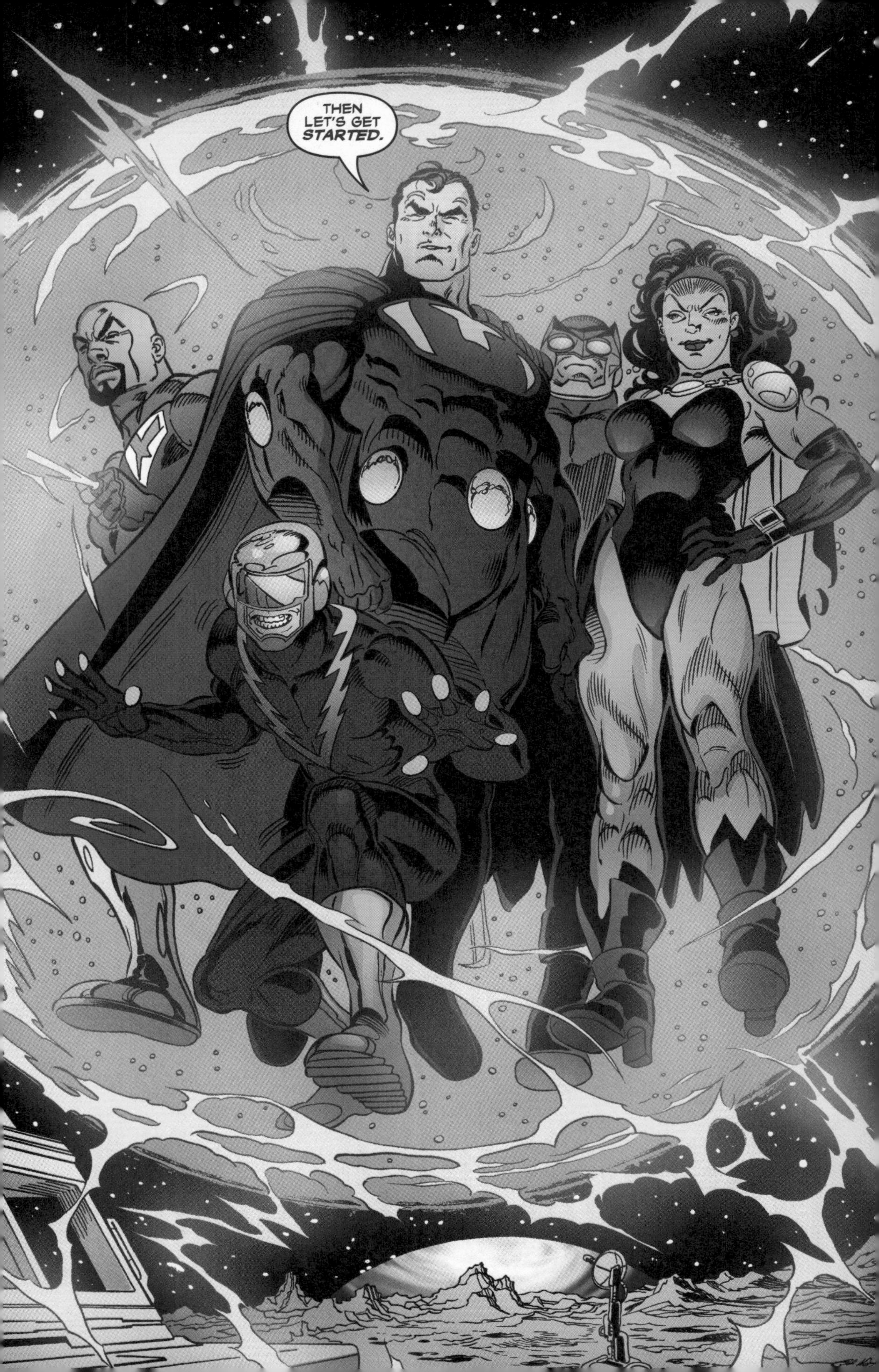
THEN LET'S GET STARTED.

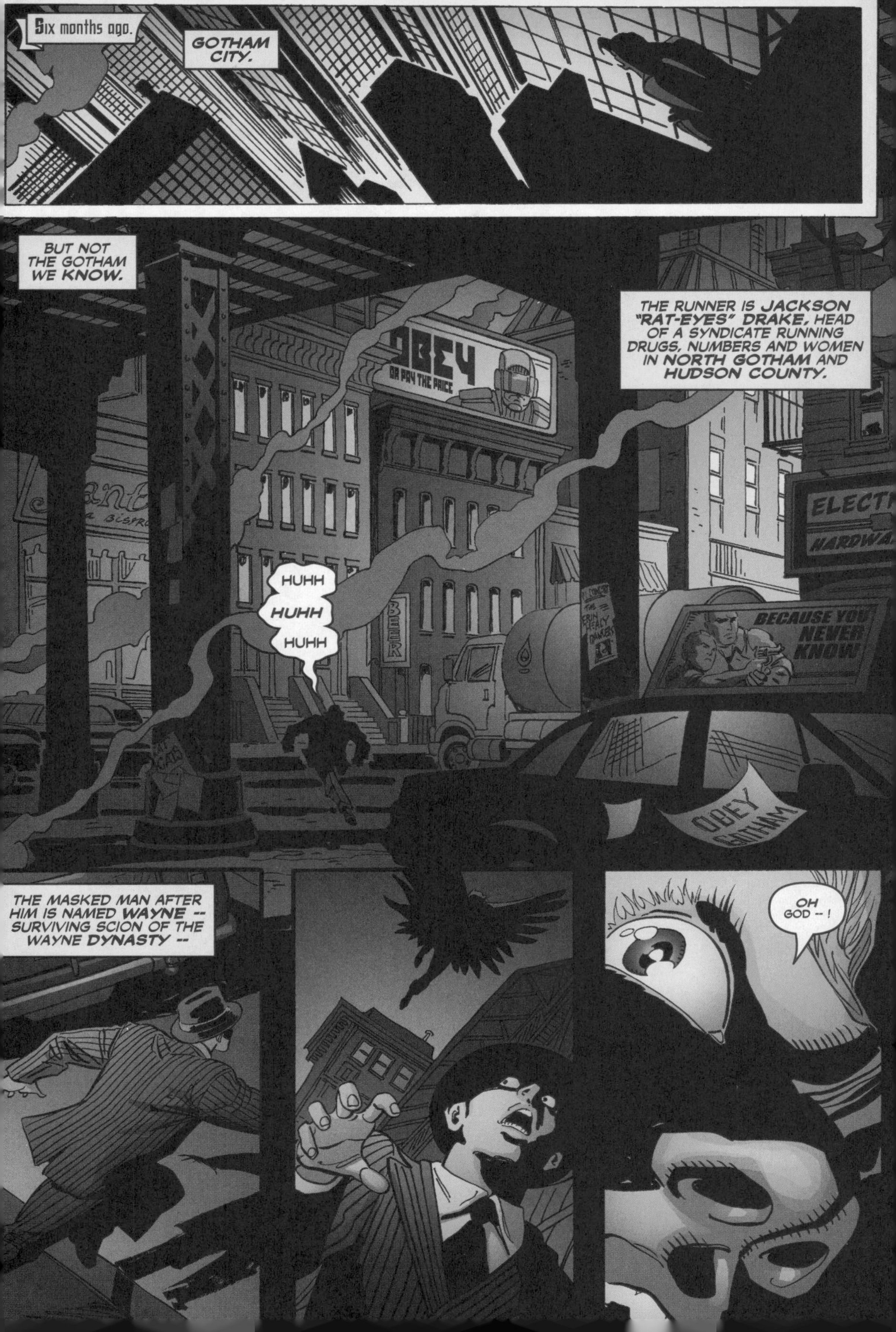
Six months ago.
GOTHAM CITY.
BUT NOT THE GOTHAM WE KNOW.
THE RUNNER IS JACKSON "RAT-EYES" DRAKE, HEAD OF A SYNDICATE RUNNING DRUGS, NUMBERS AND WOMEN IN NORTH GOTHAM AND HUDSON COUNTY.
OBEY OR PAY THE PRICE
ELECTR
HARDWA
BEER
BECAUSE YOU NEVER KNOW
HUHH
HUHH
HUHH
OBEY GOTHAM
THE MASKED MAN AFTER HIM IS NAMED WAYNE -- SURVIVING SCION OF THE WAYNE DYNASTY --
OH GOD -- !

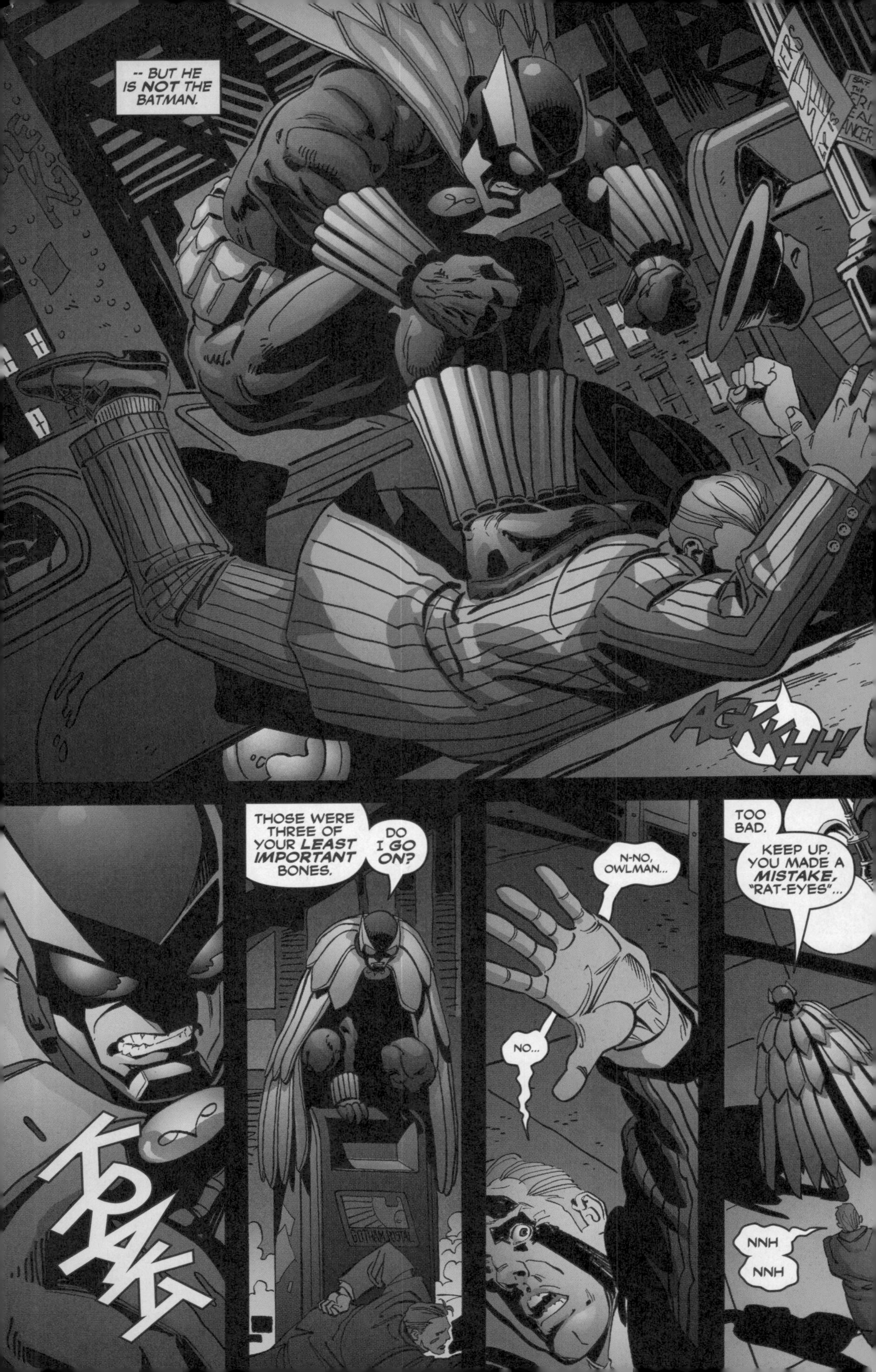
-- BUT HE IS NOT THE BATMAN.
AGKKHH!
KRAKT
THOSE WERE THREE OF YOUR LEAST IMPORTANT BONES.
DO I GO ON?
N-NO, OWLMAN...
NO...
TOO BAD.
KEEP UP. YOU MADE A MISTAKE, "RAT-EYES"...
NNH
NNH

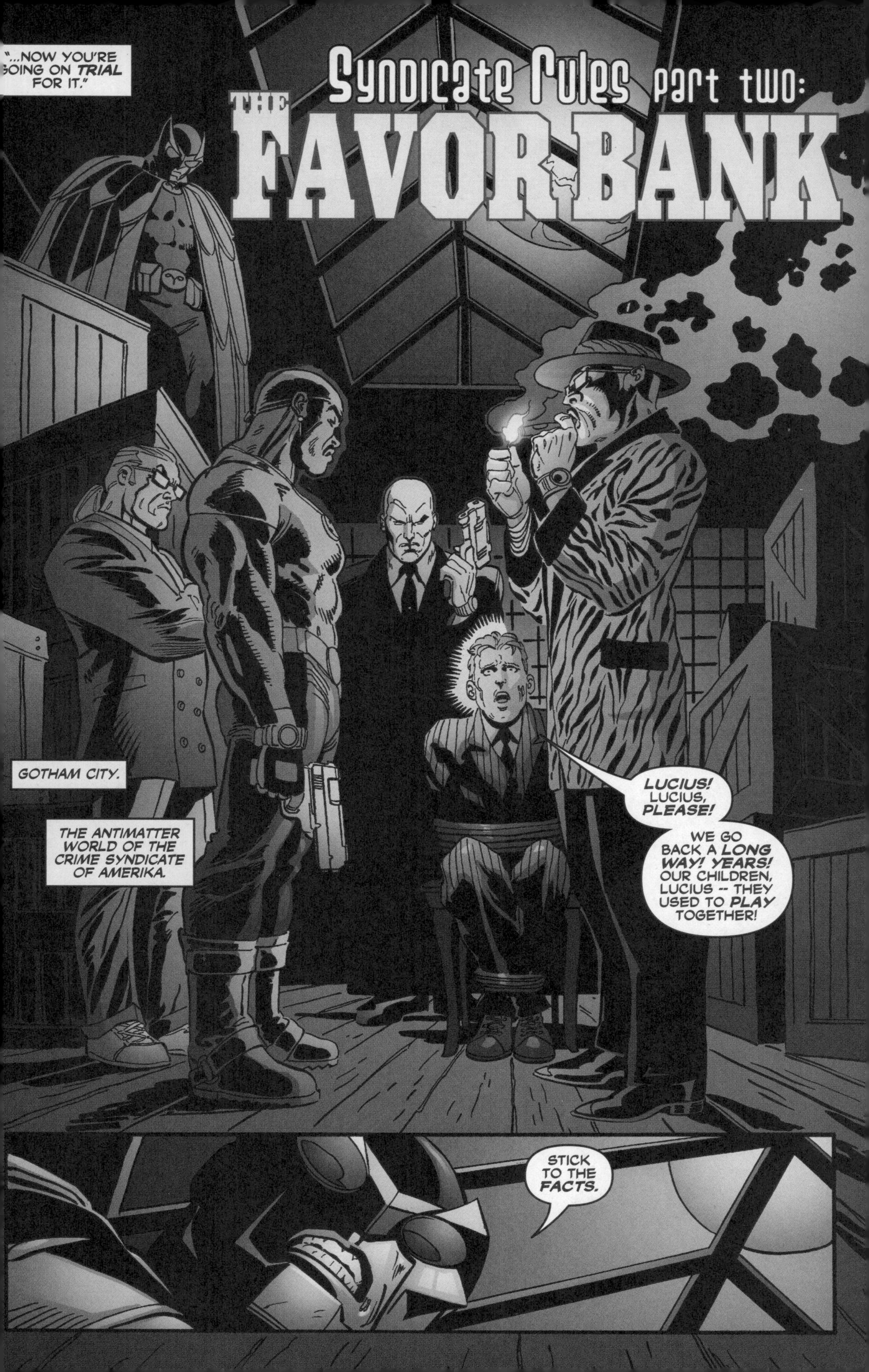
"...NOW YOU'RE GOING ON TRIAL FOR IT."
SYNDICATE RULES PART TWO:
THE FAVOR BANK
GOTHAM CITY.
THE ANTIMATTER WORLD OF THE CRIME SYNDICATE OF AMERIKA.
LUCIUS! LUCIUS, PLEASE!
WE GO BACK A LONG WAY! YEARS! OUR CHILDREN, LUCIUS -- THEY USED TO PLAY TOGETHER!
STICK TO THE FACTS.

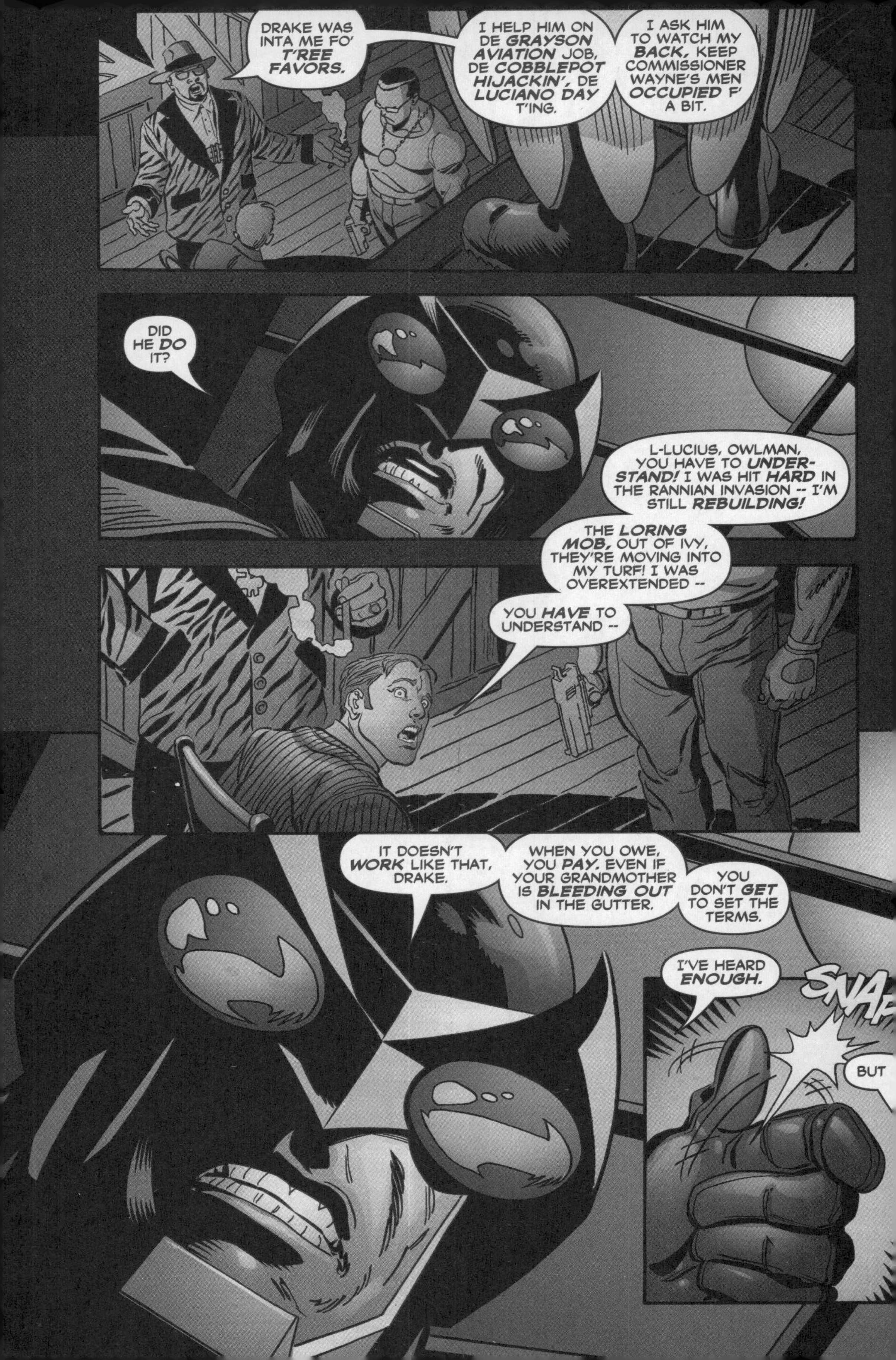
DRAKE WAS INTA ME FO' T'REE FAVORS.
I HELP HIM ON DE GRAYSON AVIATION JOB, DE COBBLEPOT HIJACKIN', DE LUCIANO DAY T'ING.
I ASK HIM TO WATCH MY BACK, KEEP COMMISSIONER WAYNE'S MEN OCCUPIED F' A BIT.
DID HE DO IT?
L-LUCIUS, OWLMAN, YOU HAVE TO UNDER-STAND! I WAS HIT HARD IN THE RANNIAN INVASION -- I'M STILL REBUILDING!
THE LORING MOB, OUT OF IVY, THEY'RE MOVING INTO MY TURF! I WAS OVEREXTENDED --
YOU HAVE TO UNDERSTAND --
IT DOESN'T WORK LIKE THAT, DRAKE.
WHEN YOU OWE, YOU PAY. EVEN IF YOUR GRANDMOTHER IS BLEEDING OUT IN THE GUTTER.
YOU DON'T GET TO SET THE TERMS.
I'VE HEARD ENOUGH.
SNAP
BUT

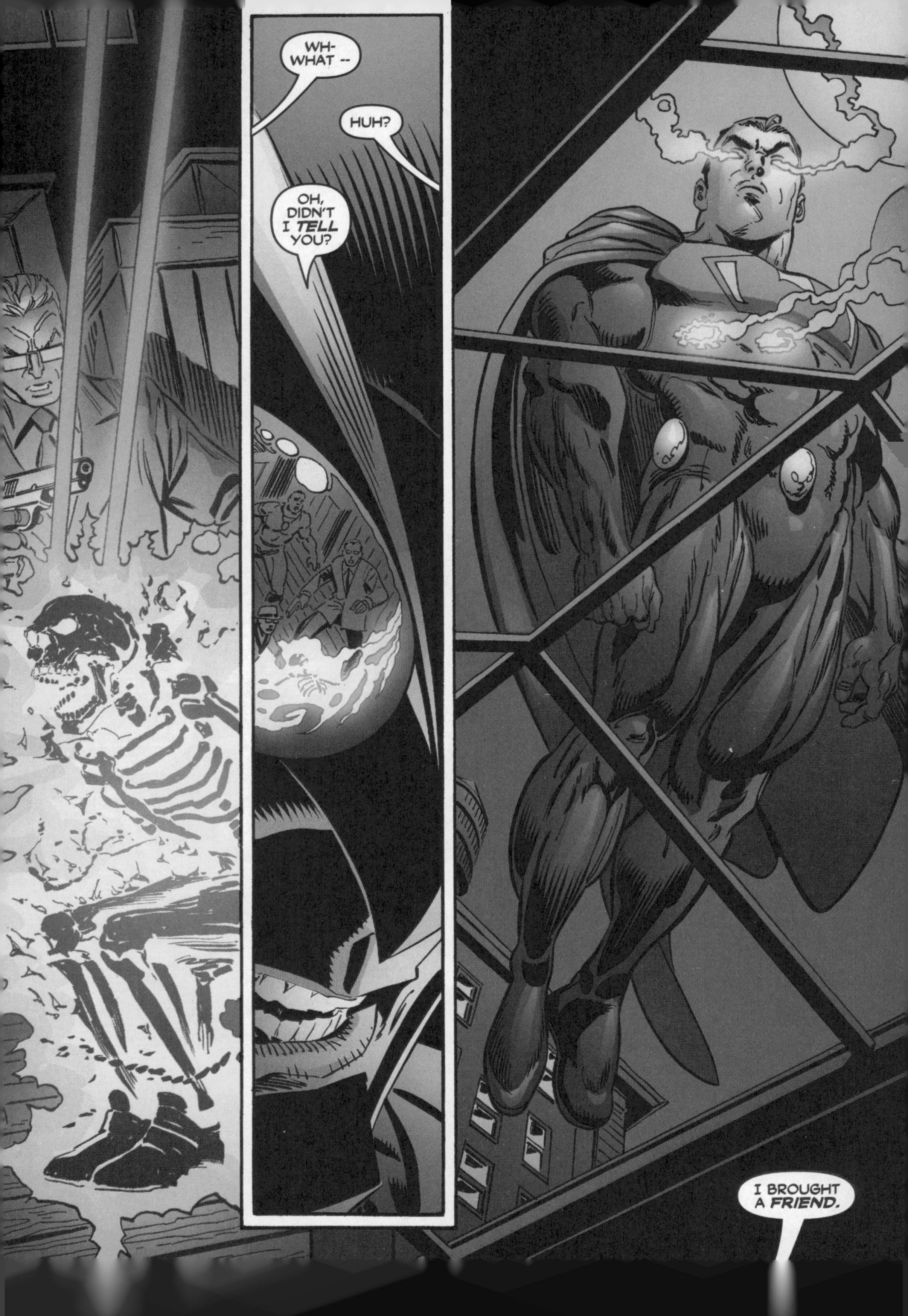
WH- WHAT --
HUH?
OH, DIDN'T I TELL YOU?
I BROUGHT A FRIEND.

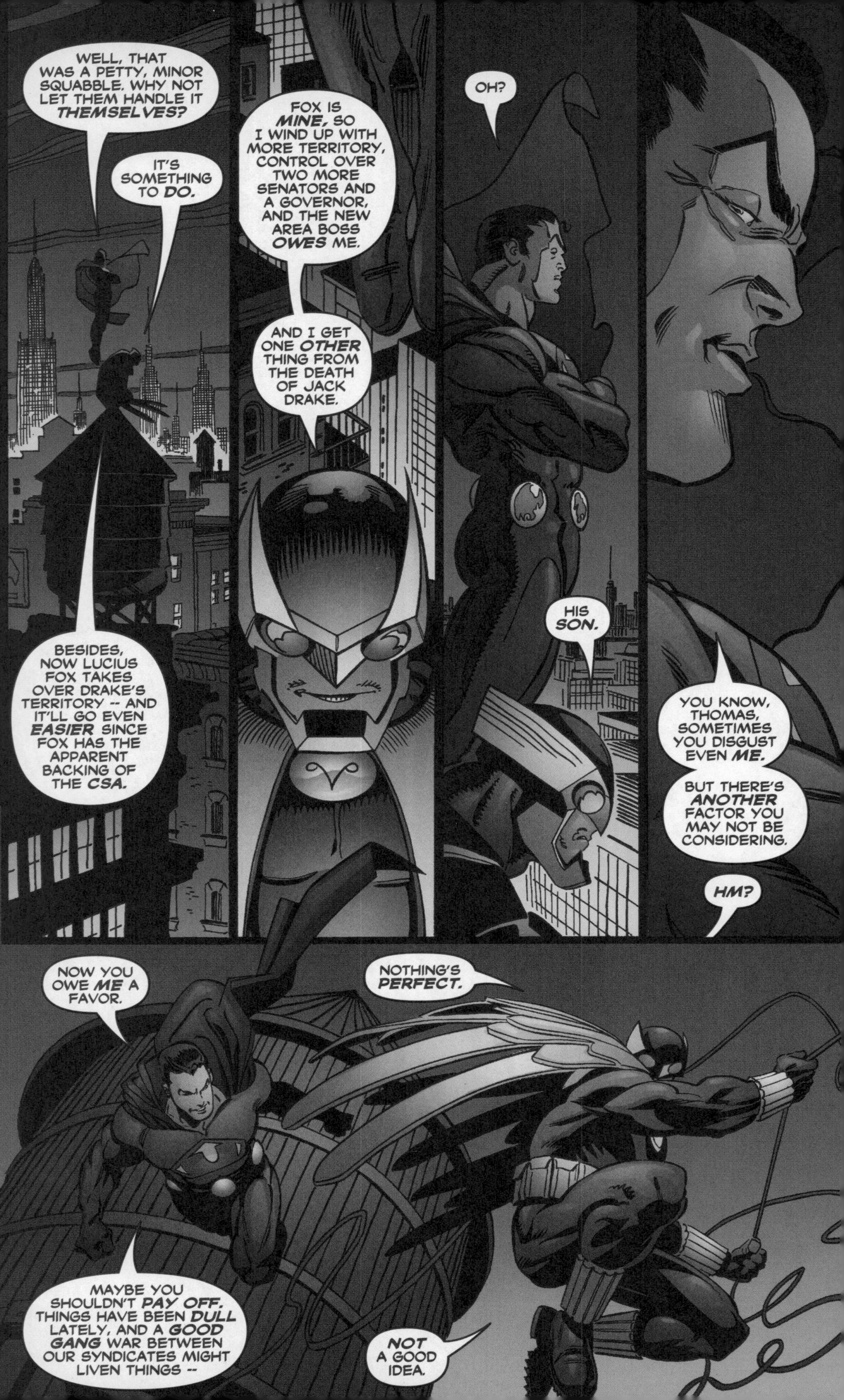
WELL, THAT WAS A PETTY, MINOR SQUABBLE. WHY NOT LET THEM HANDLE IT THEMSELVES?
IT'S SOMETHING TO DO.
BESIDES, NOW LUCIUS FOX TAKES OVER DRAKE'S TERRITORY -- AND IT'LL GO EVEN EASIER SINCE FOX HAS THE APPARENT BACKING OF THE CSA.
FOX IS MINE, SO I WIND UP WITH MORE TERRITORY, CONTROL OVER TWO MORE SENATORS AND A GOVERNOR, AND THE NEW AREA BOSS OWES ME.
AND I GET ONE OTHER THING FROM THE DEATH OF JACK DRAKE.
OH?
HIS SON.
YOU KNOW, THOMAS, SOMETIMES YOU DISGUST EVEN ME.
BUT THERE'S ANOTHER FACTOR YOU MAY NOT BE CONSIDERING.
HM?
NOW YOU OWE ME A FAVOR.
NOTHING'S PERFECT.
MAYBE YOU SHOULDN'T PAY OFF. THINGS HAVE BEEN DULL LATELY, AND A GOOD GANG WAR BETWEEN OUR SYNDICATES MIGHT LIVEN THINGS --
NOT A GOOD IDEA.

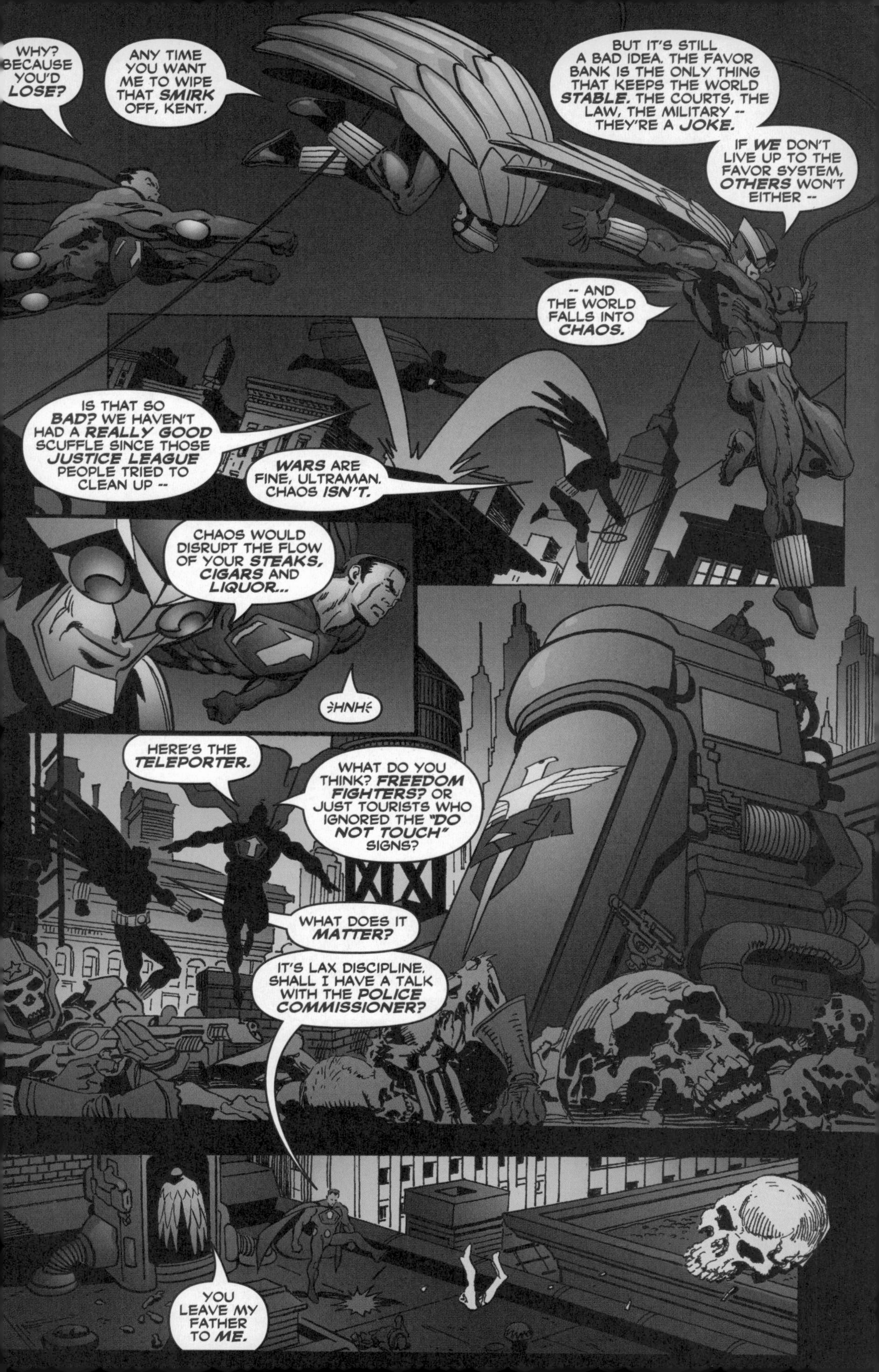
WHY? BECAUSE YOU'D LOSE?
ANY TIME YOU WANT ME TO WIPE THAT SMIRK OFF, KENT.
BUT IT'S STILL A BAD IDEA. THE FAVOR BANK IS THE ONLY THING THAT KEEPS THE WORLD STABLE. THE COURTS, THE LAW, THE MILITARY -- THEY'RE A JOKE.
IF WE DON'T LIVE UP TO THE FAVOR SYSTEM, OTHERS WON'T EITHER --
-- AND THE WORLD FALLS INTO CHAOS.
IS THAT SO BAD? WE HAVEN'T HAD A REALLY GOOD SCUFFLE SINCE THOSE JUSTICE LEAGUE PEOPLE TRIED TO CLEAN UP --
WARS ARE FINE, ULTRAMAN. CHAOS ISN'T.
CHAOS WOULD DISRUPT THE FLOW OF YOUR STEAKS, CIGARS AND LIQUOR...
HNH
HERE'S THE TELEPORTER.
WHAT DO YOU THINK? FREEDOM FIGHTERS? OR JUST TOURISTS WHO IGNORED THE "DO NOT TOUCH" SIGNS?
WHAT DOES IT MATTER?
IT'S LAX DISCIPLINE. SHALL I HAVE A TALK WITH THE POLICE COMMISSIONER?
YOU LEAVE MY FATHER TO ME.

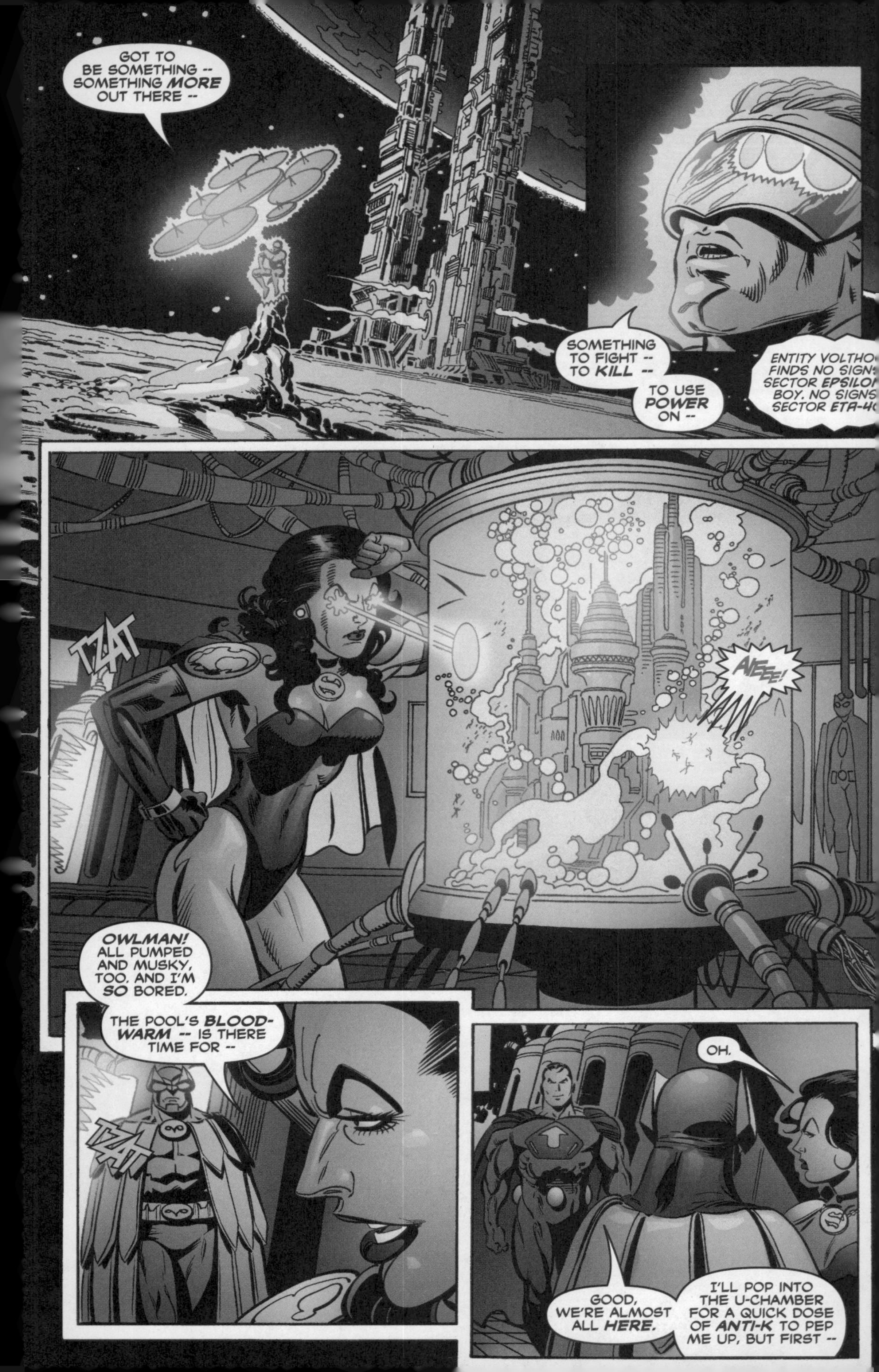
GOT TO BE SOMETHING -- SOMETHING MORE OUT THERE --
SOMETHING TO FIGHT -- TO KILL --
TO USE POWER ON --
ENTITY VOLTHO FINDS NO SIGNS SECTOR EPSILON BOY. NO SIGNS SECTOR ETA-4
TZAT
AIEEE!
OWLMAN! ALL PUMPED AND MUSKY, TOO. AND I'M SO BORED.
THE POOL'S BLOOD-WARM -- IS THERE TIME FOR --
TZAT
OH.
GOOD, WE'RE ALMOST ALL HERE.
I'LL POP INTO THE U-CHAMBER FOR A QUICK DOSE OF ANTI-K TO PEP ME UP, BUT FIRST --

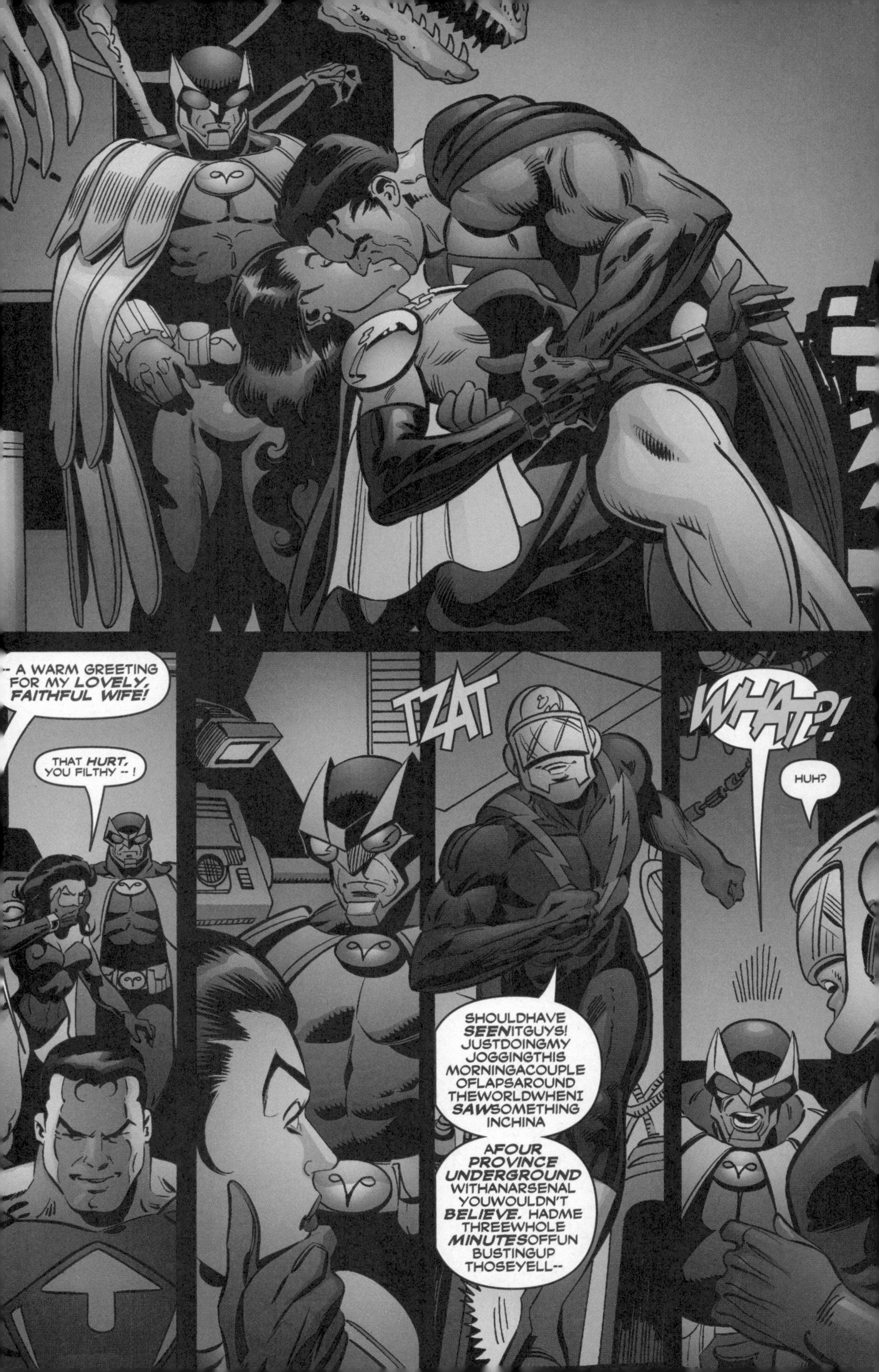

-- A WARM GREETING FOR MY LOVELY, FAITHFUL WIFE!
THAT HURT, YOU FILTHY -- !
TZAT
SHOULDHAVE SEENITGUYS! JUSTDOINGMY JOGGINGTHIS MORNINGACOUPLE OFLAPSAROUND THEWORLDWHENI SAWSOMETHING INCHINA
AFOUR PROVINCE UNDERGROUND WITHANARSENAL YOUWOULDN'T BELIEVE. HADME THREEWHOLE MINUTESOFFUN BUSTINGUP THOSEYELL--
WHAT?!
HUH?

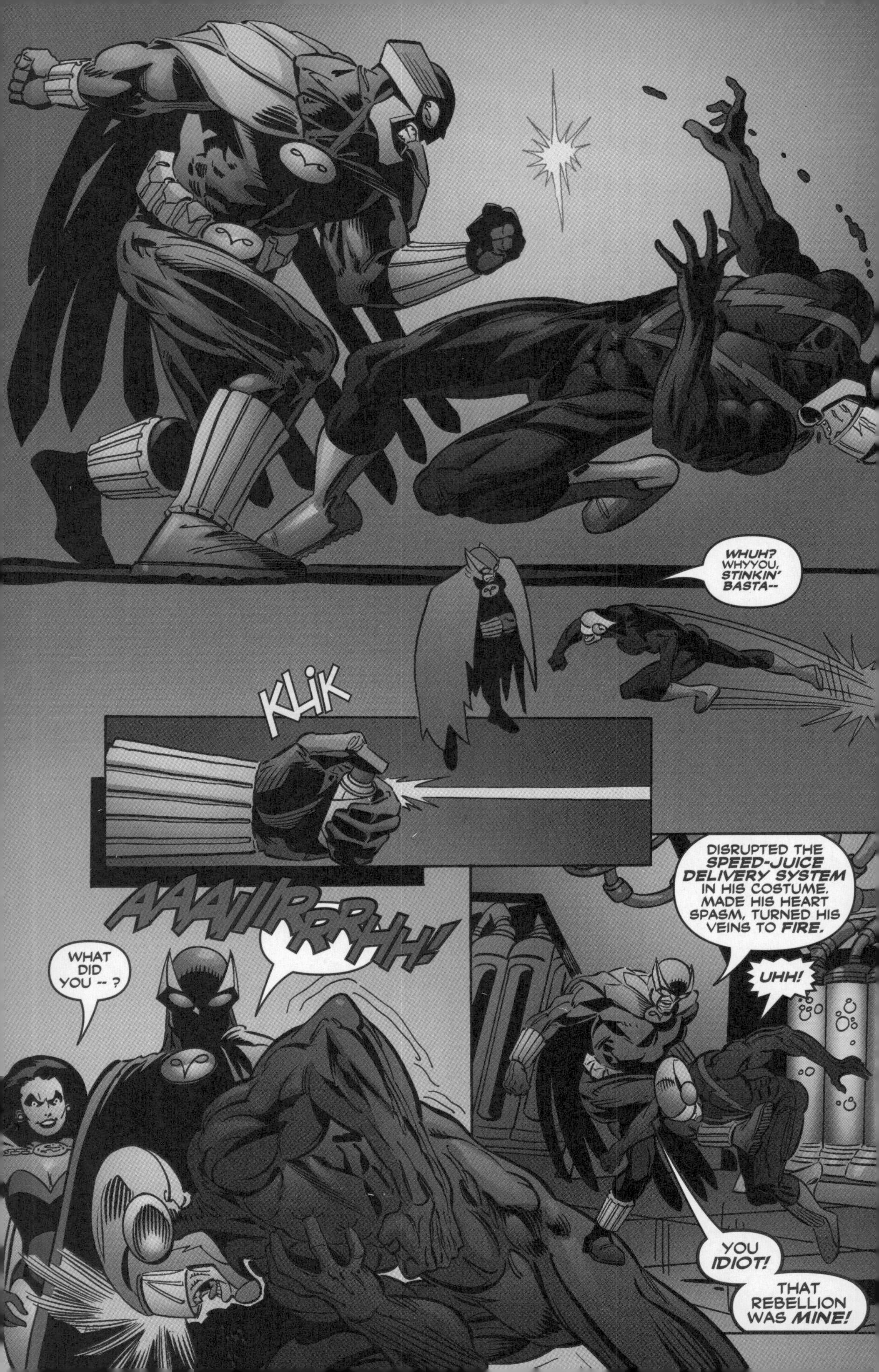
WHUH? WHYYOU, STINKIN' BASTA--
KLIK
DISRUPTED THE SPEED-JUICE DELIVERY SYSTEM IN HIS COSTUME. MADE HIS HEART SPASM, TURNED HIS VEINS TO FIRE.
AAAIIIRRRHH!
WHAT DID YOU -- ?
UHH!
YOU IDIOT!
THAT REBELLION WAS MINE!

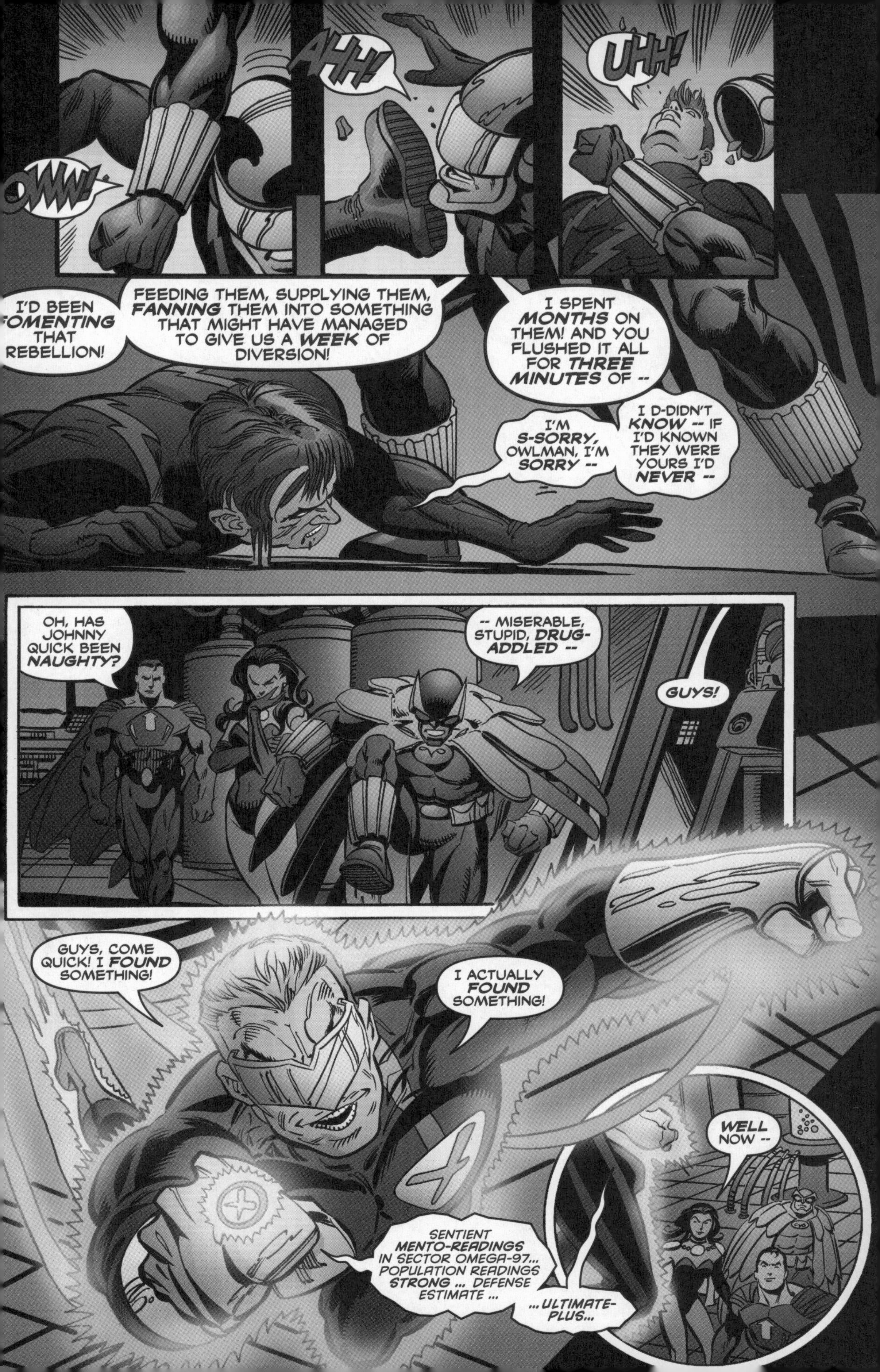
OWW!
AHH!
UHH!
I'D BEEN FOMENTING THAT REBELLION!
FEEDING THEM, SUPPLYING THEM, FANNING THEM INTO SOMETHING THAT MIGHT HAVE MANAGED TO GIVE US A WEEK OF DIVERSION!
I SPENT MONTHS ON THEM! AND YOU FLUSHED IT ALL FOR THREE MINUTES OF --
I'M S-SORRY, OWLMAN, I'M SORRY --
I D-DIDN'T KNOW -- IF I'D KNOWN THEY WERE YOURS I'D NEVER --
OH, HAS JOHNNY QUICK BEEN NAUGHTY?
-- MISERABLE, STUPID, DRUG-ADDLED --
GUYS!
GUYS, COME QUICK! I FOUND SOMETHING!
I ACTUALLY FOUND SOMETHING!
WELL NOW --
SENTIENT MENTO-READINGS IN SECTOR OMEGA-97... POPULATION READINGS STRONG ... DEFENSE ESTIMATE ...
...ULTIMATE-PLUS...

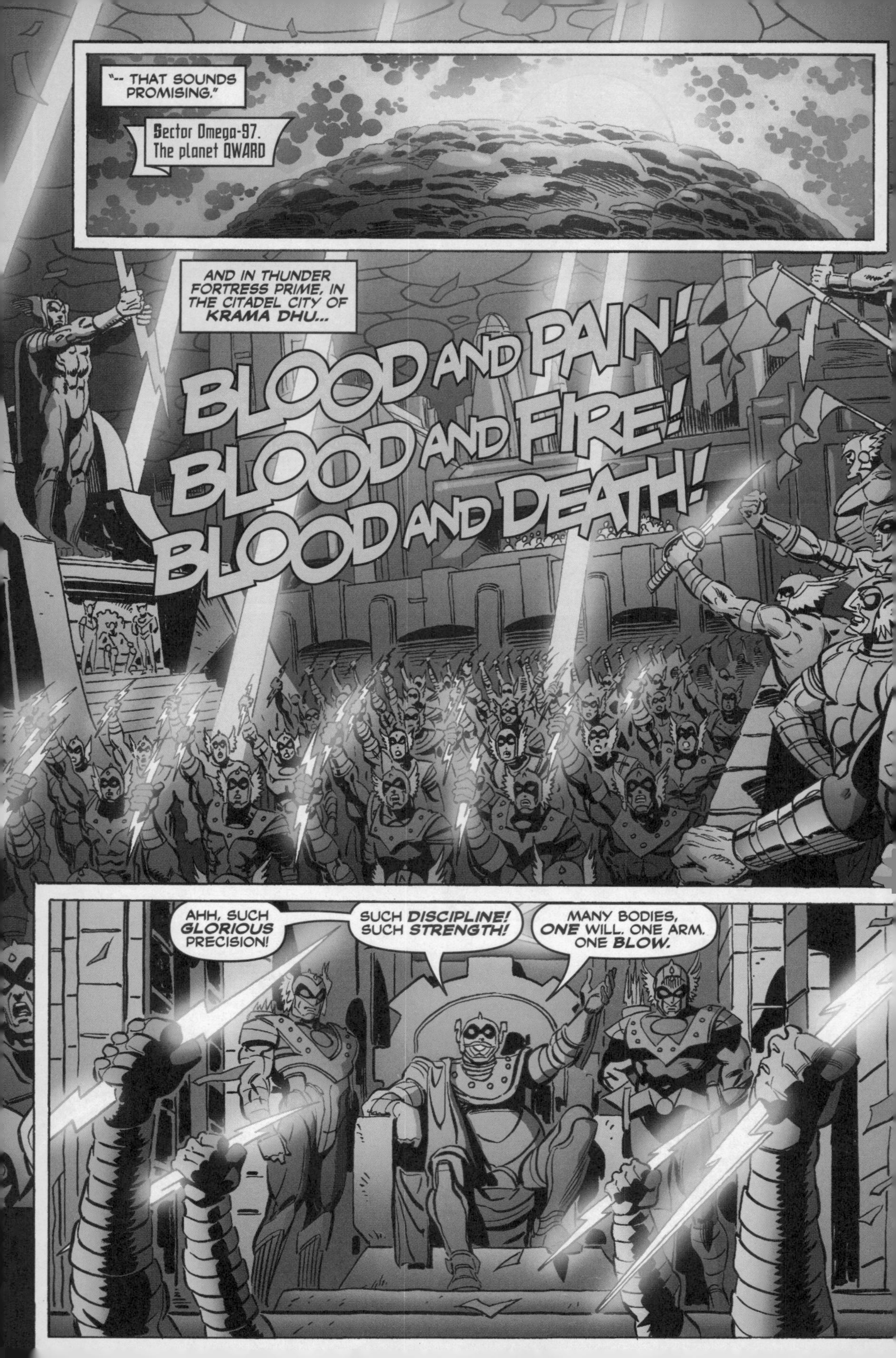
"-- THAT SOUNDS PROMISING."
Sector Omega-97. The planet QWARD
AND IN THUNDER FORTRESS PRIME, IN THE CITADEL CITY OF KRAMA DHU...
BLOOD AND PAIN! BLOOD AND FIRE! BLOOD AND DEATH!
AHH, SUCH GLORIOUS PRECISION!
SUCH DISCIPLINE! SUCH STRENGTH!
MANY BODIES, ONE WILL. ONE ARM. ONE BLOW.

THE **GREATEST** MILITARY FORCE IN THE MULTIVERSE. NEVER STRONGER, NEVER READIER, NEVER **PROUDER.**

WOULDN'T YOU **SAY,** COMMANDER ROVAL?

THEY ARE **UNPARALLELED** AT MARCHING, THUNDERLORD BRIKAN.

AFTER GENERATIONS OF **TRADE** IN ARMAMENTS RATHER THAN **CONQUEST,** HOWEVER, OUR ARMIES HAVE NOT BEEN TESTED IN --

'LL BOW! 'LL BOW!

BOW FOR THE HIGH WEAPONLORD, VARNATHON OF Q'ULD!!

VARNATHON! VARNEY, YOU OLD **LAVA-PUP,** HOW GOOD OF YOU TO DROP BY!

HAVE YOU COME TO SEE THE **TROOP REVIEW?** THEY'LL BE DISPLAYING QWA-RAMPART DEPLOYMENT AT **SPEED** NEXT.

STUNNING, I'M SURE, BUT PERHAPS ANOTHER DAY.

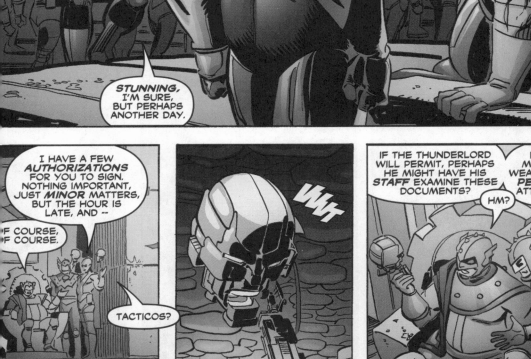

I HAVE A FEW **AUTHORIZATIONS** FOR YOU TO SIGN. NOTHING IMPORTANT, JUST **MINOR** MATTERS, BUT THE HOUR IS LATE, AND --

F COURSE, F COURSE.

TACTICOS?

WhT

IF THE THUNDERLORD WILL PERMIT, PERHAPS HE MIGHT HAVE HIS **STAFF** EXAMINE THESE DOCUMENTS?

IF THEY MERIT THE WEAPONLORD'S **PERSONAL** ATTENTION --

HM?

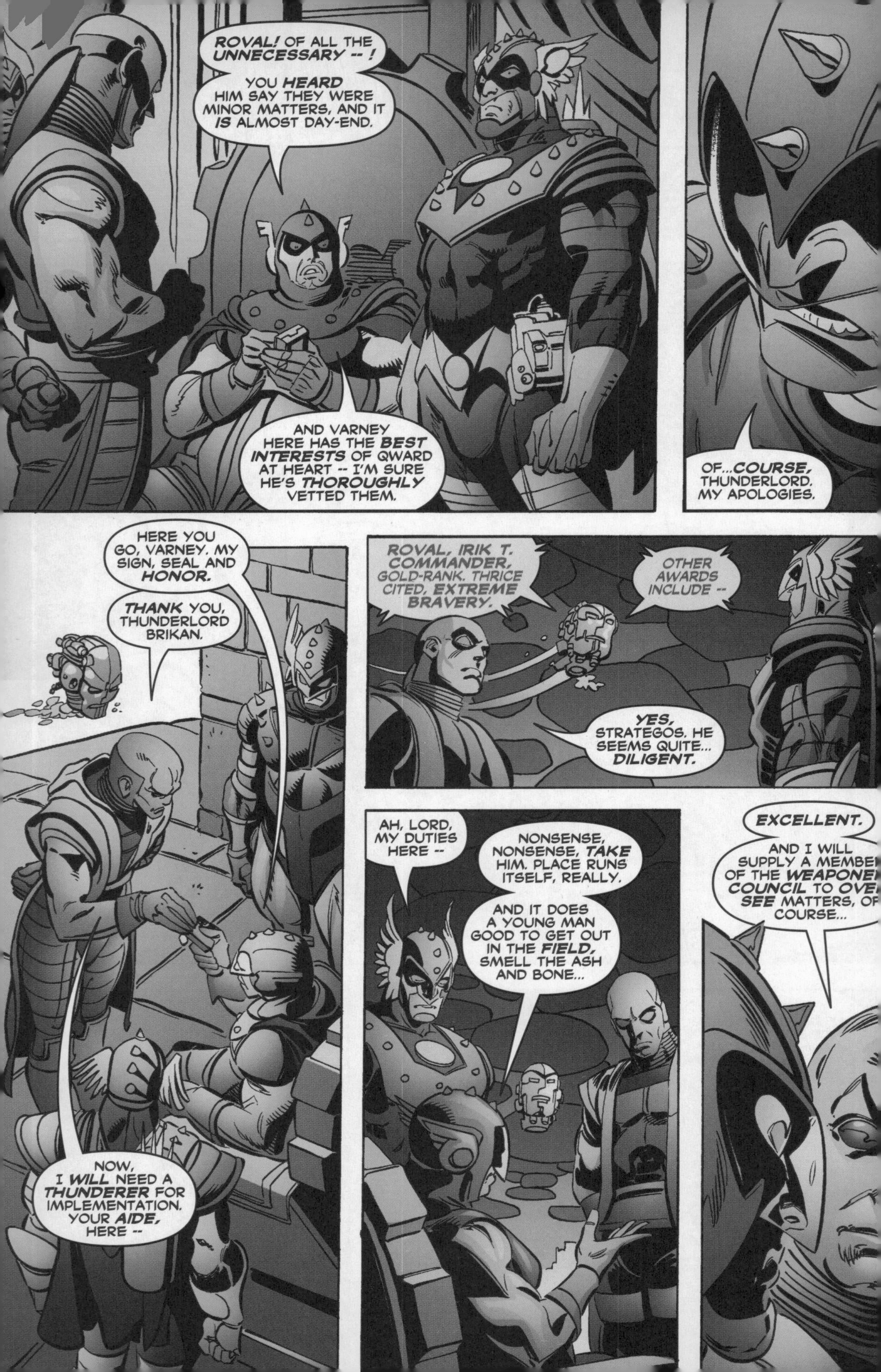
ROVAL! OF ALL THE UNNECESSARY -- !
YOU HEARD HIM SAY THEY WERE MINOR MATTERS, AND IT IS ALMOST DAY-END.
AND VARNEY HERE HAS THE BEST INTERESTS OF QWARD AT HEART -- I'M SURE HE'S THOROUGHLY VETTED THEM.
OF...COURSE, THUNDERLORD. MY APOLOGIES.
HERE YOU GO, VARNEY. MY SIGN, SEAL AND HONOR.
THANK YOU, THUNDERLORD BRIKAN.
NOW, I WILL NEED A THUNDERER FOR IMPLEMENTATION. YOUR AIDE, HERE --
ROVAL, IRIK T. COMMANDER, GOLD-RANK. THRICE CITED, EXTREME BRAVERY.
OTHER AWARDS INCLUDE --
YES, STRATEGOS. HE SEEMS QUITE... DILIGENT.
AH, LORD, MY DUTIES HERE --
NONSENSE, NONSENSE, TAKE HIM. PLACE RUNS ITSELF, REALLY.
AND IT DOES A YOUNG MAN GOOD TO GET OUT IN THE FIELD, SMELL THE ASH AND BONE...
EXCELLENT.
AND I WILL SUPPLY A MEMBE OF THE WEAPONE COUNCIL TO OVE SEE MATTERS, OF COURSE...

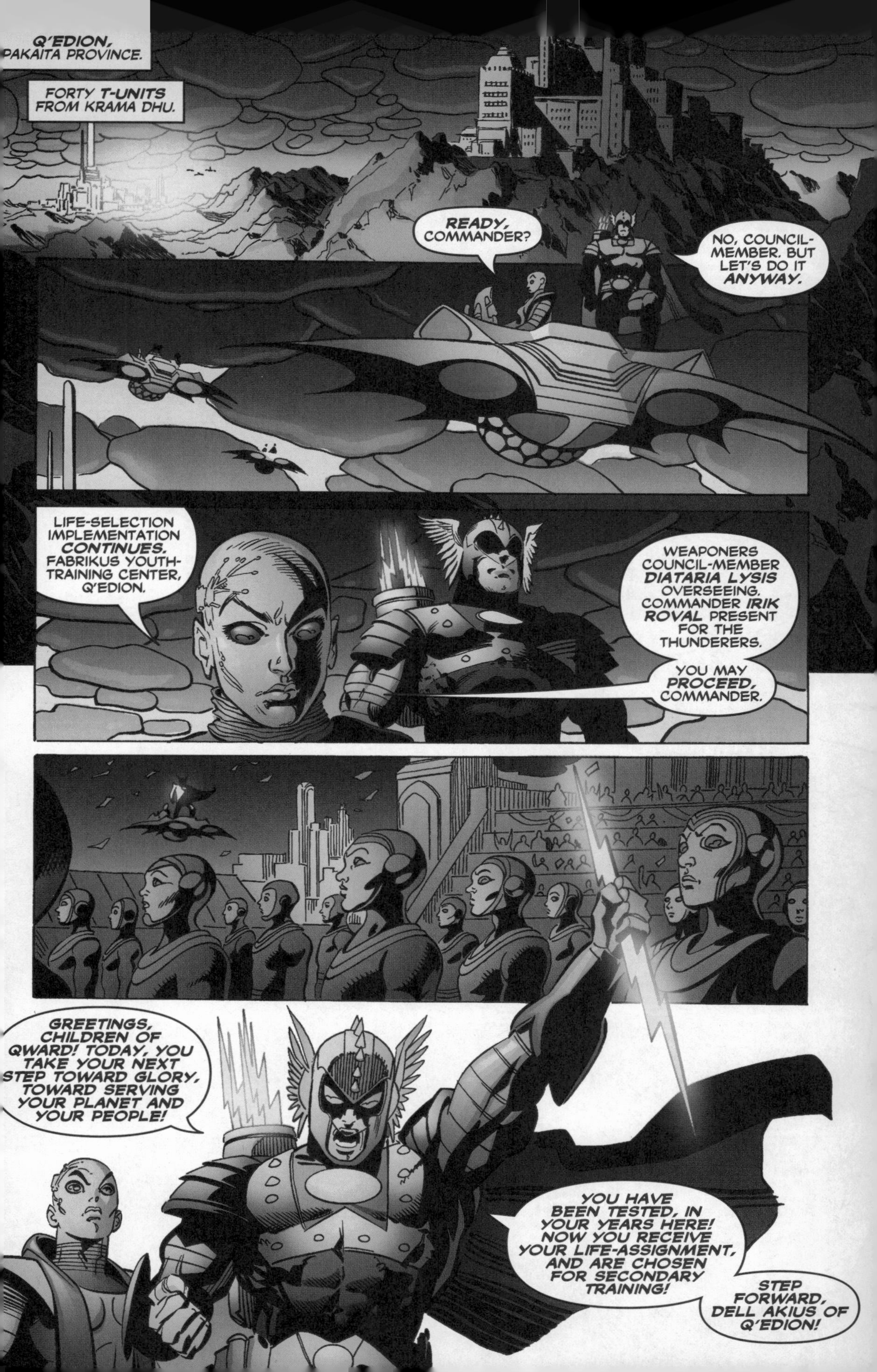
Q'EDION, PAKAITA PROVINCE.
FORTY T-UNITS FROM KRAMA DHU.
READY, COMMANDER?
NO, COUNCIL-MEMBER. BUT LET'S DO IT ANYWAY.
LIFE-SELECTION IMPLEMENTATION CONTINUES. FABRIKUS YOUTH-TRAINING CENTER, Q'EDION.
WEAPONERS COUNCIL-MEMBER DIATARIA LYSIS OVERSEEING. COMMANDER IRIK ROVAL PRESENT FOR THE THUNDERERS.
YOU MAY PROCEED, COMMANDER.
GREETINGS, CHILDREN OF QWARD! TODAY, YOU TAKE YOUR NEXT STEP TOWARD GLORY, TOWARD SERVING YOUR PLANET AND YOUR PEOPLE!
YOU HAVE BEEN TESTED, IN YOUR YEARS HERE! NOW YOU RECEIVE YOUR LIFE-ASSIGNMENT, AND ARE CHOSEN FOR SECONDARY TRAINING!
STEP FORWARD, DELL AKIUS OF Q'EDION!

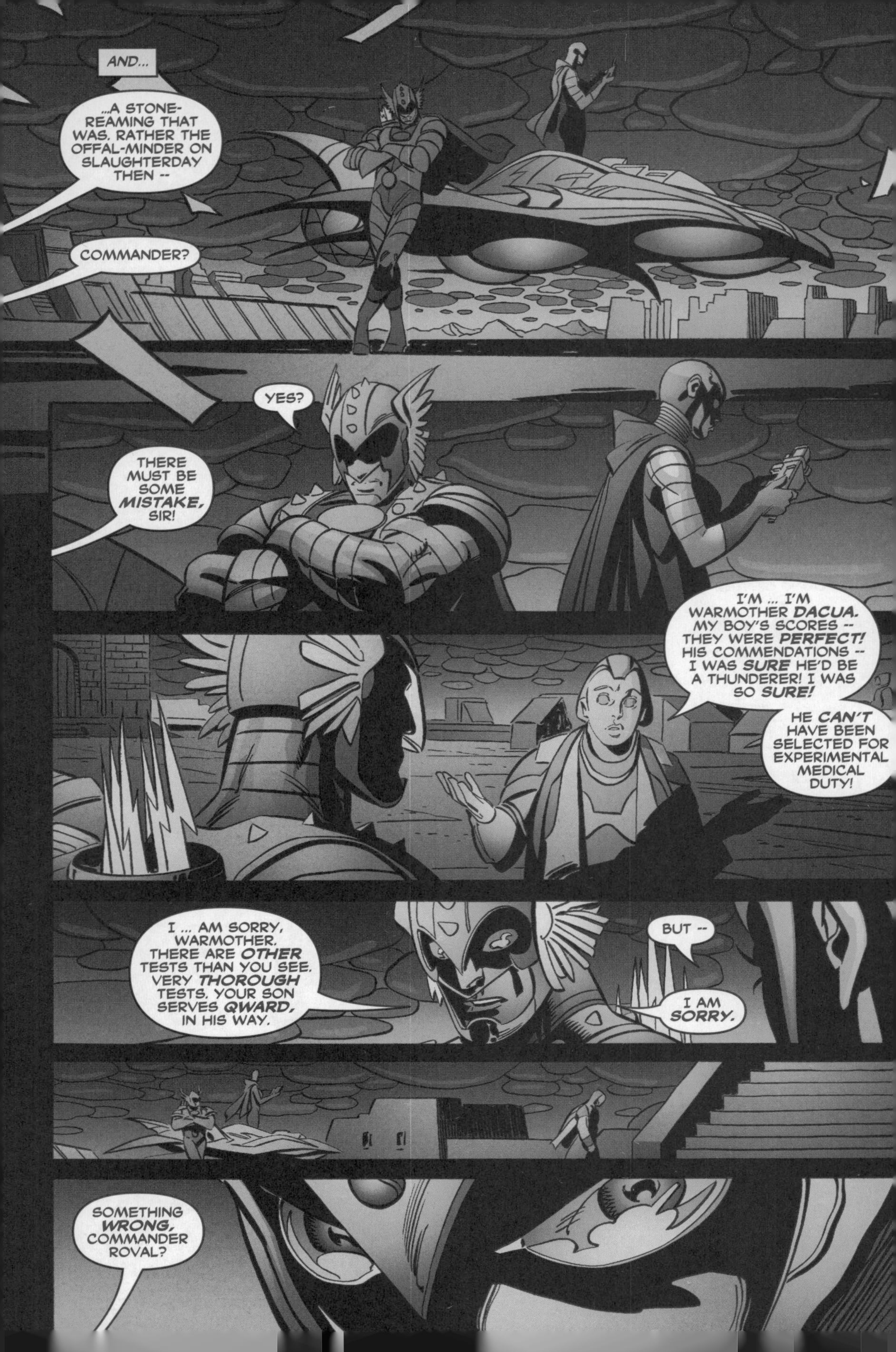
AND...
...A STONE-REAMING THAT WAS. RATHER THE OFFAL-MINDER ON SLAUGHTERDAY THEN --
COMMANDER?
YES?
THERE MUST BE SOME MISTAKE, SIR!
I'M ... I'M WARMOTHER DACUA. MY BOY'S SCORES -- THEY WERE PERFECT! HIS COMMENDATIONS -- I WAS SURE HE'D BE A THUNDERER! I WAS SO SURE!
HE CAN'T HAVE BEEN SELECTED FOR EXPERIMENTAL MEDICAL DUTY!
I ... AM SORRY, WARMOTHER. THERE ARE OTHER TESTS THAN YOU SEE. VERY THOROUGH TESTS. YOUR SON SERVES QWARD, IN HIS WAY.
BUT --
I AM SORRY.
SOMETHING WRONG, COMMANDER ROVAL?

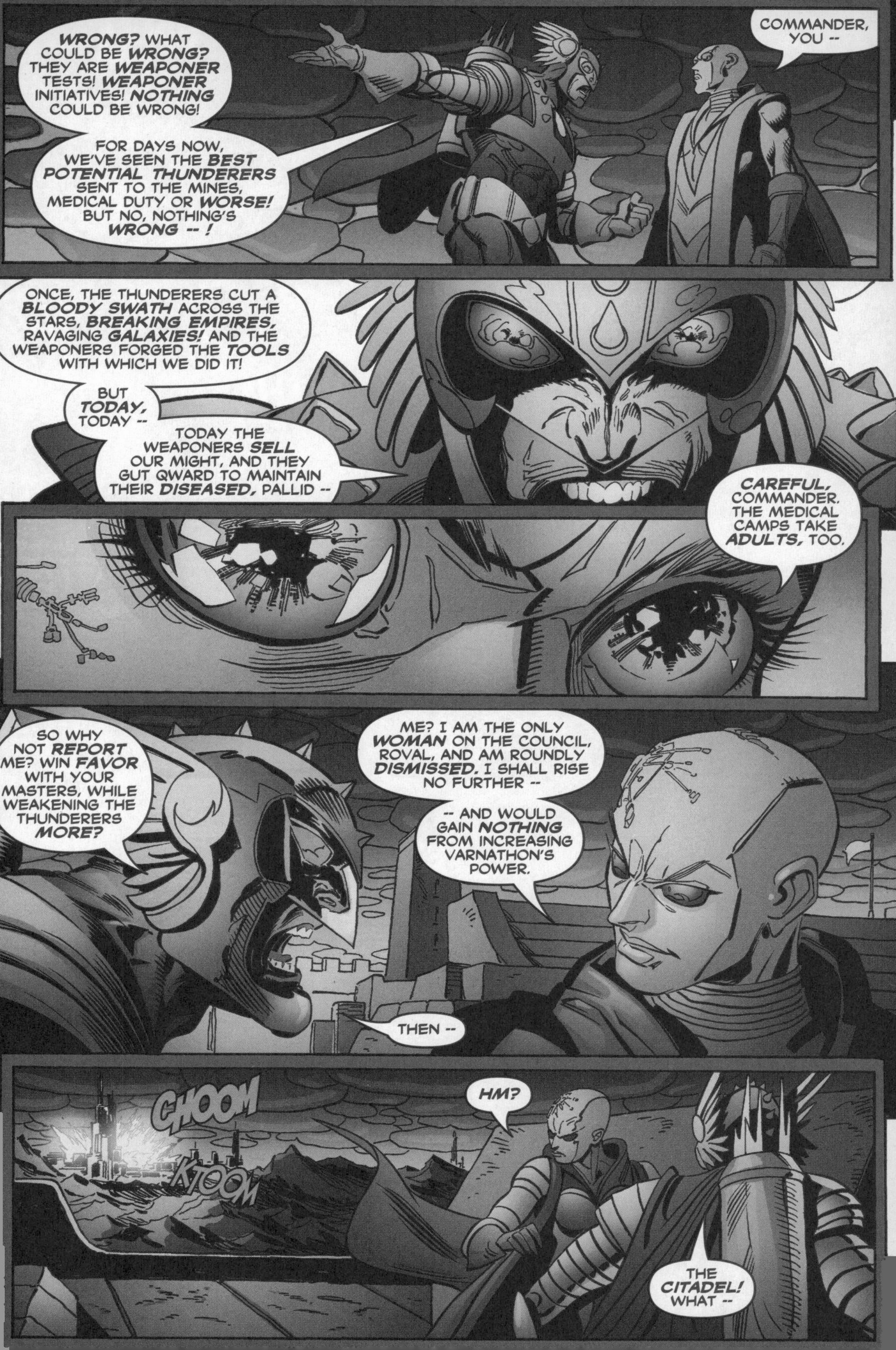

WRONG? WHAT COULD BE WRONG? THEY ARE WEAPONER TESTS! WEAPONER INITIATIVES! NOTHING COULD BE WRONG!
FOR DAYS NOW, WE'VE SEEN THE BEST POTENTIAL THUNDERERS SENT TO THE MINES, MEDICAL DUTY OR WORSE! BUT NO, NOTHING'S WRONG -- !
COMMANDER, YOU --
ONCE, THE THUNDERERS CUT A BLOODY SWATH ACROSS THE STARS, BREAKING EMPIRES, RAVAGING GALAXIES! AND THE WEAPONERS FORGED THE TOOLS WITH WHICH WE DID IT!
BUT TODAY, TODAY --
TODAY THE WEAPONERS SELL OUR MIGHT, AND THEY GUT QWARD TO MAINTAIN THEIR DISEASED, PALLID --
CAREFUL, COMMANDER. THE MEDICAL CAMPS TAKE ADULTS, TOO.
SO WHY NOT REPORT ME? WIN FAVOR WITH YOUR MASTERS, WHILE WEAKENING THE THUNDERERS MORE?
ME? I AM THE ONLY WOMAN ON THE COUNCIL, ROVAL, AND AM ROUNDLY DISMISSED. I SHALL RISE NO FURTHER --
-- AND WOULD GAIN NOTHING FROM INCREASING VARNATHON'S POWER.
THEN --
CHOOM
KTOOM
HM?
THE CITADEL! WHAT --

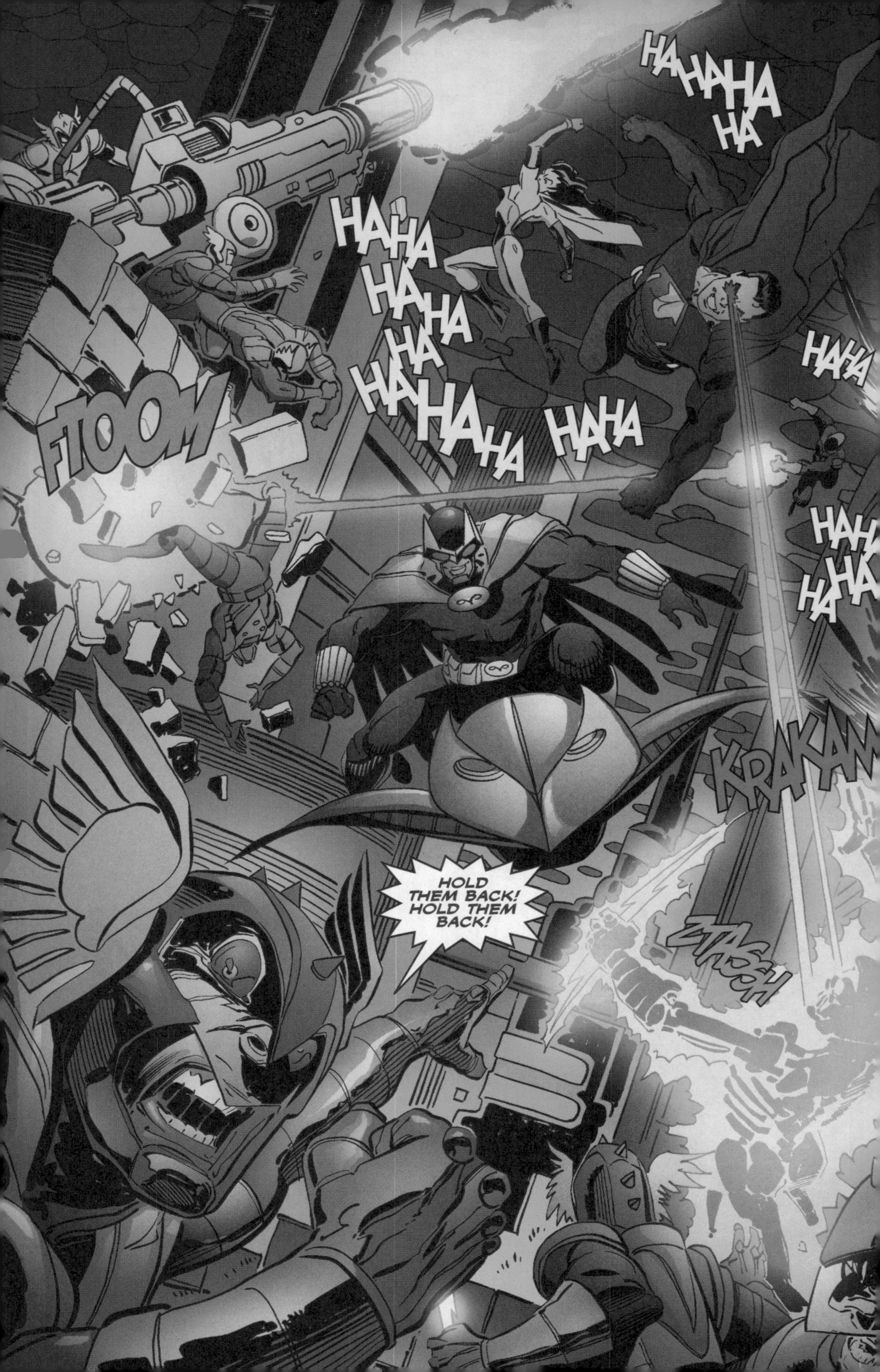
HAHAHA
HA
HAHA
HAHA
HA
HA
HAHAHAHA
FTOOM
HAHA
HAHA
HOLD THEM BACK! HOLD THEM BACK!
ZTASCH

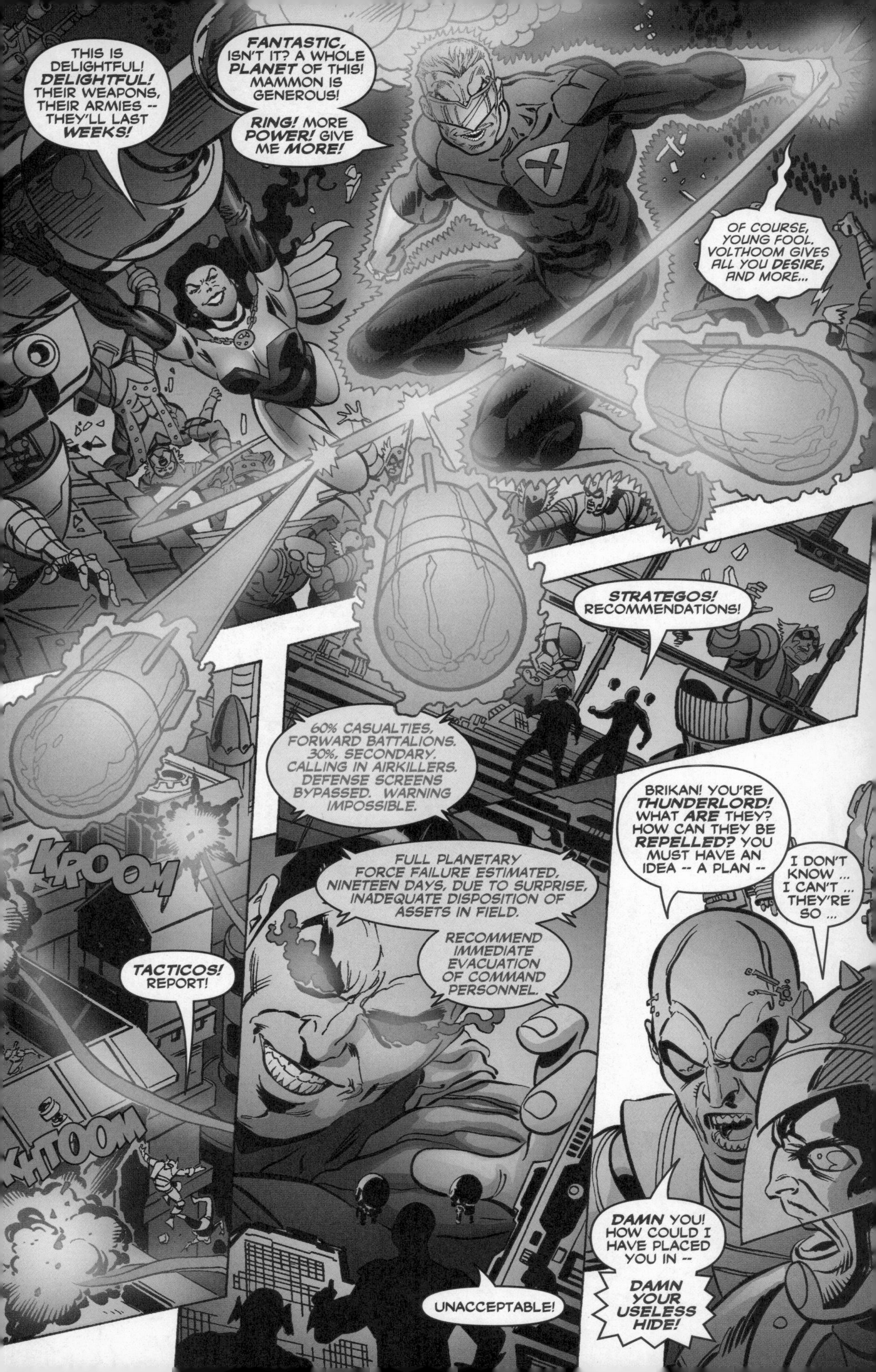
THIS IS DELIGHTFUL! DELIGHTFUL! THEIR WEAPONS, THEIR ARMIES -- THEY'LL LAST WEEKS!
FANTASTIC, ISN'T IT? A WHOLE PLANET OF THIS! MAMMON IS GENEROUS!
RING! MORE POWER! GIVE ME MORE!
OF COURSE, YOUNG FOOL. VOLTHOOM GIVES ALL YOU DESIRE, AND MORE...
STRATEGOS! RECOMMENDATIONS!
60% CASUALTIES, FORWARD BATTALIONS. 30%, SECONDARY. CALLING IN AIRKILLERS. DEFENSE SCREENS BYPASSED. WARNING IMPOSSIBLE.
KRROOM
FULL PLANETARY FORCE FAILURE ESTIMATED, NINETEEN DAYS, DUE TO SURPRISE, INADEQUATE DISPOSITION OF ASSETS IN FIELD.
RECOMMEND IMMEDIATE EVACUATION OF COMMAND PERSONNEL.
BRIKAN! YOU'RE THUNDERLORD! WHAT ARE THEY? HOW CAN THEY BE REPELLED? YOU MUST HAVE AN IDEA -- A PLAN --
I DON'T KNOW ... I CAN'T ... THEY'RE SO ...
TACTICOS! REPORT!
KHTOOM
UNACCEPTABLE!
DAMN YOU! HOW COULD I HAVE PLACED YOU IN --
DAMN YOUR USELESS HIDE!

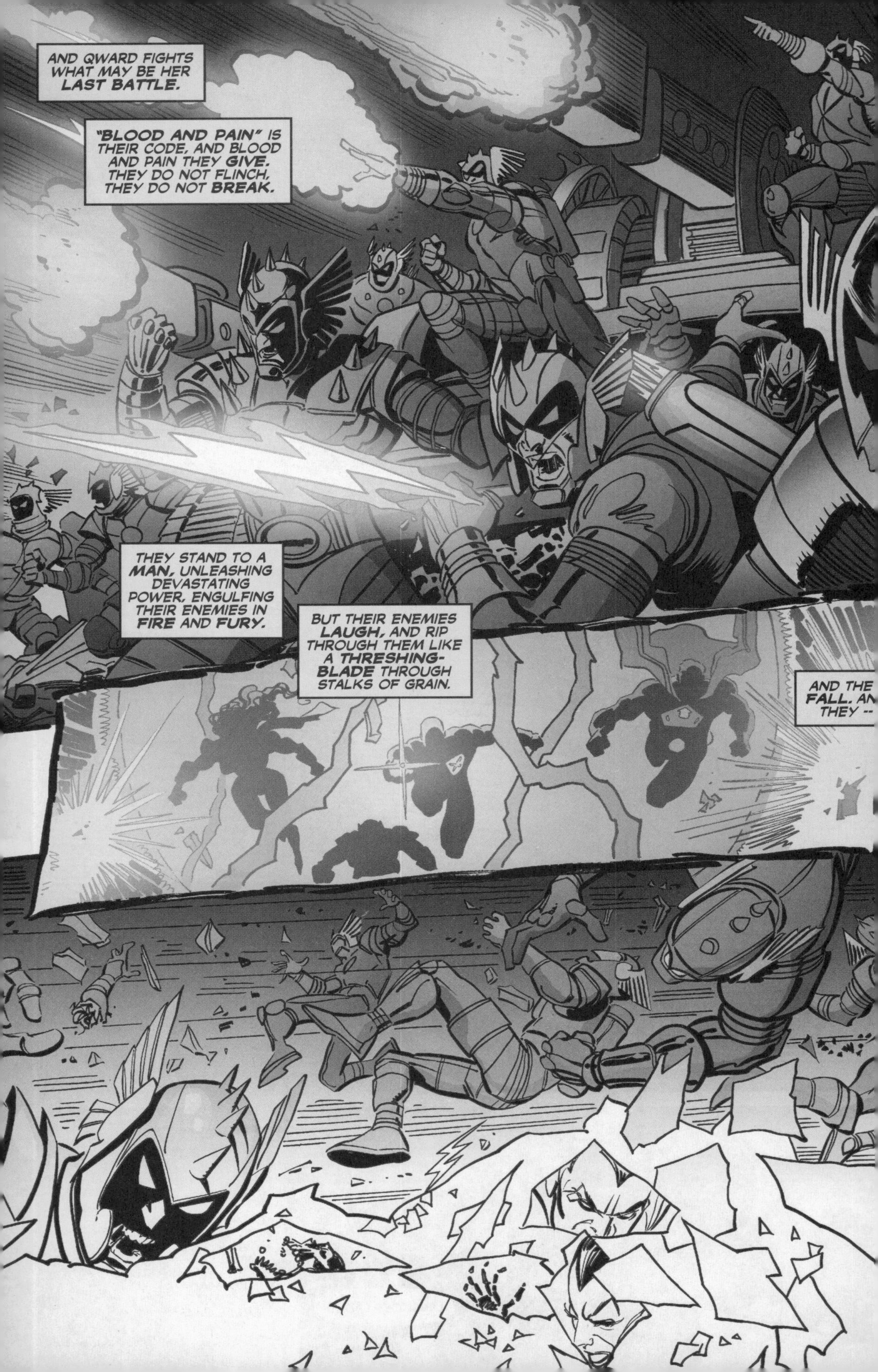
AND QWARD FIGHTS WHAT MAY BE HER LAST BATTLE.
"BLOOD AND PAIN" IS THEIR CODE, AND BLOOD AND PAIN THEY GIVE. THEY DO NOT FLINCH, THEY DO NOT BREAK.
THEY STAND TO A MAN, UNLEASHING DEVASTATING POWER, ENGULFING THEIR ENEMIES IN FIRE AND FURY.
BUT THEIR ENEMIES LAUGH, AND RIP THROUGH THEM LIKE A THRESHING-BLADE THROUGH STALKS OF GRAIN.
AND THE FALL. AN THEY --

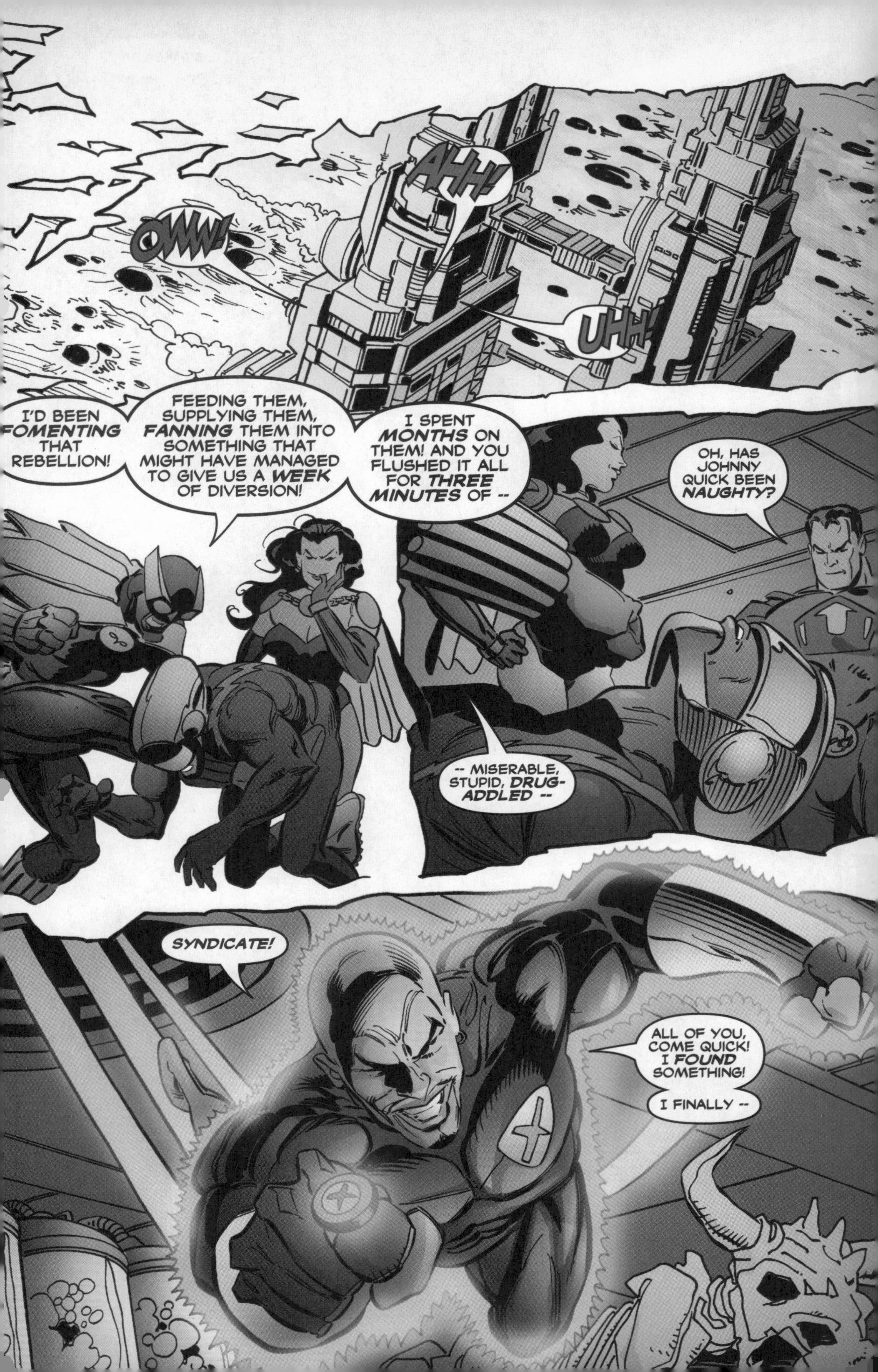
OWW!
AHH!
UHH!
I'D BEEN FOMENTING THAT REBELLION!
FEEDING THEM, SUPPLYING THEM, FANNING THEM INTO SOMETHING THAT MIGHT HAVE MANAGED TO GIVE US A WEEK OF DIVERSION!
I SPENT MONTHS ON THEM! AND YOU FLUSHED IT ALL FOR THREE MINUTES OF --
OH, HAS JOHNNY QUICK BEEN NAUGHTY?
-- MISERABLE, STUPID, DRUG-ADDLED --
SYNDICATE!
ALL OF YOU, COME QUICK! I FOUND SOMETHING!
I FINALLY --

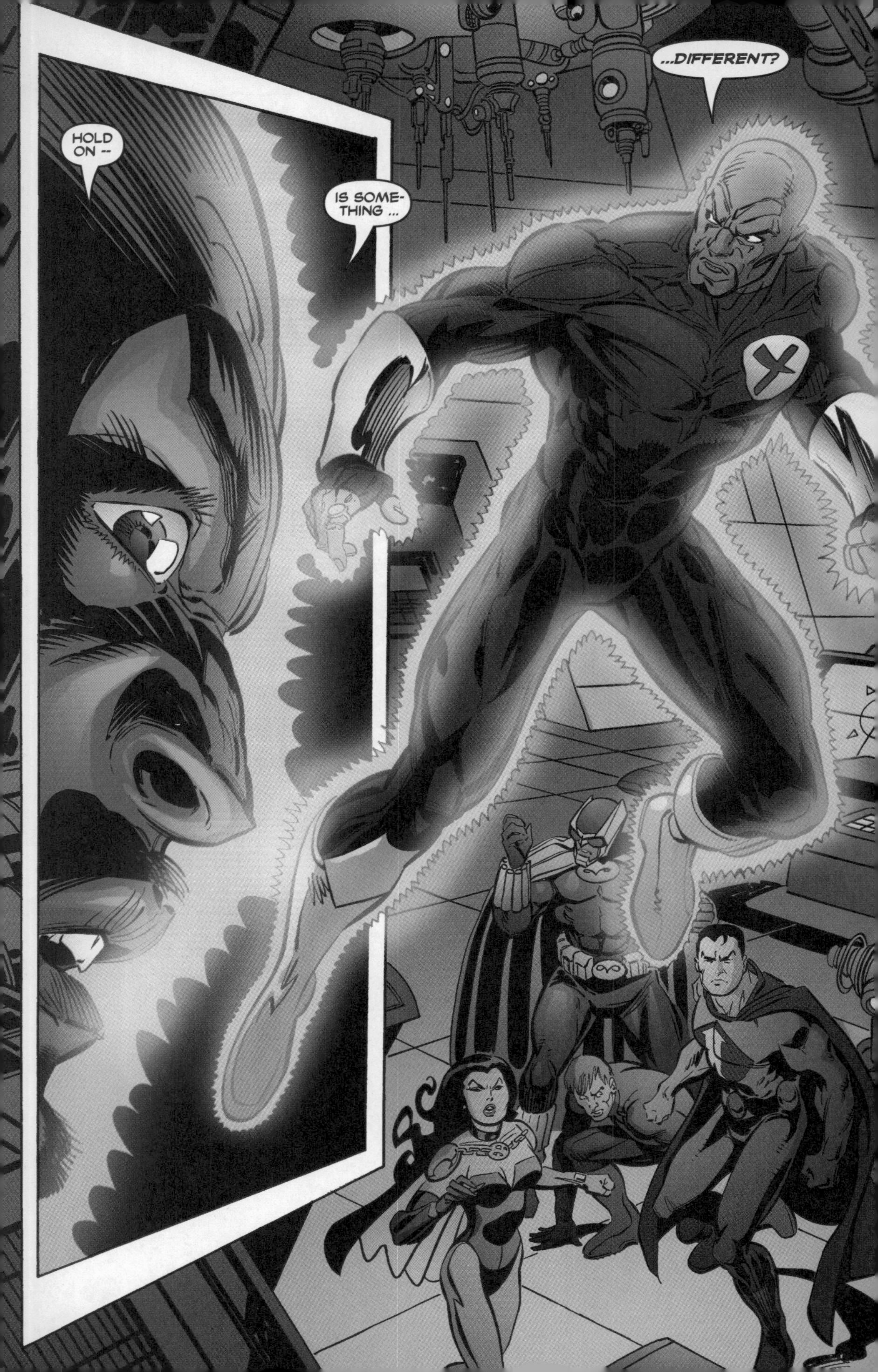
HOLD ON --
IS SOME-THING ...
...DIFFERENT?

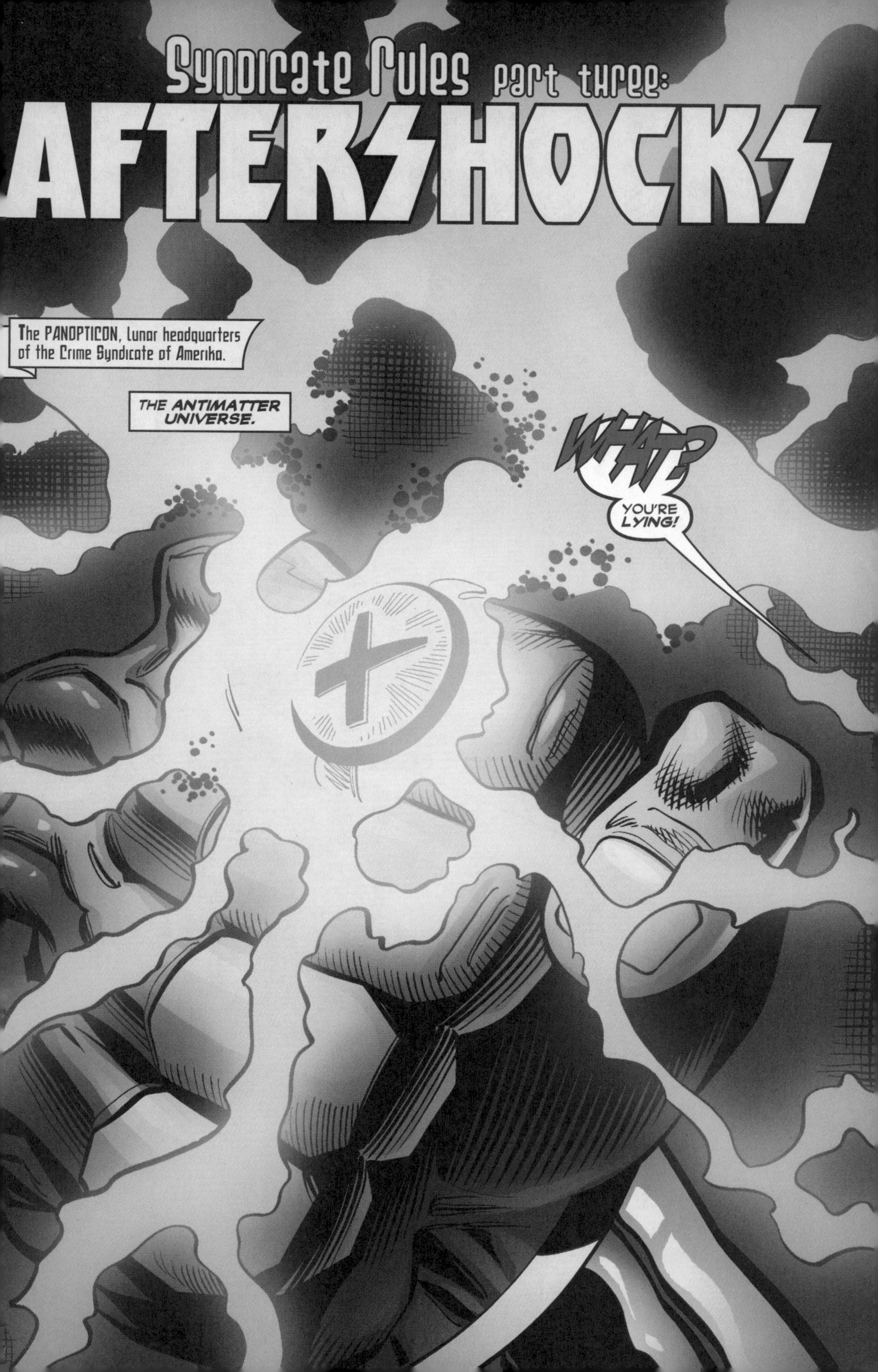
Syndicate Rules part three:
AFTERSHOCKS
The PANOPTICON, lunar headquarters of the Crime Syndicate of Amerika.
THE ANTIMATTER UNIVERSE.
WHAT?
YOU'RE LYING!

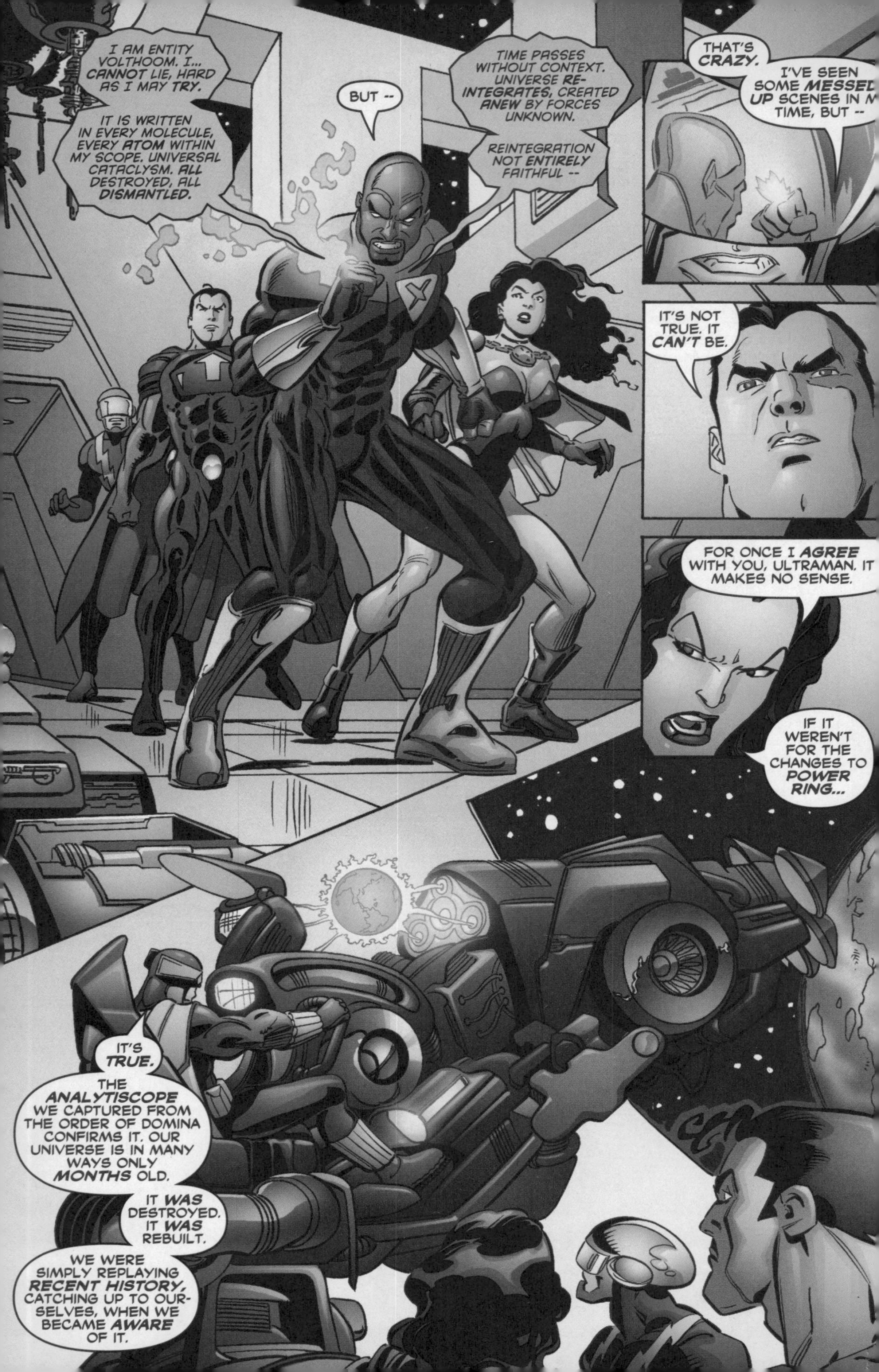

I AM ENTITY VOLTHOOM. I... CANNOT LIE, HARD AS I MAY TRY.
IT IS WRITTEN IN EVERY MOLECULE, EVERY ATOM WITHIN MY SCOPE. UNIVERSAL CATACLYSM. ALL DESTROYED, ALL DISMANTLED.
BUT --
TIME PASSES WITHOUT CONTEXT. UNIVERSE RE-INTEGRATES, CREATED ANEW BY FORCES UNKNOWN.
REINTEGRATION NOT ENTIRELY FAITHFUL --
THAT'S CRAZY.
I'VE SEEN SOME MESSED UP SCENES IN M TIME, BUT --
IT'S NOT TRUE. IT CAN'T BE.
FOR ONCE I AGREE WITH YOU, ULTRAMAN. IT MAKES NO SENSE.
IF IT WEREN'T FOR THE CHANGES TO POWER RING...
IT'S TRUE.
THE ANALYTISCOPE WE CAPTURED FROM THE ORDER OF DOMINA CONFIRMS IT. OUR UNIVERSE IS IN MANY WAYS ONLY MONTHS OLD.
IT WAS DESTROYED. IT WAS REBUILT.
WE WERE SIMPLY REPLAYING RECENT HISTORY, CATCHING UP TO OUR-SELVES, WHEN WE BECAME AWARE OF IT.

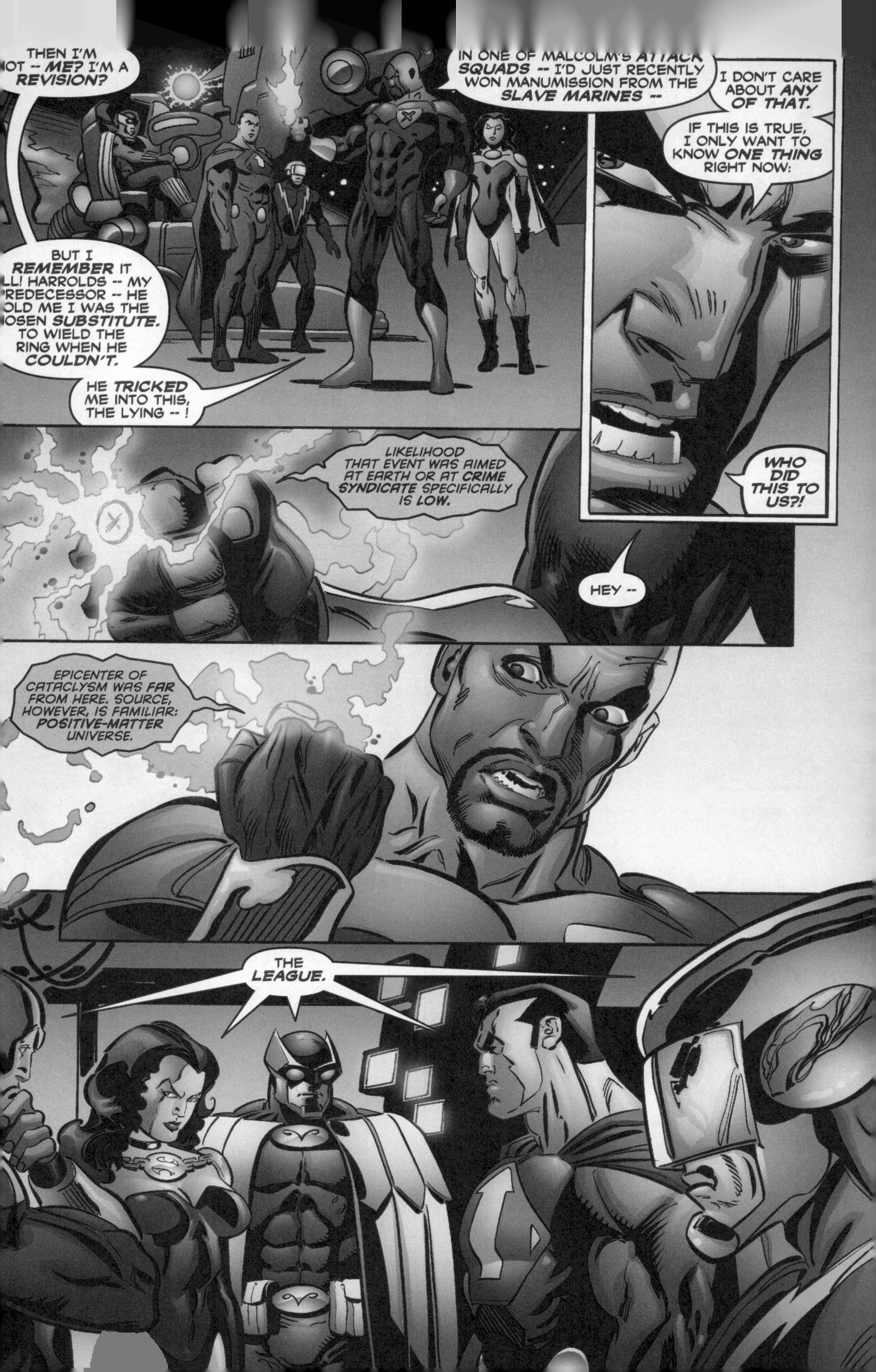

THEN I'M NOT -- ME? I'M A REVISION?
IN ONE OF MALCOLM'S ATTACK SQUADS -- I'D JUST RECENTLY WON MANUMISSION FROM THE SLAVE MARINES --
BUT I REMEMBER IT ALL! HARROLDS -- MY PREDECESSOR -- HE TOLD ME I WAS THE CHOSEN SUBSTITUTE. TO WIELD THE RING WHEN HE COULDN'T.
HE TRICKED ME INTO THIS, THE LYING -- !
I DON'T CARE ABOUT ANY OF THAT.
IF THIS IS TRUE, I ONLY WANT TO KNOW ONE THING RIGHT NOW:
WHO DID THIS TO US?!
LIKELIHOOD THAT EVENT WAS AIMED AT EARTH OR AT CRIME SYNDICATE SPECIFICALLY IS LOW.
HEY --
EPICENTER OF CATACLYSM WAS FAR FROM HERE. SOURCE, HOWEVER, IS FAMILIAR: POSITIVE-MATTER UNIVERSE.
THE LEAGUE.

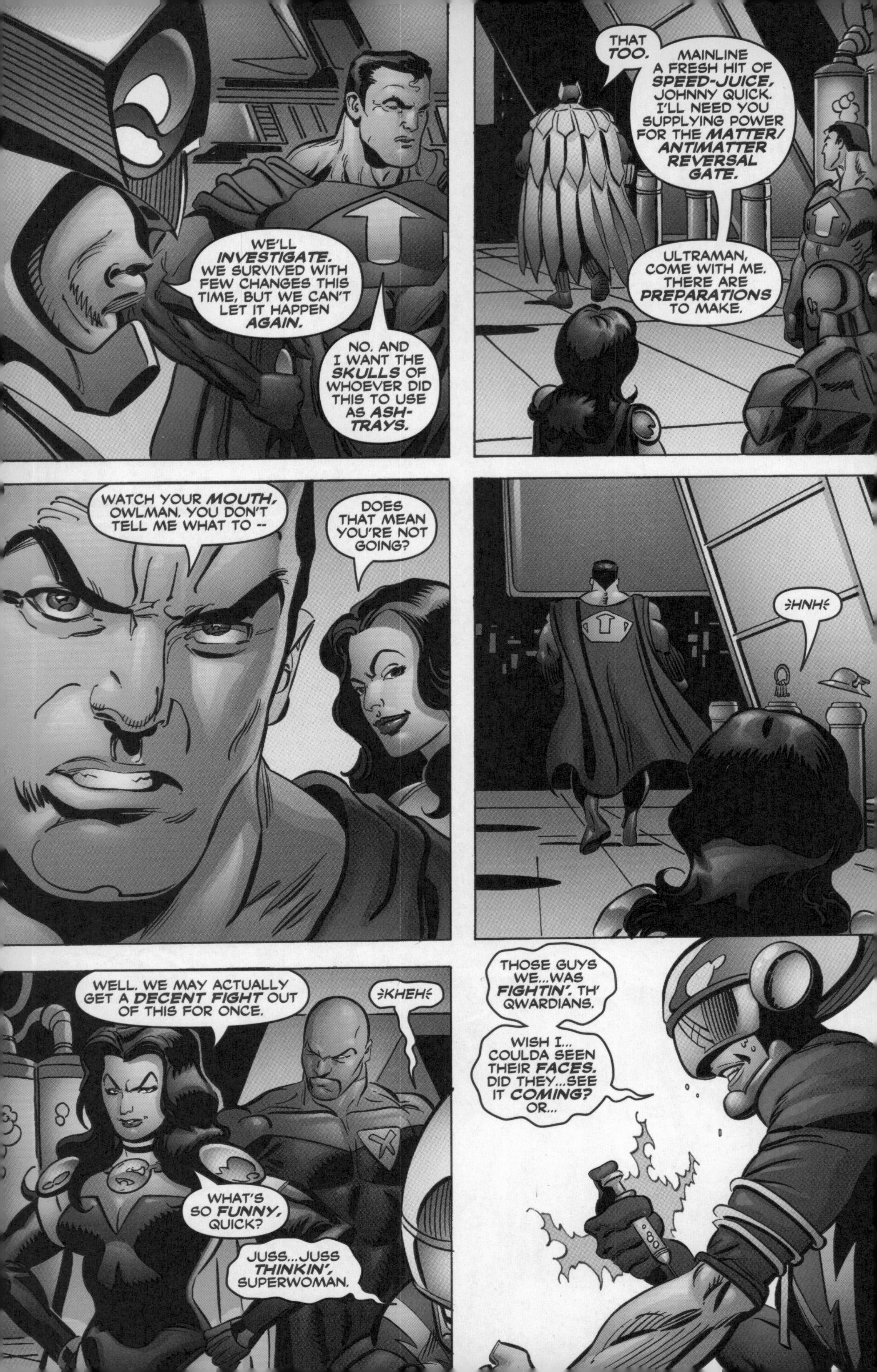
WE'LL INVESTIGATE. WE SURVIVED WITH FEW CHANGES THIS TIME, BUT WE CAN'T LET IT HAPPEN AGAIN.
NO. AND I WANT THE SKULLS OF WHOEVER DID THIS TO USE AS ASH-TRAYS.
THAT TOO.
MAINLINE A FRESH HIT OF SPEED-JUICE, JOHNNY QUICK. I'LL NEED YOU SUPPLYING POWER FOR THE MATTER/ANTIMATTER REVERSAL GATE.
ULTRAMAN, COME WITH ME. THERE ARE PREPARATIONS TO MAKE.
WATCH YOUR MOUTH, OWLMAN. YOU DON'T TELL ME WHAT TO --
DOES THAT MEAN YOU'RE NOT GOING?
HNH
WELL. WE MAY ACTUALLY GET A DECENT FIGHT OUT OF THIS FOR ONCE.
KHEH
WHAT'S SO FUNNY, QUICK?
JUSS...JUSS THINKIN', SUPERWOMAN.
THOSE GUYS WE...WAS FIGHTIN'. TH' QWARDIANS.
WISH I... COULDA SEEN THEIR FACES. DID THEY...SEE IT COMING? OR...

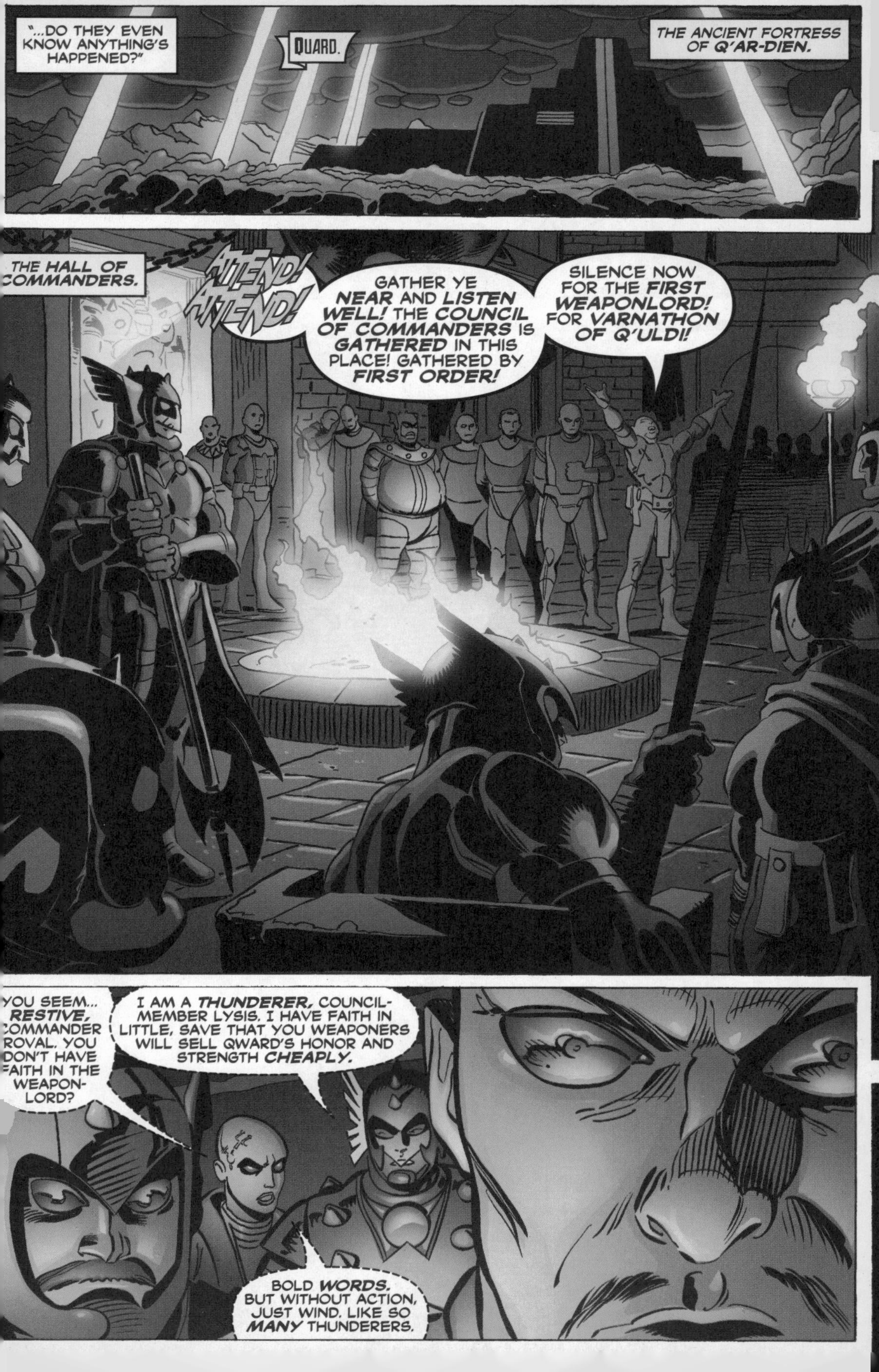

"...DO THEY EVEN KNOW ANYTHING'S HAPPENED?"
QUARD.
THE ANCIENT FORTRESS OF Q'AR-DIEN.
THE HALL OF COMMANDERS.
ATTEND! ATTEND!
GATHER YE NEAR AND LISTEN WELL! THE COUNCIL OF COMMANDERS IS GATHERED IN THIS PLACE! GATHERED BY FIRST ORDER!
SILENCE NOW FOR THE FIRST WEAPONLORD! FOR VARNATHON OF Q'ULDI!
YOU SEEM... RESTIVE, COMMANDER ROVAL. YOU DON'T HAVE FAITH IN THE WEAPON-LORD?
I AM A THUNDERER, COUNCIL-MEMBER LYSIS. I HAVE FAITH IN LITTLE, SAVE THAT YOU WEAPONERS WILL SELL QWARD'S HONOR AND STRENGTH CHEAPLY.
BOLD WORDS. BUT WITHOUT ACTION, JUST WIND. LIKE SO MANY THUNDERERS.

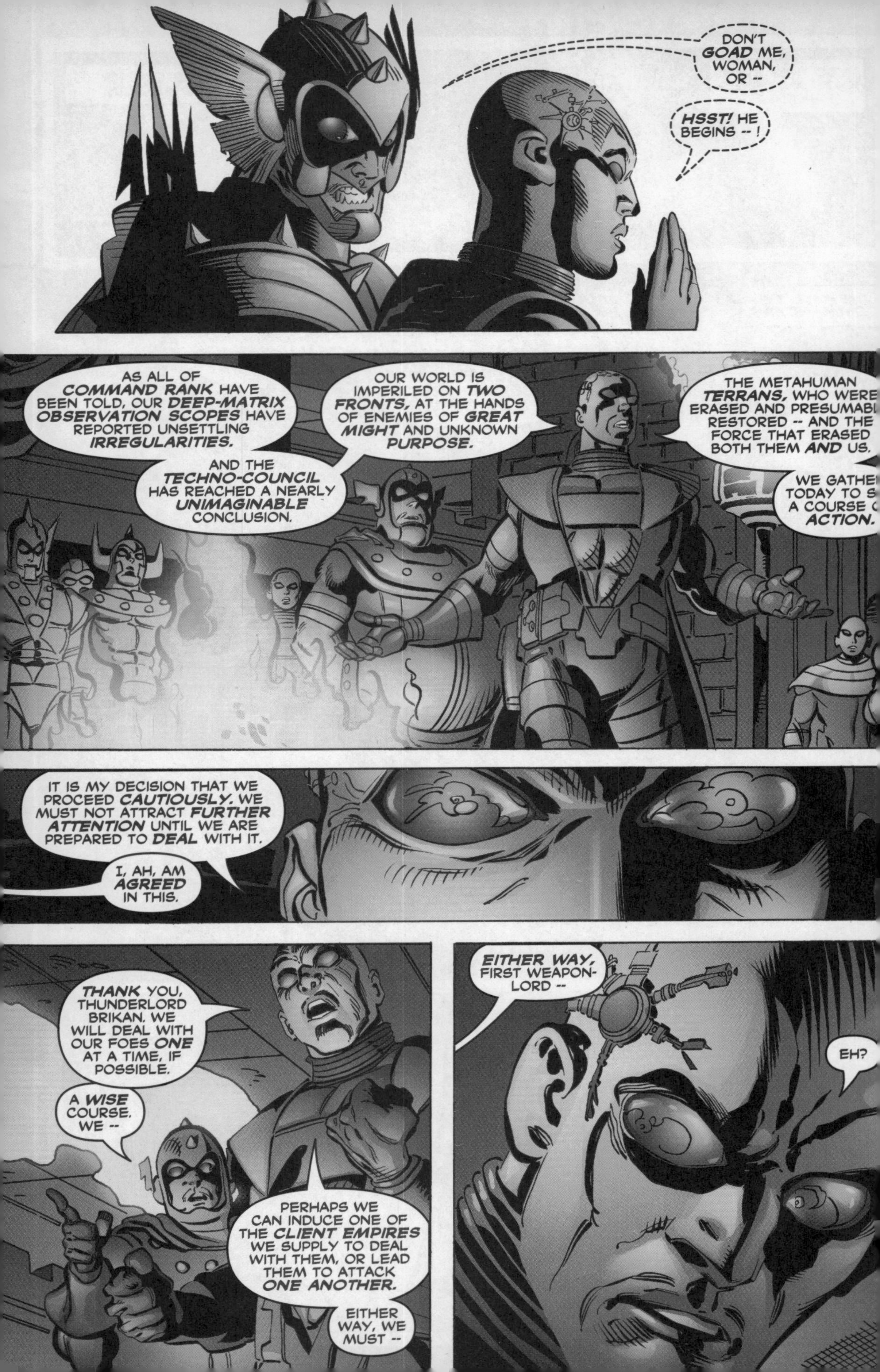
DON'T GOAD ME, WOMAN, OR --
HSST! HE BEGINS -- !
AS ALL OF COMMAND RANK HAVE BEEN TOLD, OUR DEEP-MATRIX OBSERVATION SCOPES HAVE REPORTED UNSETTLING IRREGULARITIES.
AND THE TECHNO-COUNCIL HAS REACHED A NEARLY UNIMAGINABLE CONCLUSION.
OUR WORLD IS IMPERILED ON TWO FRONTS, AT THE HANDS OF ENEMIES OF GREAT MIGHT AND UNKNOWN PURPOSE.
THE METAHUMAN TERRANS, WHO WERE ERASED AND PRESUMABL RESTORED -- AND THE FORCE THAT ERASED BOTH THEM AND US.
WE GATHE TODAY TO S A COURSE ACTION.
IT IS MY DECISION THAT WE PROCEED CAUTIOUSLY. WE MUST NOT ATTRACT FURTHER ATTENTION UNTIL WE ARE PREPARED TO DEAL WITH IT.
I, AH, AM AGREED IN THIS.
THANK YOU, THUNDERLORD BRIKAN. WE WILL DEAL WITH OUR FOES ONE AT A TIME, IF POSSIBLE.
A WISE COURSE. WE --
PERHAPS WE CAN INDUCE ONE OF THE CLIENT EMPIRES WE SUPPLY TO DEAL WITH THEM, OR LEAD THEM TO ATTACK ONE ANOTHER.
EITHER WAY, WE MUST --
EITHER WAY, FIRST WEAPON-LORD --
EH?

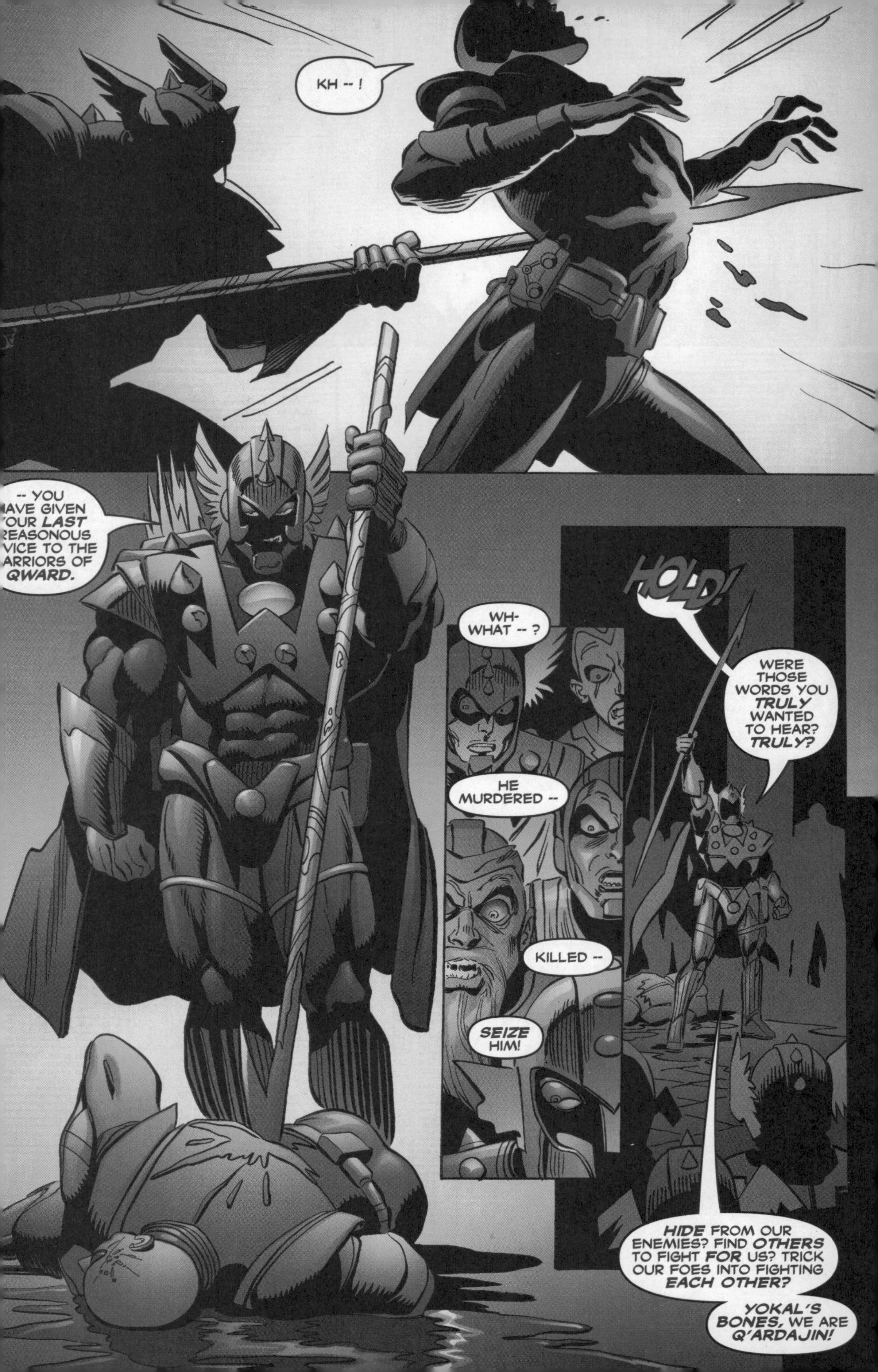

KH -- !
-- YOU
HAVE GIVEN
YOUR LAST
TREASONOUS
ADVICE TO THE
WARRIORS OF
QWARD.
HOLD!
WH-
WHAT -- ?
WERE
THOSE
WORDS YOU
TRULY
WANTED
TO HEAR?
TRULY?
HE
MURDERED --
KILLED --
SEIZE
HIM!
HIDE FROM OUR
ENEMIES? FIND OTHERS
TO FIGHT FOR US? TRICK
OUR FOES INTO FIGHTING
EACH OTHER?
YOKAL'S
BONES, WE ARE
Q'ARDAJIN!

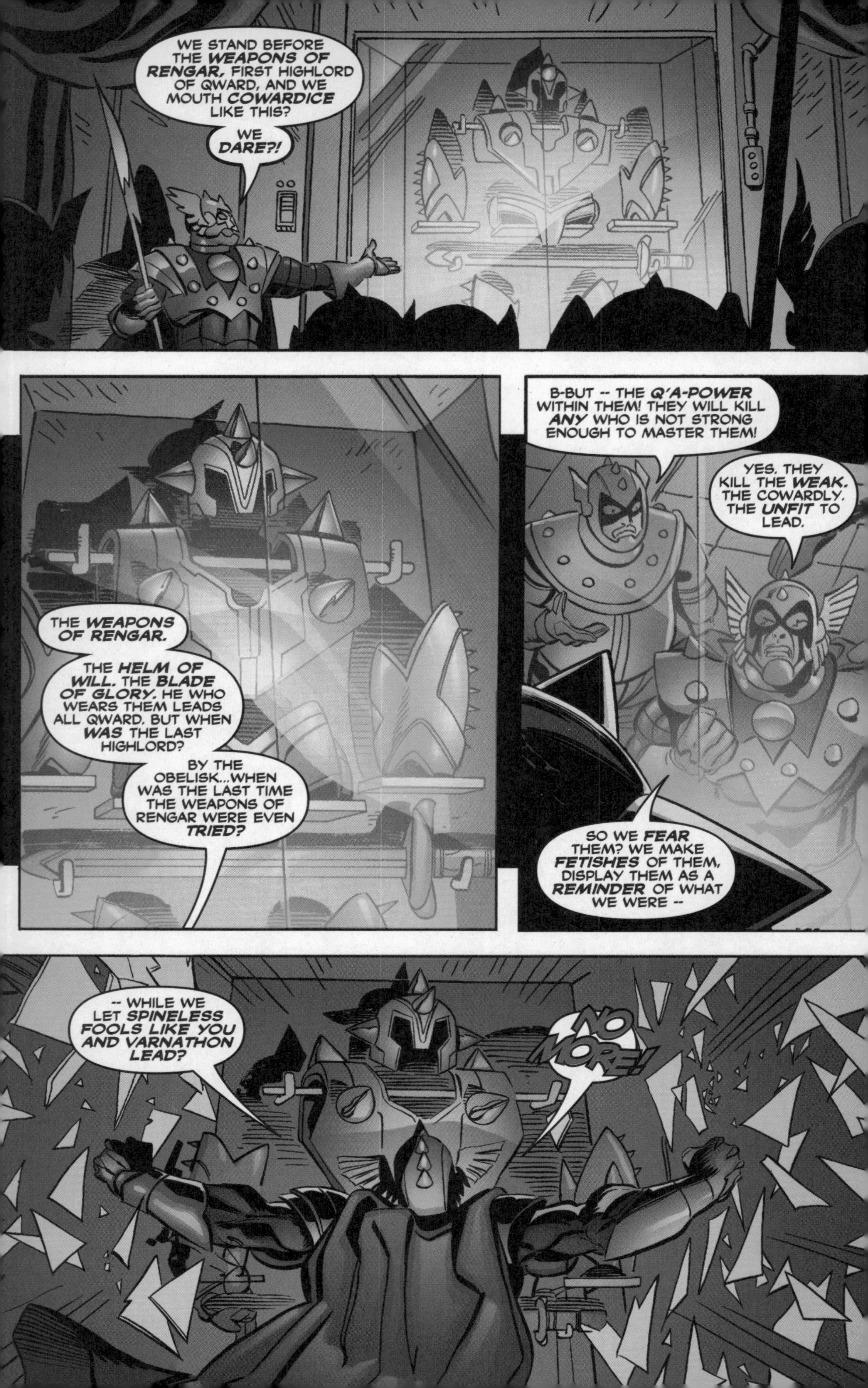
WE STAND BEFORE THE WEAPONS OF RENGAR, FIRST HIGHLORD OF QWARD, AND WE MOUTH COWARDICE LIKE THIS?
WE DARE?!
THE WEAPONS OF RENGAR.
THE HELM OF WILL. THE BLADE OF GLORY. HE WHO WEARS THEM LEADS ALL QWARD. BUT WHEN WAS THE LAST HIGHLORD?
BY THE OBELISK...WHEN WAS THE LAST TIME THE WEAPONS OF RENGAR WERE EVEN TRIED?
B-BUT -- THE Q'A-POWER WITHIN THEM! THEY WILL KILL ANY WHO IS NOT STRONG ENOUGH TO MASTER THEM!
YES. THEY KILL THE WEAK. THE COWARDLY. THE UNFIT TO LEAD.
SO WE FEAR THEM? WE MAKE FETISHES OF THEM, DISPLAY THEM AS A REMINDER OF WHAT WE WERE --
-- WHILE WE LET SPINELESS FOOLS LIKE YOU AND VARNATHON LEAD?
NO MORE!

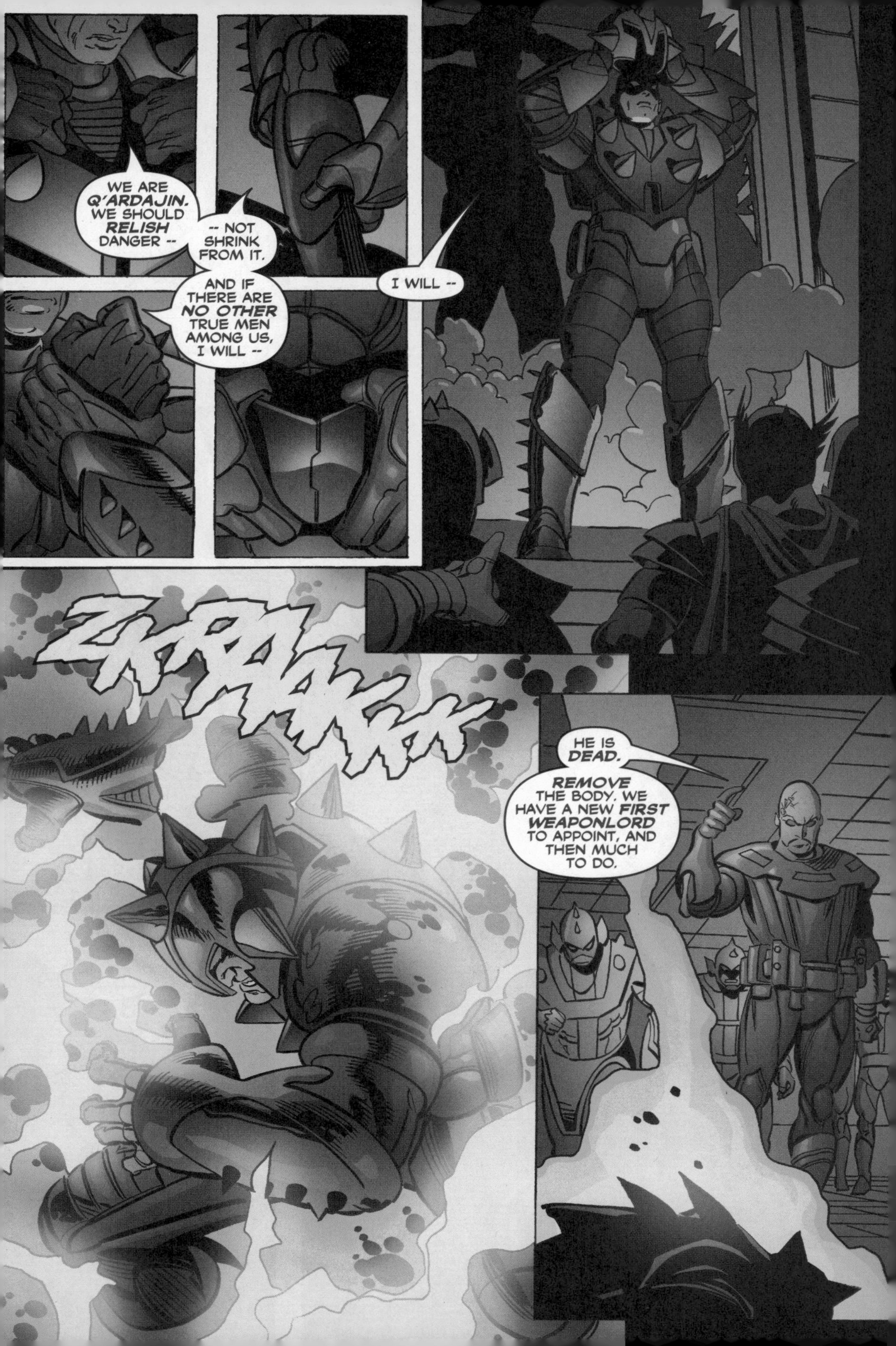

WE ARE *Q'ARDAJIN.* WE SHOULD *RELISH* DANGER --
-- NOT SHRINK FROM IT.
AND IF THERE ARE *NO OTHER* TRUE MEN AMONG US, I WILL --
I WILL --
HE IS *DEAD.*
REMOVE THE BODY. WE HAVE A NEW *FIRST WEAPONLORD* TO APPOINT, AND THEN MUCH TO DO.

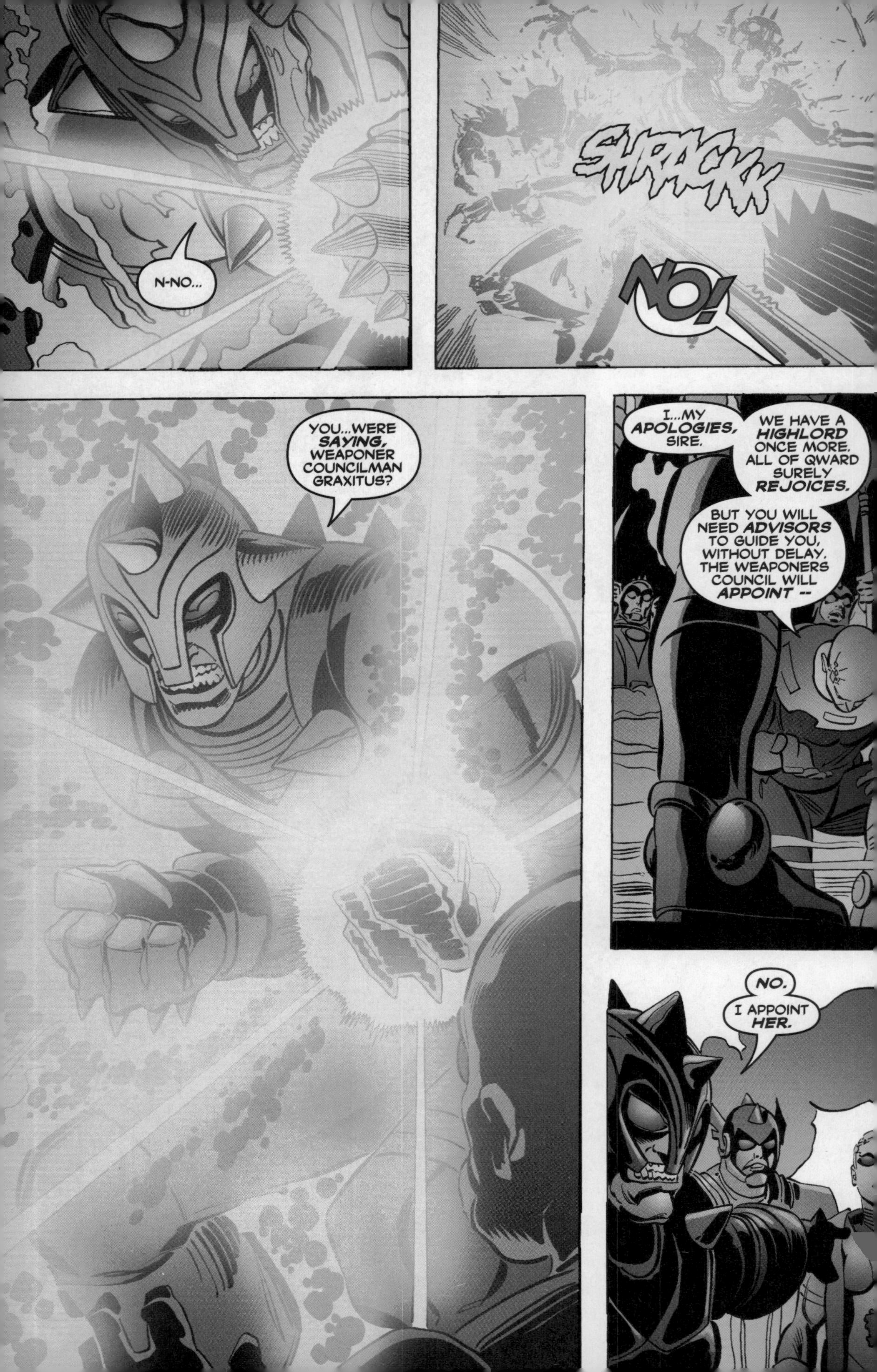
N-NO...
SHRACKK
NO!
YOU...WERE SAYING, WEAPONER COUNCILMAN GRAXITUS?
I...MY APOLOGIES, SIRE.
WE HAVE A HIGHLORD ONCE MORE. ALL OF QWARD SURELY REJOICES.
BUT YOU WILL NEED ADVISORS TO GUIDE YOU, WITHOUT DELAY. THE WEAPONERS COUNCIL WILL APPOINT --
NO. I APPOINT HER.

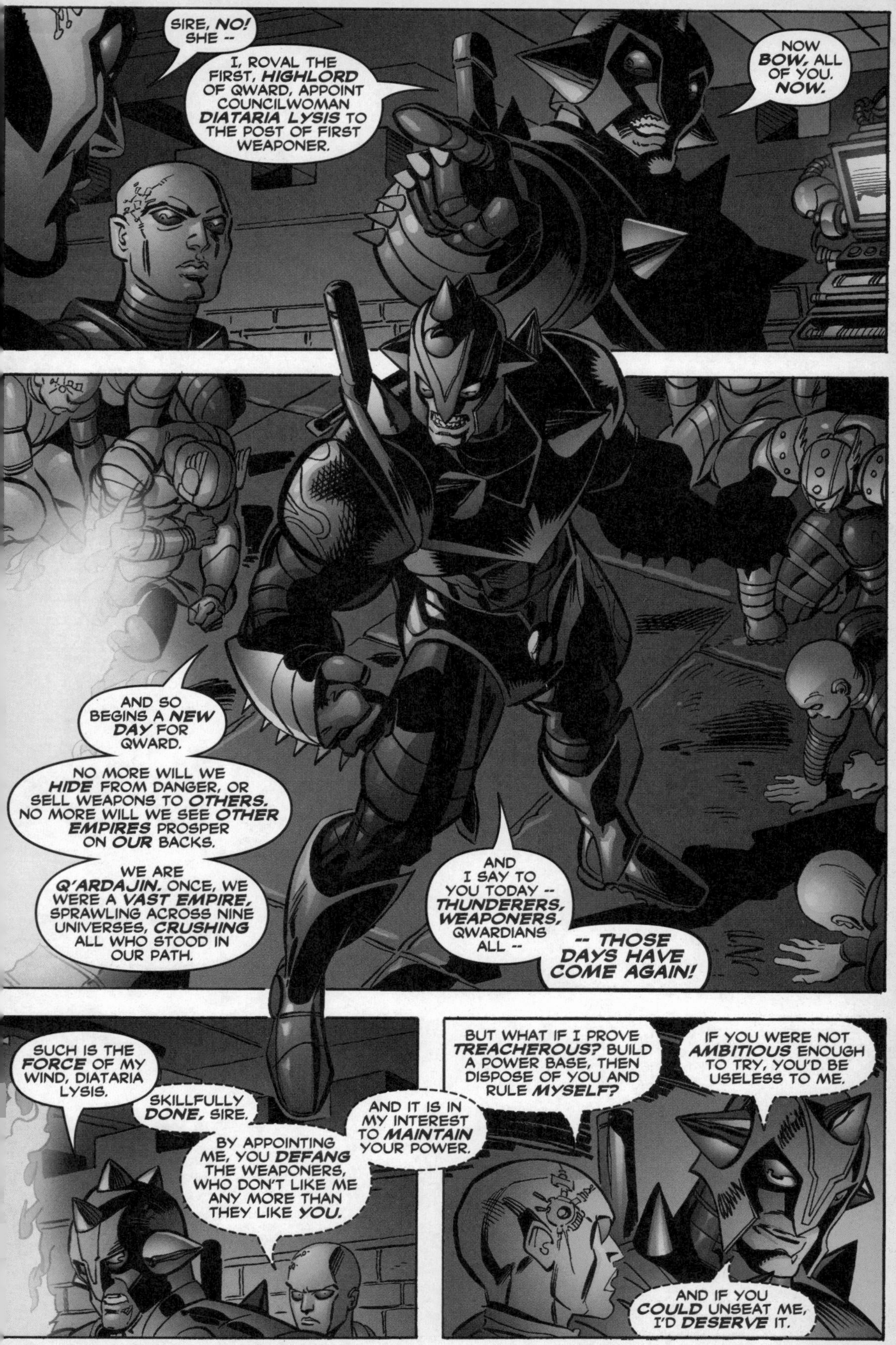
SIRE, NO! SHE --
I, ROVAL THE FIRST, HIGHLORD OF QWARD, APPOINT COUNCILWOMAN DIATARIA LYSIS TO THE POST OF FIRST WEAPONER.
NOW BOW, ALL OF YOU. NOW.
AND SO BEGINS A NEW DAY FOR QWARD.
NO MORE WILL WE HIDE FROM DANGER, OR SELL WEAPONS TO OTHERS. NO MORE WILL WE SEE OTHER EMPIRES PROSPER ON OUR BACKS.
WE ARE Q'ARDAJIN. ONCE, WE WERE A VAST EMPIRE, SPRAWLING ACROSS NINE UNIVERSES, CRUSHING ALL WHO STOOD IN OUR PATH.
AND I SAY TO YOU TODAY -- THUNDERERS, WEAPONERS, QWARDIANS ALL --
-- THOSE DAYS HAVE COME AGAIN!
SUCH IS THE FORCE OF MY WIND, DIATARIA LYSIS.
SKILLFULLY DONE, SIRE.
BY APPOINTING ME, YOU DEFANG THE WEAPONERS, WHO DON'T LIKE ME ANY MORE THAN THEY LIKE YOU.
AND IT IS IN MY INTEREST TO MAINTAIN YOUR POWER.
BUT WHAT IF I PROVE TREACHEROUS? BUILD A POWER BASE, THEN DISPOSE OF YOU AND RULE MYSELF?
IF YOU WERE NOT AMBITIOUS ENOUGH TO TRY, YOU'D BE USELESS TO ME.
AND IF YOU COULD UNSEAT ME, I'D DESERVE IT.

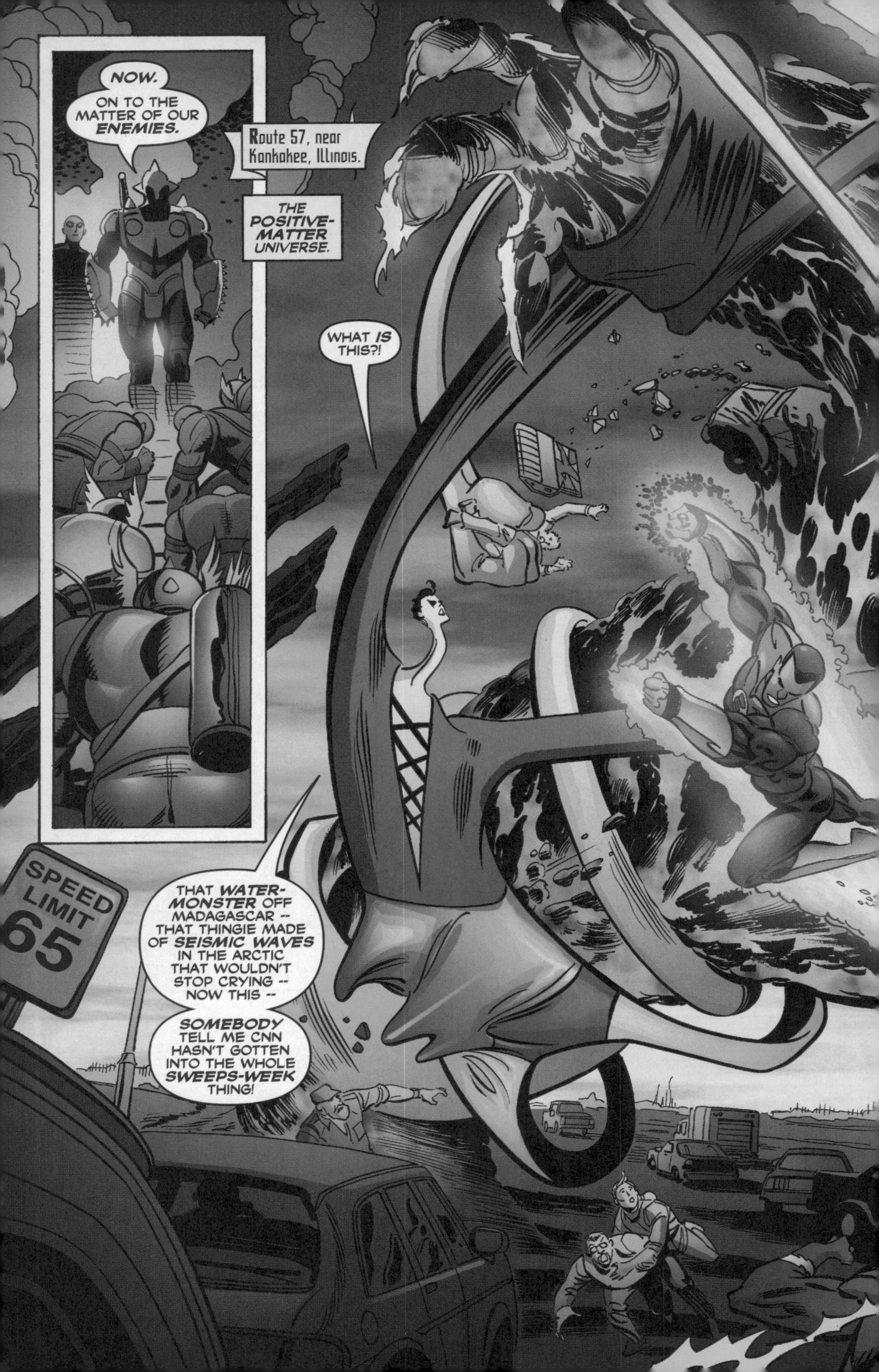
NOW.
ON TO THE MATTER OF OUR ENEMIES.
Route 57, near Kankakee, Illinois.
THE POSITIVE-MATTER UNIVERSE.
WHAT IS THIS?!
SPEED LIMIT 65
THAT WATER-MONSTER OFF MADAGASCAR -- THAT THINGIE MADE OF SEISMIC WAVES IN THE ARCTIC THAT WOULDN'T STOP CRYING -- NOW THIS --
SOMEBODY TELL ME CNN HASN'T GOTTEN INTO THE WHOLE SWEEPS-WEEK THING!

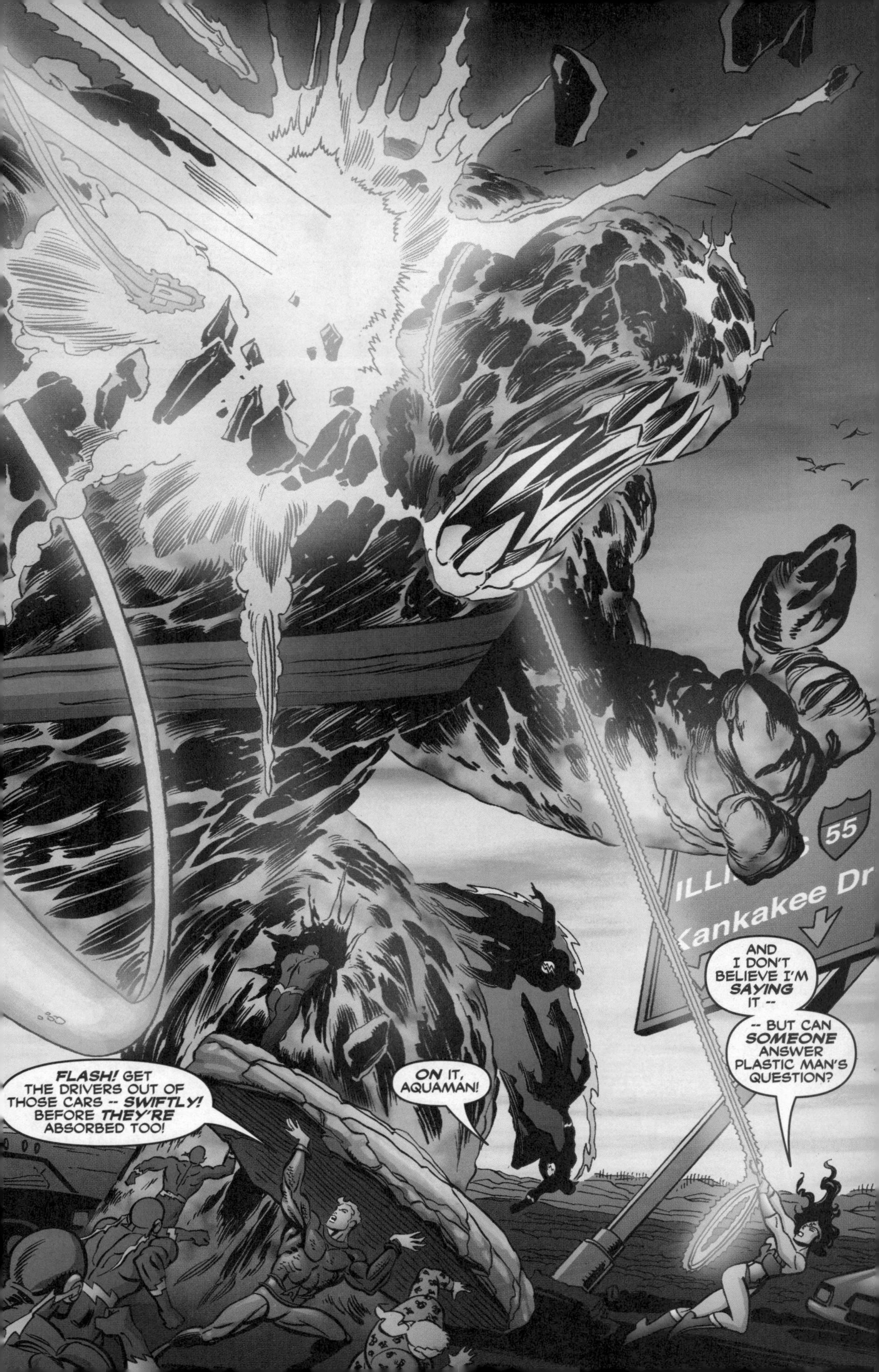
55
Kankakee Dr
FLASH! GET THE DRIVERS OUT OF THOSE CARS -- SWIFTLY! BEFORE THEY'RE ABSORBED TOO!
ON IT, AQUAMAN!
AND I DON'T BELIEVE I'M SAYING IT --
-- BUT CAN SOMEONE ANSWER PLASTIC MAN'S QUESTION?

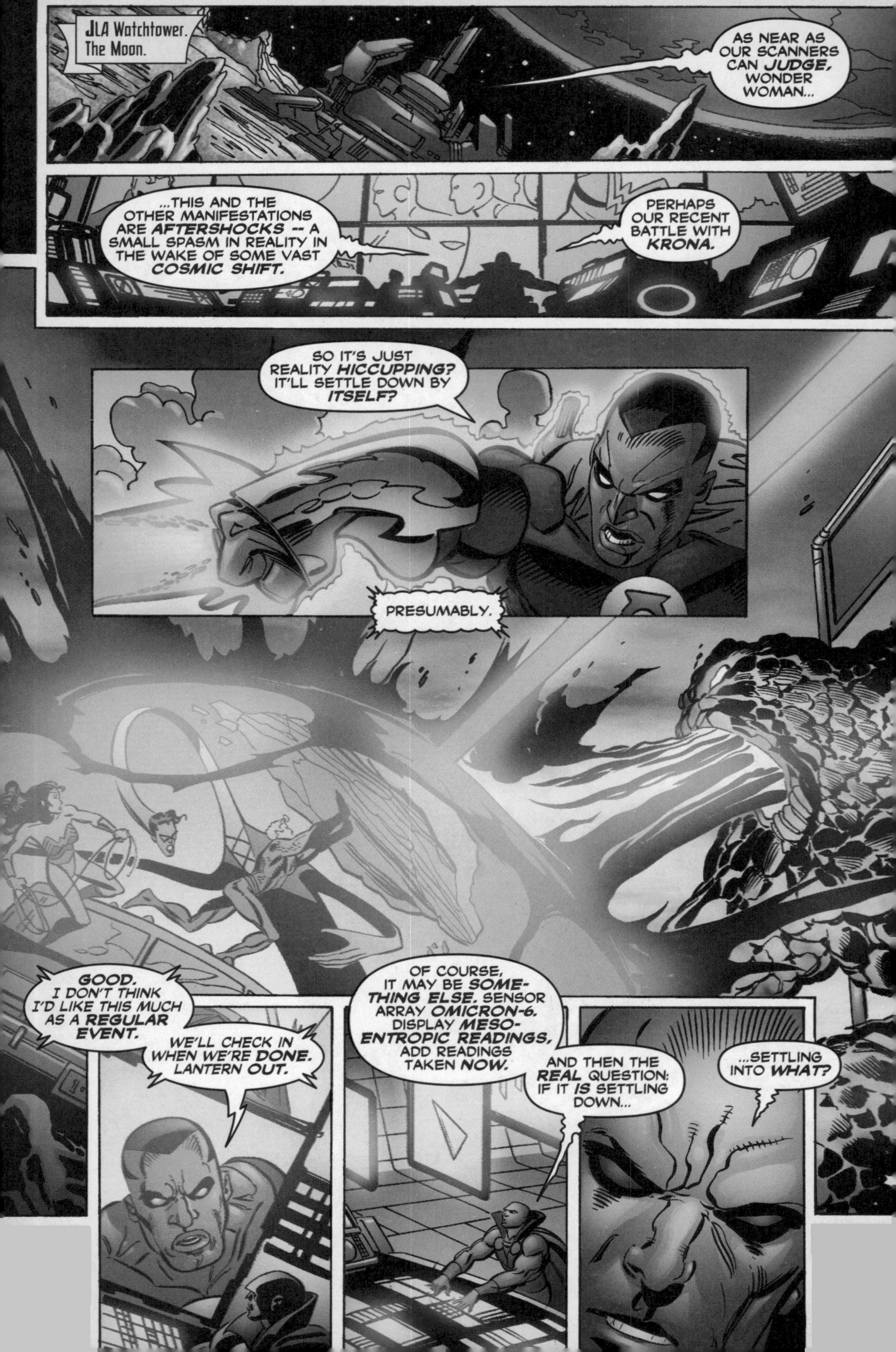
JLA Watchtower. The Moon.
AS NEAR AS OUR SCANNERS CAN JUDGE, WONDER WOMAN...
...THIS AND THE OTHER MANIFESTATIONS ARE AFTERSHOCKS -- A SMALL SPASM IN REALITY IN THE WAKE OF SOME VAST COSMIC SHIFT.
PERHAPS OUR RECENT BATTLE WITH KRONA.
SO IT'S JUST REALITY HICCUPPING? IT'LL SETTLE DOWN BY ITSELF?
PRESUMABLY.
GOOD. I DON'T THINK I'D LIKE THIS MUCH AS A REGULAR EVENT.
WE'LL CHECK IN WHEN WE'RE DONE. LANTERN OUT.
OF COURSE, IT MAY BE SOMETHING ELSE. SENSOR ARRAY OMICRON-6. DISPLAY MESO-ENTROPIC READINGS, ADD READINGS TAKEN NOW.
AND THEN THE REAL QUESTION: IF IT IS SETTLING DOWN...
...SETTLING INTO WHAT?

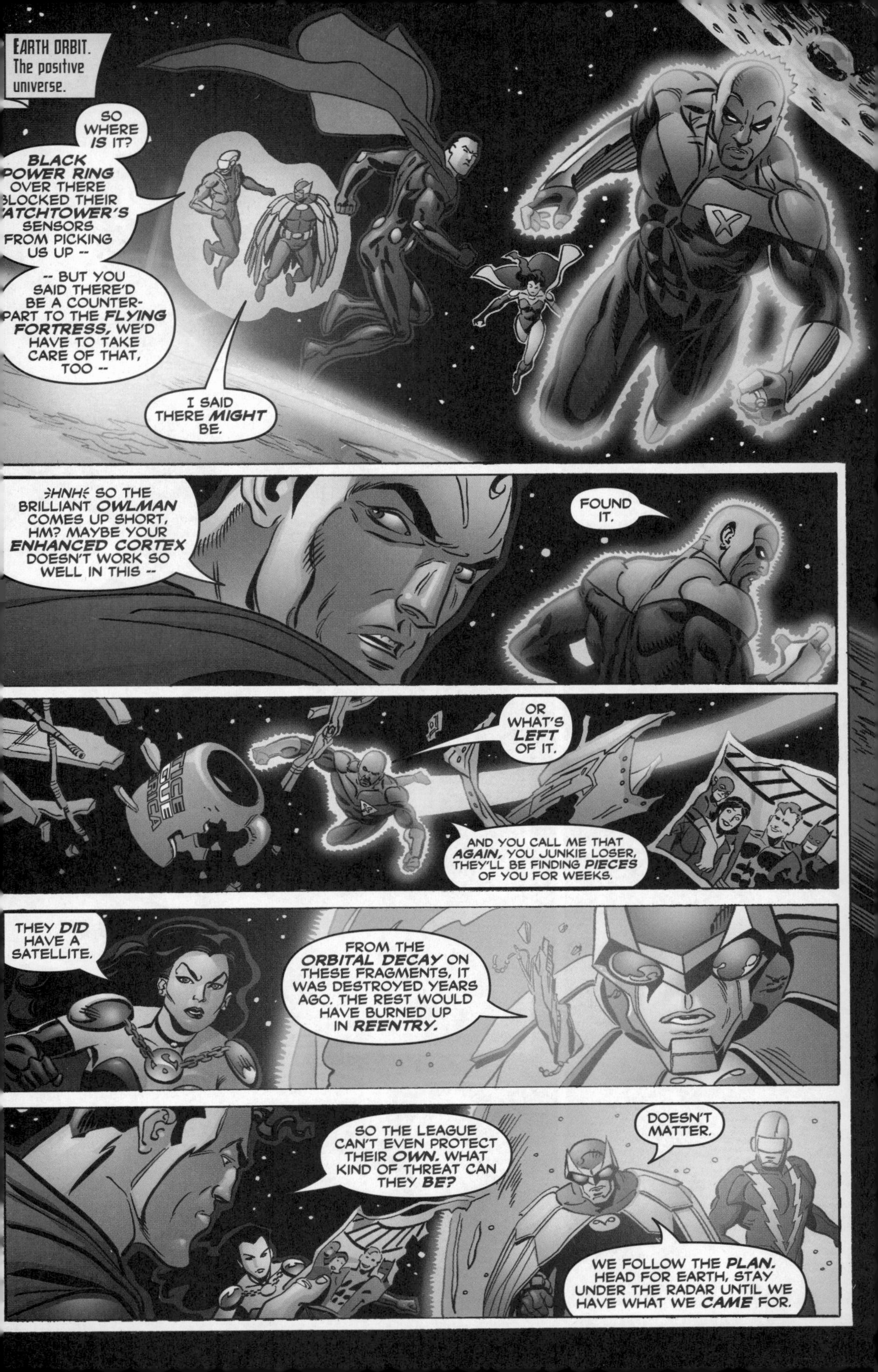
EARTH ORBIT. The positive universe.
SO WHERE *IS* IT?
BLACK POWER RING OVER THERE BLOCKED THEIR *ATCHTOWER'S* SENSORS FROM PICKING US UP --
-- BUT YOU SAID THERE'D BE A COUNTER-PART TO THE *FLYING FORTRESS,* WE'D HAVE TO TAKE CARE OF THAT, TOO --
I SAID THERE *MIGHT* BE.
HNH SO THE BRILLIANT *OWLMAN* COMES UP SHORT, HM? MAYBE YOUR *ENHANCED CORTEX* DOESN'T WORK SO WELL IN THIS --
FOUND IT.
OR WHAT'S *LEFT* OF IT.
AND YOU CALL ME THAT *AGAIN,* YOU JUNKIE LOSER, THEY'LL BE FINDING *PIECES* OF YOU FOR WEEKS.
THEY *DID* HAVE A SATELLITE.
FROM THE *ORBITAL DECAY* ON THESE FRAGMENTS, IT WAS DESTROYED YEARS AGO. THE REST WOULD HAVE BURNED UP IN *REENTRY.*
SO THE LEAGUE CAN'T EVEN PROTECT THEIR *OWN.* WHAT KIND OF THREAT CAN THEY *BE?*
DOESN'T MATTER.
WE FOLLOW THE *PLAN.* HEAD FOR EARTH, STAY UNDER THE RADAR UNTIL WE HAVE WHAT WE *CAME* FOR.

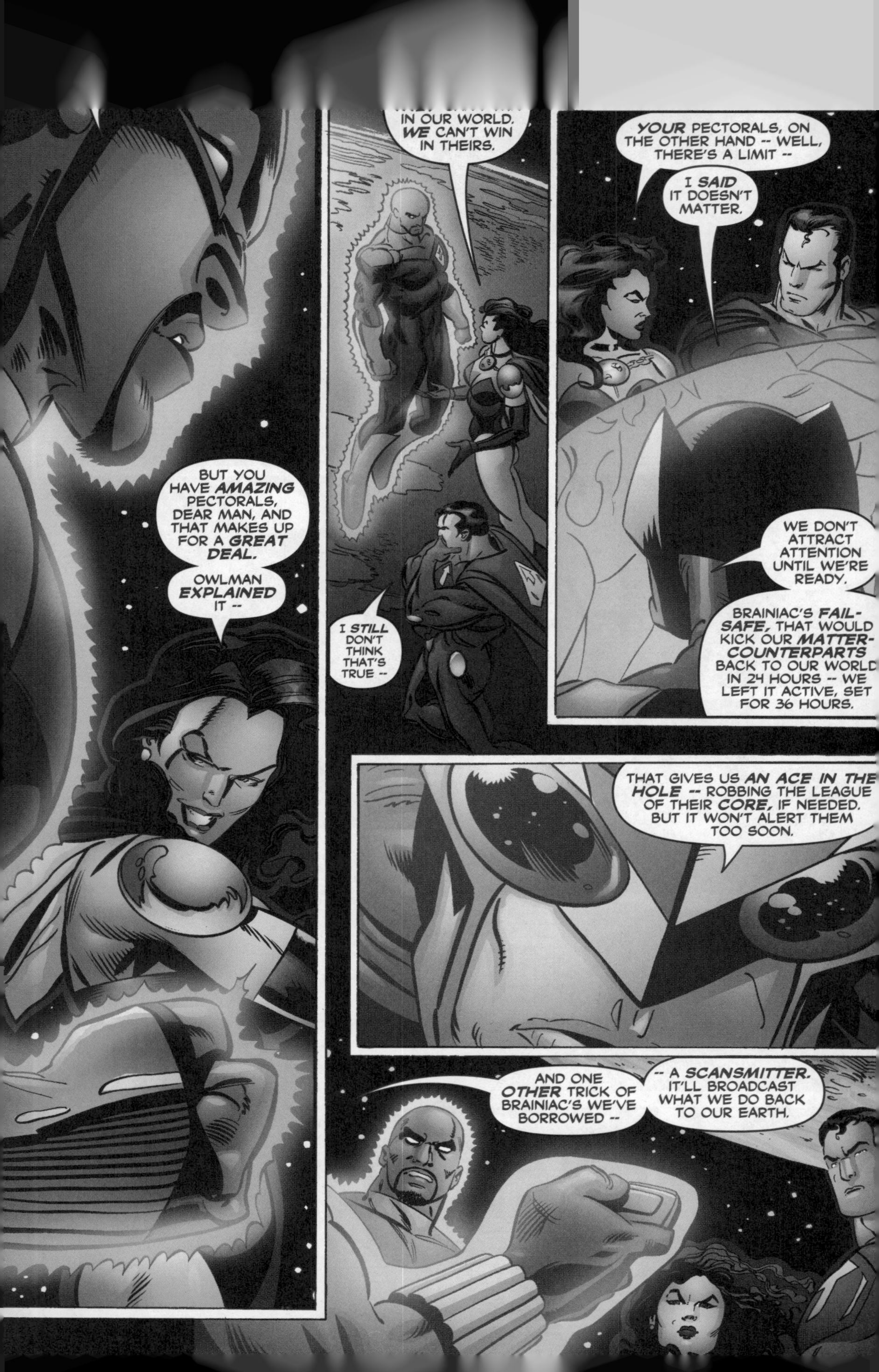
IN OUR WORLD, WE CAN'T WIN IN THEIRS.
BUT YOU HAVE AMAZING PECTORALS, DEAR MAN, AND THAT MAKES UP FOR A GREAT DEAL.
OWLMAN EXPLAINED IT --
I STILL DON'T THINK THAT'S TRUE --
YOUR PECTORALS, ON THE OTHER HAND -- WELL, THERE'S A LIMIT --
I SAID IT DOESN'T MATTER.
WE DON'T ATTRACT ATTENTION UNTIL WE'RE READY.
BRAINIAC'S FAIL-SAFE, THAT WOULD KICK OUR MATTER-COUNTERPARTS BACK TO OUR WORLD IN 24 HOURS -- WE LEFT IT ACTIVE, SET FOR 36 HOURS.
THAT GIVES US AN ACE IN THE HOLE -- ROBBING THE LEAGUE OF THEIR CORE, IF NEEDED. BUT IT WON'T ALERT THEM TOO SOON.
AND ONE OTHER TRICK OF BRAINIAC'S WE'VE BORROWED --
-- A SCANSMITTER. IT'LL BROADCAST WHAT WE DO BACK TO OUR EARTH.

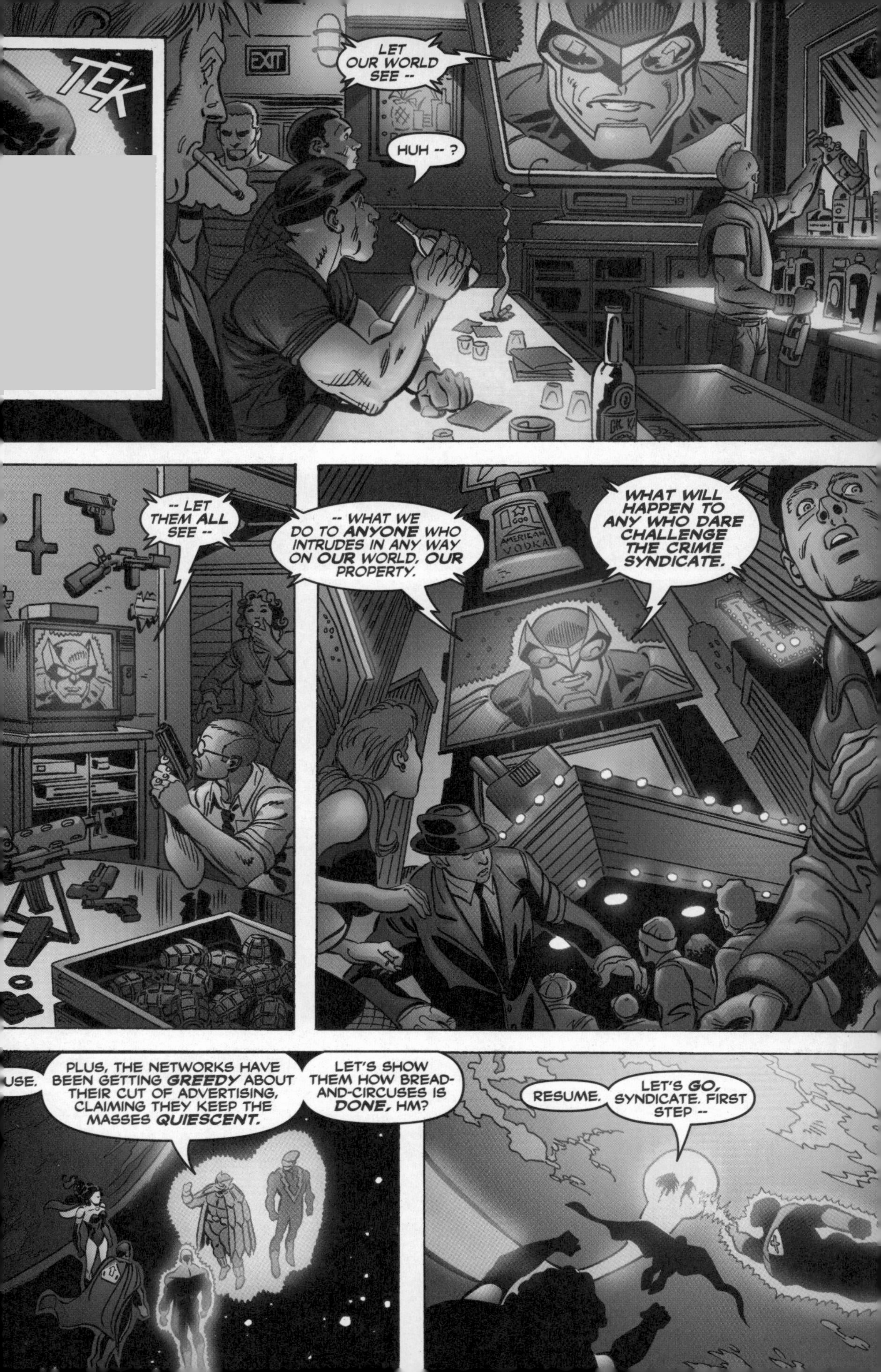
TEK
EXIT
LET OUR WORLD SEE --
HUH -- ?
-- LET THEM ALL SEE --
-- WHAT WE DO TO ANYONE WHO INTRUDES IN ANY WAY ON OUR WORLD, OUR PROPERTY.
AMERIKAN VODKA
WHAT WILL HAPPEN TO ANY WHO DARE CHALLENGE THE CRIME SYNDICATE.
USE.
PLUS, THE NETWORKS HAVE BEEN GETTING GREEDY ABOUT THEIR CUT OF ADVERTISING, CLAIMING THEY KEEP THE MASSES QUIESCENT.
LET'S SHOW THEM HOW BREAD-AND-CIRCUSES IS DONE, HM?
RESUME.
LET'S GO, SYNDICATE. FIRST STEP --

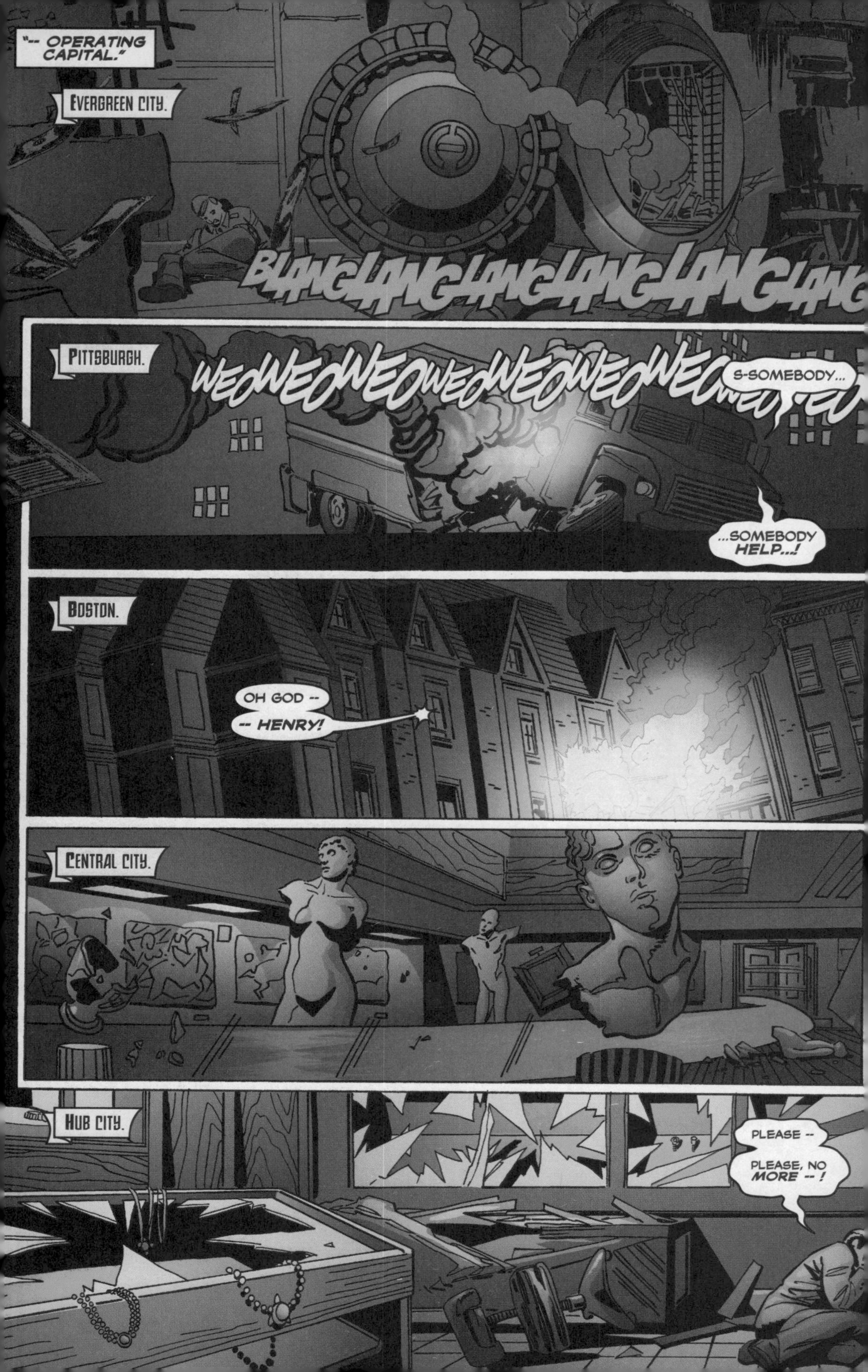
"-- OPERATING CAPITAL."
EVERGREEN CITY.
BLANGLANGLANGLANGLANGLANGLANG
PITTSBURGH.
WEOWEOWEOWEOWEOWEOWEOWEOWEO
S-SOMEBODY...
...SOMEBODY HELP...!
BOSTON.
OH GOD --
-- HENRY!
CENTRAL CITY.
HUB CITY.
PLEASE --
PLEASE, NO MORE -- !

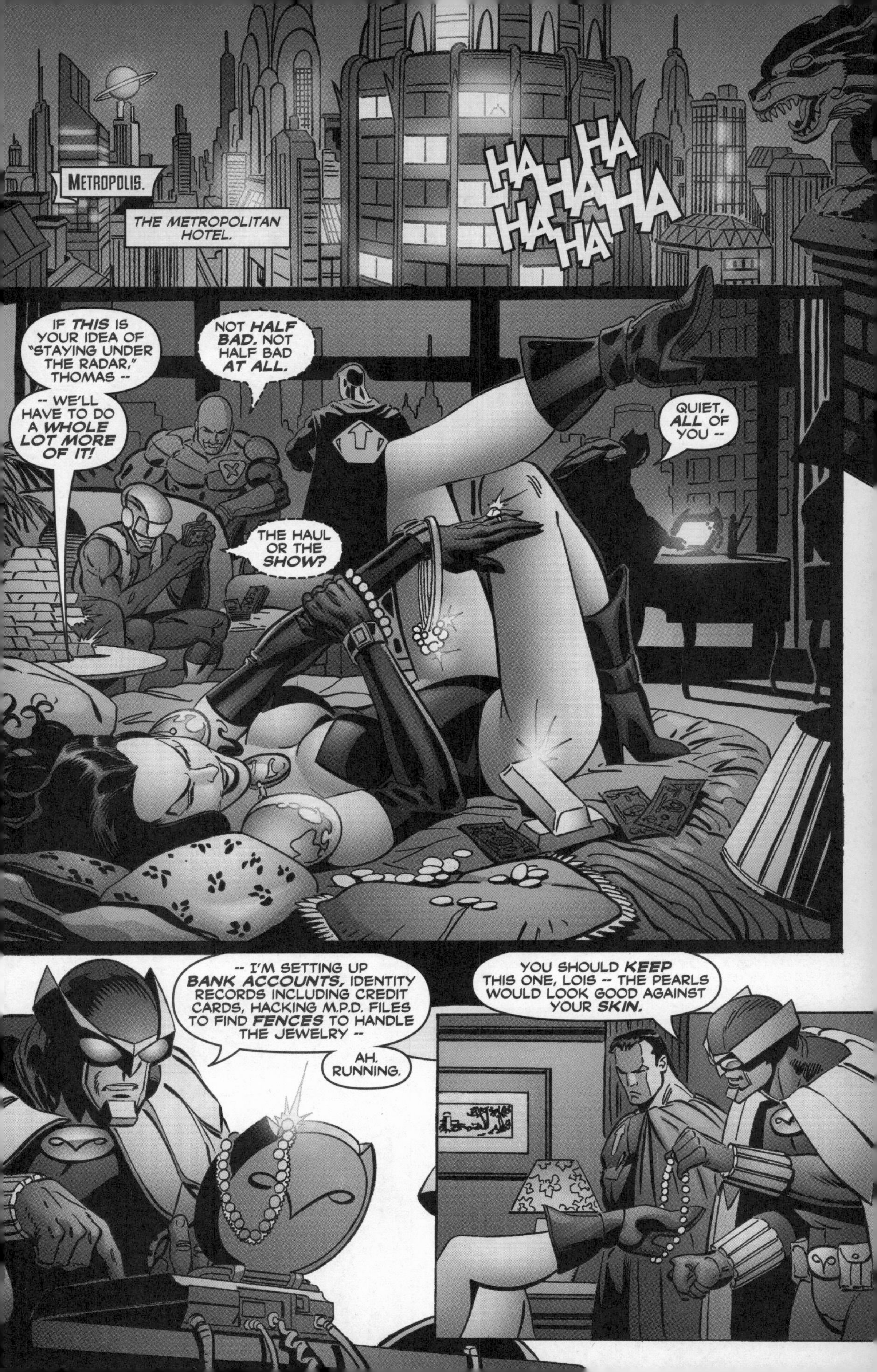

METROPOLIS.
THE METROPOLITAN HOTEL.
HA HA HA HA HA HA HA HA
IF THIS IS YOUR IDEA OF "STAYING UNDER THE RADAR," THOMAS --
-- WE'LL HAVE TO DO A WHOLE LOT MORE OF IT!
NOT HALF BAD. NOT HALF BAD AT ALL.
THE HAUL OR THE SHOW?
QUIET, ALL OF YOU --
-- I'M SETTING UP BANK ACCOUNTS, IDENTITY RECORDS INCLUDING CREDIT CARDS, HACKING M.P.D. FILES TO FIND FENCES TO HANDLE THE JEWELRY --
AH. RUNNING.
YOU SHOULD KEEP THIS ONE, LOIS -- THE PEARLS WOULD LOOK GOOD AGAINST YOUR SKIN.

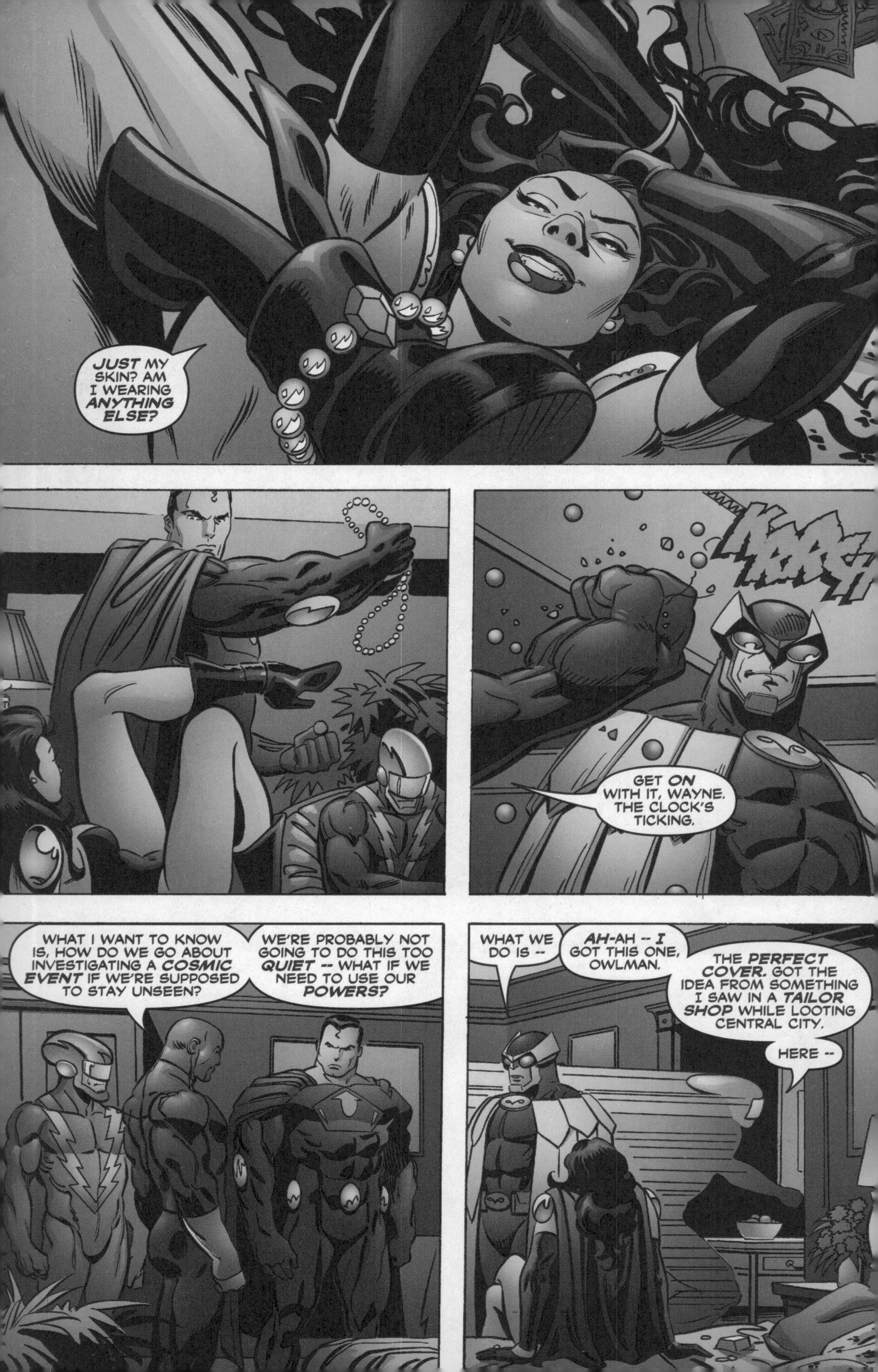
JUST MY SKIN? AM I WEARING ANYTHING ELSE?
GET ON WITH IT, WAYNE. THE CLOCK'S TICKING.
WHAT I WANT TO KNOW IS, HOW DO WE GO ABOUT INVESTIGATING A COSMIC EVENT IF WE'RE SUPPOSED TO STAY UNSEEN?
WE'RE PROBABLY NOT GOING TO DO THIS TOO QUIET -- WHAT IF WE NEED TO USE OUR POWERS?
WHAT WE DO IS --
AH-AH -- I GOT THIS ONE, OWLMAN.
THE PERFECT COVER. GOT THE IDEA FROM SOMETHING I SAW IN A TAILOR SHOP WHILE LOOTING CENTRAL CITY.
HERE --

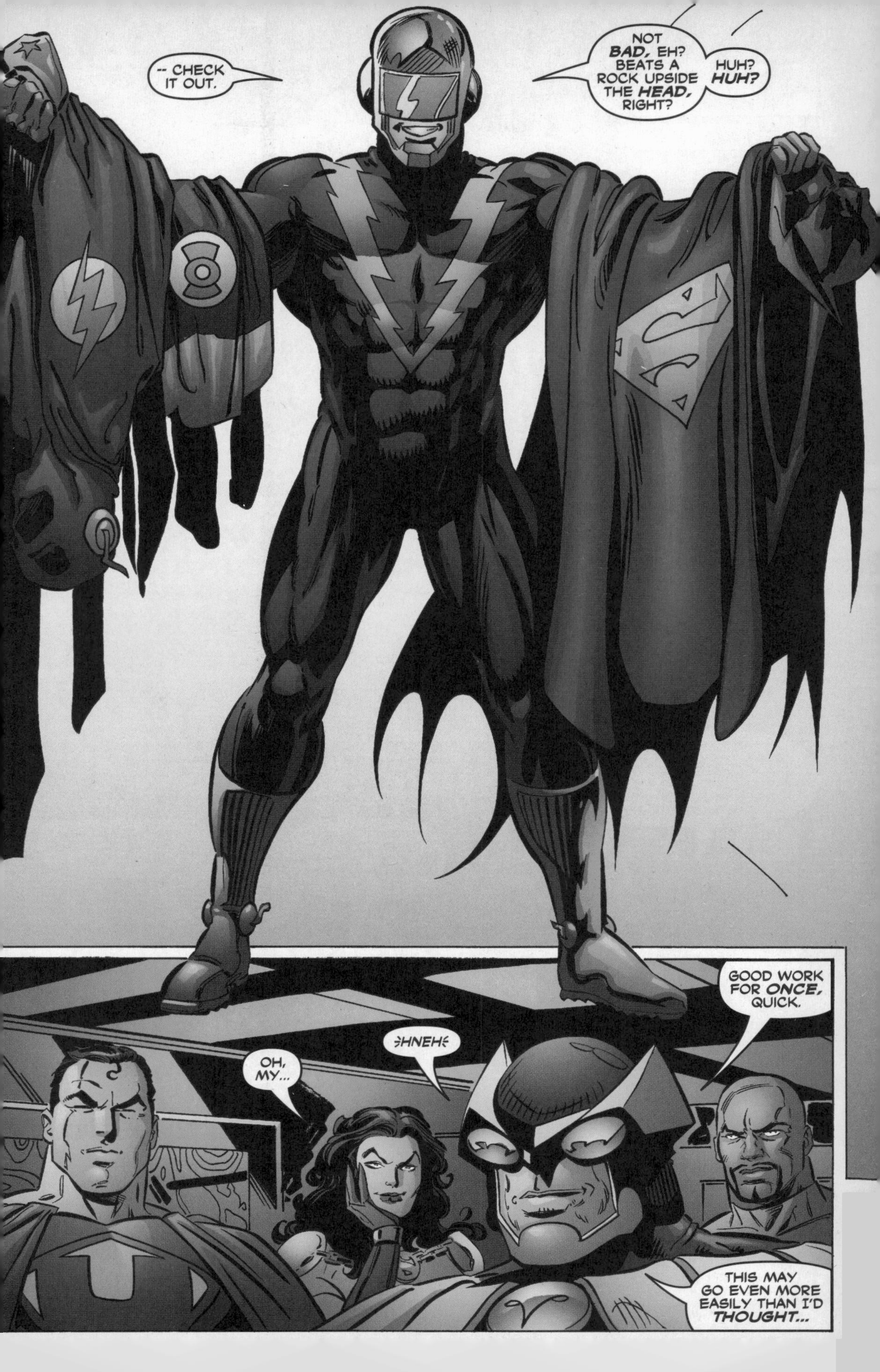

-- CHECK IT OUT.
NOT BAD, EH? BEATS A ROCK UPSIDE THE HEAD, RIGHT?
HUH? HUH?
OH, MY...
HNEH
GOOD WORK FOR ONCE, QUICK.
THIS MAY GO EVEN MORE EASILY THAN I'D THOUGHT...

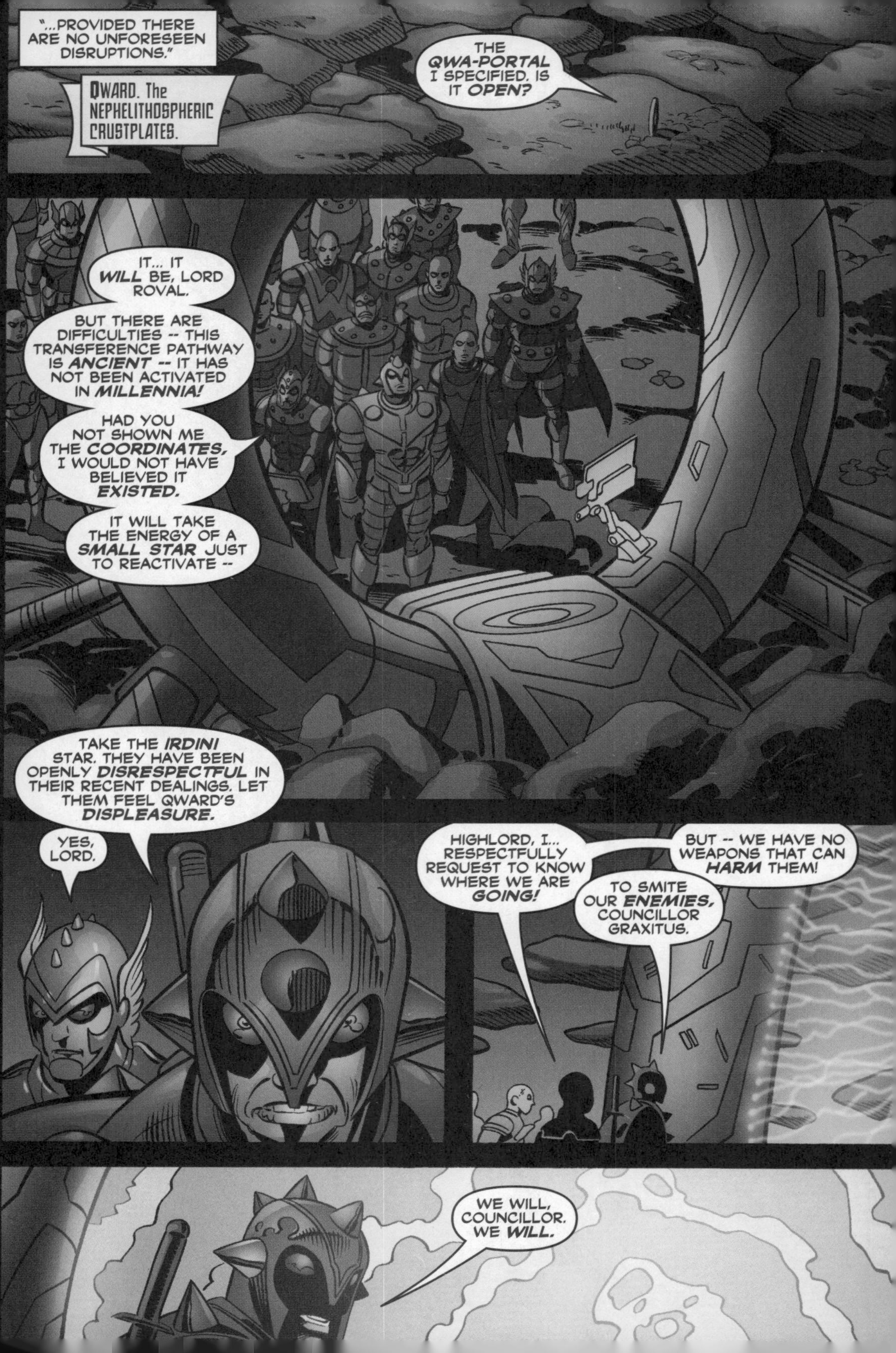
"...PROVIDED THERE ARE NO UNFORESEEN DISRUPTIONS."
QWARD. The NEPHELITHOSPHERIC CRUSTPLATES.
THE QWA-PORTAL I SPECIFIED. IS IT OPEN?
IT... IT WILL BE, LORD ROVAL.
BUT THERE ARE DIFFICULTIES -- THIS TRANSFERENCE PATHWAY IS ANCIENT -- IT HAS NOT BEEN ACTIVATED IN MILLENNIA!
HAD YOU NOT SHOWN ME THE COORDINATES, I WOULD NOT HAVE BELIEVED IT EXISTED.
IT WILL TAKE THE ENERGY OF A SMALL STAR JUST TO REACTIVATE --
TAKE THE IRDINI STAR. THEY HAVE BEEN OPENLY DISRESPECTFUL IN THEIR RECENT DEALINGS. LET THEM FEEL QWARD'S DISPLEASURE.
YES, LORD.
BUT -- WE HAVE NO WEAPONS THAT CAN HARM THEM!
HIGHLORD, I... RESPECTFULLY REQUEST TO KNOW WHERE WE ARE GOING!
TO SMITE OUR ENEMIES, COUNCILLOR GRAXITUS.
WE WILL, COUNCILLOR. WE WILL.

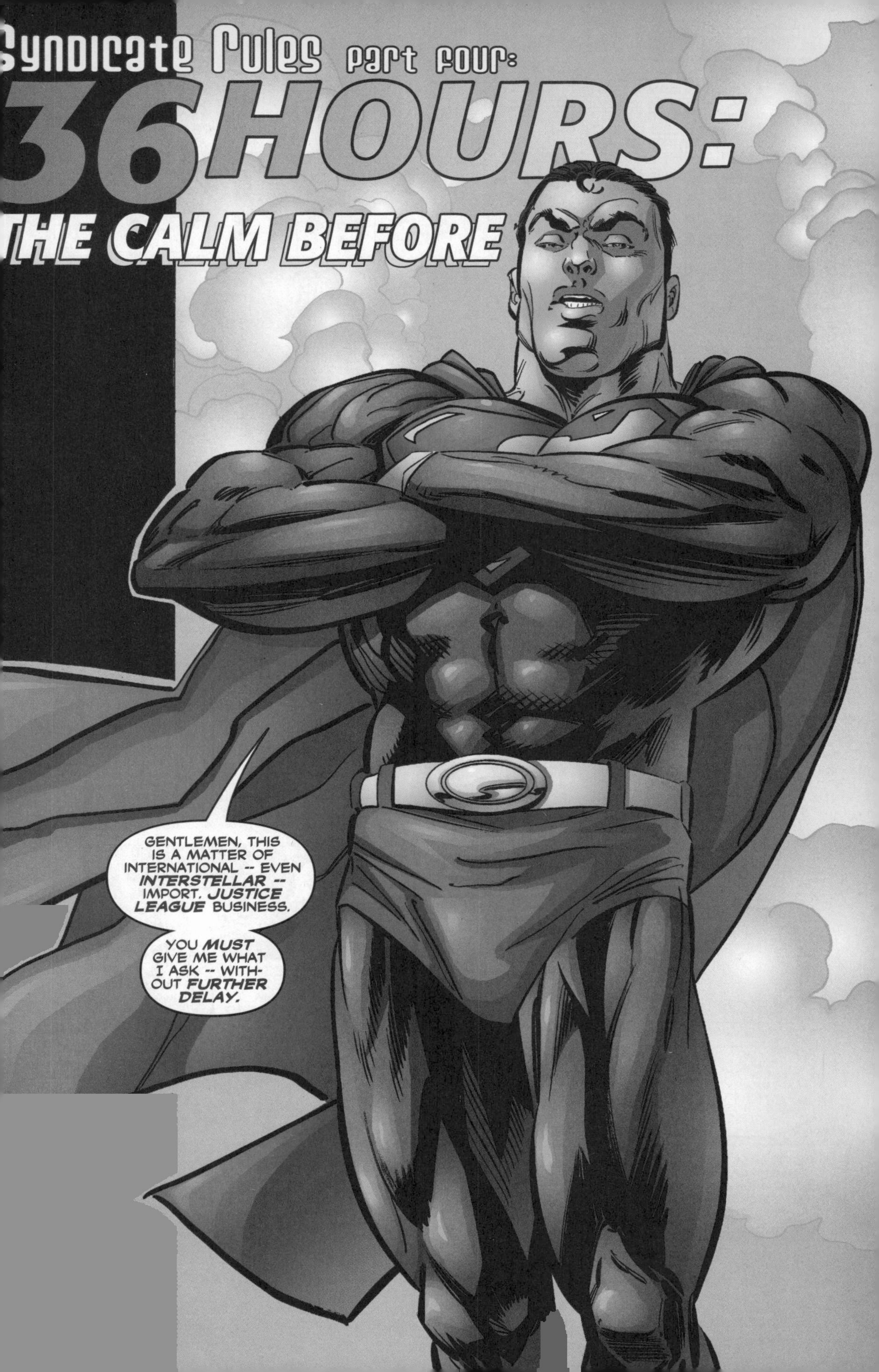
Syndicate Rules part four:
36 HOURS:
THE CALM BEFORE
GENTLEMEN, THIS IS A MATTER OF INTERNATIONAL -- EVEN INTERSTELLAR -- IMPORT. JUSTICE LEAGUE BUSINESS.
YOU MUST GIVE ME WHAT I ASK -- WITHOUT FURTHER DELAY.

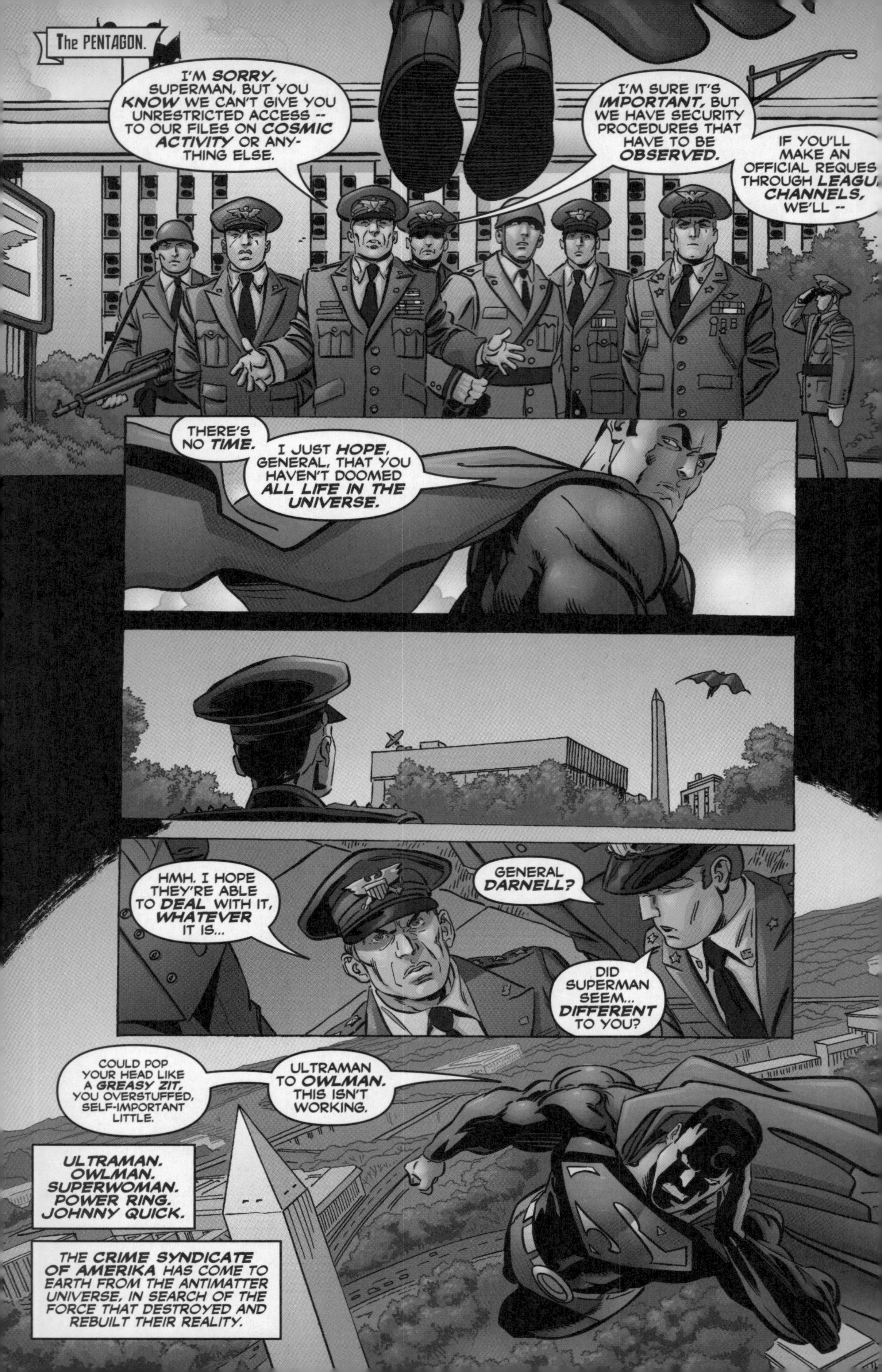
The PENTAGON.
I'M SORRY, SUPERMAN, BUT YOU KNOW WE CAN'T GIVE YOU UNRESTRICTED ACCESS -- TO OUR FILES ON COSMIC ACTIVITY OR ANY-THING ELSE.
I'M SURE IT'S IMPORTANT, BUT WE HAVE SECURITY PROCEDURES THAT HAVE TO BE OBSERVED.
IF YOU'LL MAKE AN OFFICIAL REQUE THROUGH LEAGU CHANNELS, WE'LL --
THERE'S NO TIME.
I JUST HOPE, GENERAL, THAT YOU HAVEN'T DOOMED ALL LIFE IN THE UNIVERSE.
HMH. I HOPE THEY'RE ABLE TO DEAL WITH IT, WHATEVER IT IS...
GENERAL DARNELL?
DID SUPERMAN SEEM... DIFFERENT TO YOU?
COULD POP YOUR HEAD LIKE A GREASY ZIT, YOU OVERSTUFFED, SELF-IMPORTANT LITTLE.
ULTRAMAN TO OWLMAN. THIS ISN'T WORKING.
ULTRAMAN. OWLMAN. SUPERWOMAN. POWER RING. JOHNNY QUICK.
THE CRIME SYNDICATE OF AMERIKA HAS COME TO EARTH FROM THE ANTIMATTER UNIVERSE, IN SEARCH OF THE FORCE THAT DESTROYED AND REBUILT THEIR REALITY.

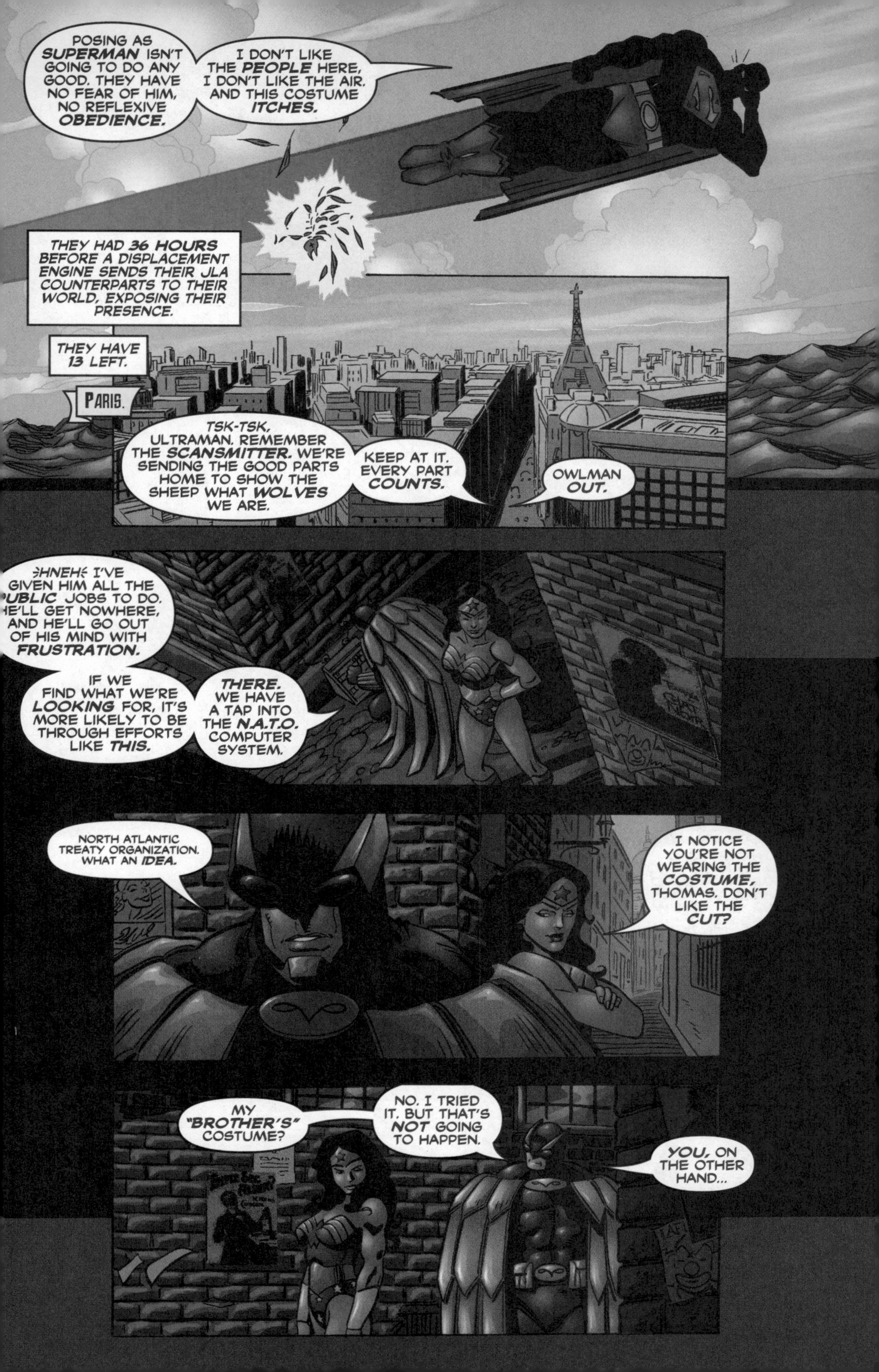
POSING AS SUPERMAN ISN'T GOING TO DO ANY GOOD. THEY HAVE NO FEAR OF HIM, NO REFLEXIVE OBEDIENCE.
I DON'T LIKE THE PEOPLE HERE, I DON'T LIKE THE AIR. AND THIS COSTUME ITCHES.
THEY HAD 36 HOURS BEFORE A DISPLACEMENT ENGINE SENDS THEIR JLA COUNTERPARTS TO THEIR WORLD, EXPOSING THEIR PRESENCE.
THEY HAVE 13 LEFT.
PARIS.
TSK-TSK, ULTRAMAN. REMEMBER THE SCANSMITTER. WE'RE SENDING THE GOOD PARTS HOME TO SHOW THE SHEEP WHAT WOLVES WE ARE.
KEEP AT IT. EVERY PART COUNTS.
OWLMAN OUT.
HNEH I'VE GIVEN HIM ALL THE PUBLIC JOBS TO DO. HE'LL GET NOWHERE, AND HE'LL GO OUT OF HIS MIND WITH FRUSTRATION.
IF WE FIND WHAT WE'RE LOOKING FOR, IT'S MORE LIKELY TO BE THROUGH EFFORTS LIKE THIS.
THERE. WE HAVE A TAP INTO THE N.A.T.O. COMPUTER SYSTEM.
NORTH ATLANTIC TREATY ORGANIZATION. WHAT AN IDEA.
I NOTICE YOU'RE NOT WEARING THE COSTUME, THOMAS. DON'T LIKE THE CUT?
MY "BROTHER'S" COSTUME?
NO. I TRIED IT. BUT THAT'S NOT GOING TO HAPPEN.
YOU, ON THE OTHER HAND...

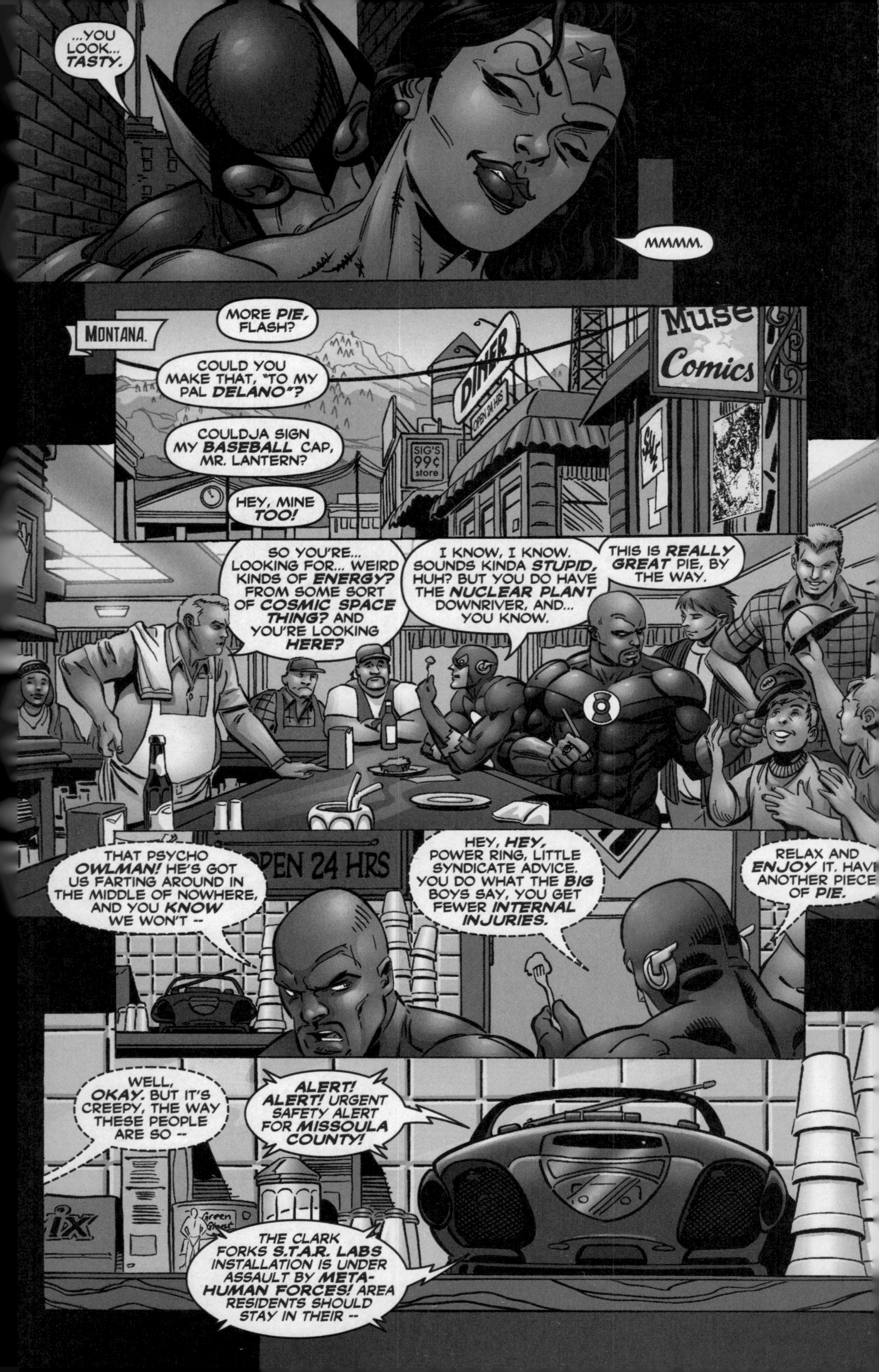

...YOU LOOK... TASTY.
MMMM.
MONTANA.
MORE PIE, FLASH?
COULD YOU MAKE THAT, "TO MY PAL DELANO"?
COULDJA SIGN MY BASEBALL CAP, MR. LANTERN?
HEY, MINE TOO!
DINER
OPEN 24 HRS
SIG'S 99¢ store
Muse Comics
SO YOU'RE... LOOKING FOR... WEIRD KINDS OF ENERGY? FROM SOME SORT OF COSMIC SPACE THING? AND YOU'RE LOOKING HERE?
I KNOW, I KNOW. SOUNDS KINDA STUPID, HUH? BUT YOU DO HAVE THE NUCLEAR PLANT DOWNRIVER, AND... YOU KNOW.
THIS IS REALLY GREAT PIE, BY THE WAY.
THAT PSYCHO OWLMAN! HE'S GOT US FARTING AROUND IN THE MIDDLE OF NOWHERE, AND YOU KNOW WE WON'T --
OPEN 24 HRS
HEY, HEY, POWER RING, LITTLE SYNDICATE ADVICE. YOU DO WHAT THE BIG BOYS SAY, YOU GET FEWER INTERNAL INJURIES.
RELAX AND ENJOY IT. HAVE ANOTHER PIECE OF PIE.
WELL, OKAY. BUT IT'S CREEPY, THE WAY THESE PEOPLE ARE SO --
ALERT! ALERT! URGENT SAFETY ALERT FOR MISSOULA COUNTY!
THE CLARK FORKS S.T.A.R. LABS INSTALLATION IS UNDER ASSAULT BY META-HUMAN FORCES! AREA RESIDENTS SHOULD STAY IN THEIR --

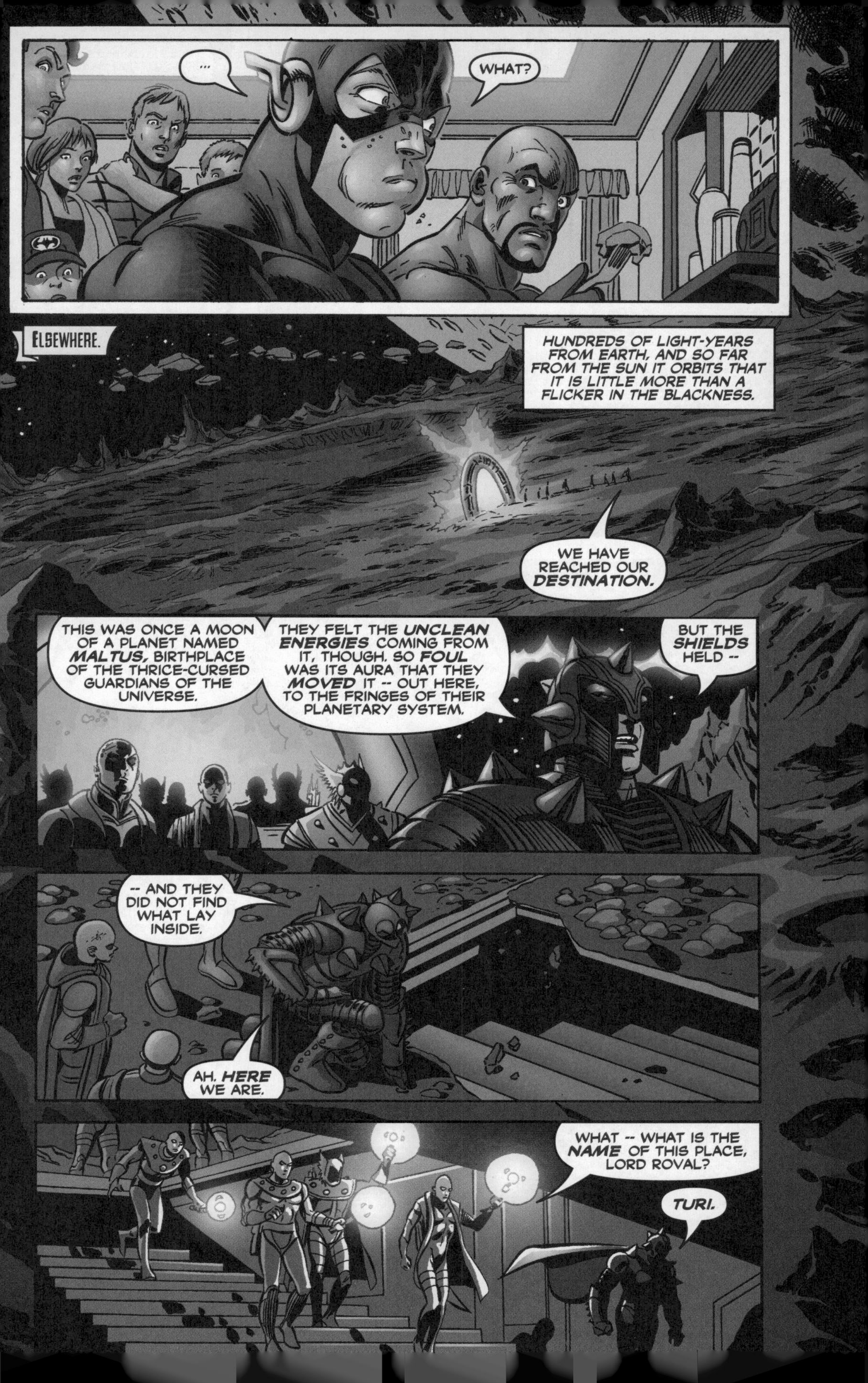
...
WHAT?
ELSEWHERE.
HUNDREDS OF LIGHT-YEARS FROM EARTH, AND SO FAR FROM THE SUN IT ORBITS THAT IT IS LITTLE MORE THAN A FLICKER IN THE BLACKNESS.
WE HAVE REACHED OUR DESTINATION.
THIS WAS ONCE A MOON OF A PLANET NAMED MALTUS, BIRTHPLACE OF THE THRICE-CURSED GUARDIANS OF THE UNIVERSE.
THEY FELT THE UNCLEAN ENERGIES COMING FROM IT, THOUGH. SO FOUL WAS ITS AURA THAT THEY MOVED IT -- OUT HERE, TO THE FRINGES OF THEIR PLANETARY SYSTEM.
BUT THE SHIELDS HELD --
-- AND THEY DID NOT FIND WHAT LAY INSIDE.
AH. HERE WE ARE.
WHAT -- WHAT IS THE NAME OF THIS PLACE, LORD ROVAL?
TURI.

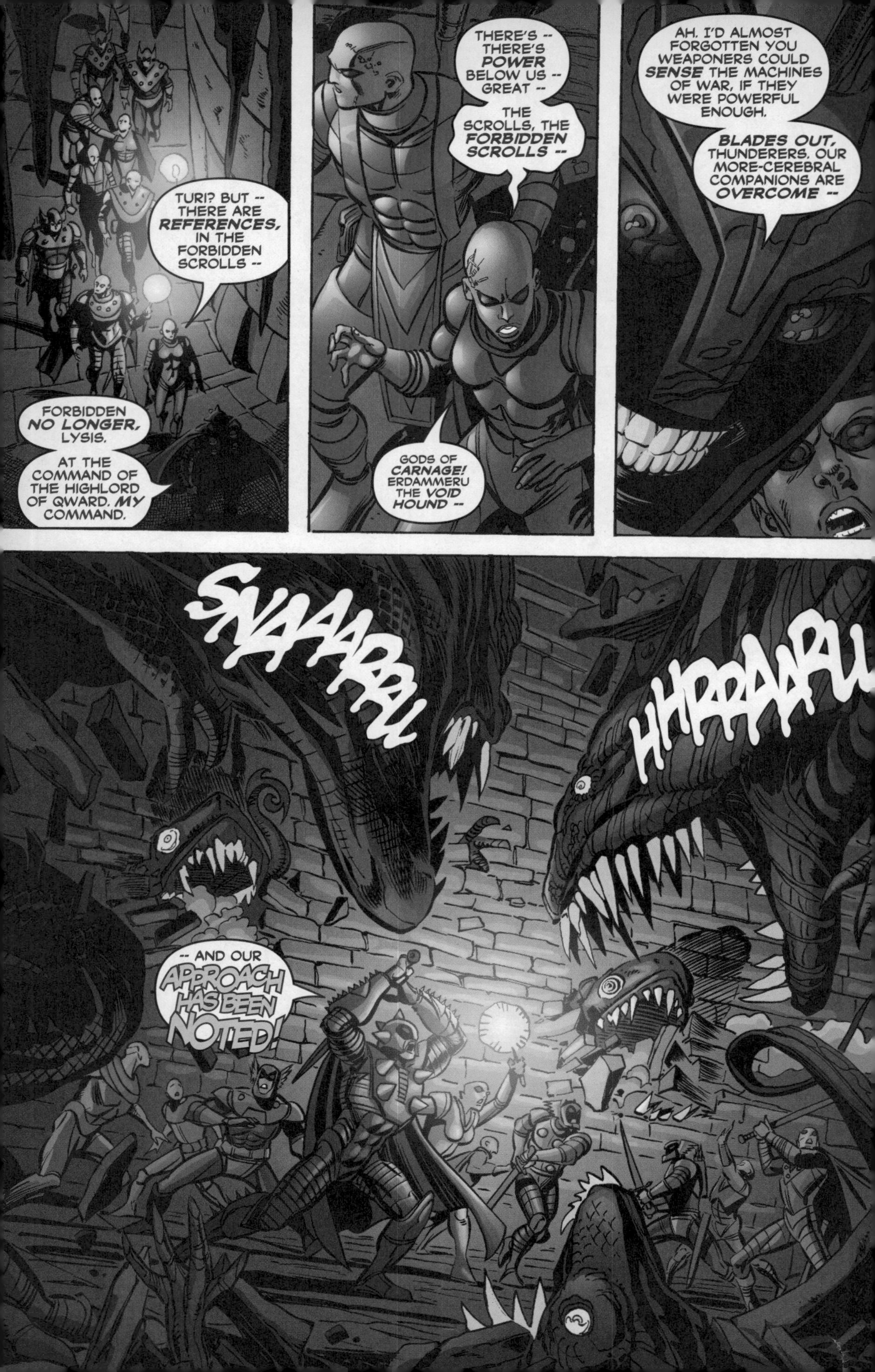
TURI? BUT -- THERE ARE REFERENCES, IN THE FORBIDDEN SCROLLS --
FORBIDDEN NO LONGER, LYSIS.
AT THE COMMAND OF THE HIGHLORD OF QWARD. MY COMMAND.
THERE'S -- THERE'S POWER BELOW US -- GREAT --
THE SCROLLS, THE FORBIDDEN SCROLLS --
GODS OF CARNAGE! ERDAMMERU THE VOID HOUND --
AH. I'D ALMOST FORGOTTEN YOU WEAPONERS COULD SENSE THE MACHINES OF WAR, IF THEY WERE POWERFUL ENOUGH.
BLADES OUT, THUNDERERS. OUR MORE-CEREBRAL COMPANIONS ARE OVERCOME --
SNAAARRW
HHRRAARU
-- AND OUR APPROACH HAS BEEN NOTED!

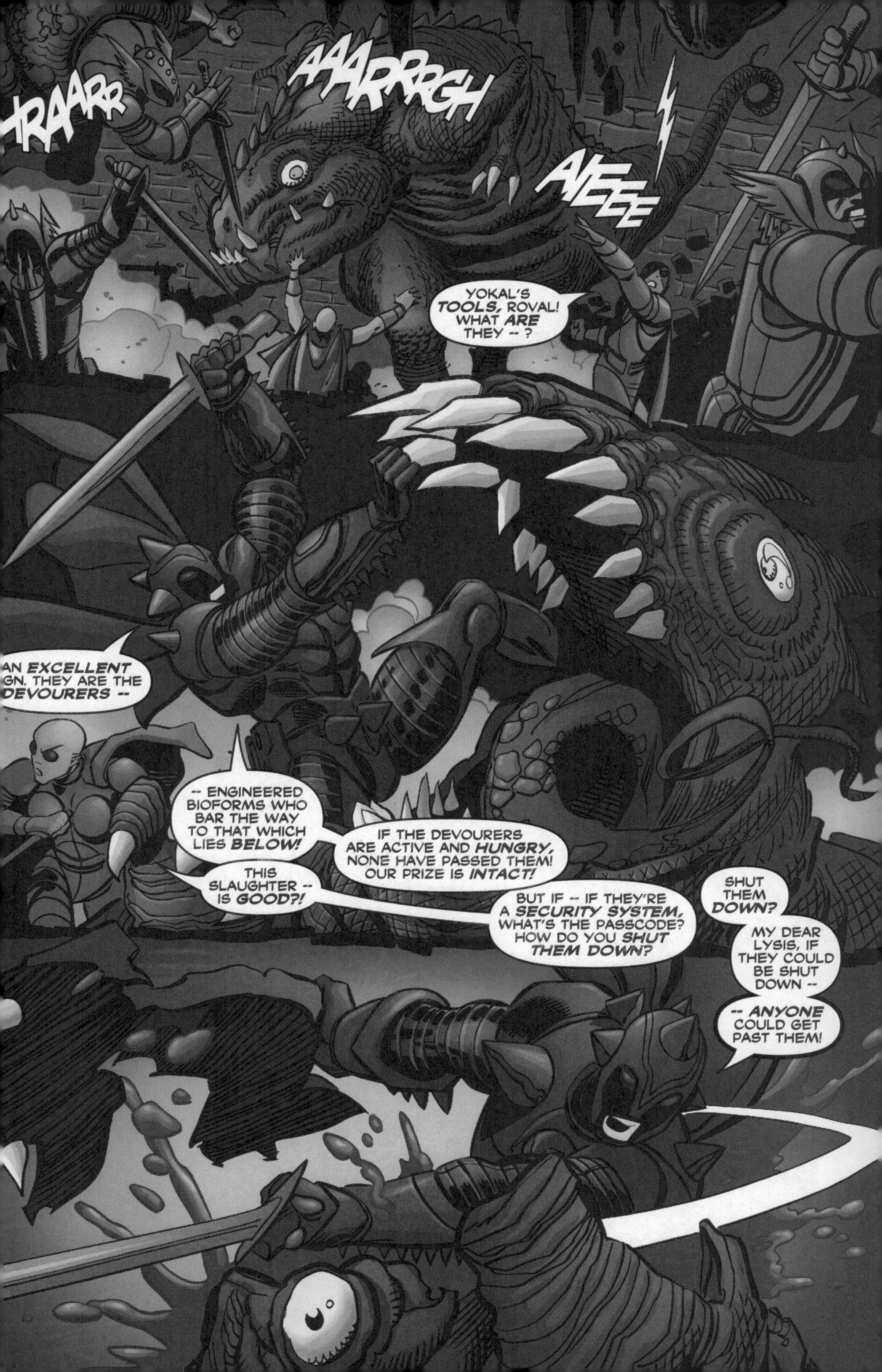
TRAARR
AAAARRRGH
AIEEE
YOKAL'S TOOLS, ROVAL! WHAT ARE THEY -- ?
AN EXCELLENT GN. THEY ARE THE DEVOURERS --
-- ENGINEERED BIOFORMS WHO BAR THE WAY TO THAT WHICH LIES BELOW!
IF THE DEVOURERS ARE ACTIVE AND HUNGRY, NONE HAVE PASSED THEM! OUR PRIZE IS INTACT!
THIS SLAUGHTER -- IS GOOD?!
BUT IF -- IF THEY'RE A SECURITY SYSTEM, WHAT'S THE PASSCODE? HOW DO YOU SHUT THEM DOWN?
SHUT THEM DOWN?
MY DEAR LYSIS, IF THEY COULD BE SHUT DOWN --
-- ANYONE COULD GET PAST THEM!

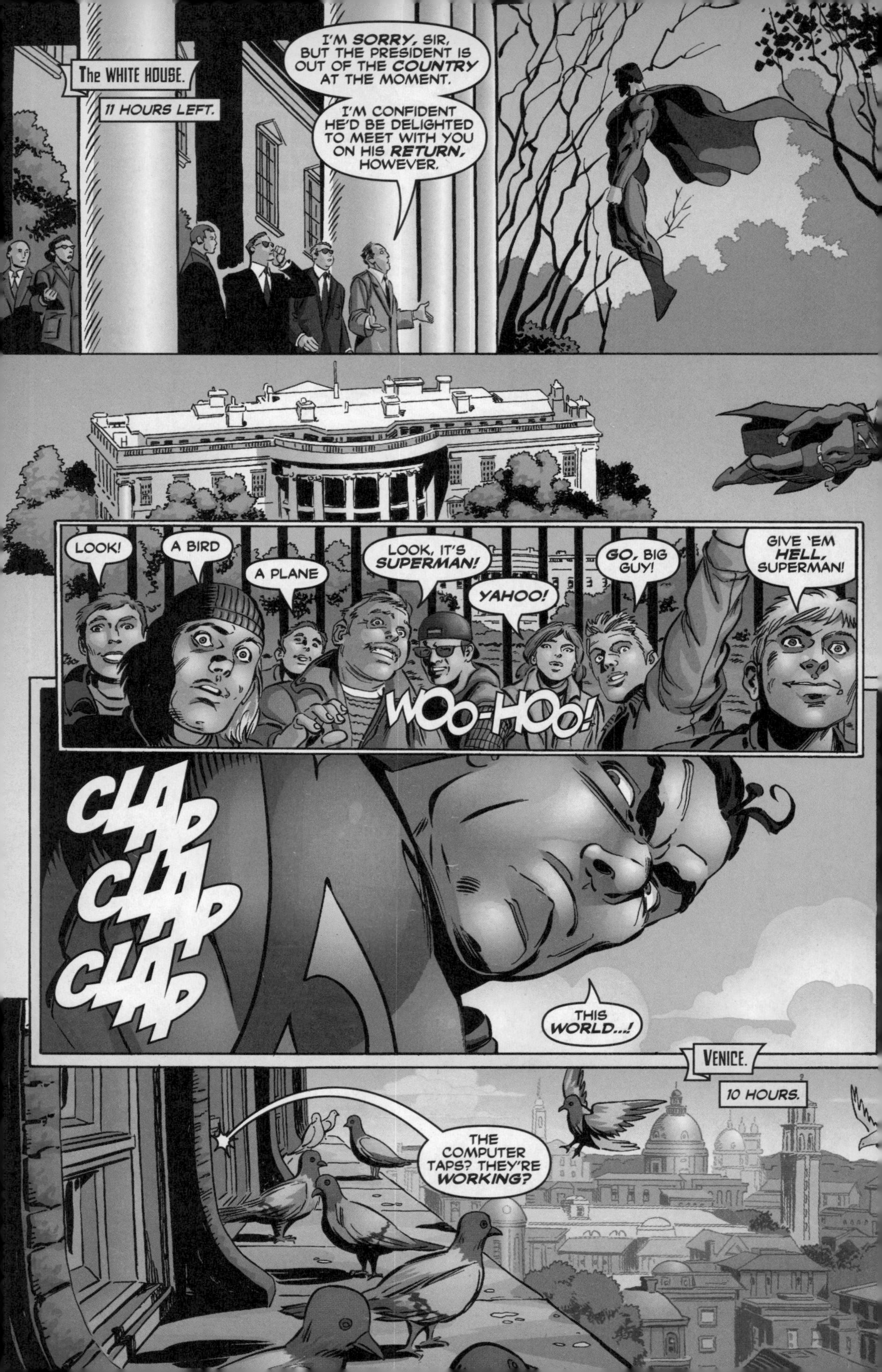
The WHITE HOUSE.
11 HOURS LEFT.
I'M SORRY, SIR, BUT THE PRESIDENT IS OUT OF THE COUNTRY AT THE MOMENT.
I'M CONFIDENT HE'D BE DELIGHTED TO MEET WITH YOU ON HIS RETURN, HOWEVER.
LOOK!
A BIRD
A PLANE
LOOK, IT'S SUPERMAN!
YAHOO!
GO, BIG GUY!
GIVE 'EM HELL, SUPERMAN!
WOO-HOO!
CLAP CLAP CLAP
THIS WORLD...!
VENICE.
10 HOURS.
THE COMPUTER TAPS? THEY'RE WORKING?

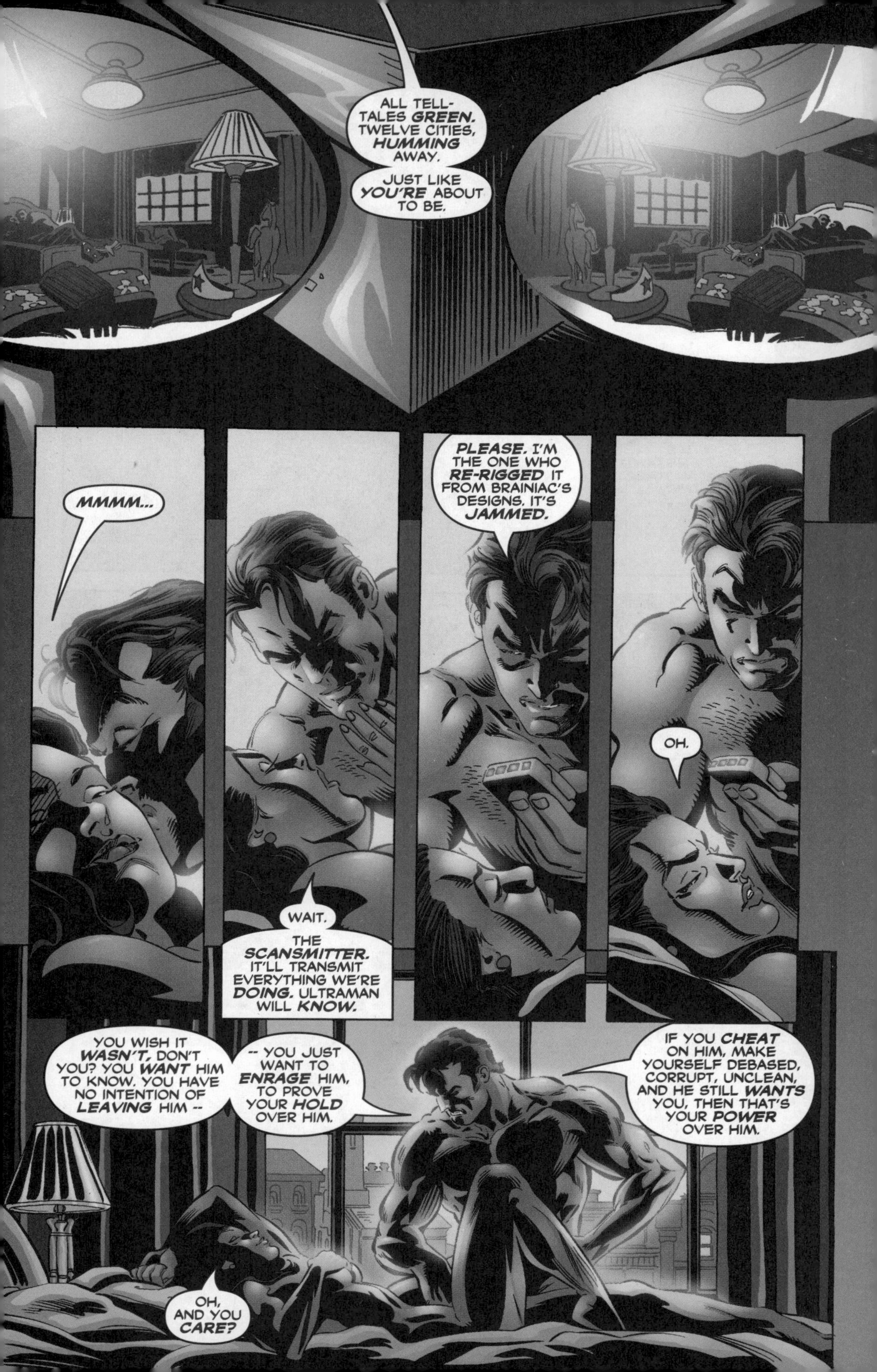
ALL TELL-TALES GREEN. TWELVE CITIES, HUMMING AWAY.
JUST LIKE YOU'RE ABOUT TO BE.
MMMM...
WAIT.
THE SCANSMITTER. IT'LL TRANSMIT EVERYTHING WE'RE DOING. ULTRAMAN WILL KNOW.
PLEASE. I'M THE ONE WHO RE-RIGGED IT FROM BRAINIAC'S DESIGNS. IT'S JAMMED.
OH.
YOU WISH IT WASN'T, DON'T YOU? YOU WANT HIM TO KNOW. YOU HAVE NO INTENTION OF LEAVING HIM --
-- YOU JUST WANT TO ENRAGE HIM, TO PROVE YOUR HOLD OVER HIM.
OH, AND YOU CARE?
IF YOU CHEAT ON HIM, MAKE YOURSELF DEBASED, CORRUPT, UNCLEAN, AND HE STILL WANTS YOU, THEN THAT'S YOUR POWER OVER HIM.

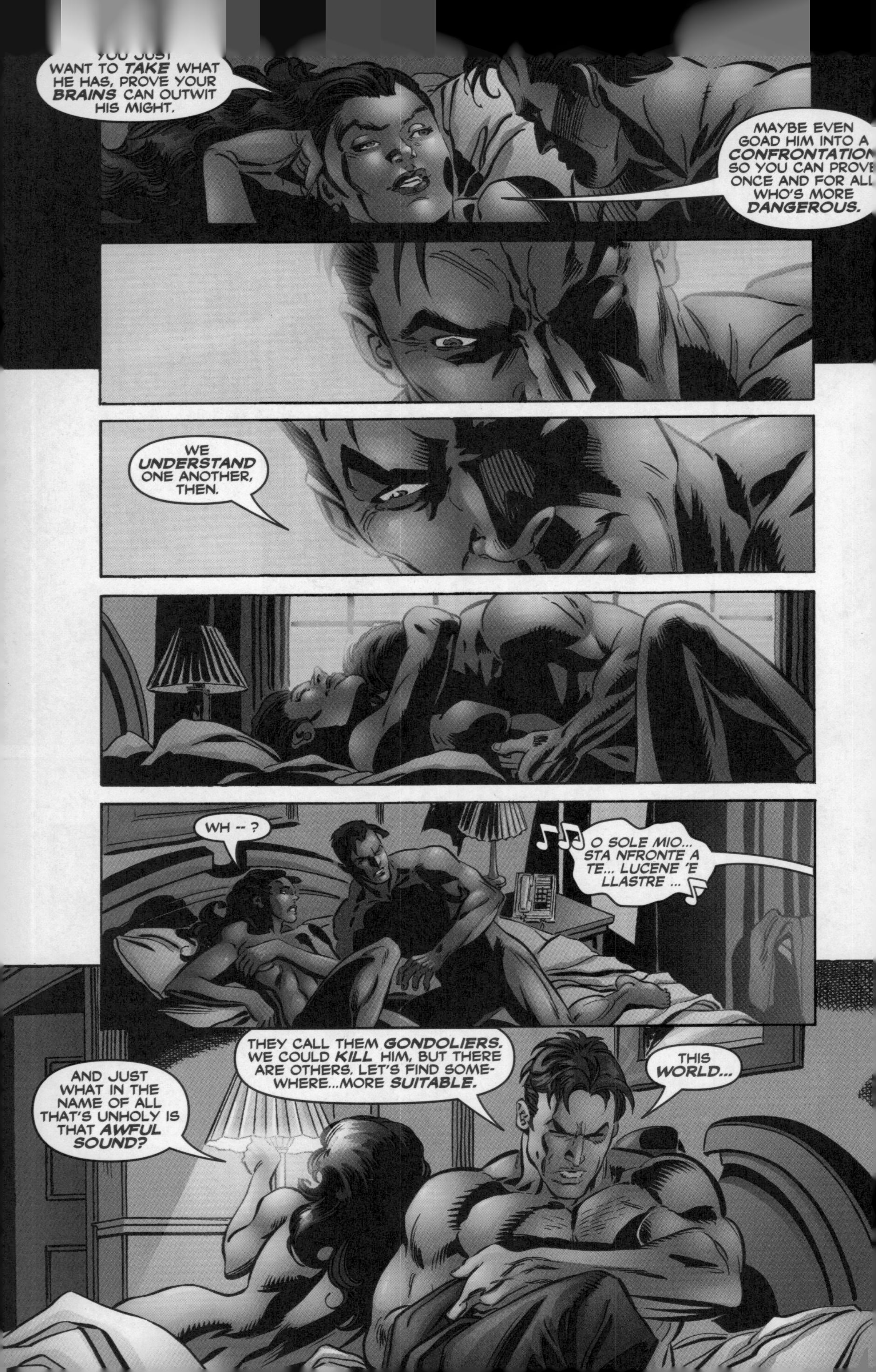
YOU JUST WANT TO TAKE WHAT HE HAS, PROVE YOUR BRAINS CAN OUTWIT HIS MIGHT.
MAYBE EVEN GOAD HIM INTO A CONFRONTATION SO YOU CAN PROVE ONCE AND FOR ALL WHO'S MORE DANGEROUS.
WE UNDERSTAND ONE ANOTHER, THEN.
WH -- ?
O SOLE MIO... STA NFRONTE A TE... LUCENE 'E LLASTRE ...
AND JUST WHAT IN THE NAME OF ALL THAT'S UNHOLY IS THAT AWFUL SOUND?
THEY CALL THEM GONDOLIERS. WE COULD KILL HIM, BUT THERE ARE OTHERS. LET'S FIND SOMEWHERE...MORE SUITABLE.
THIS WORLD...

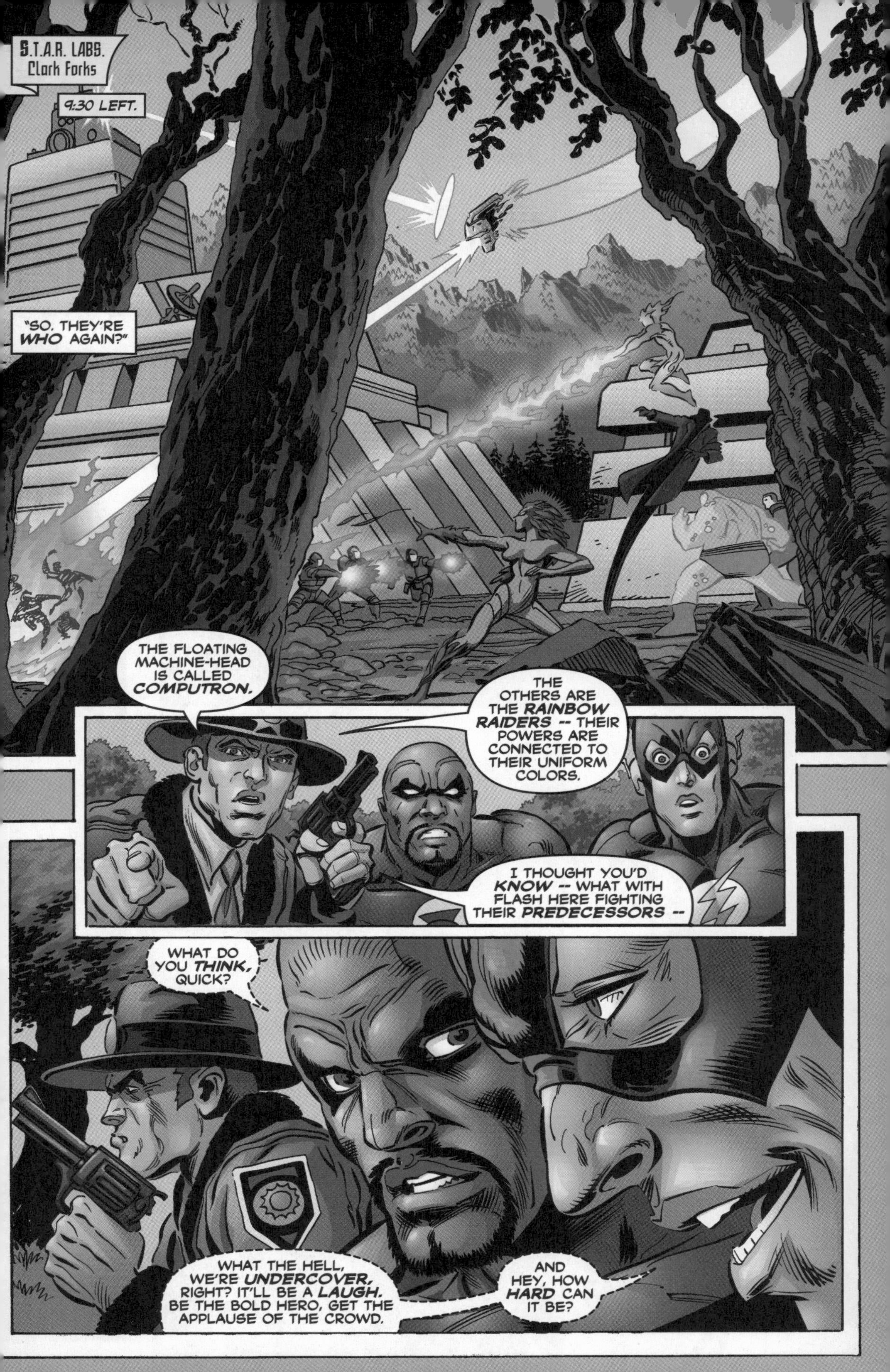
S.T.A.R. LABS.
Clark Forks
9:30 LEFT.
"SO. THEY'RE WHO AGAIN?"
THE FLOATING MACHINE-HEAD IS CALLED COMPUTRON.
THE OTHERS ARE THE RAINBOW RAIDERS -- THEIR POWERS ARE CONNECTED TO THEIR UNIFORM COLORS.
I THOUGHT YOU'D KNOW -- WHAT WITH FLASH HERE FIGHTING THEIR PREDECESSORS --
WHAT DO YOU THINK, QUICK?
WHAT THE HELL, WE'RE UNDERCOVER, RIGHT? IT'LL BE A LAUGH. BE THE BOLD HERO, GET THE APPLAUSE OF THE CROWD.
AND HEY, HOW HARD CAN IT BE?

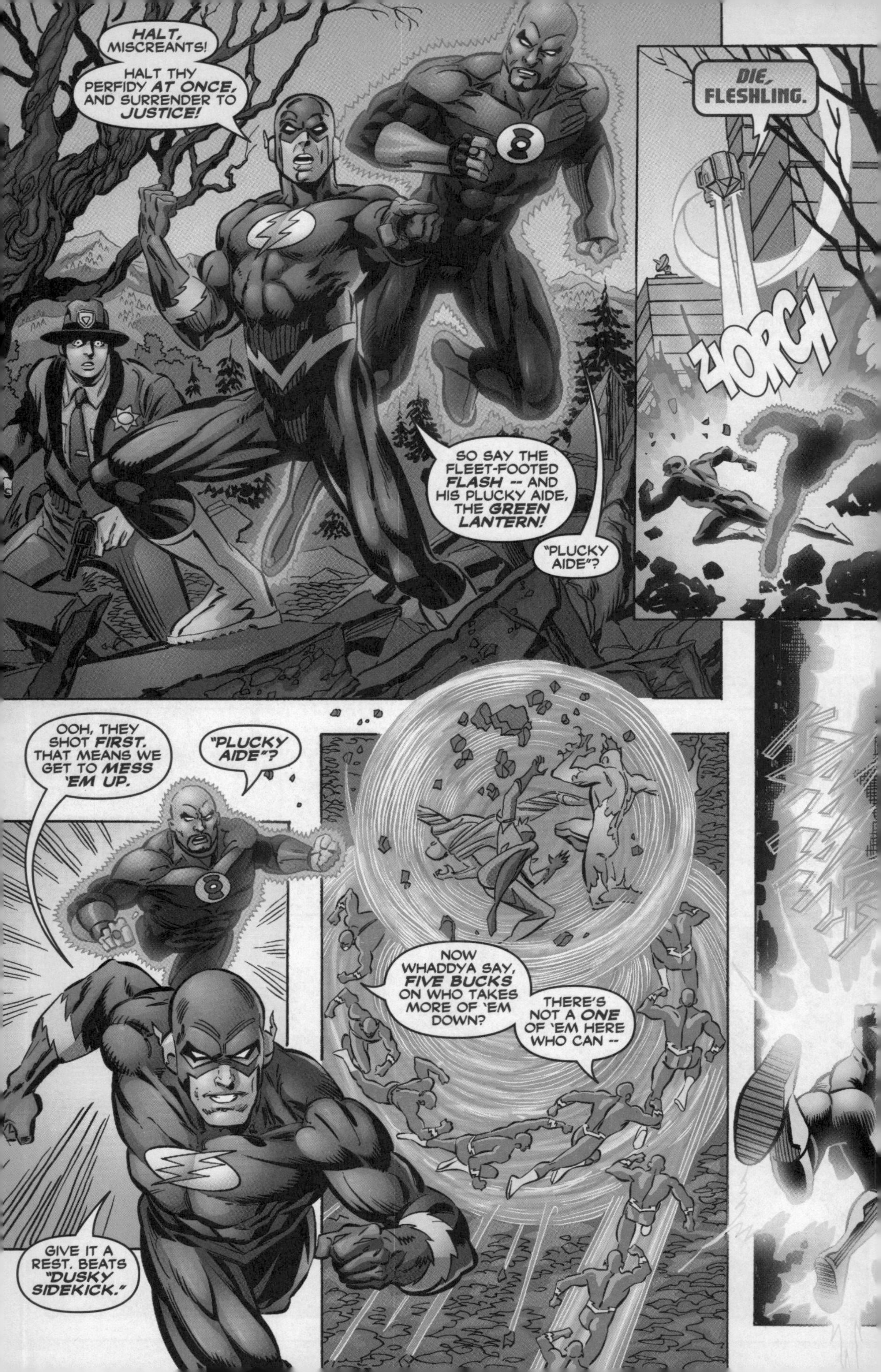
HALT, MISCREANTS!
HALT THY PERFIDY AT ONCE, AND SURRENDER TO JUSTICE!
SO SAY THE FLEET-FOOTED FLASH -- AND HIS PLUCKY AIDE, THE GREEN LANTERN!
"PLUCKY AIDE"?
DIE, FLESHLING.
ZORCH
OOH, THEY SHOT FIRST. THAT MEANS WE GET TO MESS 'EM UP.
"PLUCKY AIDE"?
GIVE IT A REST. BEATS "DUSKY SIDEKICK."
NOW WHADDYA SAY, FIVE BUCKS ON WHO TAKES MORE OF 'EM DOWN?
THERE'S NOT A ONE OF 'EM HERE WHO CAN --

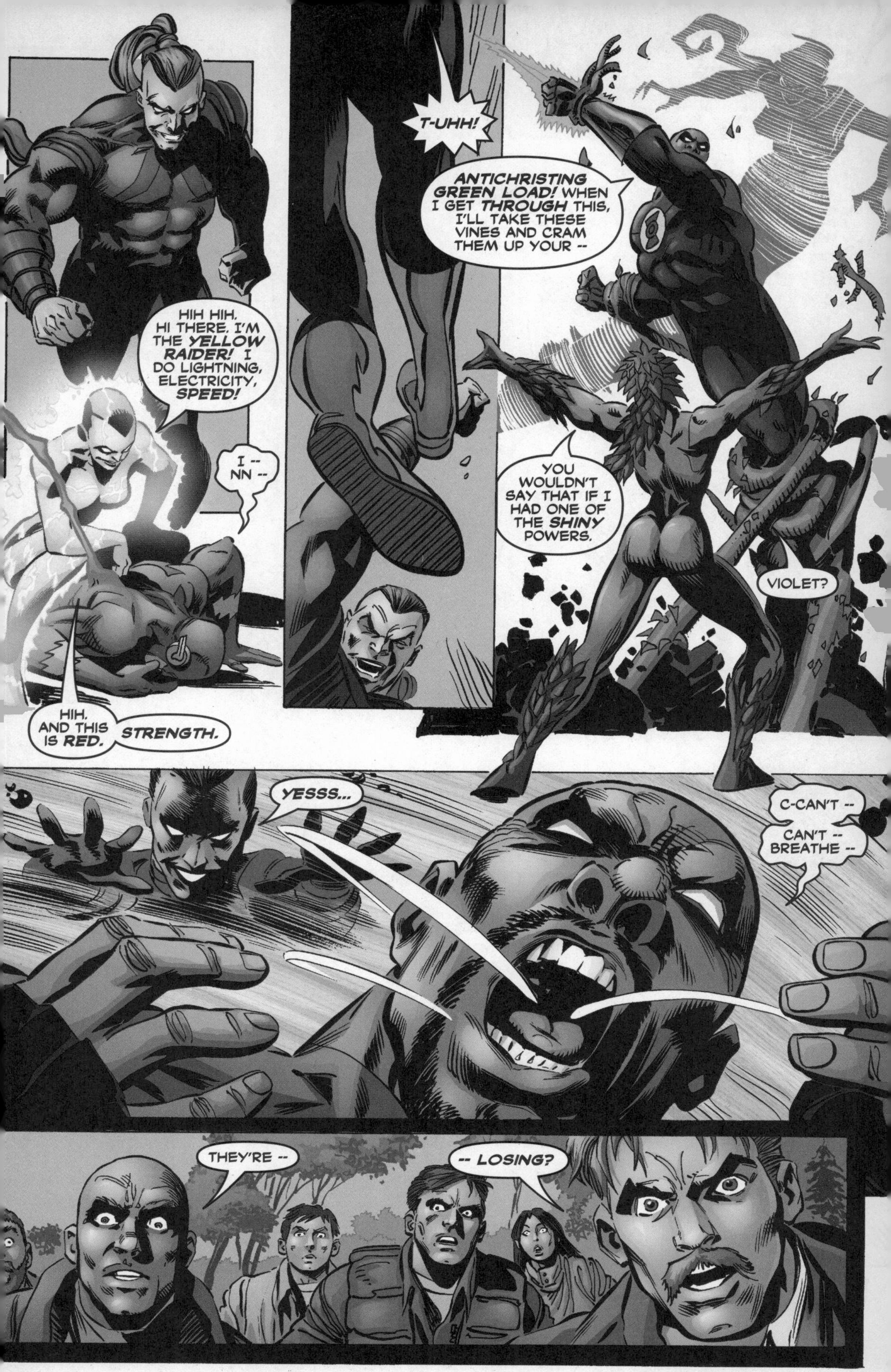
HIH HIH. HI THERE. I'M THE YELLOW RAIDER! I DO LIGHTNING, ELECTRICITY, SPEED!
I -- NN --
HIH. AND THIS IS RED.
STRENGTH.
T-UHH!
ANTICHRISTING GREEN LOAD! WHEN I GET THROUGH THIS, I'LL TAKE THESE VINES AND CRAM THEM UP YOUR --
YOU WOULDN'T SAY THAT IF I HAD ONE OF THE SHINY POWERS.
VIOLET?
YESSS...
C-CAN'T --
CAN'T -- BREATHE --
THEY'RE --
-- LOSING?

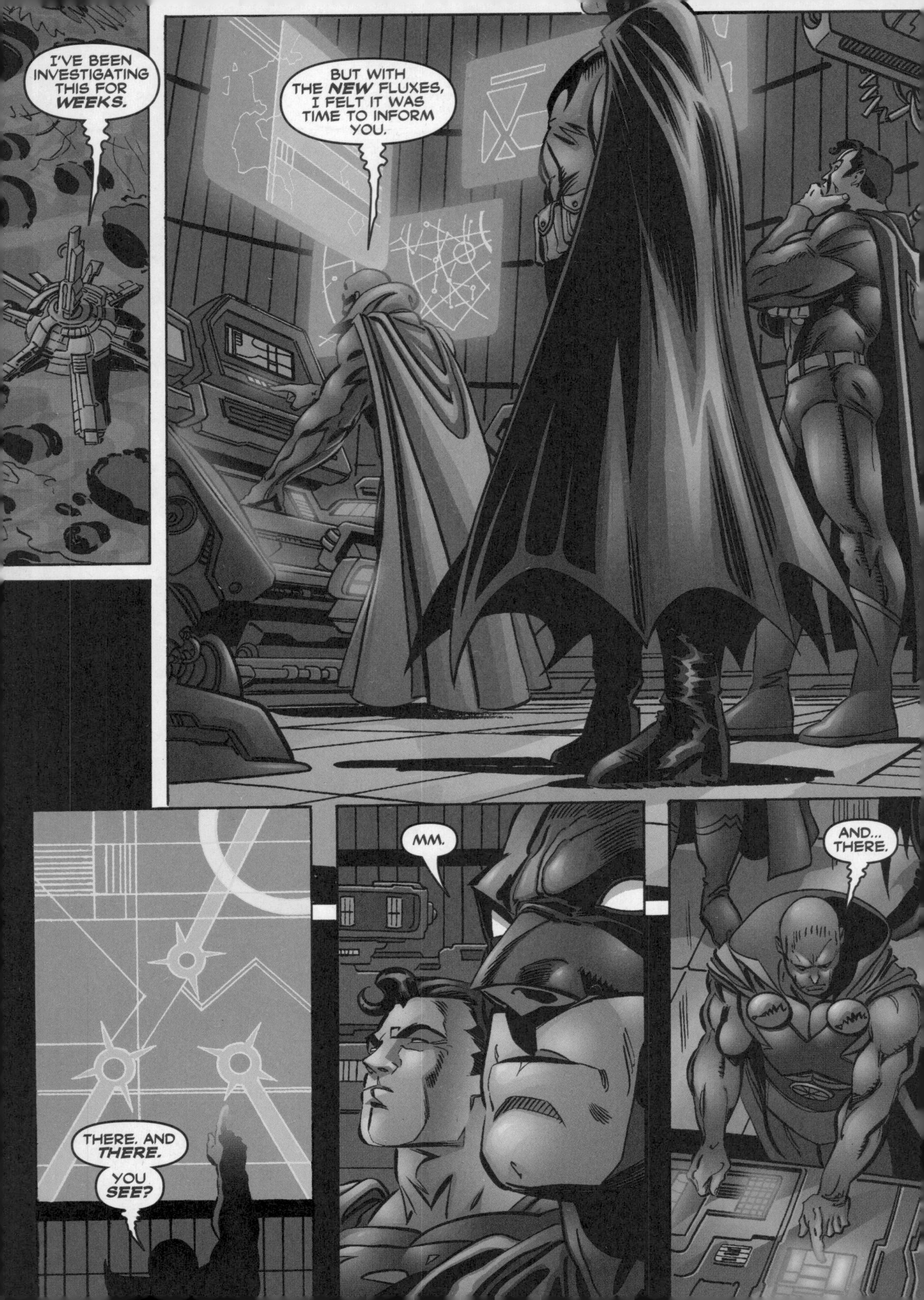
I'VE BEEN INVESTIGATING THIS FOR WEEKS.
BUT WITH THE NEW FLUXES, I FELT IT WAS TIME TO INFORM YOU.
THERE. AND THERE.
YOU SEE?
MM.
AND... THERE.

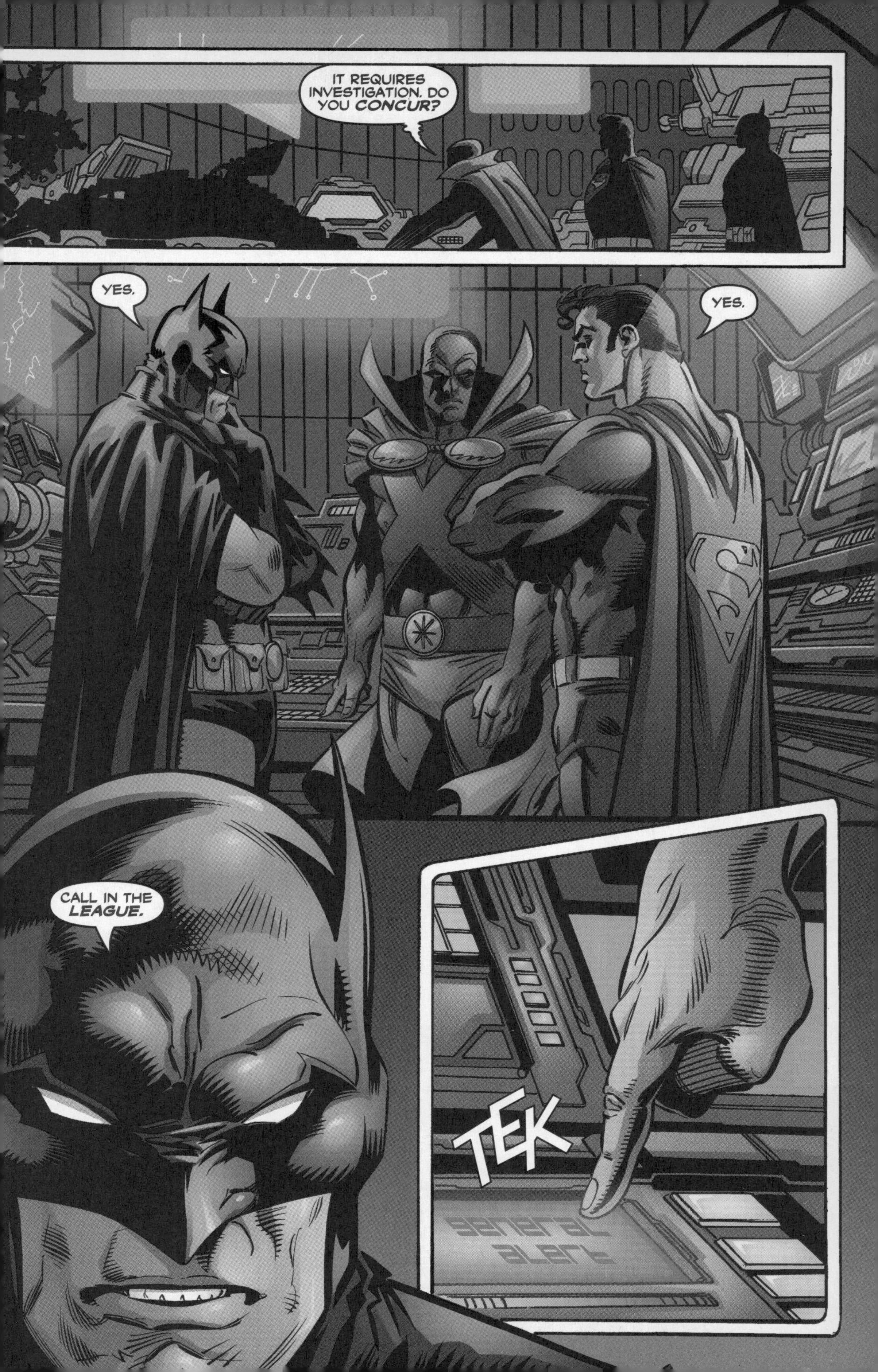
IT REQUIRES INVESTIGATION. DO YOU CONCUR?
YES.
YES.
CALL IN THE LEAGUE.
TEK
GENERAL ALERT

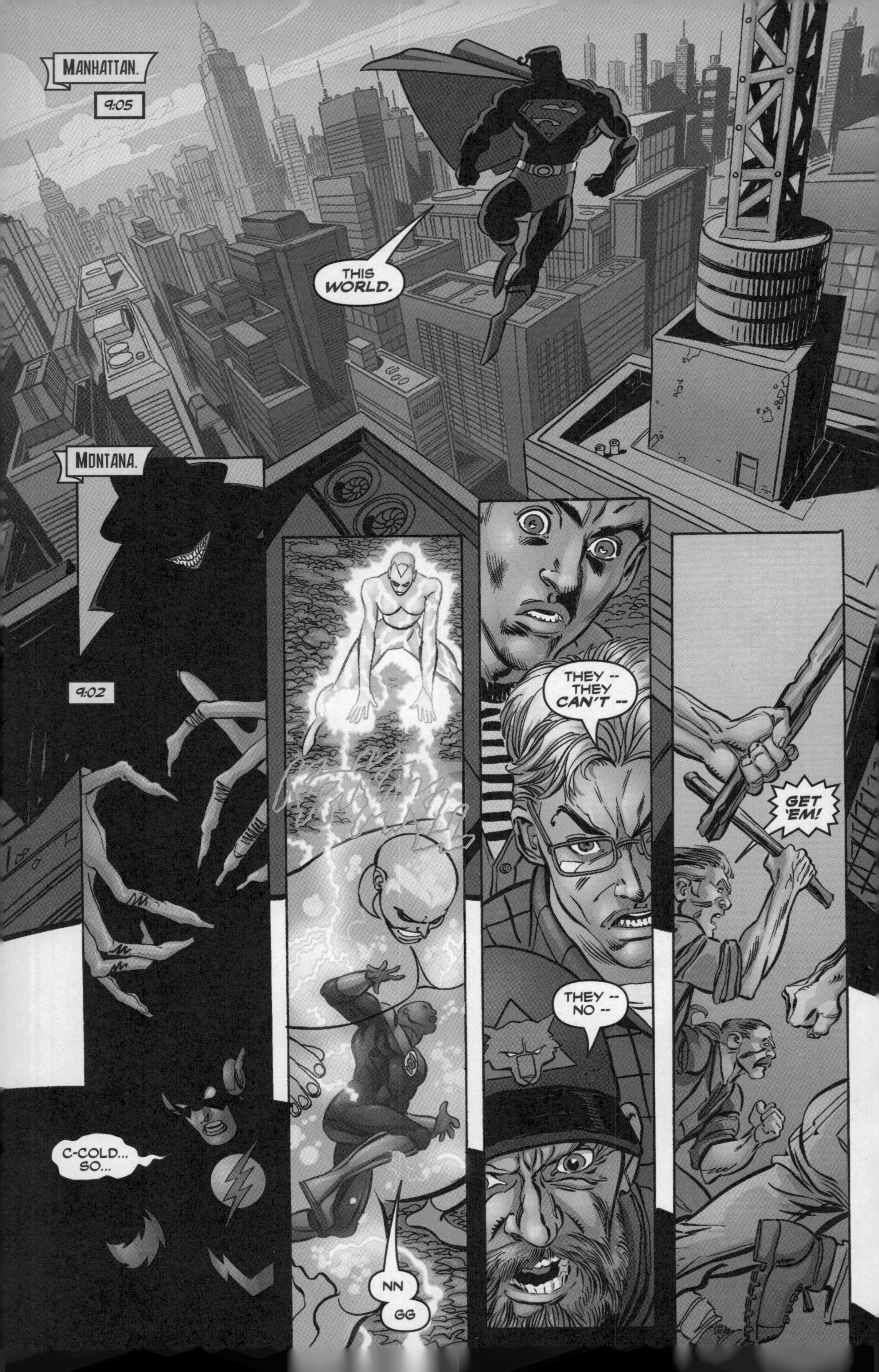
MANHATTAN.
9:05
THIS WORLD.
MONTANA.
9:02
C-COLD... SO...
NN
GG
THEY -- THEY CAN'T --
THEY -- NO --
GET 'EM!

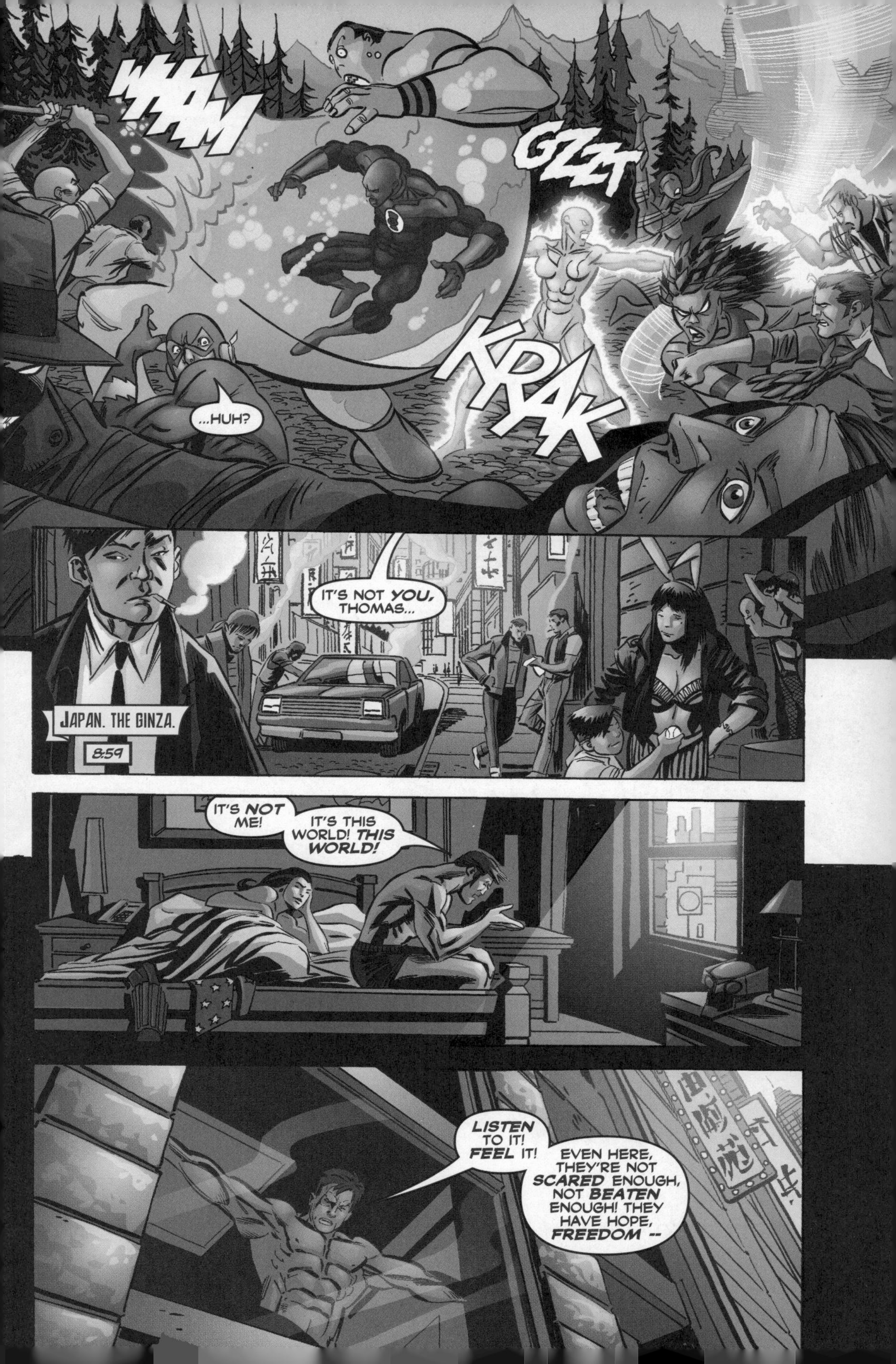
WHAM
GZZT
KRAK
...HUH?
IT'S NOT YOU, THOMAS...
JAPAN. THE GINZA.
8:59
IT'S NOT ME!
IT'S THIS WORLD! THIS WORLD!
LISTEN TO IT! FEEL IT!
EVEN HERE, THEY'RE NOT SCARED ENOUGH, NOT BEATEN ENOUGH! THEY HAVE HOPE, FREEDOM --

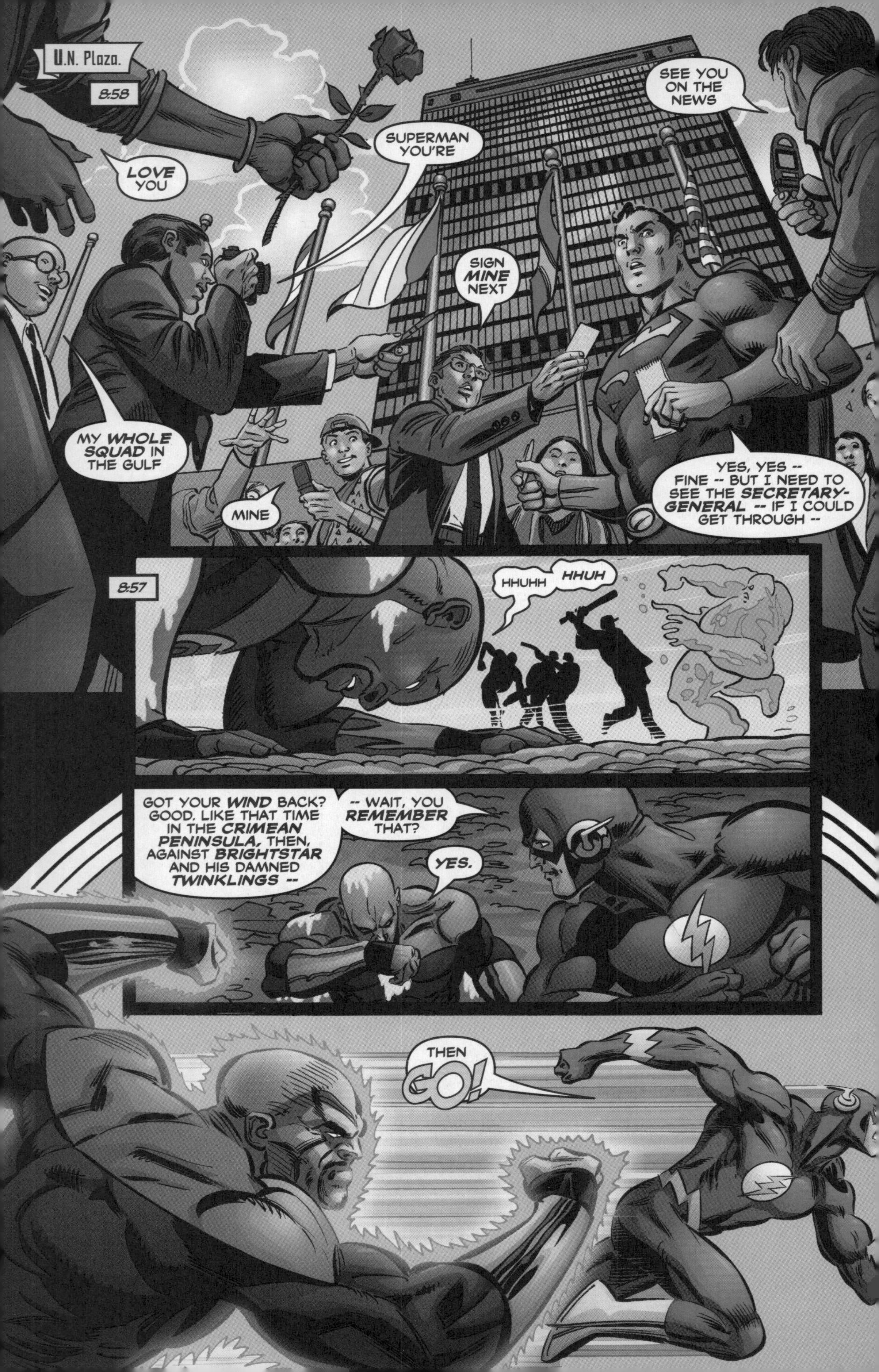
U.N. Plaza.
8:58
LOVE YOU
SUPERMAN YOU'RE
SEE YOU ON THE NEWS
SIGN MINE NEXT
MY WHOLE SQUAD IN THE GULF
MINE
YES, YES -- FINE -- BUT I NEED TO SEE THE SECRETARY-GENERAL -- IF I COULD GET THROUGH --
8:57
HHUHH HHUH
GOT YOUR WIND BACK? GOOD. LIKE THAT TIME IN THE CRIMEAN PENINSULA, THEN, AGAINST BRIGHTSTAR AND HIS DAMNED TWINKLINGS --
-- WAIT, YOU REMEMBER THAT?
YES.
THEN GO!

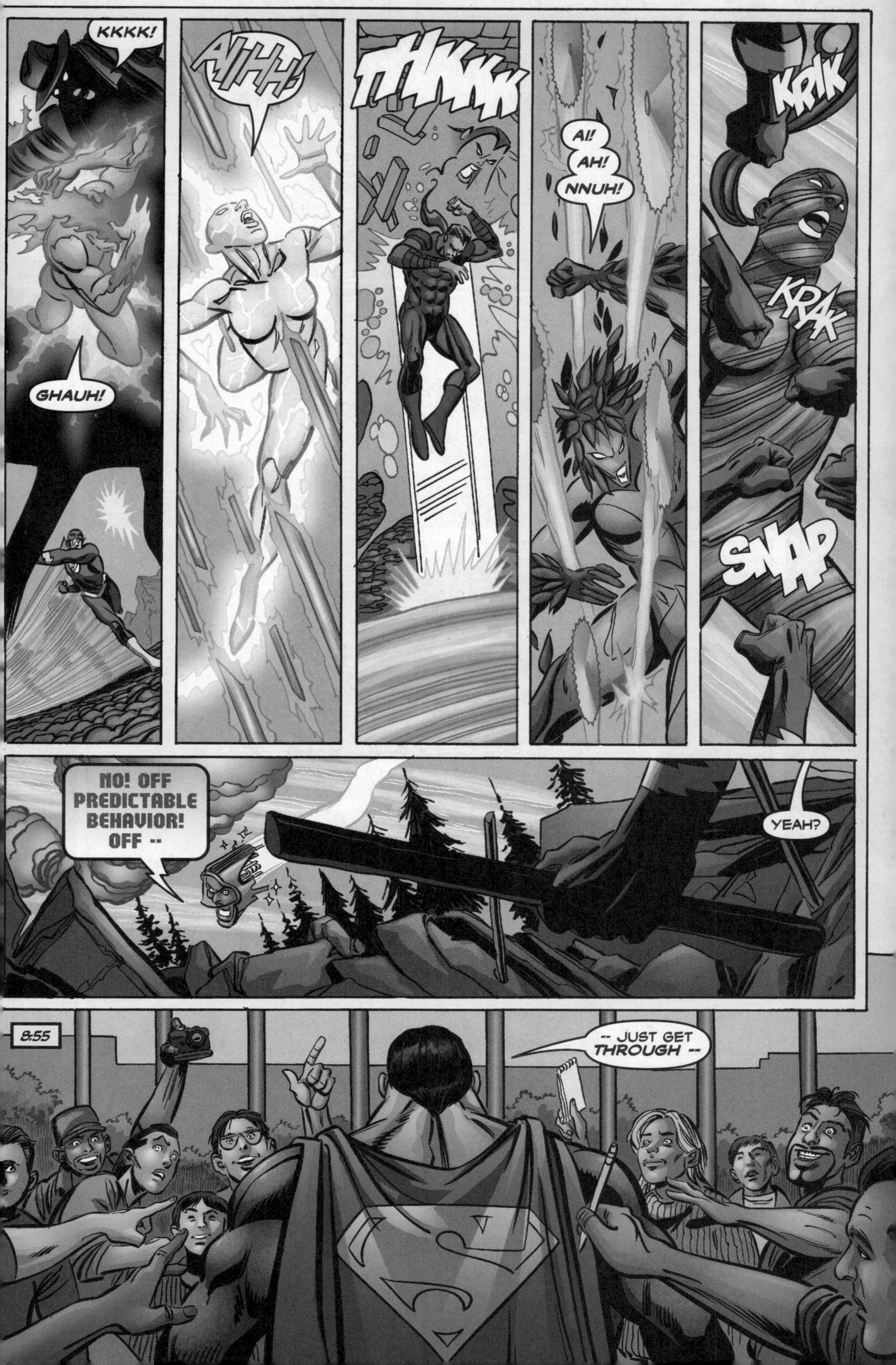
KKKK!
GHAUH!
AIIHH!
THKKKK
AI!
AH!
NNUH!
KRIK
KRAK
SNAP
NO! OFF
PREDICTABLE
BEHAVIOR!
OFF --
YEAH?
8:55
-- JUST GET
THROUGH --

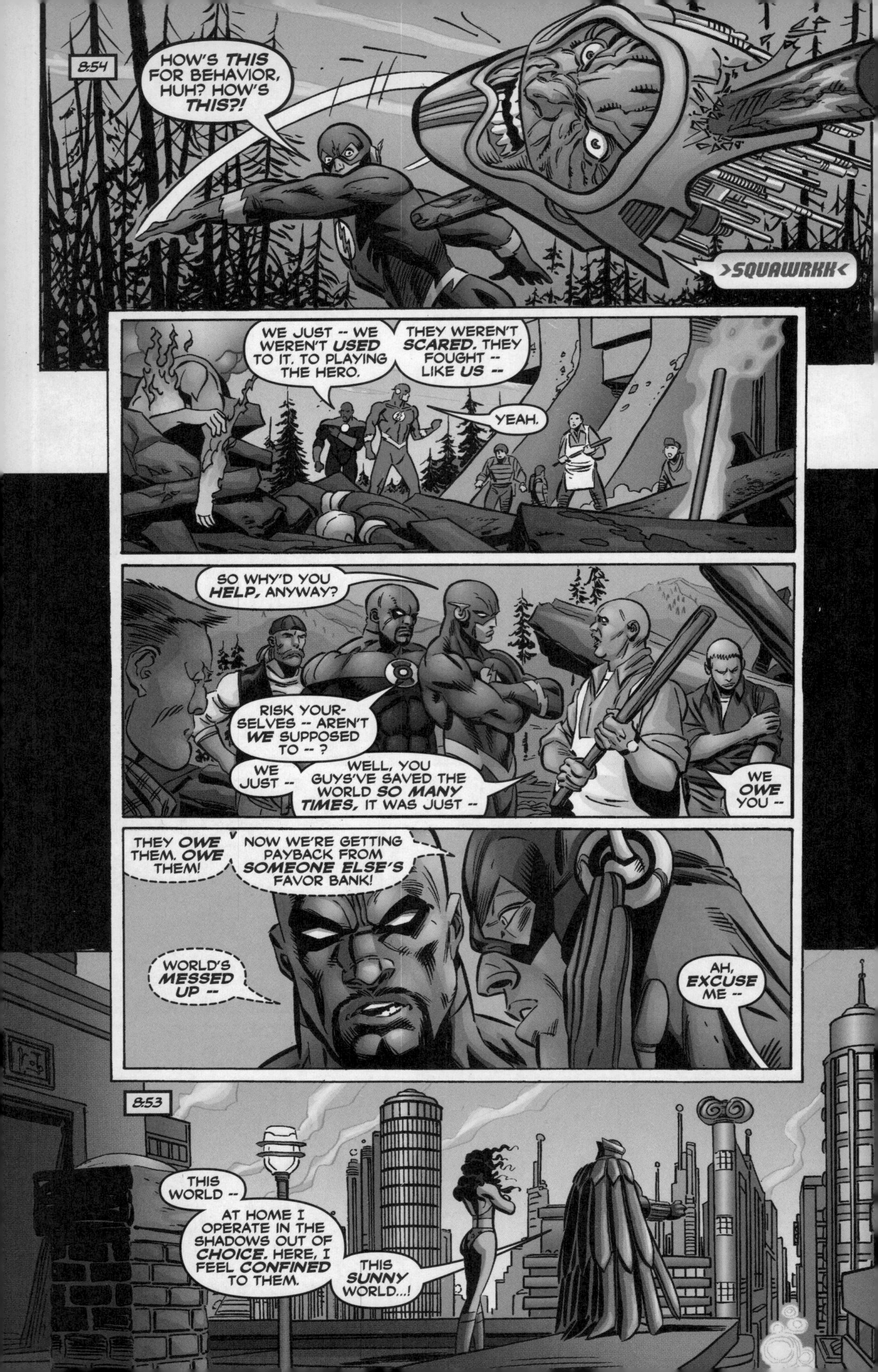

8:54
HOW'S THIS FOR BEHAVIOR, HUH? HOW'S THIS?!
>SQUAWRKK<
WE JUST -- WE WEREN'T USED TO IT. TO PLAYING THE HERO.
THEY WEREN'T SCARED. THEY FOUGHT -- LIKE US --
YEAH.
SO WHY'D YOU HELP, ANYWAY?
RISK YOURSELVES -- AREN'T WE SUPPOSED TO -- ?
WE JUST --
WELL, YOU GUYS'VE SAVED THE WORLD SO MANY TIMES, IT WAS JUST --
WE OWE YOU --
THEY OWE THEM. OWE THEM!
NOW WE'RE GETTING PAYBACK FROM SOMEONE ELSE'S FAVOR BANK!
WORLD'S MESSED UP --
AH, EXCUSE ME --
8:53
THIS WORLD --
AT HOME I OPERATE IN THE SHADOWS OUT OF CHOICE. HERE, I FEEL CONFINED TO THEM.
THIS SUNNY WORLD...!

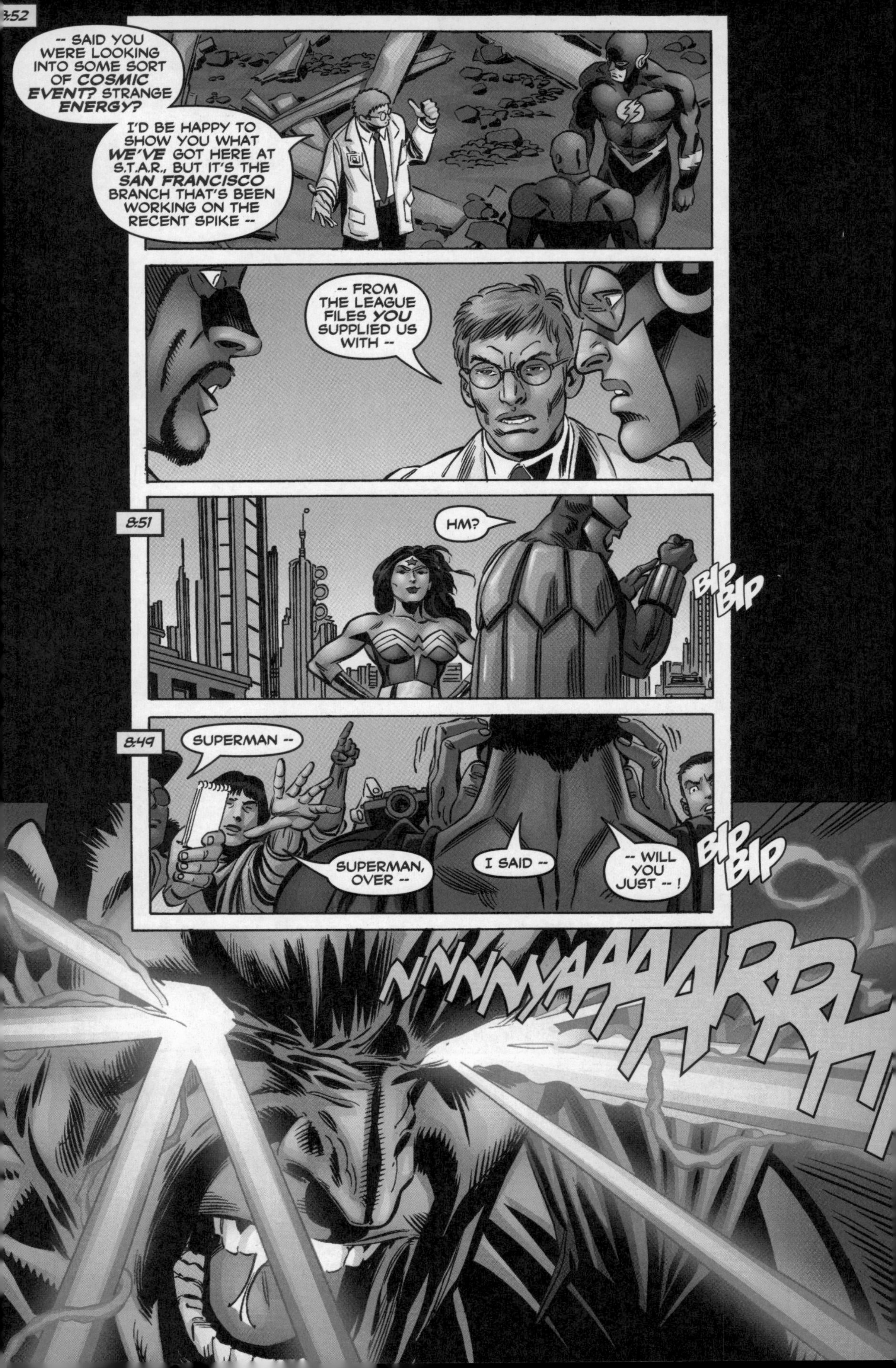
8:52
-- SAID YOU WERE LOOKING INTO SOME SORT OF COSMIC EVENT? STRANGE ENERGY?
I'D BE HAPPY TO SHOW YOU WHAT WE'VE GOT HERE AT S.T.A.R., BUT IT'S THE SAN FRANCISCO BRANCH THAT'S BEEN WORKING ON THE RECENT SPIKE --
-- FROM THE LEAGUE FILES YOU SUPPLIED US WITH --
8:51
HM?
BIP BIP
8:49
SUPERMAN --
SUPERMAN, OVER --
I SAID --
-- WILL YOU JUST -- !
BIP BIP
NNNNYAAAARRRR

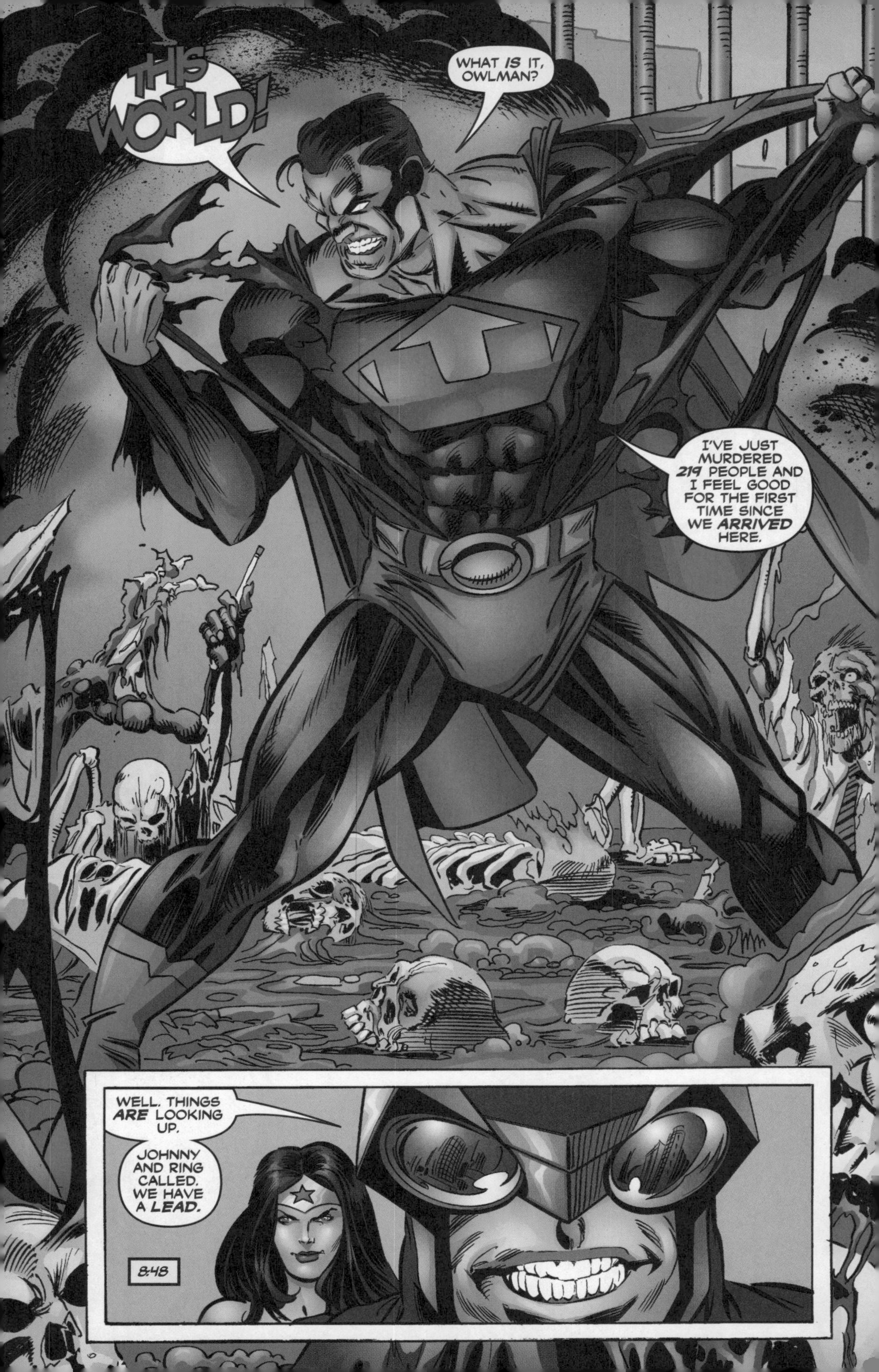
THIS WORLD!
WHAT IS IT, OWLMAN?
I'VE JUST MURDERED 219 PEOPLE AND I FEEL GOOD FOR THE FIRST TIME SINCE WE ARRIVED HERE.
WELL. THINGS ARE LOOKING UP.
JOHNNY AND RING CALLED. WE HAVE A LEAD.
8:48

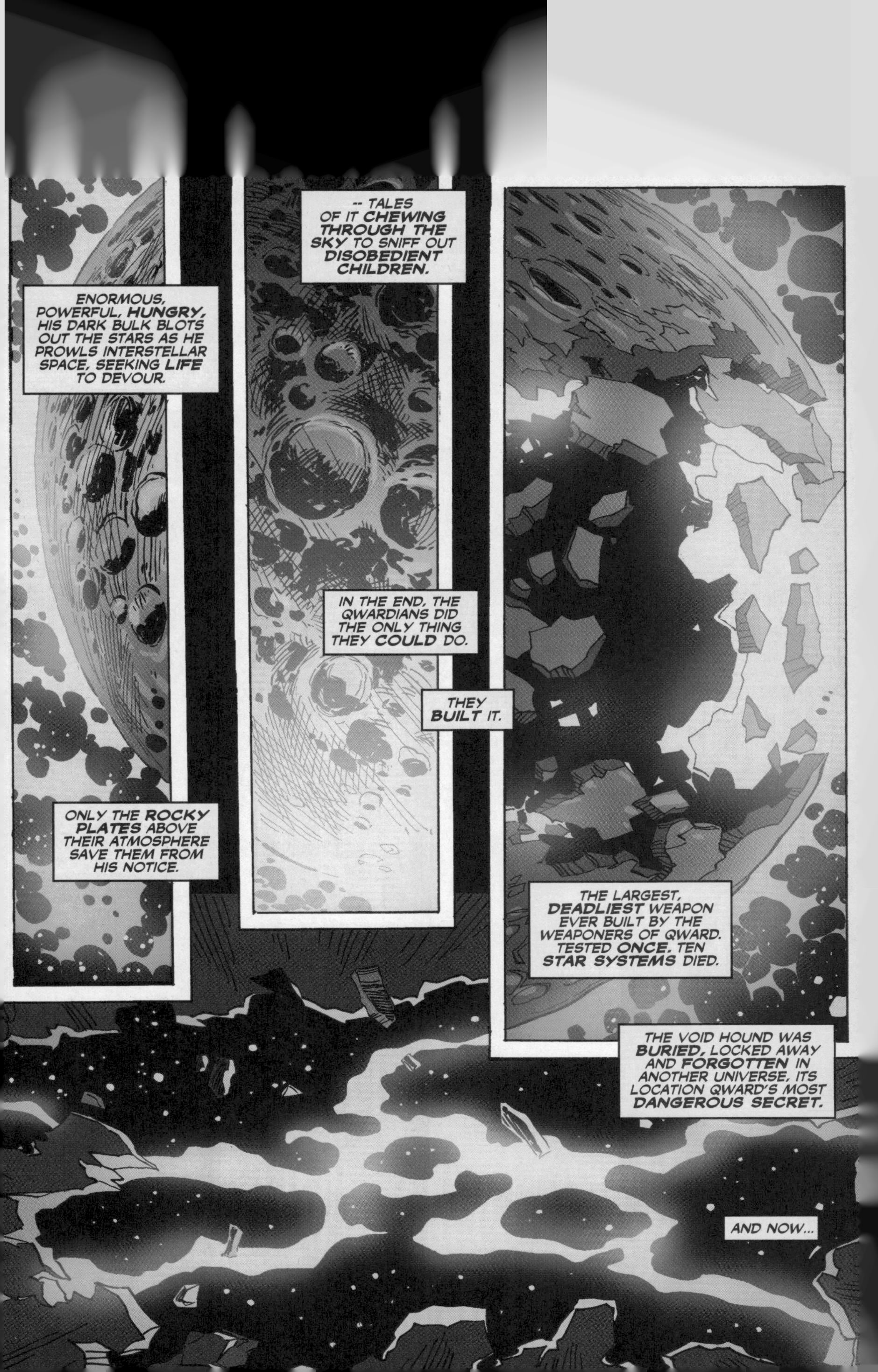
ENORMOUS, POWERFUL, HUNGRY, HIS DARK BULK BLOTS OUT THE STARS AS HE PROWLS INTERSTELLAR SPACE, SEEKING LIFE TO DEVOUR.
ONLY THE ROCKY PLATES ABOVE THEIR ATMOSPHERE SAVE THEM FROM HIS NOTICE.
-- TALES OF IT CHEWING THROUGH THE SKY TO SNIFF OUT DISOBEDIENT CHILDREN.
IN THE END, THE QWARDIANS DID THE ONLY THING THEY COULD DO.
THEY BUILT IT.
THE LARGEST, DEADLIEST WEAPON EVER BUILT BY THE WEAPONERS OF QWARD. TESTED ONCE. TEN STAR SYSTEMS DIED.
THE VOID HOUND WAS BURIED, LOCKED AWAY AND FORGOTTEN IN ANOTHER UNIVERSE, ITS LOCATION QWARD'S MOST DANGEROUS SECRET.
AND NOW...

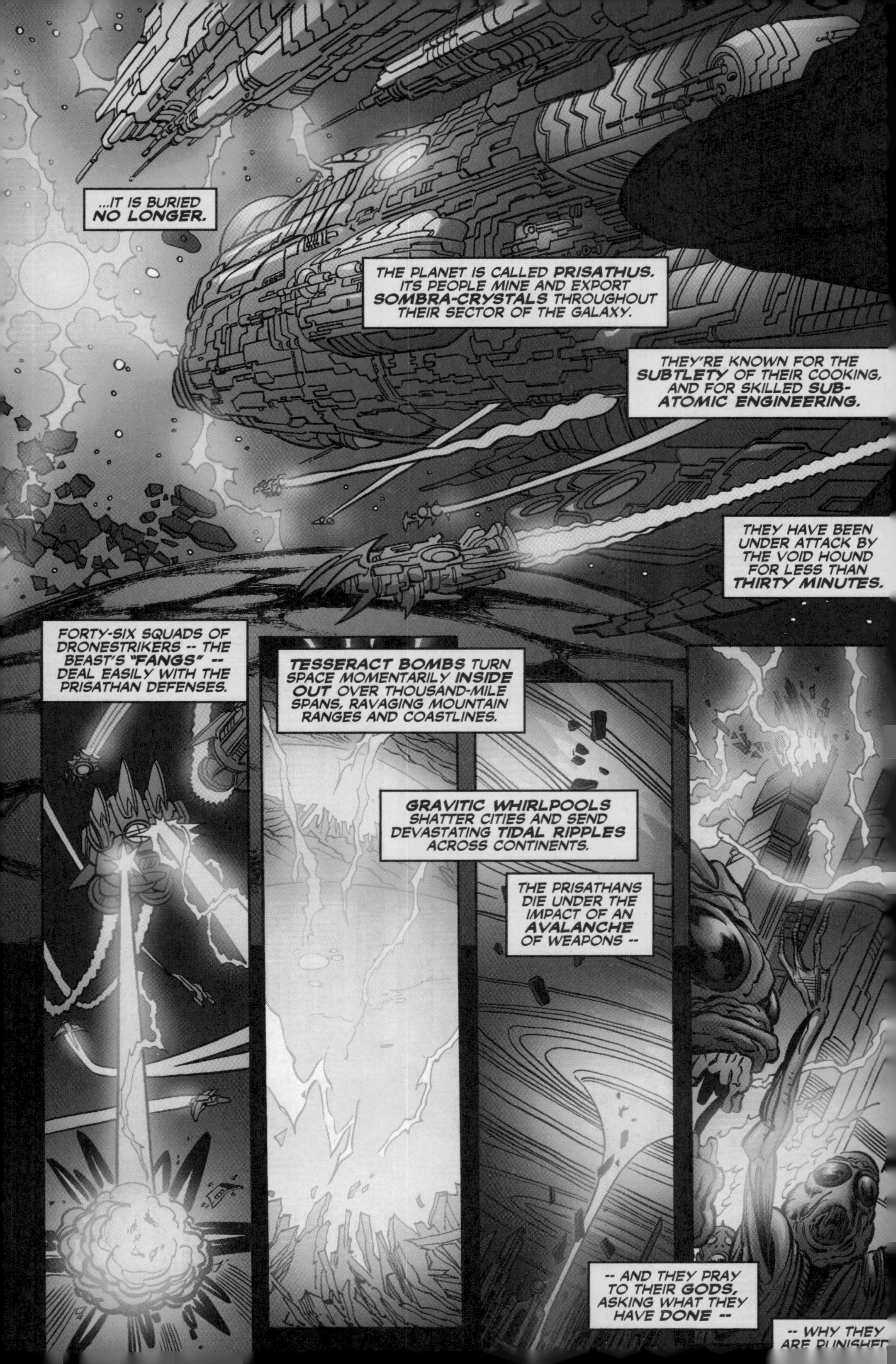
...IT IS BURIED NO LONGER.
THE PLANET IS CALLED PRISATHUS. ITS PEOPLE MINE AND EXPORT SOMBRA-CRYSTALS THROUGHOUT THEIR SECTOR OF THE GALAXY.
THEY'RE KNOWN FOR THE SUBTLETY OF THEIR COOKING, AND FOR SKILLED SUB-ATOMIC ENGINEERING.
THEY HAVE BEEN UNDER ATTACK BY THE VOID HOUND FOR LESS THAN THIRTY MINUTES.
FORTY-SIX SQUADS OF DRONESTRIKERS -- THE BEAST'S "FANGS" -- DEAL EASILY WITH THE PRISATHAN DEFENSES.
TESSERACT BOMBS TURN SPACE MOMENTARILY INSIDE OUT OVER THOUSAND-MILE SPANS, RAVAGING MOUNTAIN RANGES AND COASTLINES.
GRAVITIC WHIRLPOOLS SHATTER CITIES AND SEND DEVASTATING TIDAL RIPPLES ACROSS CONTINENTS.
THE PRISATHANS DIE UNDER THE IMPACT OF AN AVALANCHE OF WEAPONS --
-- AND THEY PRAY TO THEIR GODS, ASKING WHAT THEY HAVE DONE --
-- WHY THEY

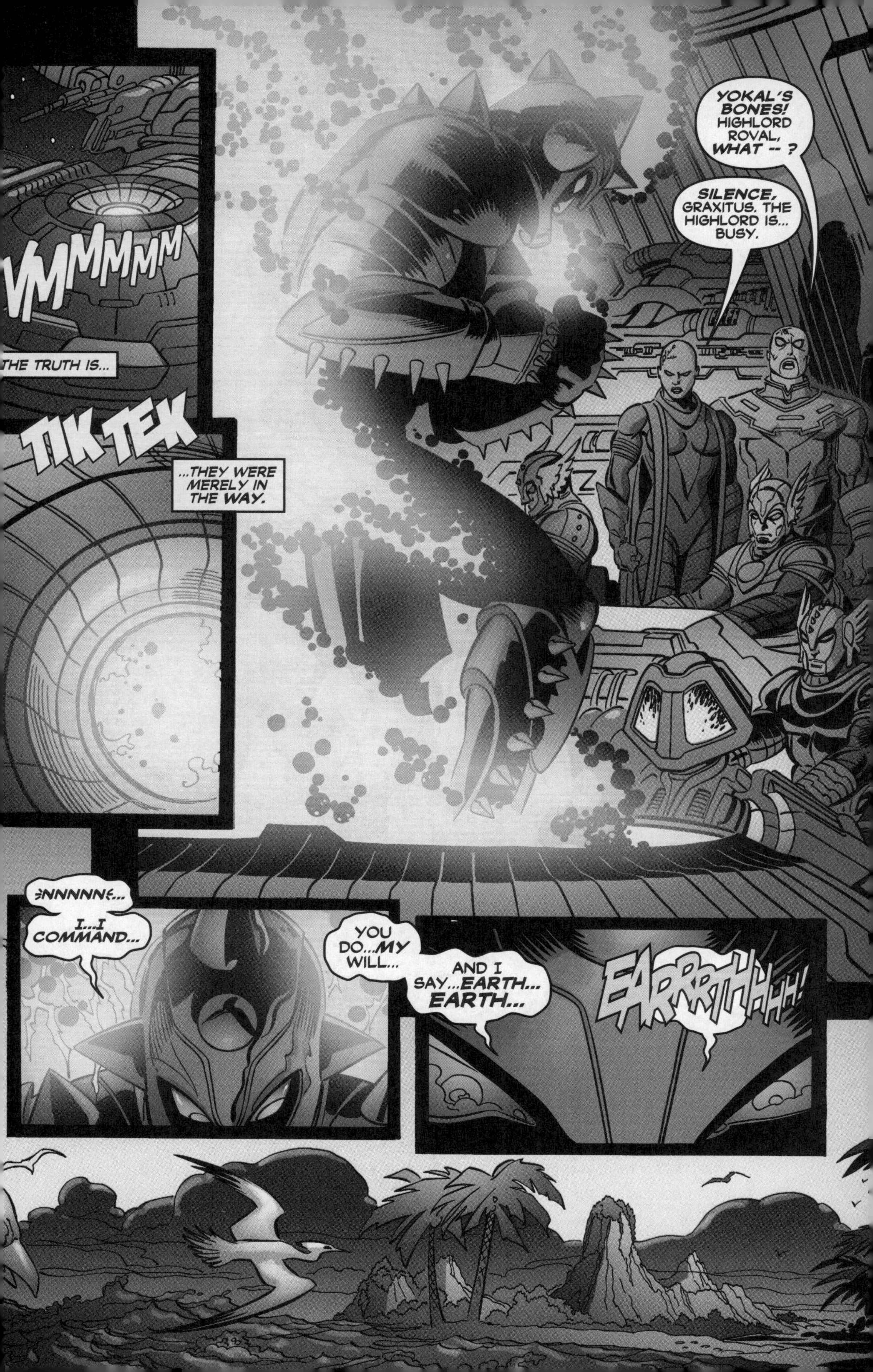
VMMMMMM
THE TRUTH IS...
TIK TEK
...THEY WERE MERELY IN THE WAY.
YOKAL'S BONES! HIGHLORD ROVAL, WHAT -- ?
SILENCE, GRAXITUS. THE HIGHLORD IS... BUSY.
NNNNN...
I...I COMMAND...
YOU DO...MY WILL...
AND I SAY...EARTH... EARTH...
EARRRTHHHH!

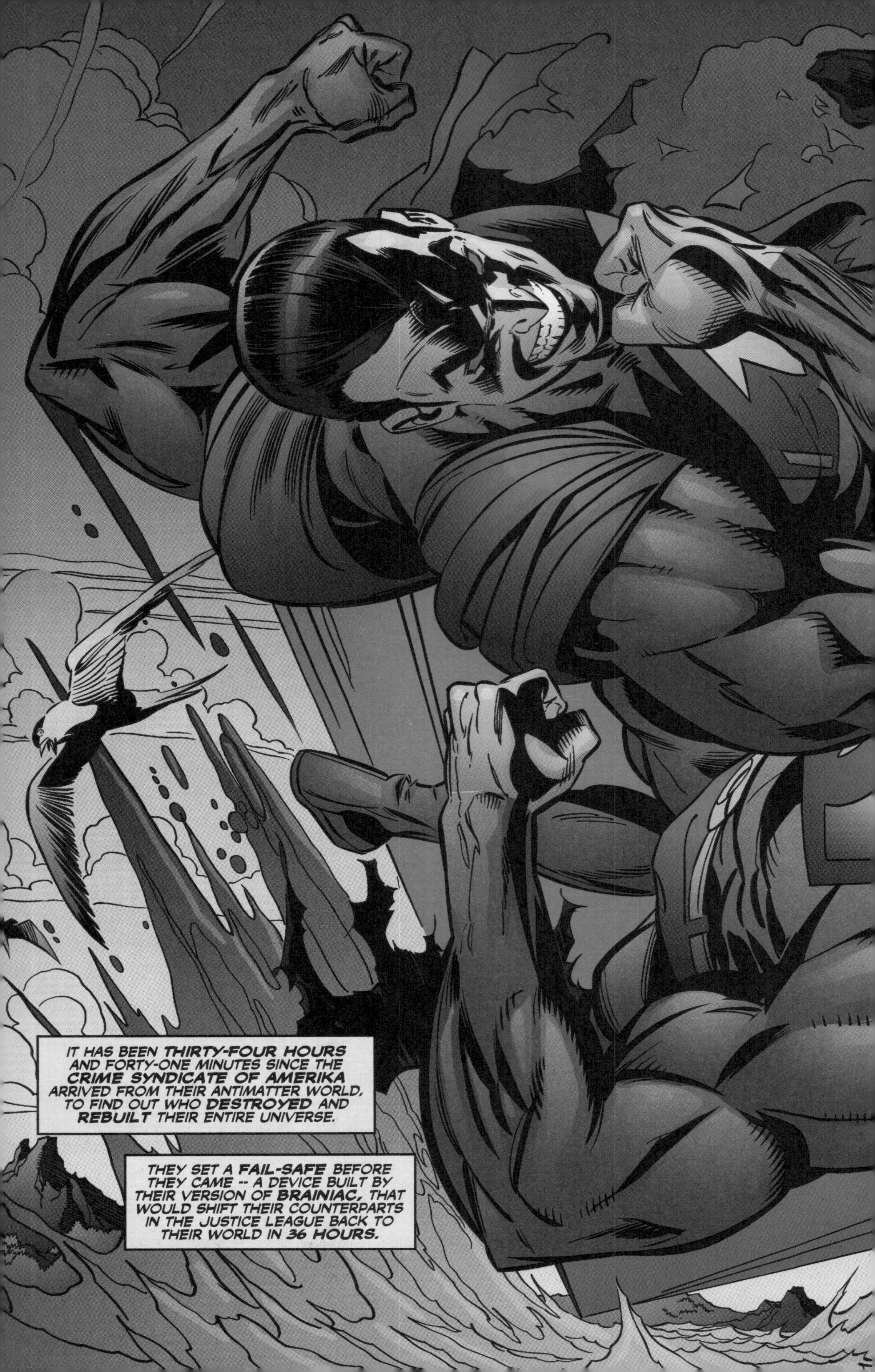
IT HAS BEEN THIRTY-FOUR HOURS AND FORTY-ONE MINUTES SINCE THE CRIME SYNDICATE OF AMERIKA ARRIVED FROM THEIR ANTIMATTER WORLD, TO FIND OUT WHO DESTROYED AND REBUILT THEIR ENTIRE UNIVERSE.
THEY SET A FAIL-SAFE BEFORE THEY CAME -- A DEVICE BUILT BY THEIR VERSION OF BRAINIAC, THAT WOULD SHIFT THEIR COUNTERPARTS IN THE JUSTICE LEAGUE BACK TO THEIR WORLD IN 36 HOURS.

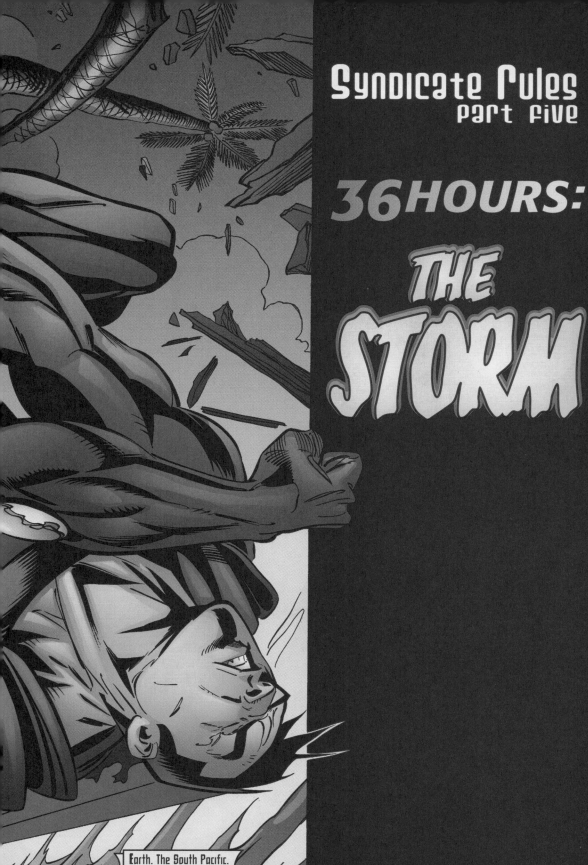

Syndicate Rules
Part Five

36HOURS:

THE STORM

Earth. The South Pacific.

ONE HOUR, NINETEEN
MINUTES TO GO.

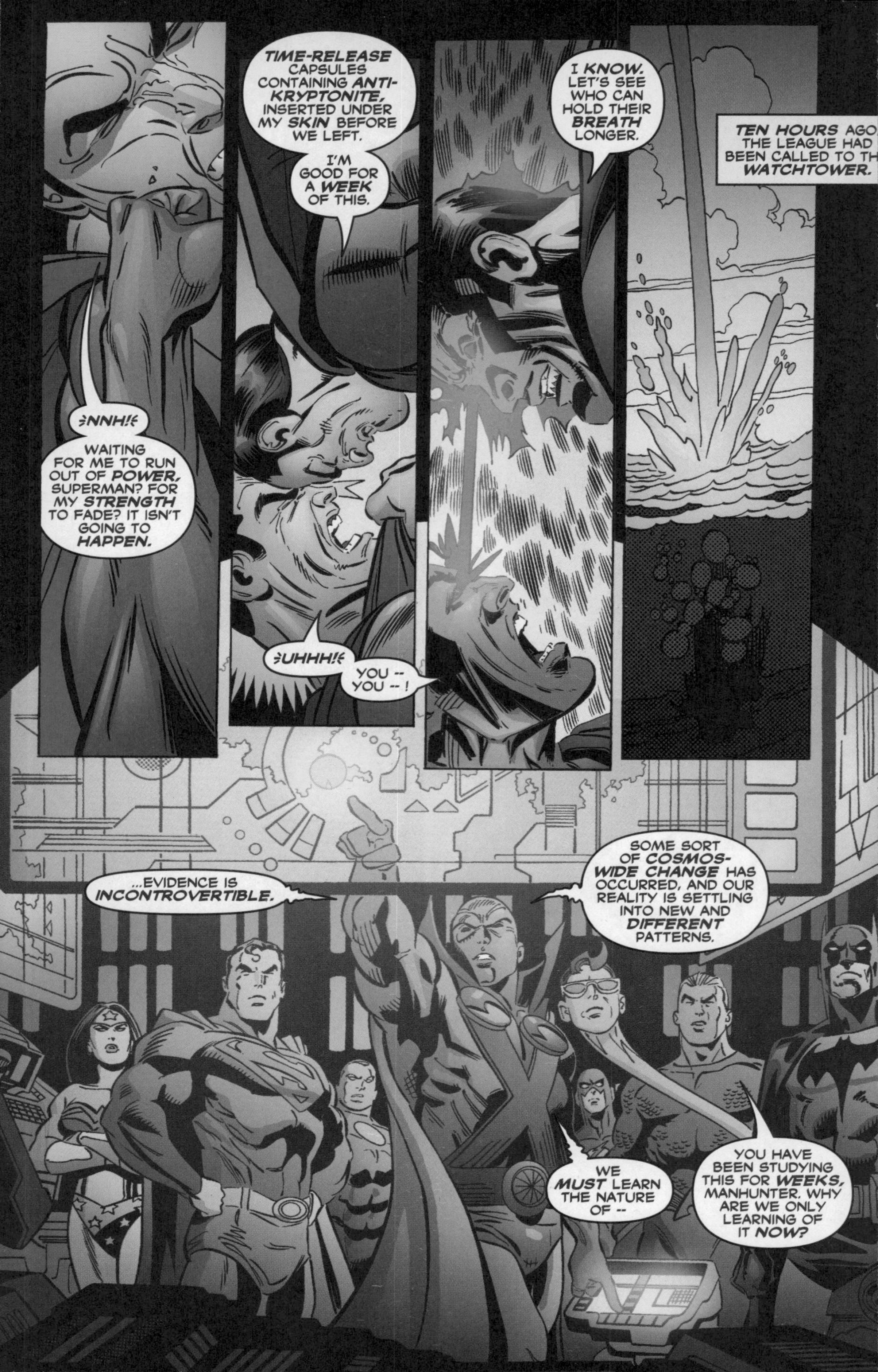

TIME-RELEASE CAPSULES CONTAINING ANTI-KRYPTONITE, INSERTED UNDER MY SKIN BEFORE WE LEFT.
I'M GOOD FOR A WEEK OF THIS.
I KNOW. LET'S SEE WHO CAN HOLD THEIR BREATH LONGER.
TEN HOURS AGO THE LEAGUE HAD BEEN CALLED TO THE WATCHTOWER.
NNH!
WAITING FOR ME TO RUN OUT OF POWER, SUPERMAN? FOR MY STRENGTH TO FADE? IT ISN'T GOING TO HAPPEN.
UHHH!
YOU -- YOU -- !
...EVIDENCE IS INCONTROVERTIBLE.
SOME SORT OF COSMOS-WIDE CHANGE HAS OCCURRED, AND OUR REALITY IS SETTLING INTO NEW AND DIFFERENT PATTERNS.
WE MUST LEARN THE NATURE OF --
YOU HAVE BEEN STUDYING THIS FOR WEEKS, MANHUNTER. WHY ARE WE ONLY LEARNING OF IT NOW?

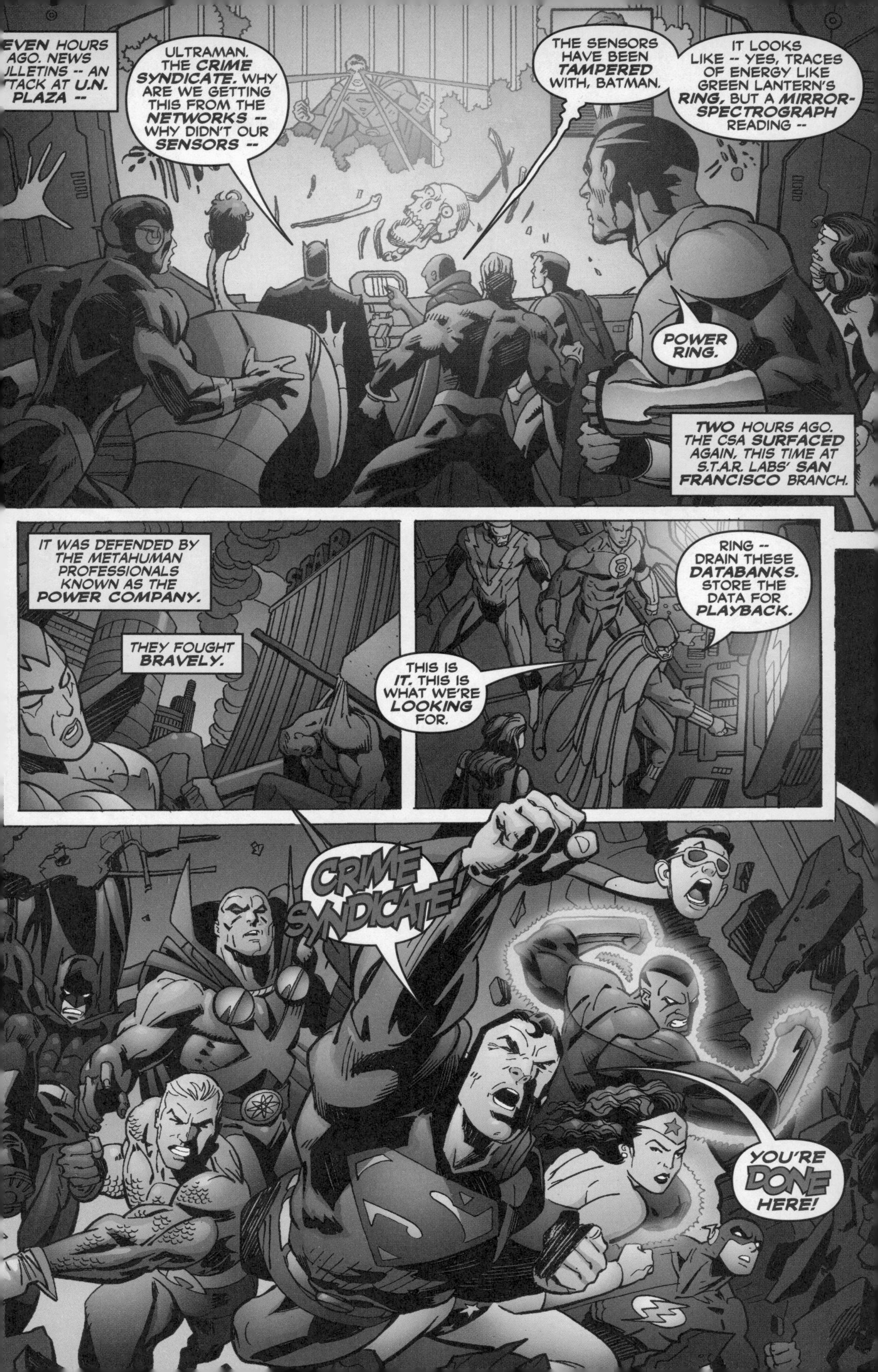
EVEN HOURS AGO. NEWS ULLETINS -- AN TTACK AT U.N. PLAZA --
ULTRAMAN. THE CRIME SYNDICATE. WHY ARE WE GETTING THIS FROM THE NETWORKS -- WHY DIDN'T OUR SENSORS --
THE SENSORS HAVE BEEN TAMPERED WITH, BATMAN.
IT LOOKS LIKE -- YES, TRACES OF ENERGY LIKE GREEN LANTERN'S RING, BUT A MIRROR-SPECTROGRAPH READING --
POWER RING.
TWO HOURS AGO. THE CSA SURFACED AGAIN, THIS TIME AT S.T.A.R. LABS' SAN FRANCISCO BRANCH.
IT WAS DEFENDED BY THE METAHUMAN PROFESSIONALS KNOWN AS THE POWER COMPANY.
THEY FOUGHT BRAVELY.
RING -- DRAIN THESE DATABANKS. STORE THE DATA FOR PLAYBACK.
THIS IS IT. THIS IS WHAT WE'RE LOOKING FOR.
CRIME SYNDICATE!
YOU'RE DONE HERE!

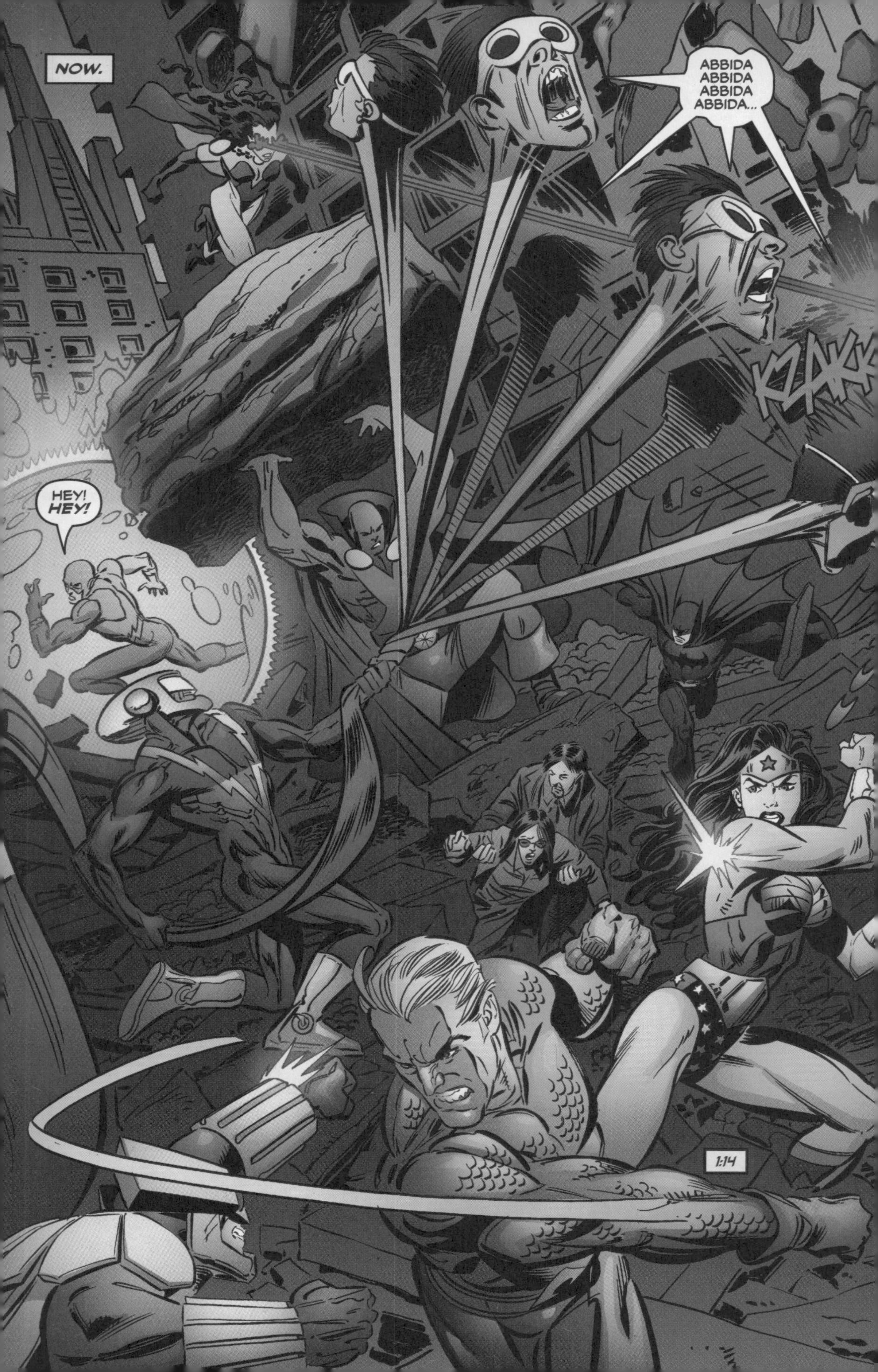
NOW.
ABBIDA ABBIDA ABBIDA ABBIDA...
KZAKK
HEY! HEY!
1:14

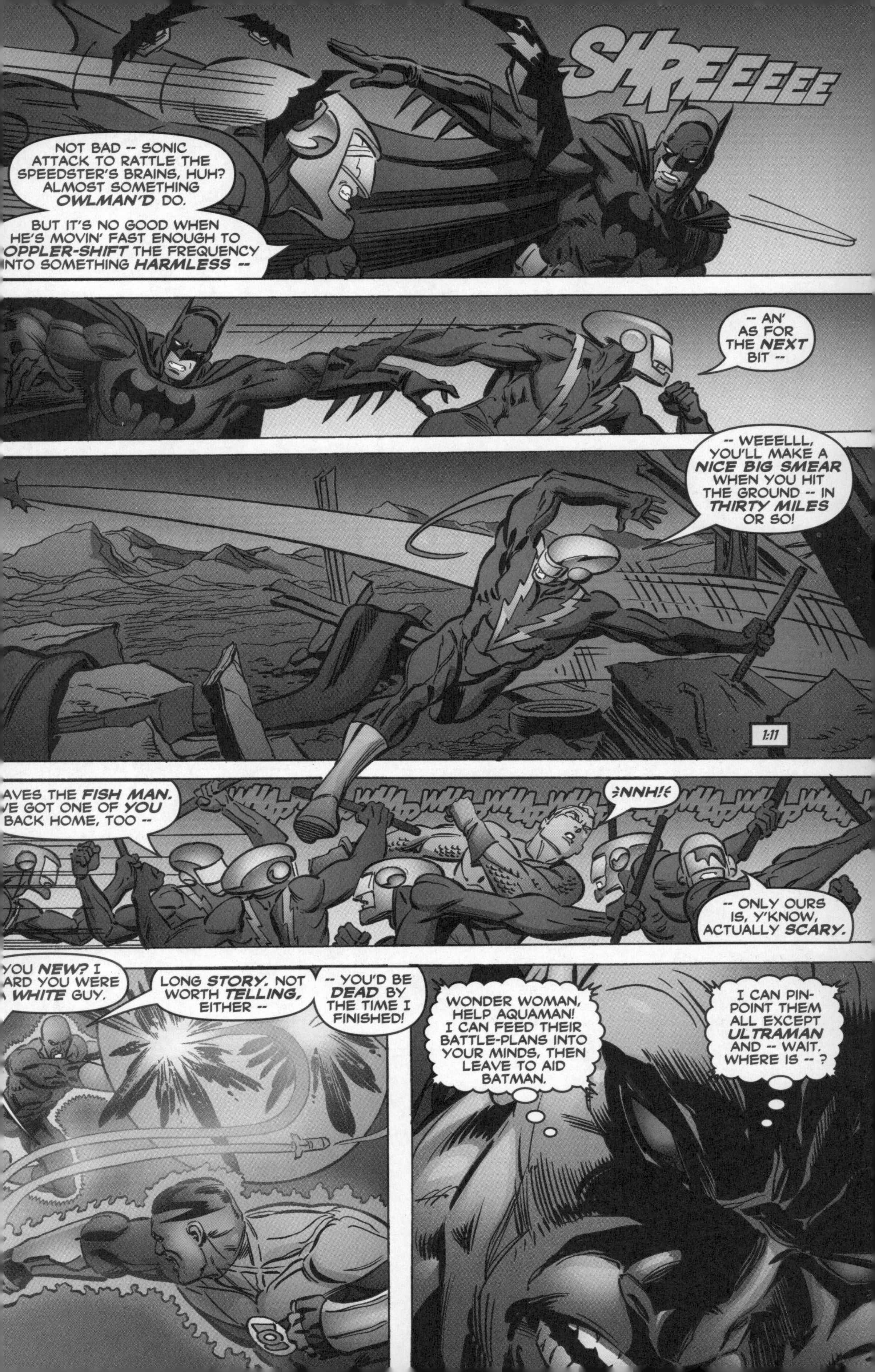
SHREEEEE
NOT BAD -- SONIC ATTACK TO RATTLE THE SPEEDSTER'S BRAINS, HUH? ALMOST SOMETHING OWLMAN'D DO.
BUT IT'S NO GOOD WHEN HE'S MOVIN' FAST ENOUGH TO OPPLER-SHIFT THE FREQUENCY INTO SOMETHING HARMLESS --
-- AN' AS FOR THE NEXT BIT --
-- WEEELLL, YOU'LL MAKE A NICE BIG SMEAR WHEN YOU HIT THE GROUND -- IN THIRTY MILES OR SO!
1:11
AVES THE FISH MAN. VE GOT ONE OF YOU BACK HOME, TOO --
NNH!
-- ONLY OURS IS, Y'KNOW, ACTUALLY SCARY.
YOU NEW? I ARD YOU WERE WHITE GUY.
LONG STORY. NOT WORTH TELLING, EITHER --
-- YOU'D BE DEAD BY THE TIME I FINISHED!
WONDER WOMAN, HELP AQUAMAN! I CAN FEED THEIR BATTLE-PLANS INTO YOUR MINDS, THEN LEAVE TO AID BATMAN.
I CAN PIN-POINT THEM ALL EXCEPT ULTRAMAN AND -- WAIT. WHERE IS -- ?

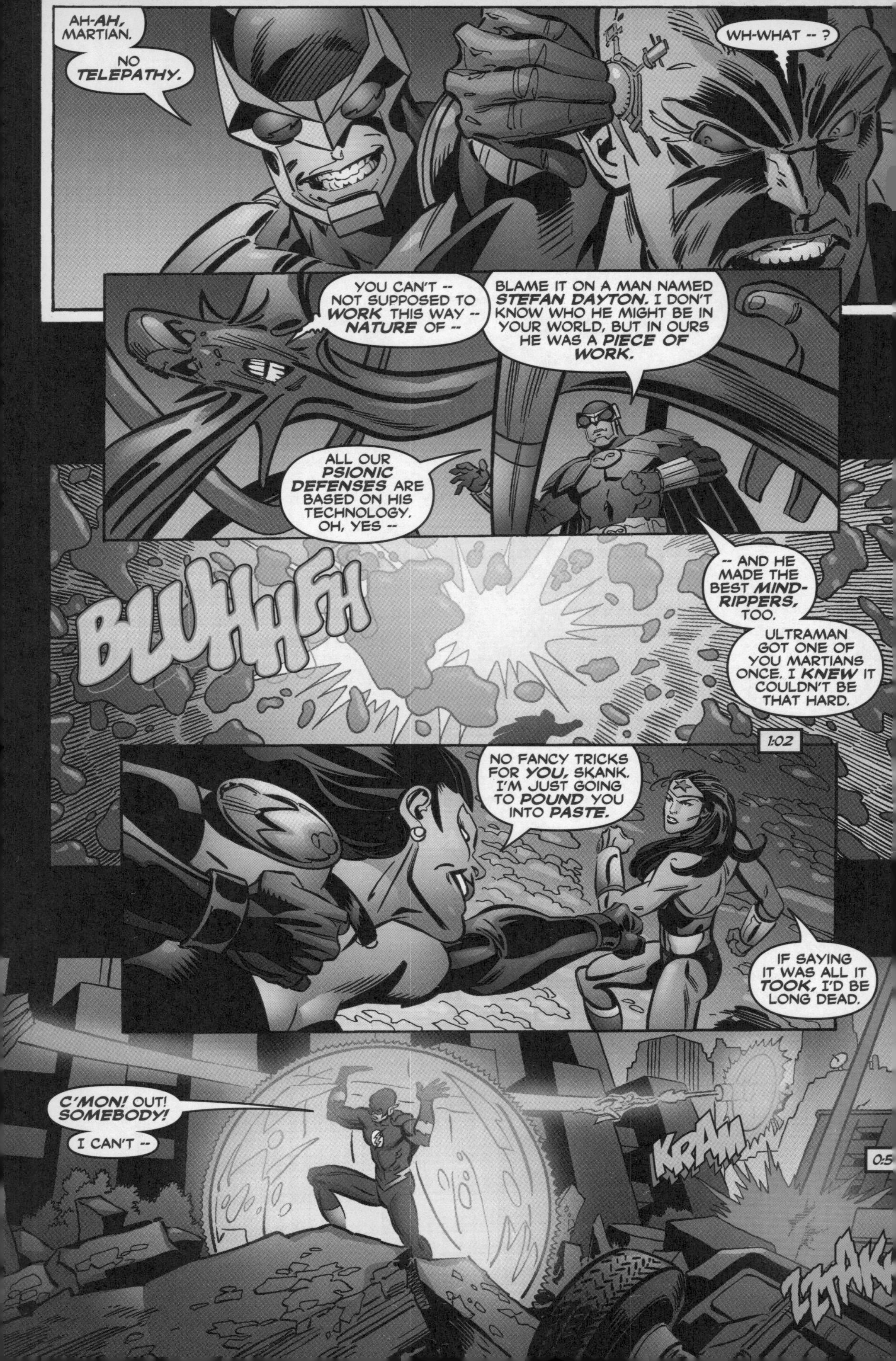
AH-AH, MARTIAN. NO TELEPATHY.
WH-WHAT -- ?
YOU CAN'T -- NOT SUPPOSED TO WORK THIS WAY -- NATURE OF --
BLAME IT ON A MAN NAMED STEFAN DAYTON. I DON'T KNOW WHO HE MIGHT BE IN YOUR WORLD, BUT IN OURS HE WAS A PIECE OF WORK.
ALL OUR PSIONIC DEFENSES ARE BASED ON HIS TECHNOLOGY. OH, YES --
-- AND HE MADE THE BEST MIND-RIPPERS, TOO.
ULTRAMAN GOT ONE OF YOU MARTIANS ONCE. I KNEW IT COULDN'T BE THAT HARD.
BLUHHFH
1:02
NO FANCY TRICKS FOR YOU, SKANK. I'M JUST GOING TO POUND YOU INTO PASTE.
IF SAYING IT WAS ALL IT TOOK, I'D BE LONG DEAD.
C'MON! OUT! SOMEBODY!
I CAN'T --
KRAM

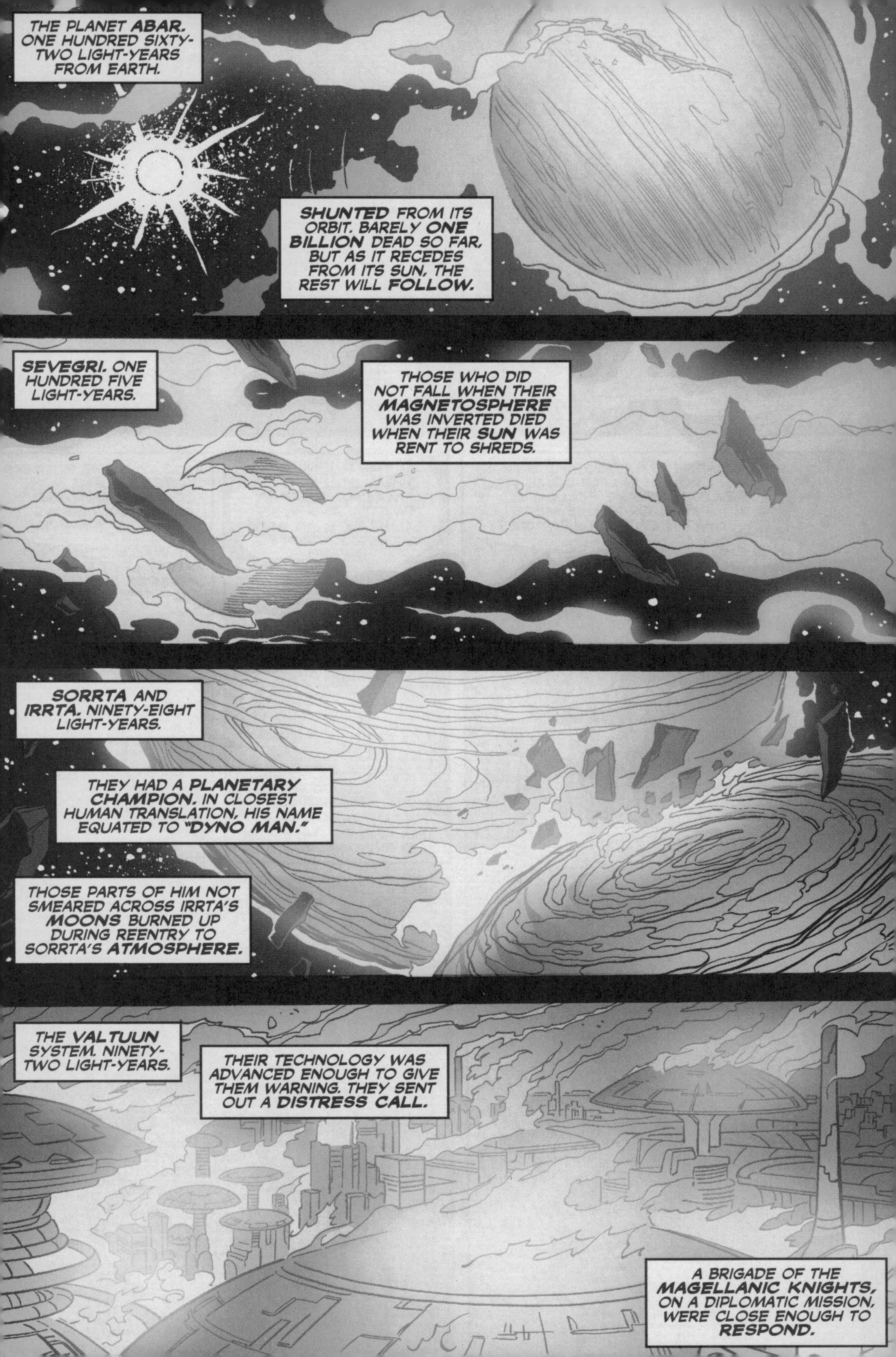
THE PLANET ABAR. ONE HUNDRED SIXTY-TWO LIGHT-YEARS FROM EARTH.
SHUNTED FROM ITS ORBIT. BARELY ONE BILLION DEAD SO FAR, BUT AS IT RECEDES FROM ITS SUN, THE REST WILL FOLLOW.
SEVEGRI. ONE HUNDRED FIVE LIGHT-YEARS.
THOSE WHO DID NOT FALL WHEN THEIR MAGNETOSPHERE WAS INVERTED DIED WHEN THEIR SUN WAS RENT TO SHREDS.
SORRTA AND IRRTA. NINETY-EIGHT LIGHT-YEARS.
THEY HAD A PLANETARY CHAMPION. IN CLOSEST HUMAN TRANSLATION, HIS NAME EQUATED TO "DYNO MAN."
THOSE PARTS OF HIM NOT SMEARED ACROSS IRRTA'S MOONS BURNED UP DURING REENTRY TO SORRTA'S ATMOSPHERE.
THE VALTUUN SYSTEM. NINETY-TWO LIGHT-YEARS.
THEIR TECHNOLOGY WAS ADVANCED ENOUGH TO GIVE THEM WARNING. THEY SENT OUT A DISTRESS CALL.
A BRIGADE OF THE MAGELLANIC KNIGHTS, ON A DIPLOMATIC MISSION, WERE CLOSE ENOUGH TO RESPOND.

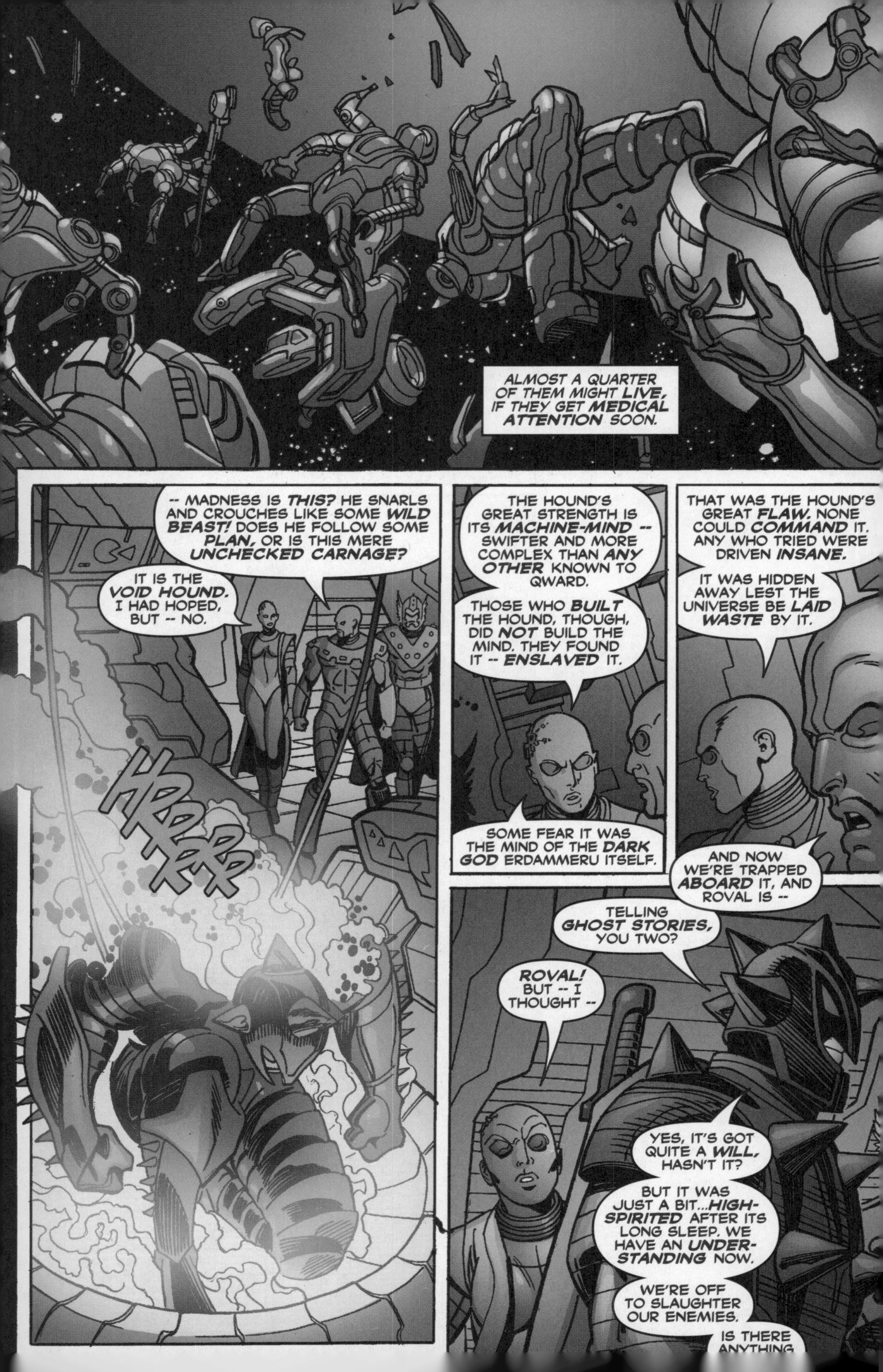
ALMOST A QUARTER OF THEM MIGHT LIVE, IF THEY GET MEDICAL ATTENTION SOON.
-- MADNESS IS THIS? HE SNARLS AND CROUCHES LIKE SOME WILD BEAST! DOES HE FOLLOW SOME PLAN, OR IS THIS MERE UNCHECKED CARNAGE?
IT IS THE VOID HOUND. I HAD HOPED, BUT -- NO.
HRRRRR
THE HOUND'S GREAT STRENGTH IS ITS MACHINE-MIND -- SWIFTER AND MORE COMPLEX THAN ANY OTHER KNOWN TO QWARD.
THOSE WHO BUILT THE HOUND, THOUGH, DID NOT BUILD THE MIND. THEY FOUND IT -- ENSLAVED IT.
SOME FEAR IT WAS THE MIND OF THE DARK GOD ERDAMMERU ITSELF.
THAT WAS THE HOUND'S GREAT FLAW. NONE COULD COMMAND IT. ANY WHO TRIED WERE DRIVEN INSANE.
IT WAS HIDDEN AWAY LEST THE UNIVERSE BE LAID WASTE BY IT.
AND NOW WE'RE TRAPPED ABOARD IT, AND ROVAL IS --
TELLING GHOST STORIES, YOU TWO?
ROVAL! BUT -- I THOUGHT --
YES, IT'S GOT QUITE A WILL, HASN'T IT?
BUT IT WAS JUST A BIT...HIGH-SPIRITED AFTER ITS LONG SLEEP. WE HAVE AN UNDER-STANDING NOW.
WE'RE OFF TO SLAUGHTER OUR ENEMIES.
IS THERE ANYTHING

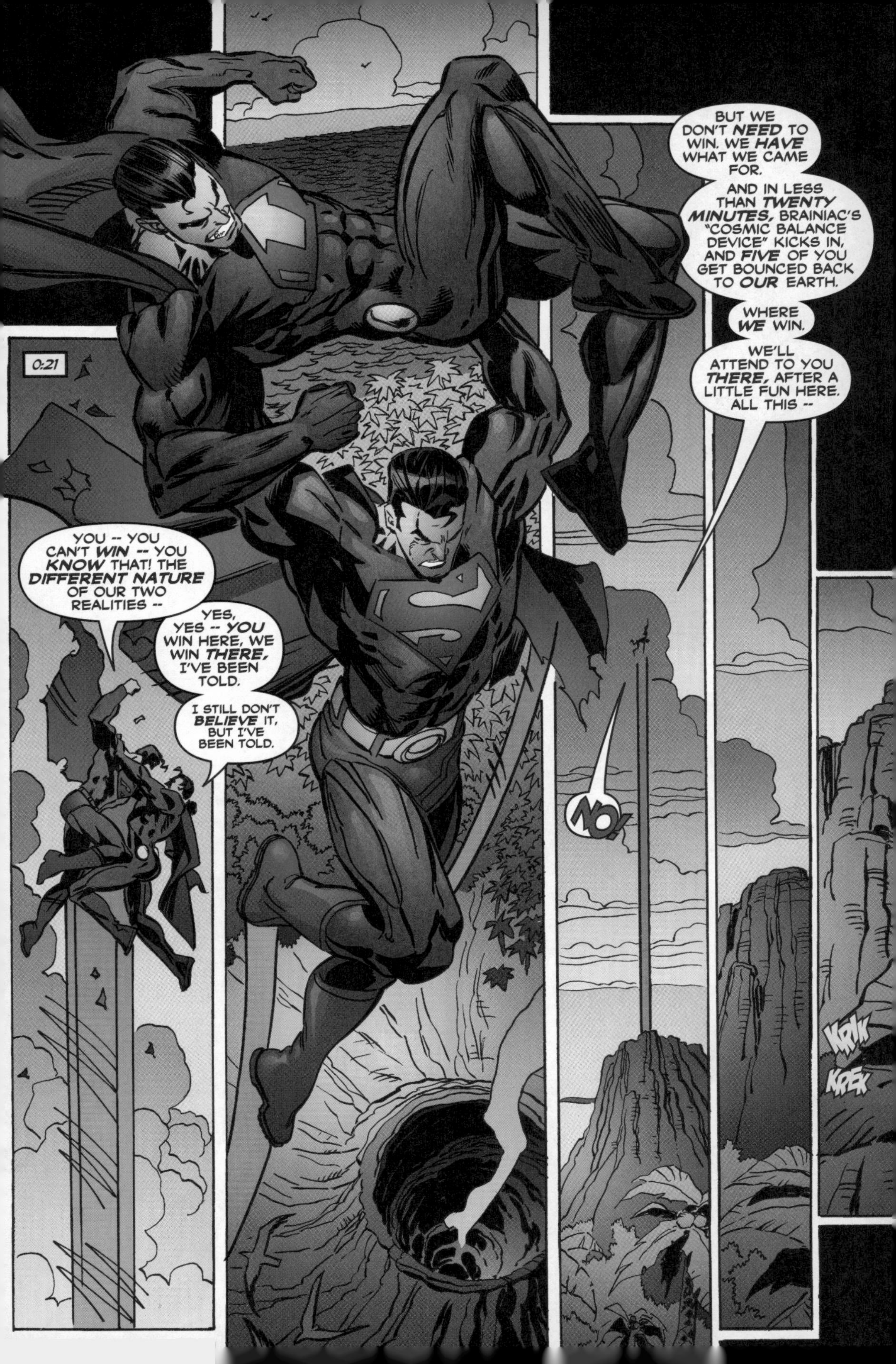
0:21
YOU -- YOU CAN'T WIN -- YOU KNOW THAT! THE DIFFERENT NATURE OF OUR TWO REALITIES --
YES, YES -- YOU WIN HERE, WE WIN THERE, I'VE BEEN TOLD.
I STILL DON'T BELIEVE IT, BUT I'VE BEEN TOLD.
BUT WE DON'T NEED TO WIN. WE HAVE WHAT WE CAME FOR.
AND IN LESS THAN TWENTY MINUTES, BRAINIAC'S "COSMIC BALANCE DEVICE" KICKS IN, AND FIVE OF YOU GET BOUNCED BACK TO OUR EARTH.
WHERE WE WIN.
WE'LL ATTEND TO YOU THERE, AFTER A LITTLE FUN HERE. ALL THIS --
NO!
KRAK
KREK

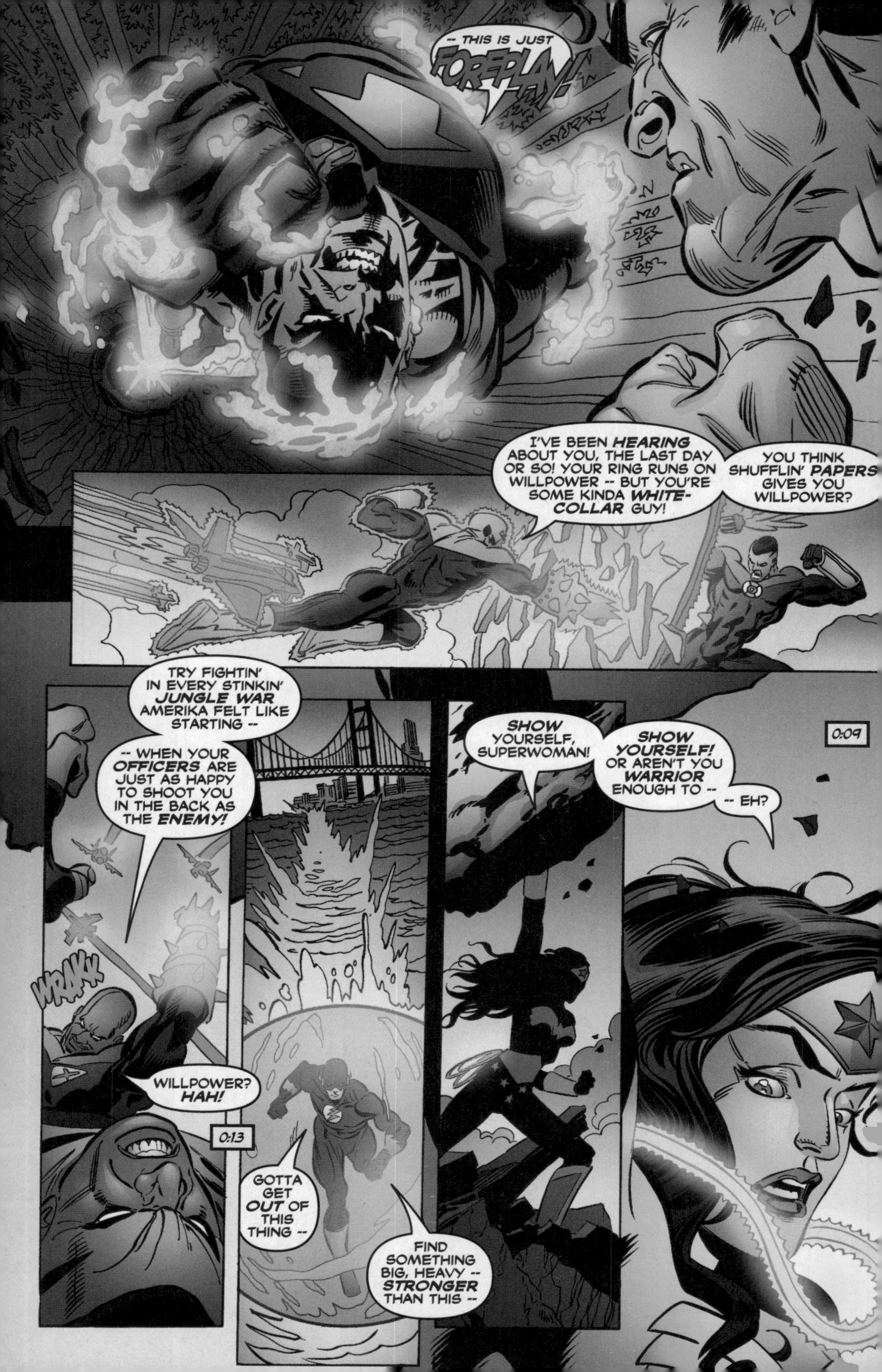

-- THIS IS JUST
FOREPLAY!
I'VE BEEN HEARING ABOUT YOU, THE LAST DAY OR SO! YOUR RING RUNS ON WILLPOWER -- BUT YOU'RE SOME KINDA WHITE-COLLAR GUY!
YOU THINK SHUFFLIN' PAPERS GIVES YOU WILLPOWER?
TRY FIGHTIN' IN EVERY STINKIN' JUNGLE WAR AMERIKA FELT LIKE STARTING --
-- WHEN YOUR OFFICERS ARE JUST AS HAPPY TO SHOOT YOU IN THE BACK AS THE ENEMY!
WRAKK
WILLPOWER? HAH!
0:13
GOTTA GET OUT OF THIS THING --
FIND SOMETHING BIG, HEAVY -- STRONGER THAN THIS --
SHOW YOURSELF, SUPERWOMAN!
SHOW YOURSELF! OR AREN'T YOU WARRIOR ENOUGH TO --
-- EH?
0:09

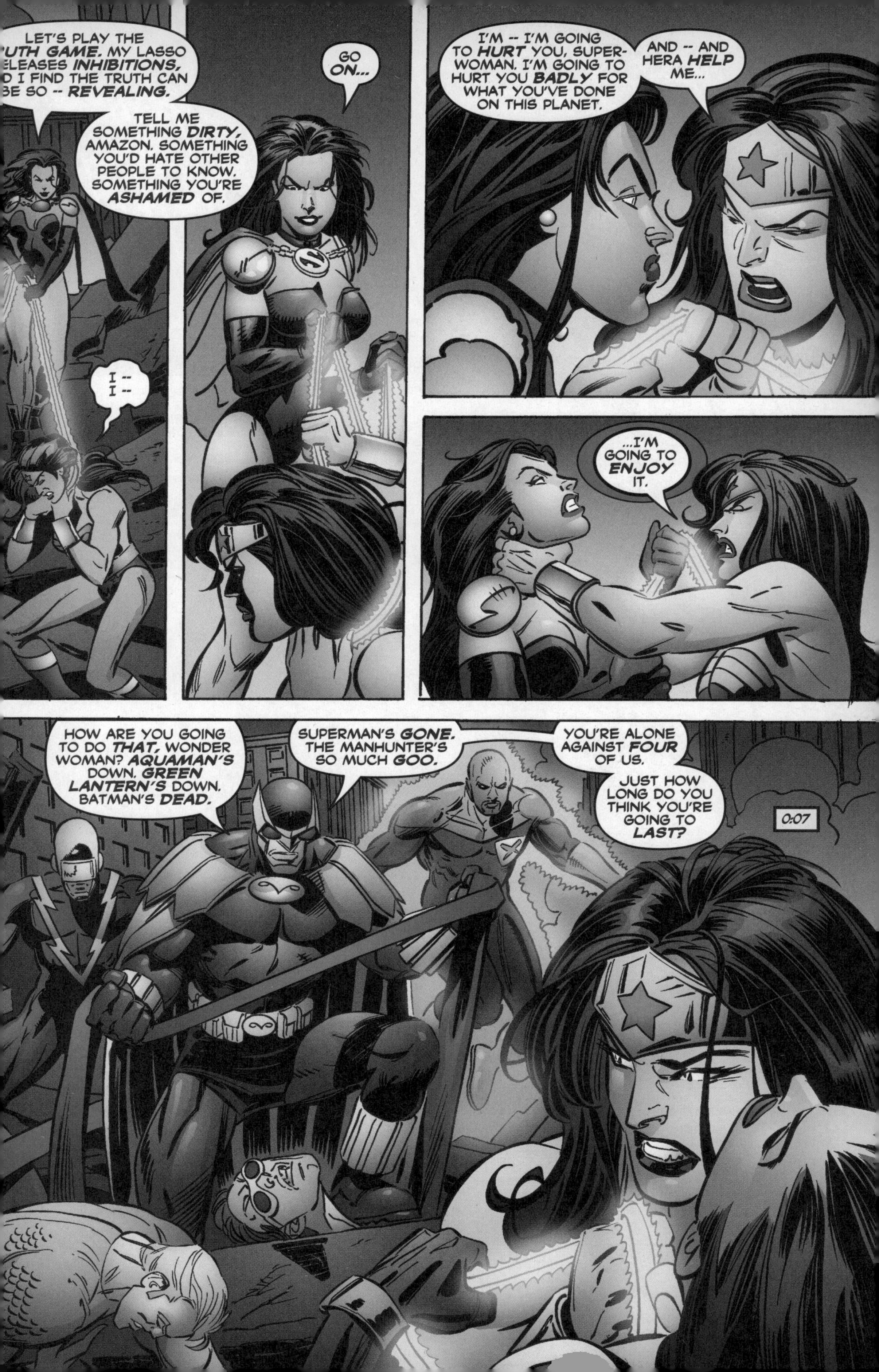
LET'S PLAY THE
UTH GAME. MY LASSO
ELEASES INHIBITIONS,
D I FIND THE TRUTH CAN
BE SO -- REVEALING.
GO ON...
TELL ME SOMETHING DIRTY, AMAZON. SOMETHING YOU'D HATE OTHER PEOPLE TO KNOW. SOMETHING YOU'RE ASHAMED OF.
I -- I --
I'M -- I'M GOING TO HURT YOU, SUPER-WOMAN. I'M GOING TO HURT YOU BADLY FOR WHAT YOU'VE DONE ON THIS PLANET.
AND -- AND HERA HELP ME...
...I'M GOING TO ENJOY IT.
HOW ARE YOU GOING TO DO THAT, WONDER WOMAN? AQUAMAN'S DOWN. GREEN LANTERN'S DOWN. BATMAN'S DEAD.
SUPERMAN'S GONE. THE MANHUNTER'S SO MUCH GOO.
YOU'RE ALONE AGAINST FOUR OF US.
JUST HOW LONG DO YOU THINK YOU'RE GOING TO LAST?
0:07

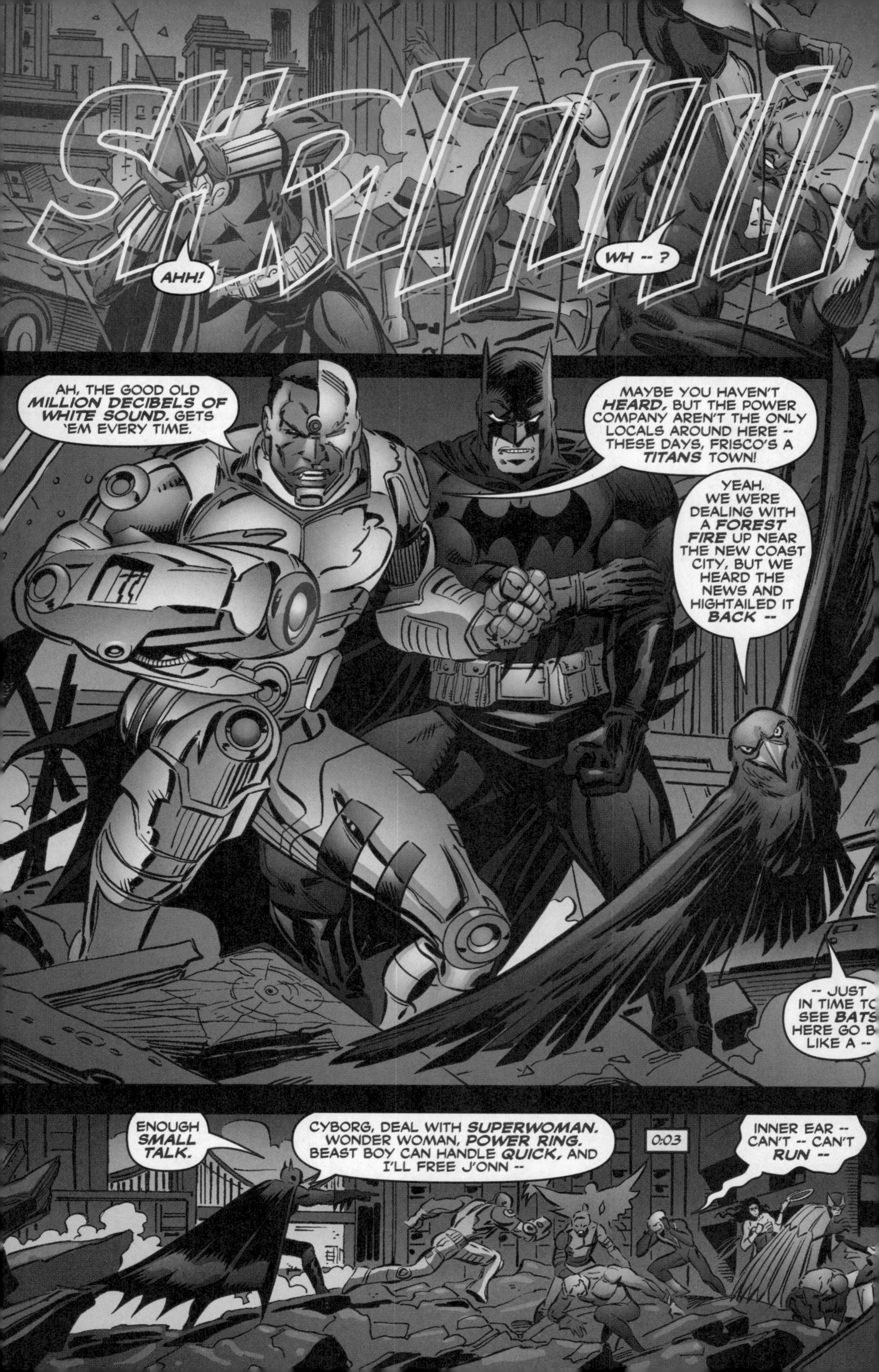
SHRIIIIIII
AHH!
WH -- ?
AH, THE GOOD OLD MILLION DECIBELS OF WHITE SOUND. GETS 'EM EVERY TIME.
MAYBE YOU HAVEN'T HEARD, BUT THE POWER COMPANY AREN'T THE ONLY LOCALS AROUND HERE -- THESE DAYS, FRISCO'S A TITANS TOWN!
YEAH. WE WERE DEALING WITH A FOREST FIRE UP NEAR THE NEW COAST CITY, BUT WE HEARD THE NEWS AND HIGHTAILED IT BACK --
-- JUST IN TIME TO SEE BATS HERE GO B LIKE A --
ENOUGH SMALL TALK.
CYBORG, DEAL WITH SUPERWOMAN. WONDER WOMAN, POWER RING. BEAST BOY CAN HANDLE QUICK, AND I'LL FREE J'ONN --
0:03
INNER EAR -- CAN'T -- CAN'T RUN --

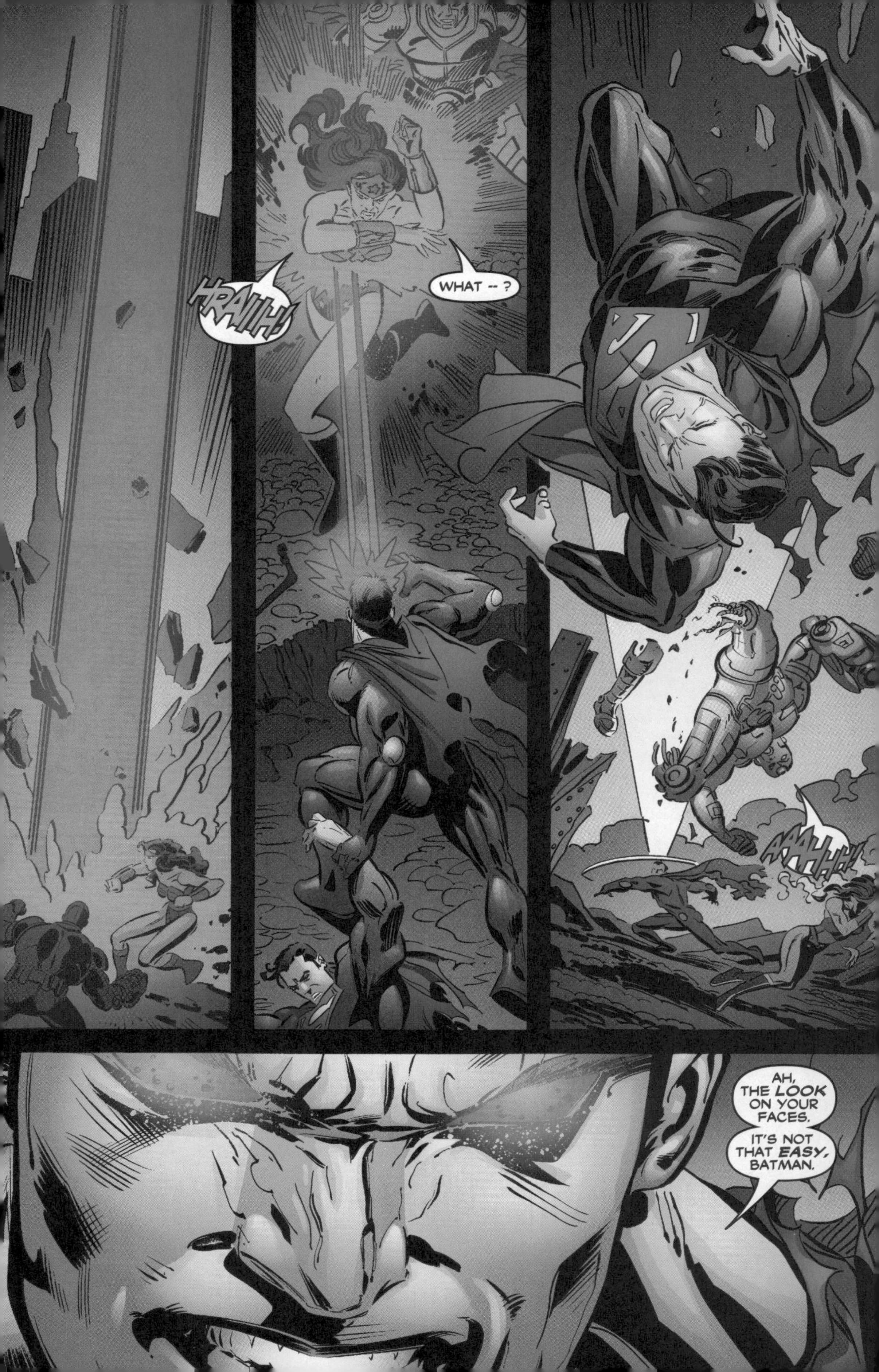

HRAIIH!
WHAT -- ?
AAAHHH!
AH, THE LOOK ON YOUR FACES.
IT'S NOT THAT EASY, BATMAN.

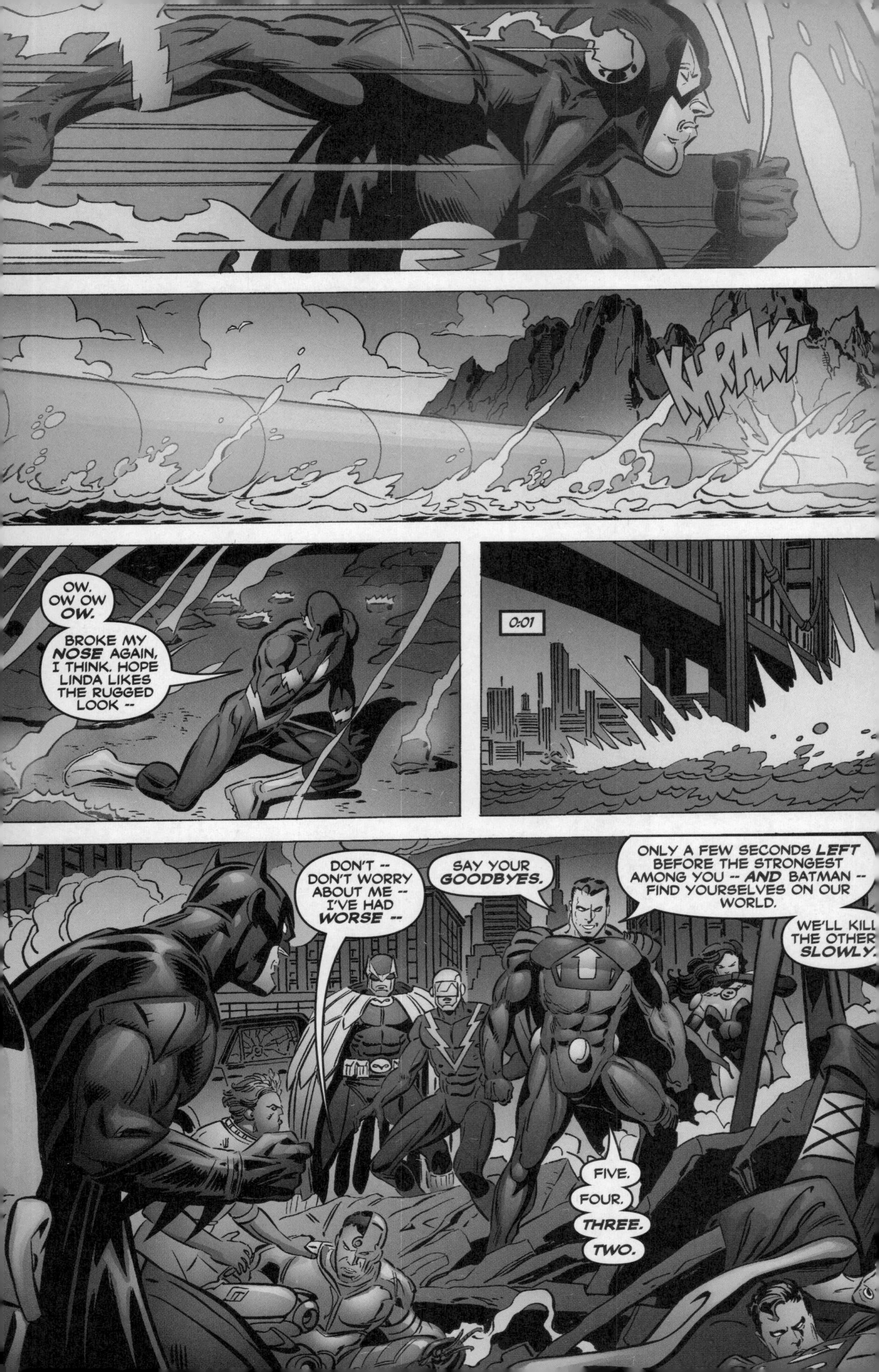
KHRAK!
OW. OW OW OW.
BROKE MY NOSE AGAIN, I THINK. HOPE LINDA LIKES THE RUGGED LOOK --
0:01
DON'T -- DON'T WORRY ABOUT ME -- I'VE HAD WORSE --
SAY YOUR GOODBYES.
ONLY A FEW SECONDS LEFT BEFORE THE STRONGEST AMONG YOU -- AND BATMAN -- FIND YOURSELVES ON OUR WORLD.
WE'LL KILL THE OTHER SLOWLY.
FIVE.
FOUR.
THREE.
TWO.

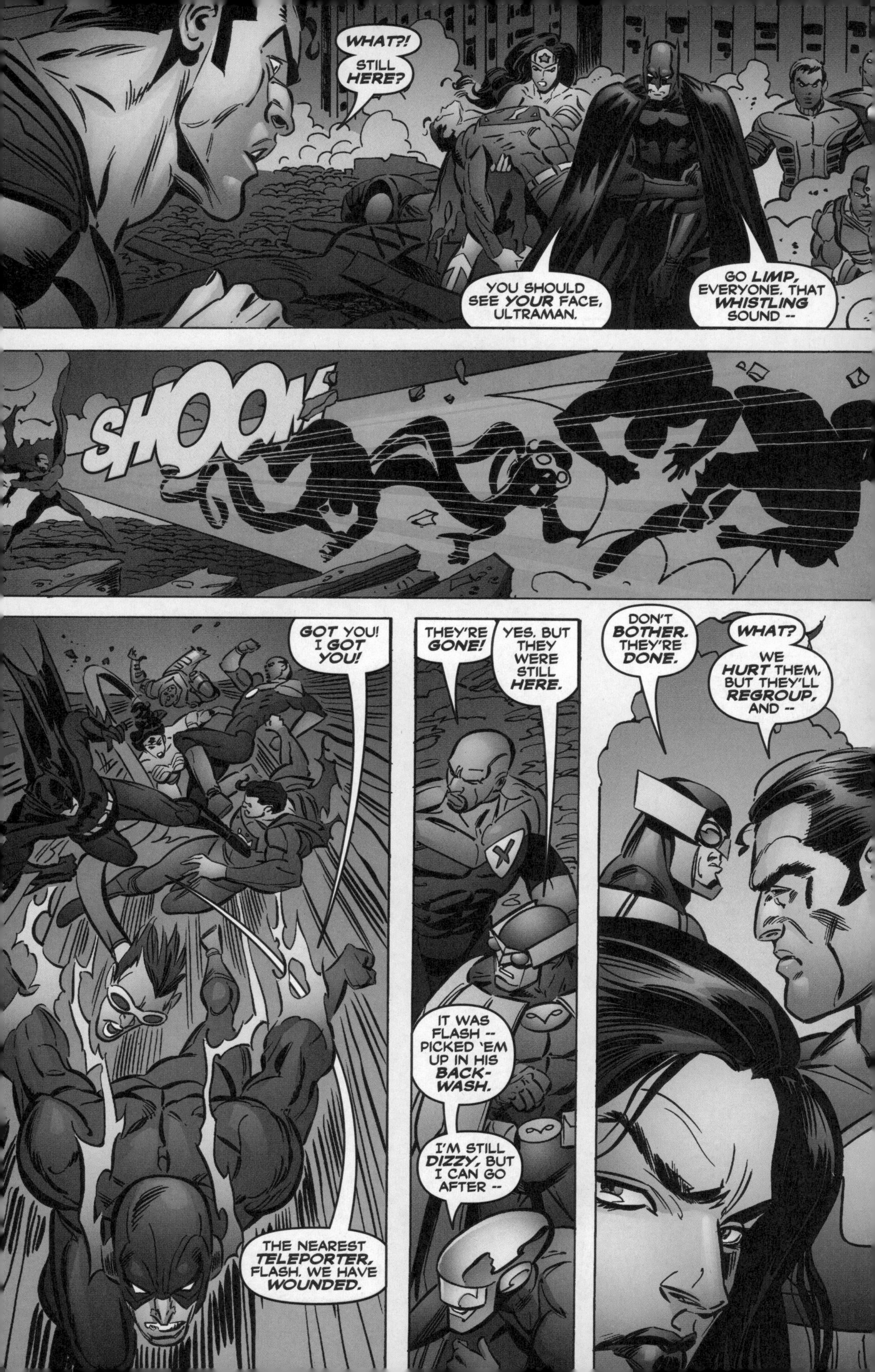
WHAT?! STILL HERE?
YOU SHOULD SEE YOUR FACE, ULTRAMAN.
GO LIMP, EVERYONE. THAT WHISTLING SOUND --
SHOOM
GOT YOU! I GOT YOU!
THE NEAREST TELEPORTER, FLASH. WE HAVE WOUNDED.
THEY'RE GONE!
YES. BUT THEY WERE STILL HERE.
IT WAS FLASH -- PICKED 'EM UP IN HIS BACK-WASH.
I'M STILL DIZZY, BUT I CAN GO AFTER --
DON'T BOTHER. THEY'RE DONE.
WHAT?
WE HURT THEM, BUT THEY'LL REGROUP, AND --

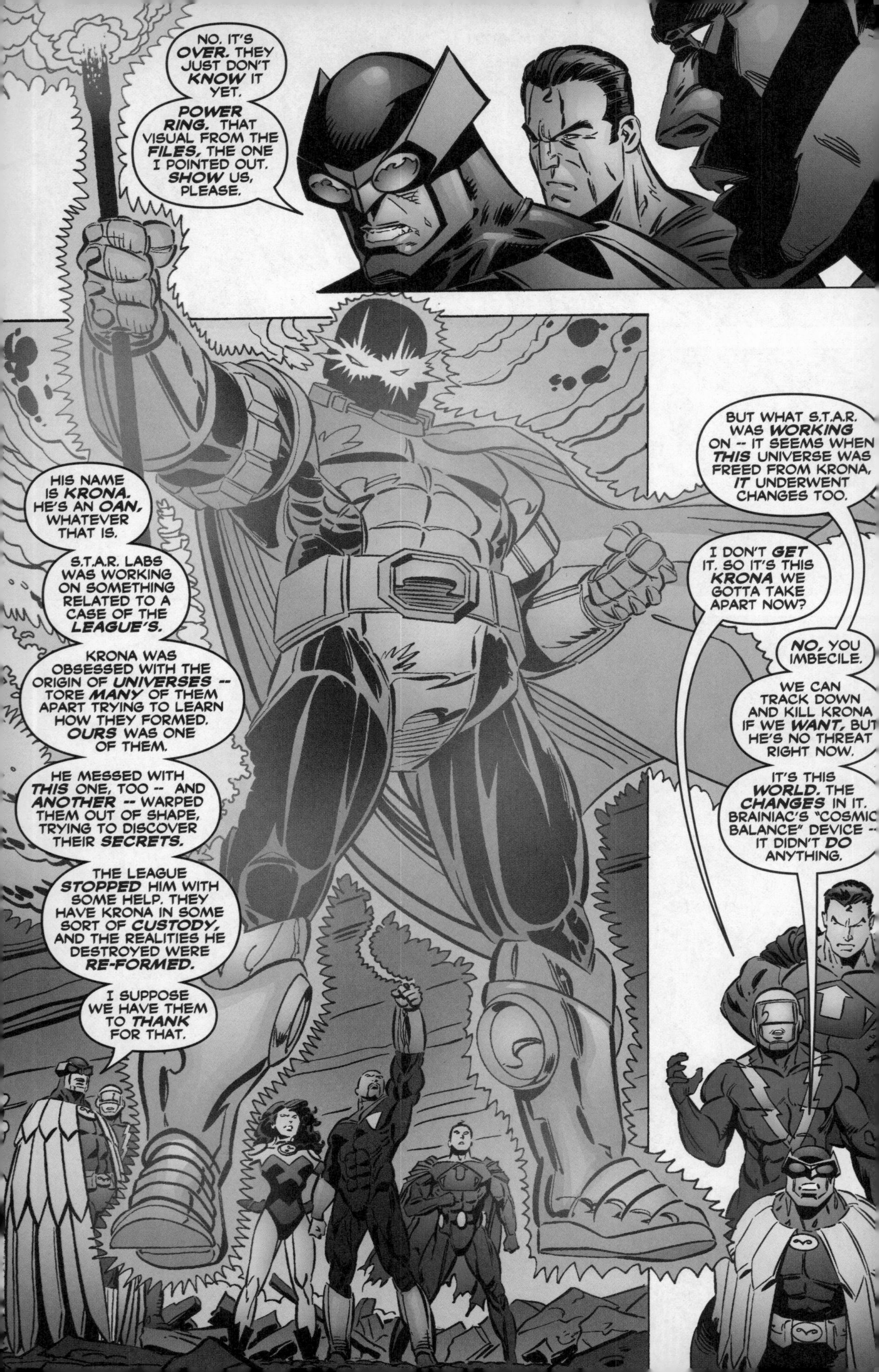
NO. IT'S OVER. THEY JUST DON'T KNOW IT YET.
POWER RING. THAT VISUAL FROM THE FILES, THE ONE I POINTED OUT. SHOW US, PLEASE.
HIS NAME IS KRONA. HE'S AN OAN, WHATEVER THAT IS.
S.T.A.R. LABS WAS WORKING ON SOMETHING RELATED TO A CASE OF THE LEAGUE'S.
KRONA WAS OBSESSED WITH THE ORIGIN OF UNIVERSES -- TORE MANY OF THEM APART TRYING TO LEARN HOW THEY FORMED. OURS WAS ONE OF THEM.
HE MESSED WITH THIS ONE, TOO -- AND ANOTHER -- WARPED THEM OUT OF SHAPE, TRYING TO DISCOVER THEIR SECRETS.
THE LEAGUE STOPPED HIM WITH SOME HELP. THEY HAVE KRONA IN SOME SORT OF CUSTODY, AND THE REALITIES HE DESTROYED WERE RE-FORMED.
I SUPPOSE WE HAVE THEM TO THANK FOR THAT.
BUT WHAT S.T.A.R. WAS WORKING ON -- IT SEEMS WHEN THIS UNIVERSE WAS FREED FROM KRONA, IT UNDERWENT CHANGES TOO.
I DON'T GET IT. SO IT'S THIS KRONA WE GOTTA TAKE APART NOW?
NO, YOU IMBECILE.
WE CAN TRACK DOWN AND KILL KRONA IF WE WANT, BUT HE'S NO THREAT RIGHT NOW.
IT'S THIS WORLD. THE CHANGES IN IT. BRAINIAC'S "COSMIC BALANCE" DEVICE -- IT DIDN'T DO ANYTHING.

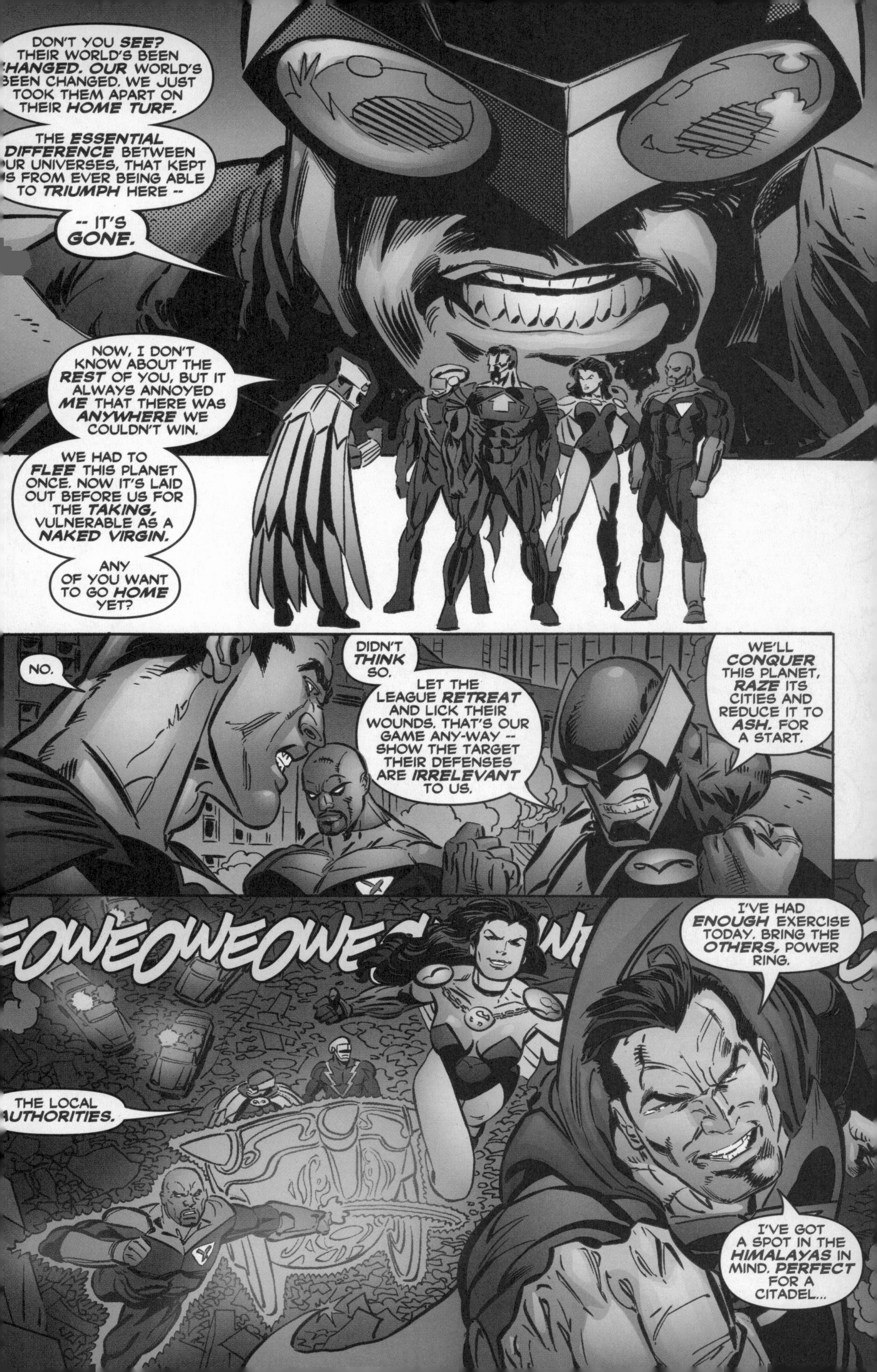
DON'T YOU SEE? THEIR WORLD'S BEEN CHANGED. OUR WORLD'S BEEN CHANGED. WE JUST TOOK THEM APART ON THEIR HOME TURF.
THE ESSENTIAL DIFFERENCE BETWEEN OUR UNIVERSES, THAT KEPT US FROM EVER BEING ABLE TO TRIUMPH HERE --
-- IT'S GONE.
NOW, I DON'T KNOW ABOUT THE REST OF YOU, BUT IT ALWAYS ANNOYED ME THAT THERE WAS ANYWHERE WE COULDN'T WIN.
WE HAD TO FLEE THIS PLANET ONCE. NOW IT'S LAID OUT BEFORE US FOR THE TAKING, VULNERABLE AS A NAKED VIRGIN.
ANY OF YOU WANT TO GO HOME YET?
NO.
DIDN'T THINK SO.
LET THE LEAGUE RETREAT AND LICK THEIR WOUNDS. THAT'S OUR GAME ANY-WAY -- SHOW THE TARGET THEIR DEFENSES ARE IRRELEVANT TO US.
WE'LL CONQUER THIS PLANET, RAZE ITS CITIES AND REDUCE IT TO ASH. FOR A START.
EOWEOWEOWEOWE
I'VE HAD ENOUGH EXERCISE TODAY. BRING THE OTHERS, POWER RING.
THE LOCAL AUTHORITIES.
I'VE GOT A SPOT IN THE HIMALAYAS IN MIND. PERFECT FOR A CITADEL...

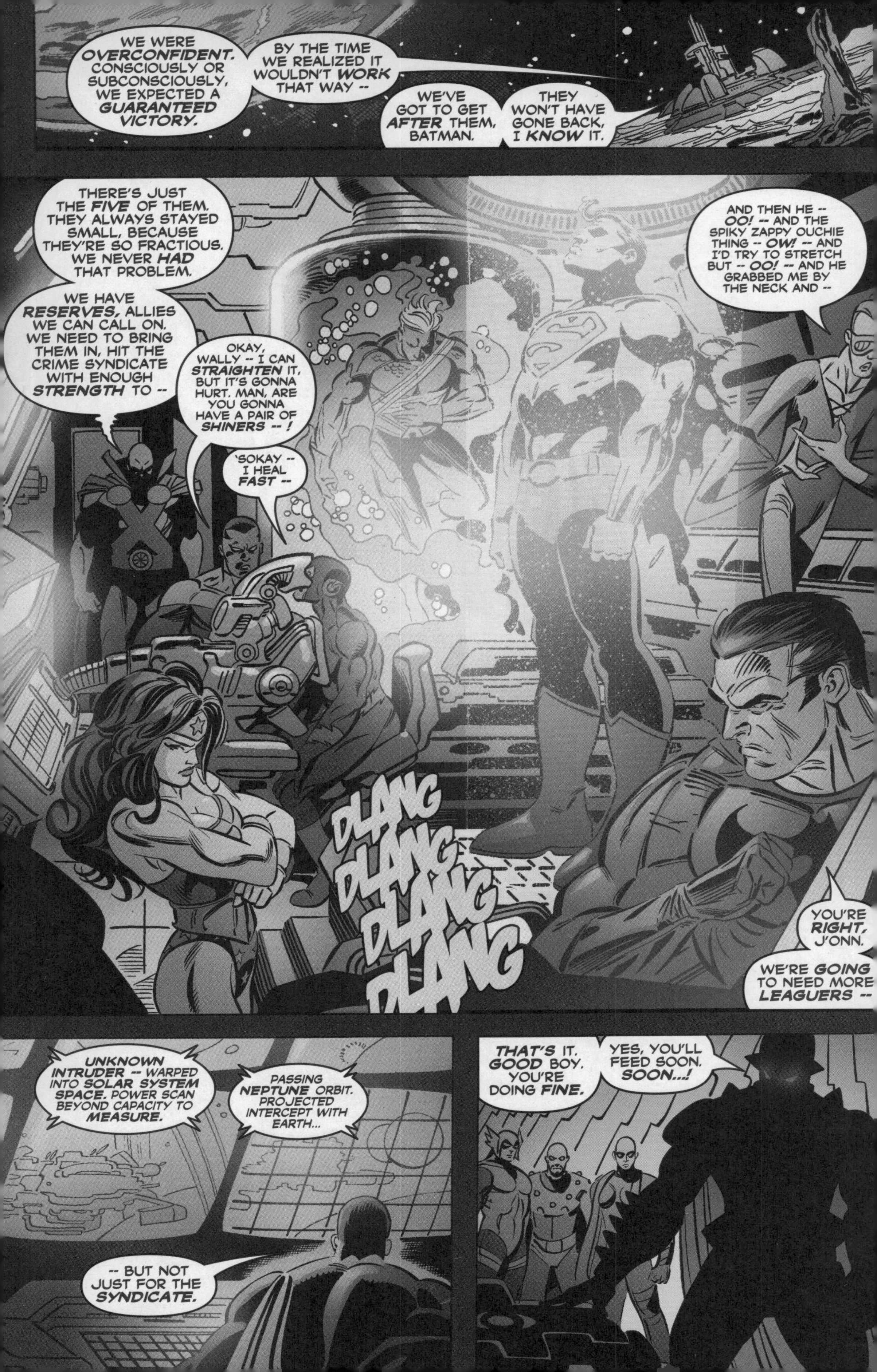
WE WERE OVERCONFIDENT. CONSCIOUSLY OR SUBCONSCIOUSLY, WE EXPECTED A GUARANTEED VICTORY.
BY THE TIME WE REALIZED IT WOULDN'T WORK THAT WAY --
WE'VE GOT TO GET AFTER THEM, BATMAN.
THEY WON'T HAVE GONE BACK, I KNOW IT.
THERE'S JUST THE FIVE OF THEM. THEY ALWAYS STAYED SMALL, BECAUSE THEY'RE SO FRACTIOUS. WE NEVER HAD THAT PROBLEM.
WE HAVE RESERVES, ALLIES WE CAN CALL ON. WE NEED TO BRING THEM IN, HIT THE CRIME SYNDICATE WITH ENOUGH STRENGTH TO --
OKAY, WALLY -- I CAN STRAIGHTEN IT, BUT IT'S GONNA HURT. MAN, ARE YOU GONNA HAVE A PAIR OF SHINERS -- !
'SOKAY -- I HEAL FAST --
AND THEN HE -- OO! -- AND THE SPIKY ZAPPY OUCHIE THING -- OW! -- AND I'D TRY TO STRETCH BUT -- OO! -- AND HE GRABBED ME BY THE NECK AND --
DLANG DLANG DLANG DLANG DLANG
YOU'RE RIGHT, J'ONN.
WE'RE GOING TO NEED MORE LEAGUERS --
UNKNOWN INTRUDER -- WARPED INTO SOLAR SYSTEM SPACE. POWER SCAN BEYOND CAPACITY TO MEASURE.
PASSING NEPTUNE ORBIT. PROJECTED INTERCEPT WITH EARTH...
-- BUT NOT JUST FOR THE SYNDICATE.
THAT'S IT. GOOD BOY. YOU'RE DOING FINE.
YES, YOU'LL FEED SOON. SOON...!

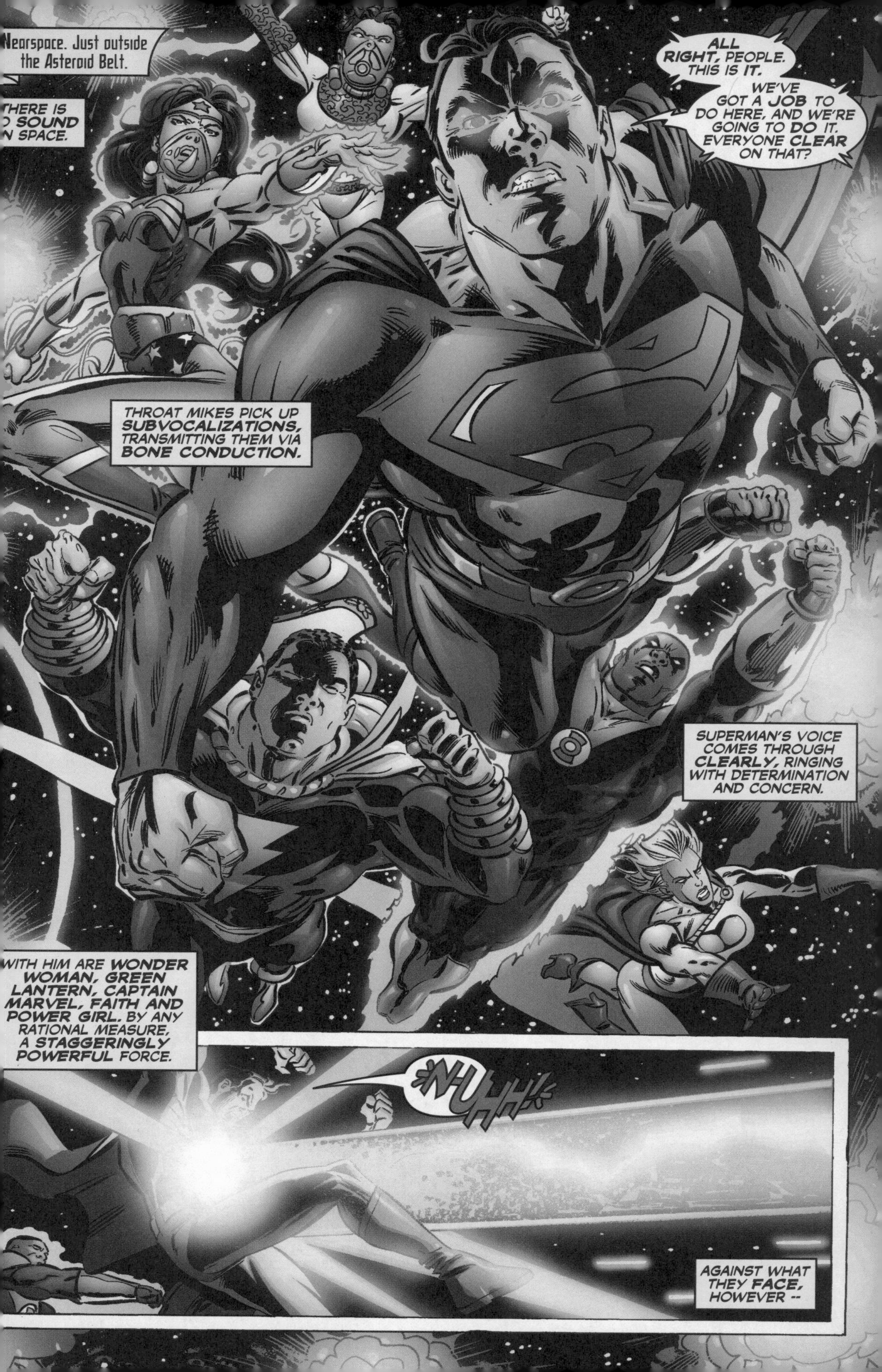
Nearspace. Just outside the Asteroid Belt.
THERE IS NO SOUND IN SPACE.
ALL RIGHT, PEOPLE. THIS IS IT.
WE'VE GOT A JOB TO DO HERE, AND WE'RE GOING TO DO IT. EVERYONE CLEAR ON THAT?
THROAT MIKES PICK UP SUBVOCALIZATIONS, TRANSMITTING THEM VIA BONE CONDUCTION.
SUPERMAN'S VOICE COMES THROUGH CLEARLY, RINGING WITH DETERMINATION AND CONCERN.
WITH HIM ARE WONDER WOMAN, GREEN LANTERN, CAPTAIN MARVEL, FAITH AND POWER GIRL. BY ANY RATIONAL MEASURE, A STAGGERINGLY POWERFUL FORCE.
N-UHH!
AGAINST WHAT THEY FACE, HOWEVER --

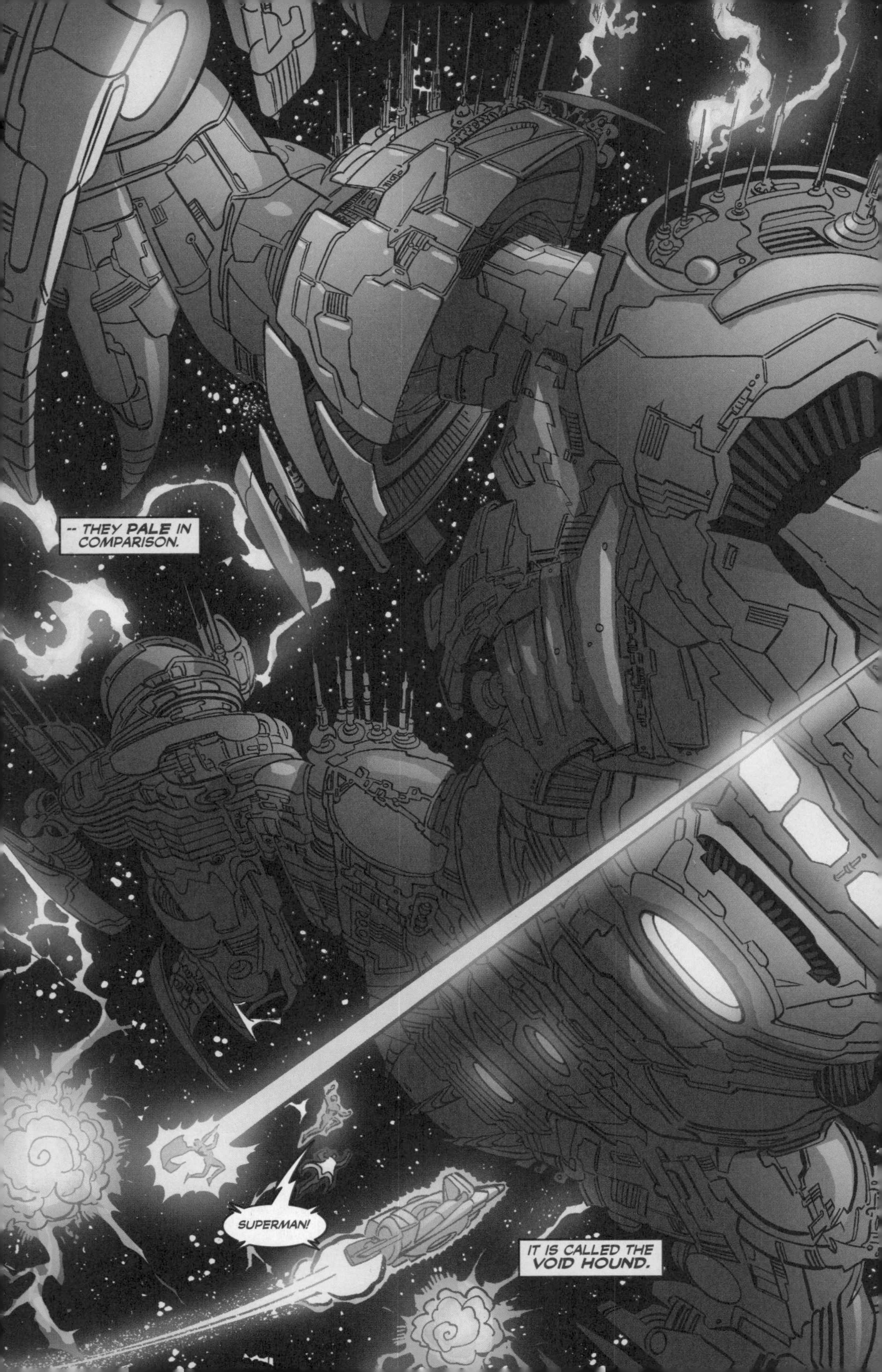
-- THEY PALE IN COMPARISON.
SUPERMAN!
IT IS CALLED THE VOID HOUND.

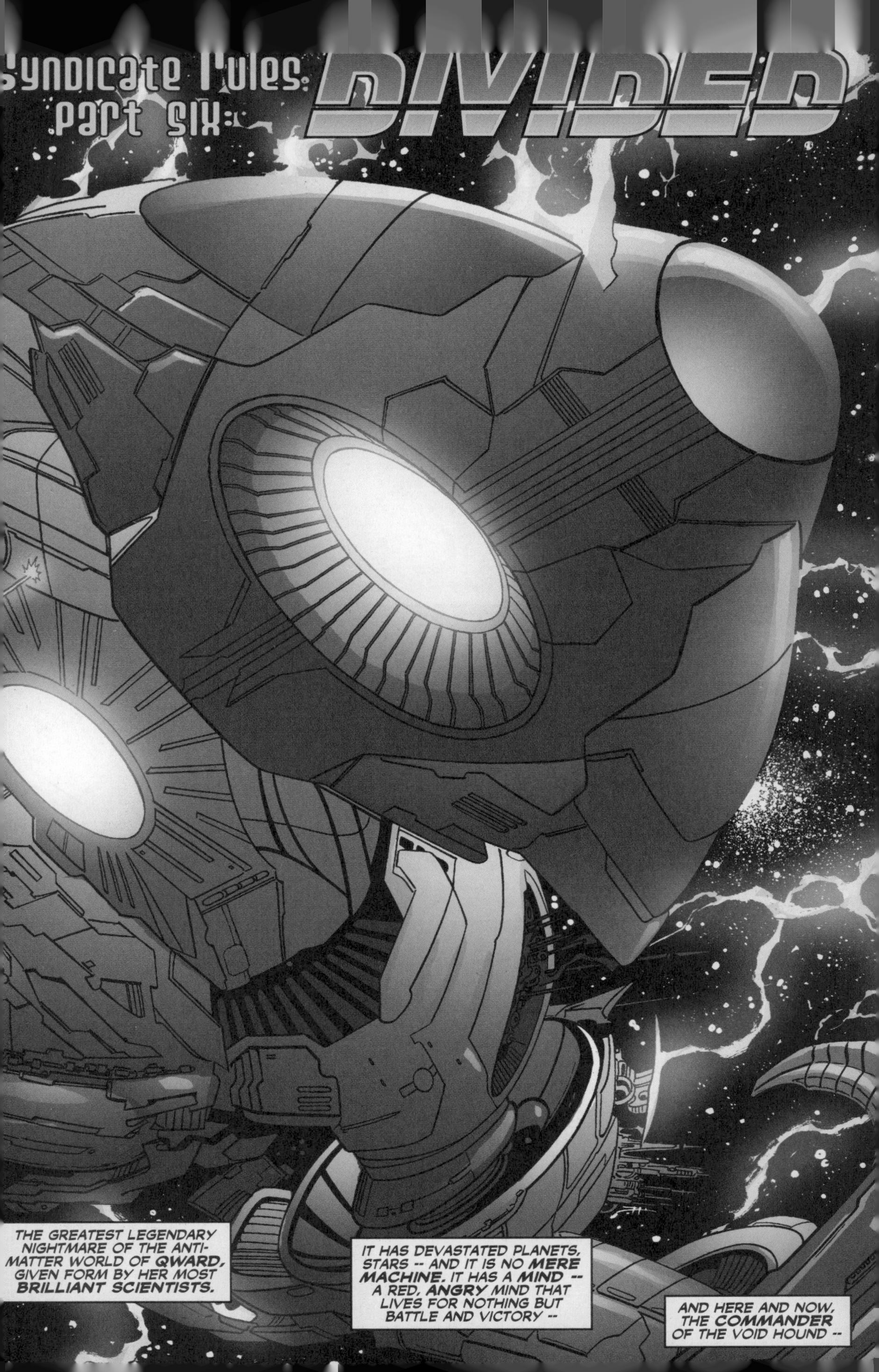

Syndicate Rules Part Six:
DIVIDED
THE GREATEST LEGENDARY NIGHTMARE OF THE ANTI-MATTER WORLD OF QWARD, GIVEN FORM BY HER MOST BRILLIANT SCIENTISTS.
IT HAS DEVASTATED PLANETS, STARS -- AND IT IS NO MERE MACHINE. IT HAS A MIND -- A RED, ANGRY MIND THAT LIVES FOR NOTHING BUT BATTLE AND VICTORY --
AND HERE AND NOW, THE COMMANDER OF THE VOID HOUND --

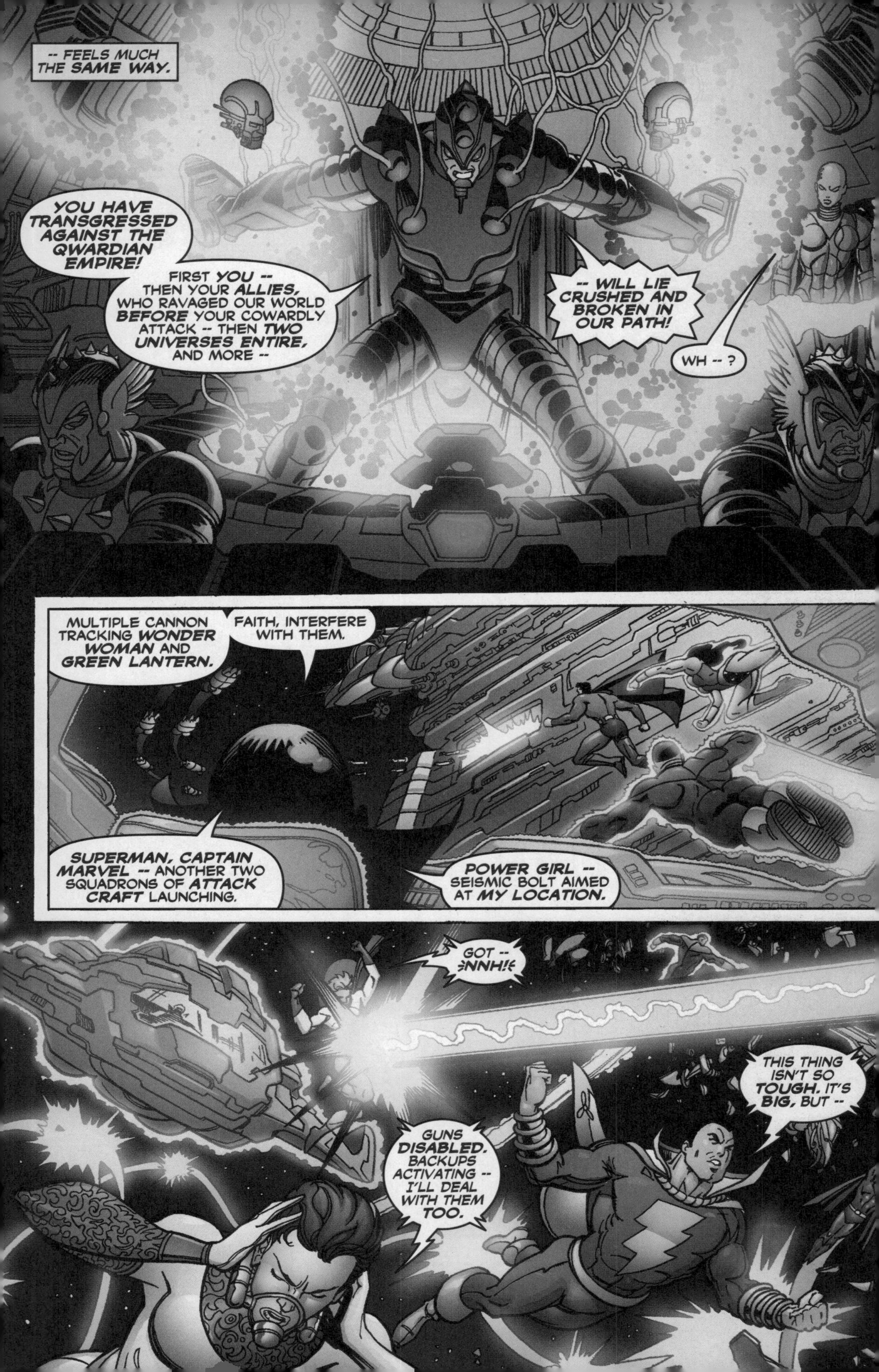
-- FEELS MUCH THE SAME WAY.
YOU HAVE TRANSGRESSED AGAINST THE QWARDIAN EMPIRE!
FIRST YOU -- THEN YOUR ALLIES, WHO RAVAGED OUR WORLD BEFORE YOUR COWARDLY ATTACK -- THEN TWO UNIVERSES ENTIRE, AND MORE --
-- WILL LIE CRUSHED AND BROKEN IN OUR PATH!
WH -- ?
MULTIPLE CANNON TRACKING WONDER WOMAN AND GREEN LANTERN.
FAITH, INTERFERE WITH THEM.
SUPERMAN, CAPTAIN MARVEL -- ANOTHER TWO SQUADRONS OF ATTACK CRAFT LAUNCHING.
POWER GIRL -- SEISMIC BOLT AIMED AT MY LOCATION.
GOT -- NNH!
THIS THING ISN'T SO TOUGH. IT'S BIG, BUT --
GUNS DISABLED. BACKUPS ACTIVATING -- I'LL DEAL WITH THEM TOO.

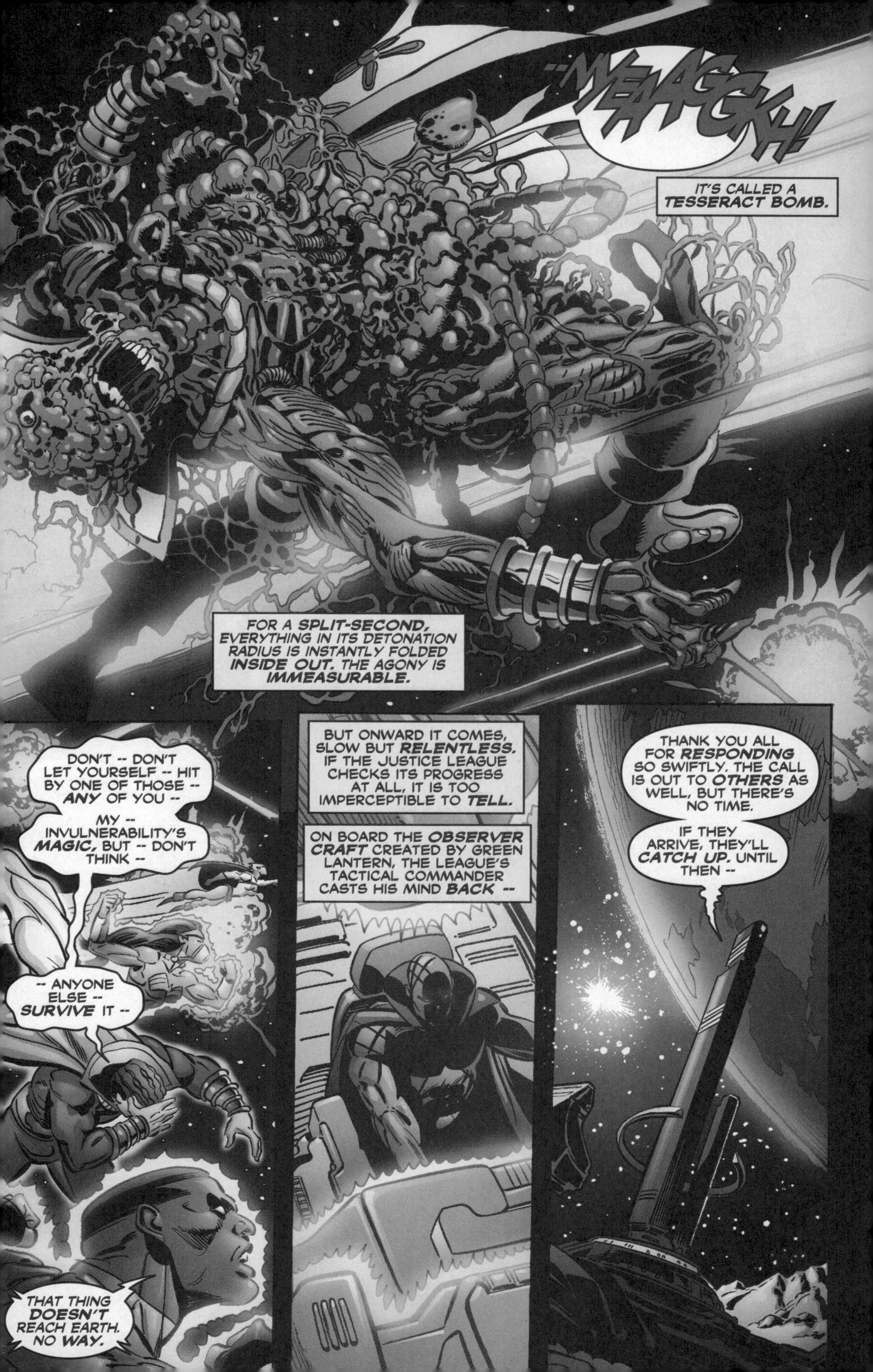
--NYEAAGGKH!
IT'S CALLED A TESSERACT BOMB.
FOR A SPLIT-SECOND, EVERYTHING IN ITS DETONATION RADIUS IS INSTANTLY FOLDED INSIDE OUT. THE AGONY IS IMMEASURABLE.
DON'T -- DON'T LET YOURSELF -- HIT BY ONE OF THOSE -- ANY OF YOU --
MY -- INVULNERABILITY'S MAGIC, BUT -- DON'T THINK --
-- ANYONE ELSE -- SURVIVE IT --
THAT THING DOESN'T REACH EARTH. NO WAY.
BUT ONWARD IT COMES, SLOW BUT RELENTLESS. IF THE JUSTICE LEAGUE CHECKS ITS PROGRESS AT ALL, IT IS TOO IMPERCEPTIBLE TO TELL.
ON BOARD THE OBSERVER CRAFT CREATED BY GREEN LANTERN, THE LEAGUE'S TACTICAL COMMANDER CASTS HIS MIND BACK --
THANK YOU ALL FOR RESPONDING SO SWIFTLY. THE CALL IS OUT TO OTHERS AS WELL, BUT THERE'S NO TIME.
IF THEY ARRIVE, THEY'LL CATCH UP. UNTIL THEN --

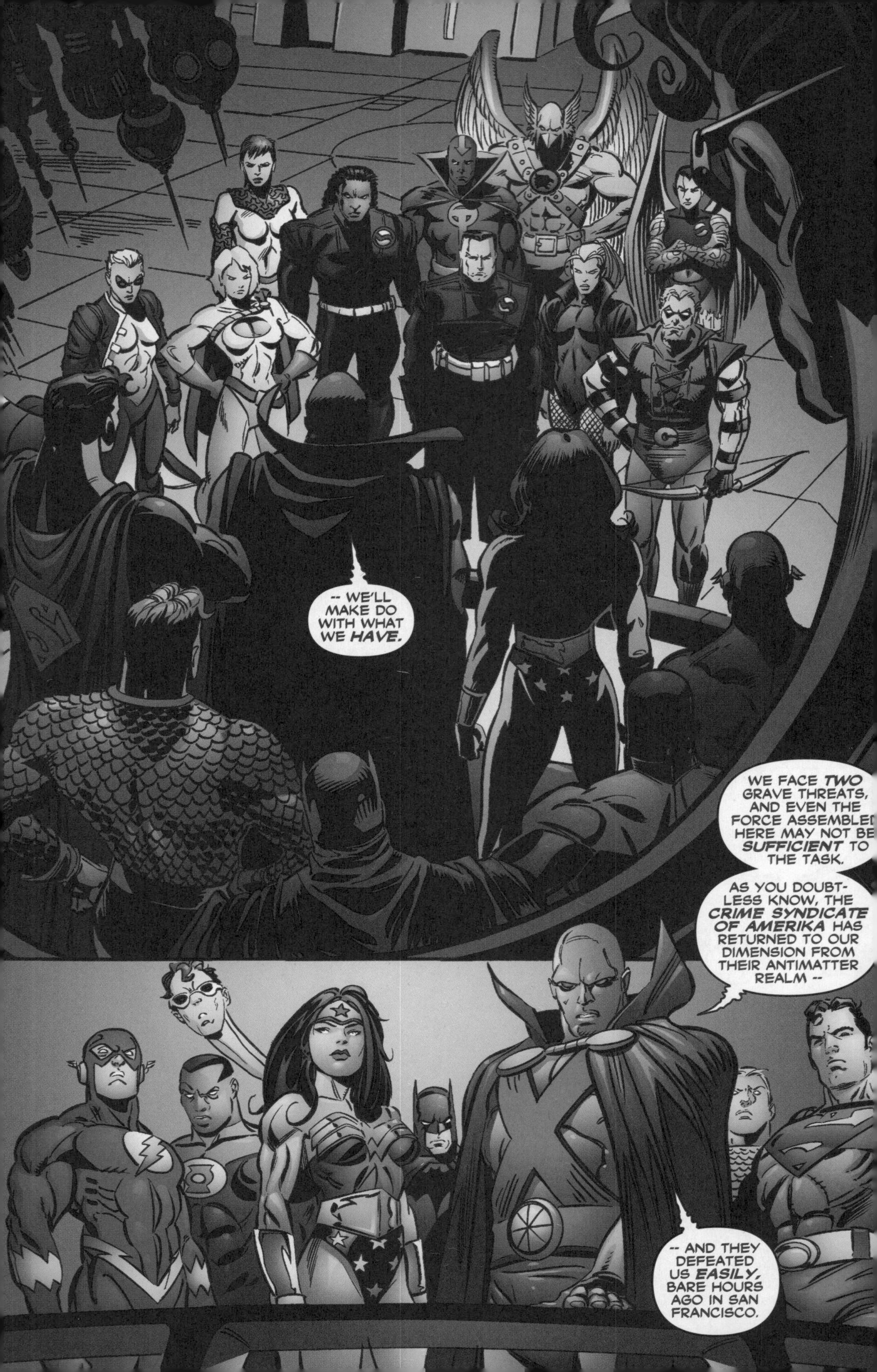
-- WE'LL MAKE DO WITH WHAT WE *HAVE.*
WE FACE *TWO* GRAVE THREATS, AND EVEN THE FORCE ASSEMBLED HERE MAY NOT BE *SUFFICIENT* TO THE TASK.
AS YOU DOUBTLESS KNOW, THE *CRIME SYNDICATE OF AMERIKA* HAS RETURNED TO OUR DIMENSION FROM THEIR ANTIMATTER REALM --
-- AND THEY DEFEATED US *EASILY,* BARE HOURS AGO IN SAN FRANCISCO.

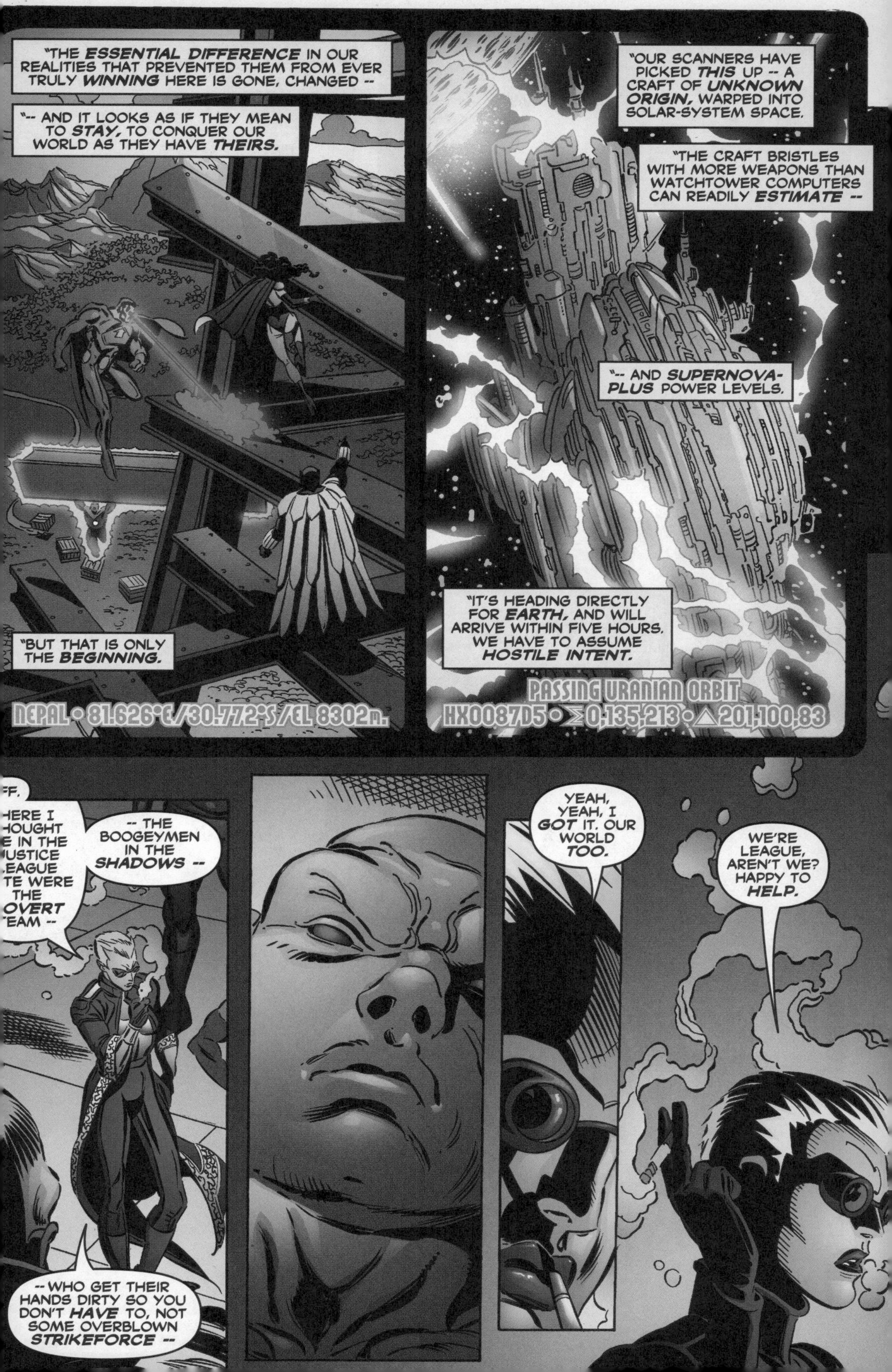
"THE ESSENTIAL DIFFERENCE IN OUR REALITIES THAT PREVENTED THEM FROM EVER TRULY WINNING HERE IS GONE, CHANGED --
"-- AND IT LOOKS AS IF THEY MEAN TO STAY, TO CONQUER OUR WORLD AS THEY HAVE THEIRS.
"BUT THAT IS ONLY THE BEGINNING.
NEPAL • 81.626°E/30.772°S/EL 8302m.
"OUR SCANNERS HAVE PICKED THIS UP -- A CRAFT OF UNKNOWN ORIGIN, WARPED INTO SOLAR-SYSTEM SPACE.
"THE CRAFT BRISTLES WITH MORE WEAPONS THAN WATCHTOWER COMPUTERS CAN READILY ESTIMATE --
"-- AND SUPERNOVA-PLUS POWER LEVELS.
"IT'S HEADING DIRECTLY FOR EARTH, AND WILL ARRIVE WITHIN FIVE HOURS. WE HAVE TO ASSUME HOSTILE INTENT.
PASSING URANIAN ORBIT
HX0087D5 • Σ0,135,213 • △201,100,83
-- THE BOOGEYMEN IN THE SHADOWS --
-- WHO GET THEIR HANDS DIRTY SO YOU DON'T HAVE TO, NOT SOME OVERBLOWN STRIKEFORCE --
YEAH, YEAH, I GOT IT. OUR WORLD TOO.
WE'RE LEAGUE, AREN'T WE? HAPPY TO HELP.

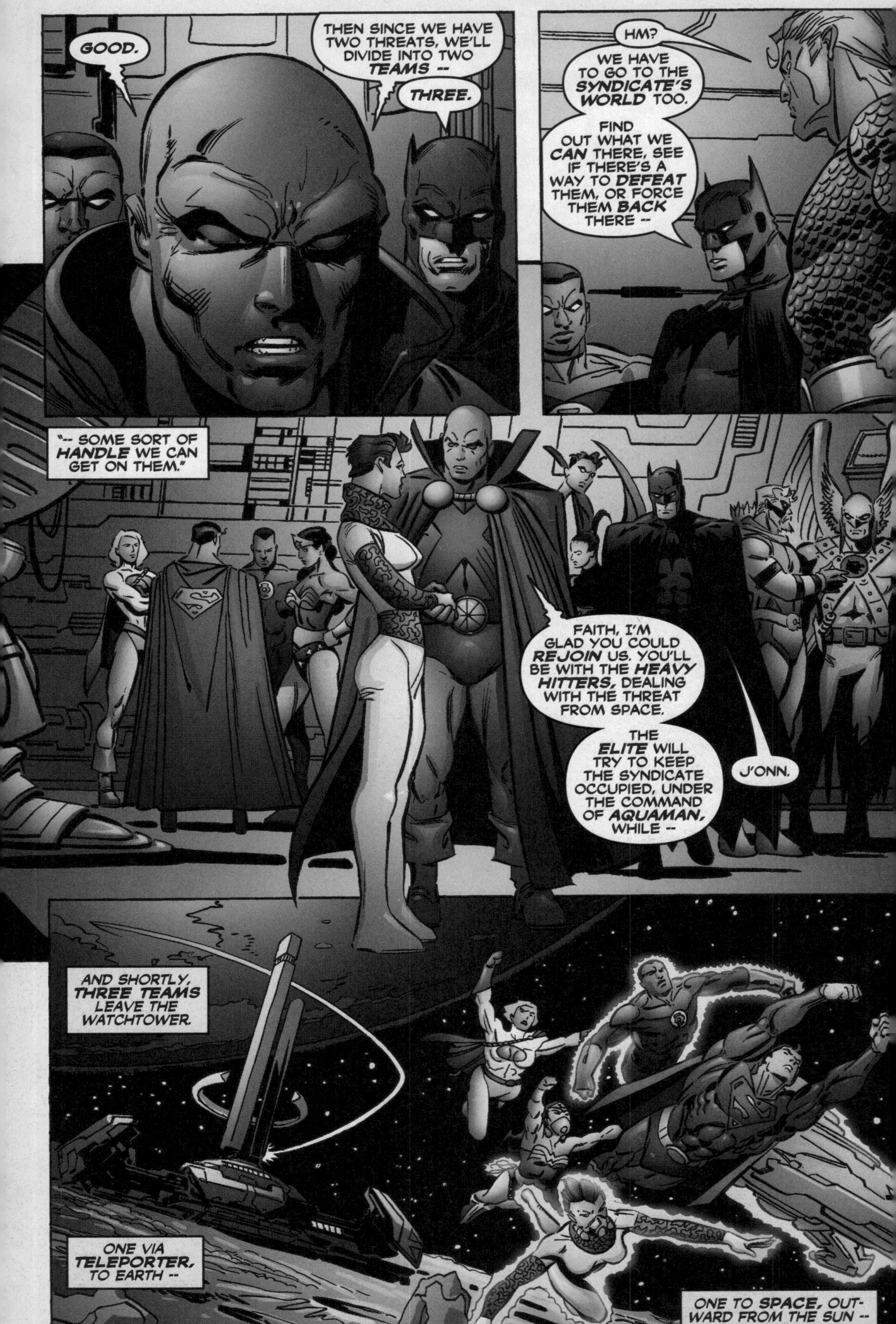
GOOD.
THEN SINCE WE HAVE TWO THREATS, WE'LL DIVIDE INTO TWO TEAMS --
THREE.
HM?
WE HAVE TO GO TO THE SYNDICATE'S WORLD TOO.
FIND OUT WHAT WE CAN THERE, SEE IF THERE'S A WAY TO DEFEAT THEM, OR FORCE THEM BACK THERE --
"-- SOME SORT OF HANDLE WE CAN GET ON THEM."
FAITH, I'M GLAD YOU COULD REJOIN US. YOU'LL BE WITH THE HEAVY HITTERS, DEALING WITH THE THREAT FROM SPACE.
THE ELITE WILL TRY TO KEEP THE SYNDICATE OCCUPIED, UNDER THE COMMAND OF AQUAMAN, WHILE --
J'ONN.
AND SHORTLY, THREE TEAMS LEAVE THE WATCHTOWER.
ONE VIA TELEPORTER, TO EARTH --
ONE TO SPACE, OUTWARD FROM THE SUN --

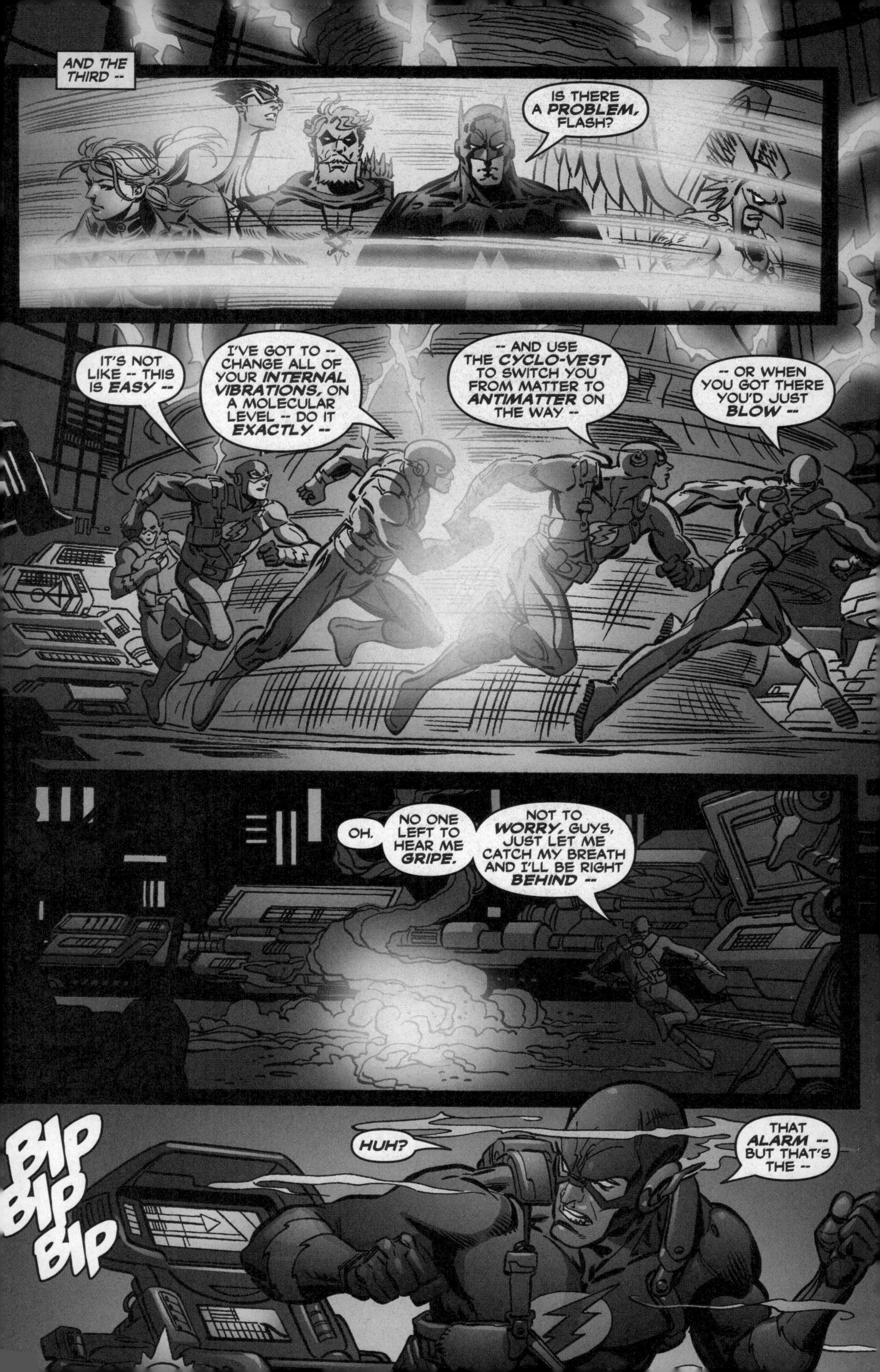
AND THE THIRD --
IS THERE A PROBLEM, FLASH?
IT'S NOT LIKE -- THIS IS EASY --
I'VE GOT TO -- CHANGE ALL OF YOUR INTERNAL VIBRATIONS, ON A MOLECULAR LEVEL -- DO IT EXACTLY --
-- AND USE THE CYCLO-VEST TO SWITCH YOU FROM MATTER TO ANTIMATTER ON THE WAY --
-- OR WHEN YOU GOT THERE YOU'D JUST BLOW --
OH.
NO ONE LEFT TO HEAR ME GRIPE.
NOT TO WORRY, GUYS, JUST LET ME CATCH MY BREATH AND I'LL BE RIGHT BEHIND --
BIP BIP BIP
HUH?
THAT ALARM -- BUT THAT'S THE --

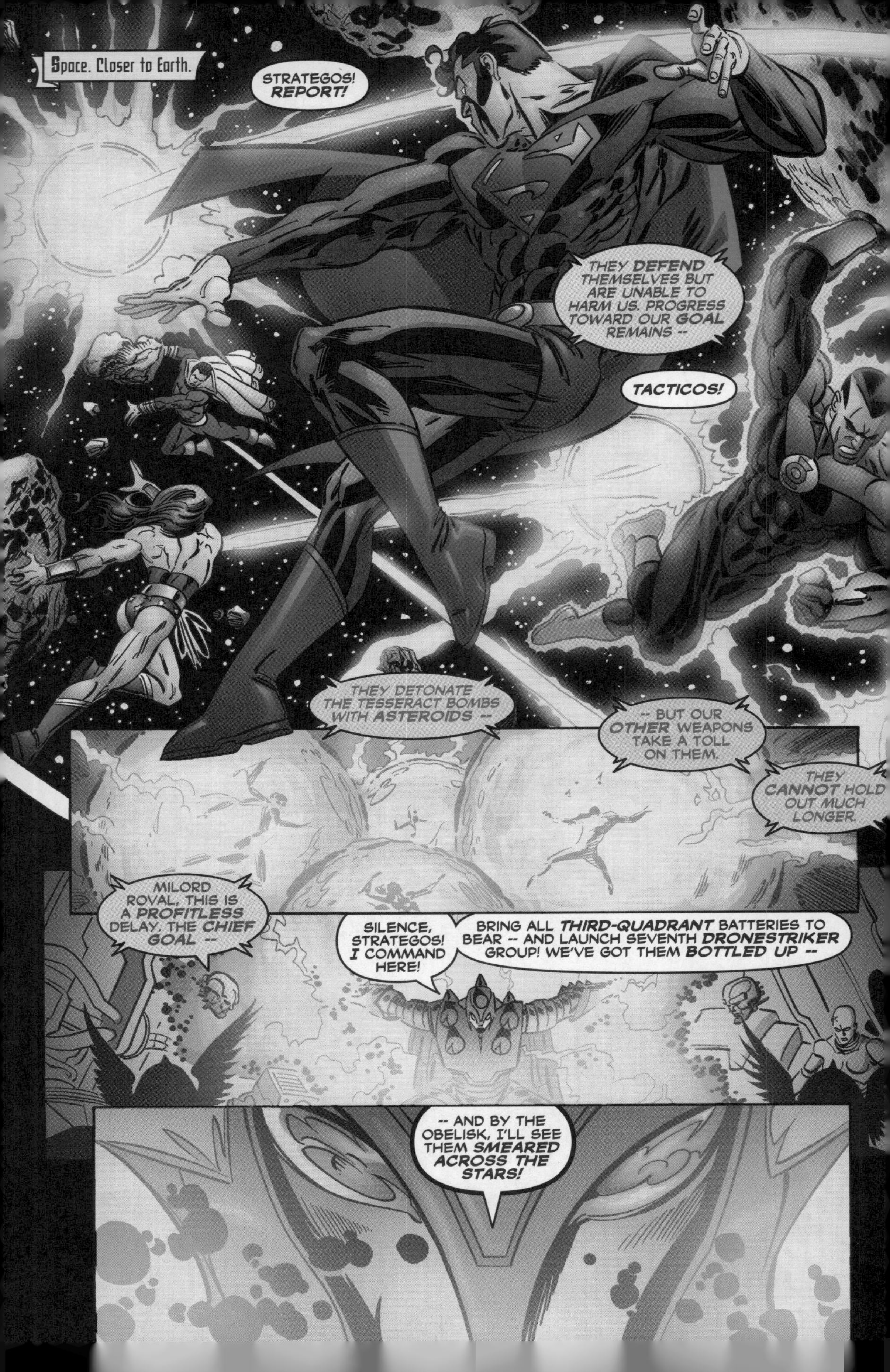
Space. Closer to Earth.
STRATEGOS! REPORT!
THEY DEFEND THEMSELVES BUT ARE UNABLE TO HARM US. PROGRESS TOWARD OUR GOAL REMAINS --
TACTICOS!
THEY DETONATE THE TESSERACT BOMBS WITH ASTEROIDS --
-- BUT OUR OTHER WEAPONS TAKE A TOLL ON THEM.
THEY CANNOT HOLD OUT MUCH LONGER.
MILORD ROVAL, THIS IS A PROFITLESS DELAY. THE CHIEF GOAL --
SILENCE, STRATEGOS! I COMMAND HERE!
BRING ALL THIRD-QUADRANT BATTERIES TO BEAR -- AND LAUNCH SEVENTH DRONESTRIKER GROUP! WE'VE GOT THEM BOTTLED UP --
-- AND BY THE OBELISK, I'LL SEE THEM SMEARED ACROSS THE STARS!

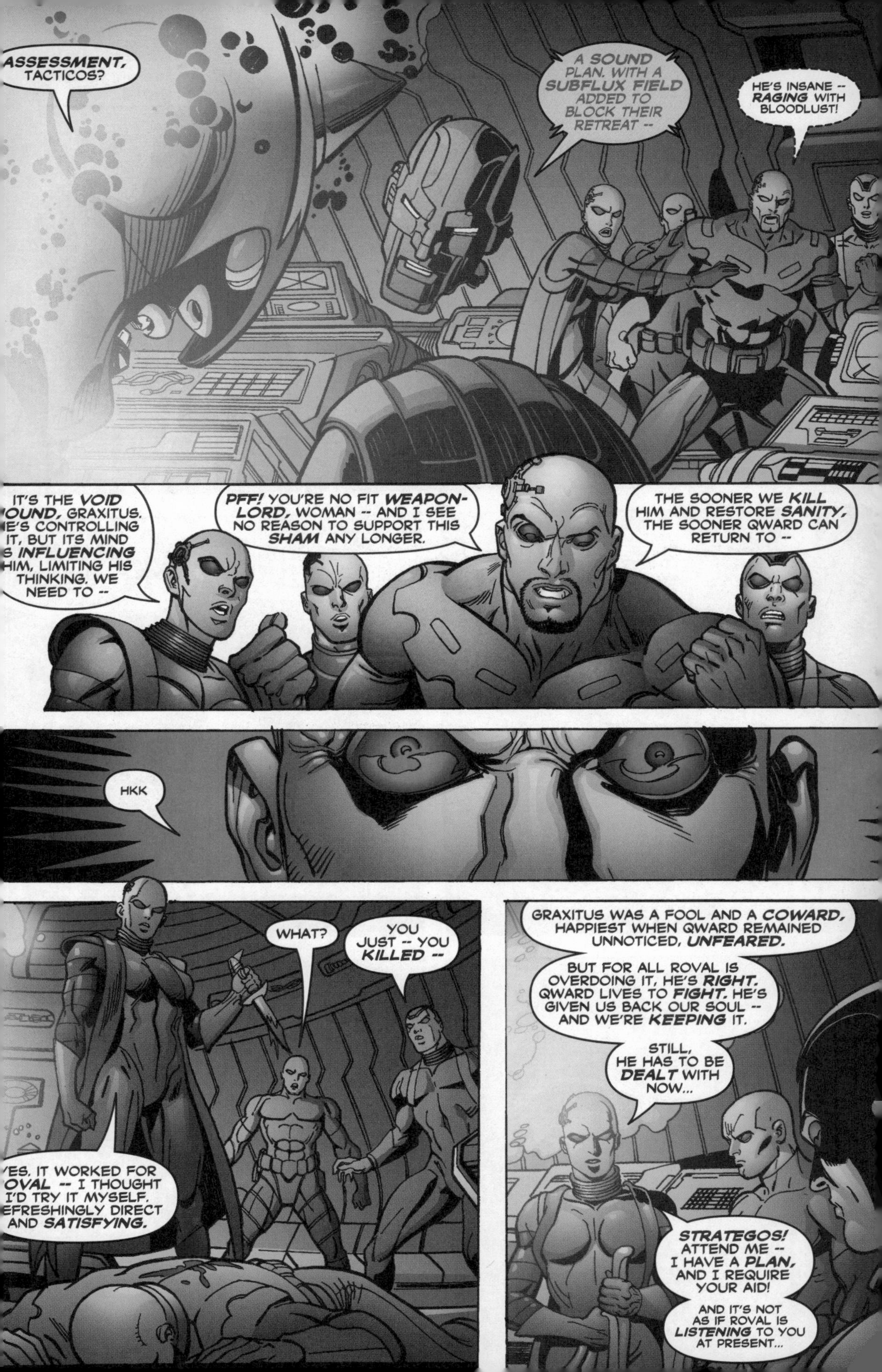
ASSESSMENT, TACTICOS?
A SOUND PLAN. WITH A SUBFLUX FIELD ADDED TO BLOCK THEIR RETREAT --
HE'S INSANE -- RAGING WITH BLOODLUST!
IT'S THE VOID OUND, GRAXITUS. E'S CONTROLLING IT, BUT ITS MIND S INFLUENCING HIM, LIMITING HIS THINKING. WE NEED TO --
PFF! YOU'RE NO FIT WEAPON-LORD, WOMAN -- AND I SEE NO REASON TO SUPPORT THIS SHAM ANY LONGER.
THE SOONER WE KILL HIM AND RESTORE SANITY, THE SOONER QWARD CAN RETURN TO --
HKK
WHAT?
YOU JUST -- YOU KILLED --
YES. IT WORKED FOR OVAL -- I THOUGHT I'D TRY IT MYSELF. EFRESHINGLY DIRECT AND SATISFYING.
GRAXITUS WAS A FOOL AND A COWARD, HAPPIEST WHEN QWARD REMAINED UNNOTICED, UNFEARED.
BUT FOR ALL ROVAL IS OVERDOING IT, HE'S RIGHT. QWARD LIVES TO FIGHT. HE'S GIVEN US BACK OUR SOUL -- AND WE'RE KEEPING IT.
STILL, HE HAS TO BE DEALT WITH NOW...
STRATEGOS! ATTEND ME -- I HAVE A PLAN, AND I REQUIRE YOUR AID!
AND IT'S NOT AS IF ROVAL IS LISTENING TO YOU AT PRESENT...

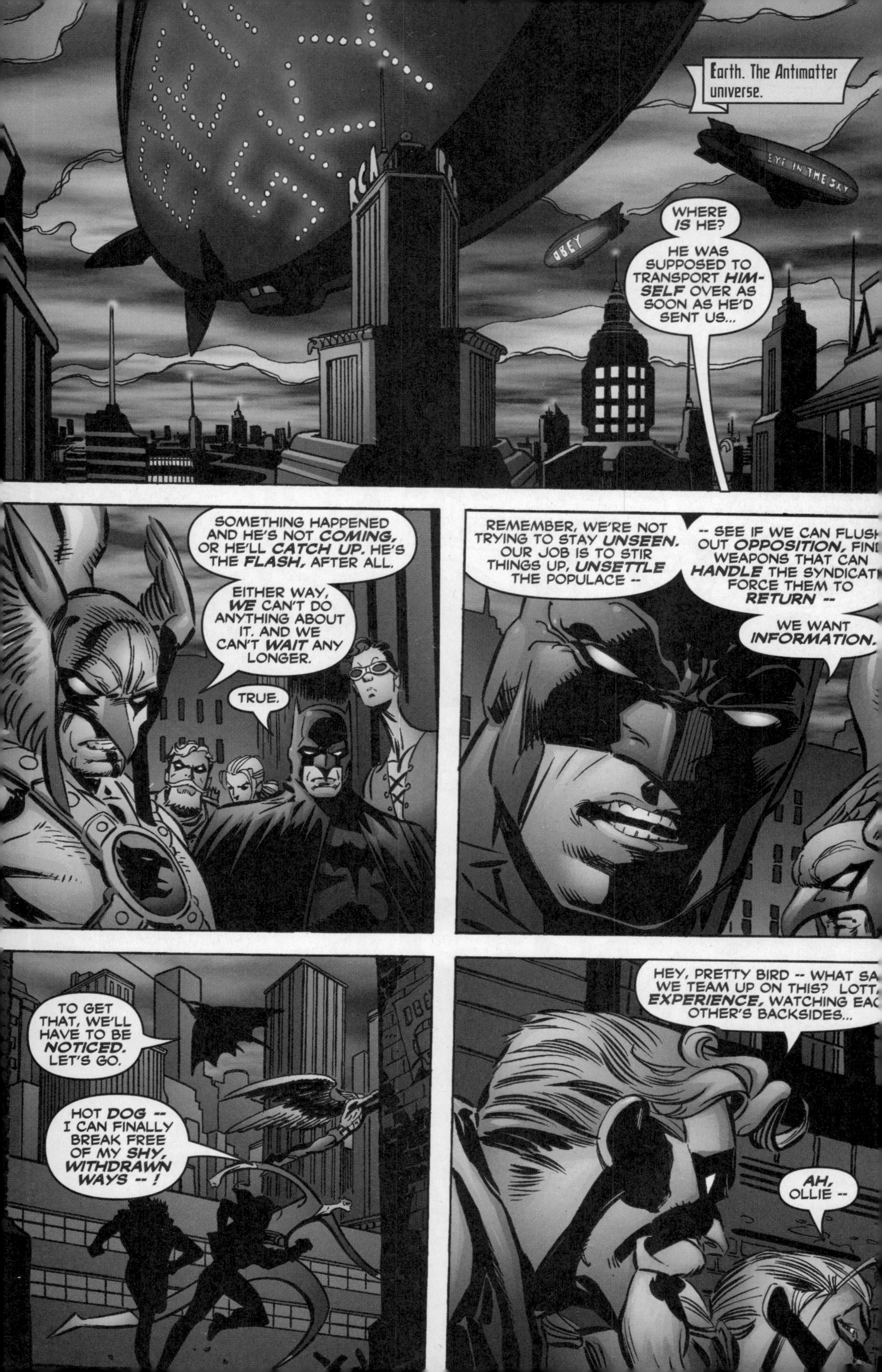
Earth. The Antimatter universe.
EYE IN THE SKY
OBEY
RCA
WHERE IS HE?
HE WAS SUPPOSED TO TRANSPORT HIMSELF OVER AS SOON AS HE'D SENT US...
SOMETHING HAPPENED AND HE'S NOT COMING, OR HE'LL CATCH UP. HE'S THE FLASH, AFTER ALL.
EITHER WAY, WE CAN'T DO ANYTHING ABOUT IT. AND WE CAN'T WAIT ANY LONGER.
TRUE.
REMEMBER, WE'RE NOT TRYING TO STAY UNSEEN. OUR JOB IS TO STIR THINGS UP, UNSETTLE THE POPULACE --
-- SEE IF WE CAN FLUSH OUT OPPOSITION, FIND WEAPONS THAT CAN HANDLE THE SYNDICATE, FORCE THEM TO RETURN --
WE WANT INFORMATION.
TO GET THAT, WE'LL HAVE TO BE NOTICED. LET'S GO.
HOT DOG -- I CAN FINALLY BREAK FREE OF MY SHY, WITHDRAWN WAYS -- !
HEY, PRETTY BIRD -- WHAT SA WE TEAM UP ON THIS? LOTT EXPERIENCE, WATCHING EAC OTHER'S BACKSIDES...
AH, OLLIE --

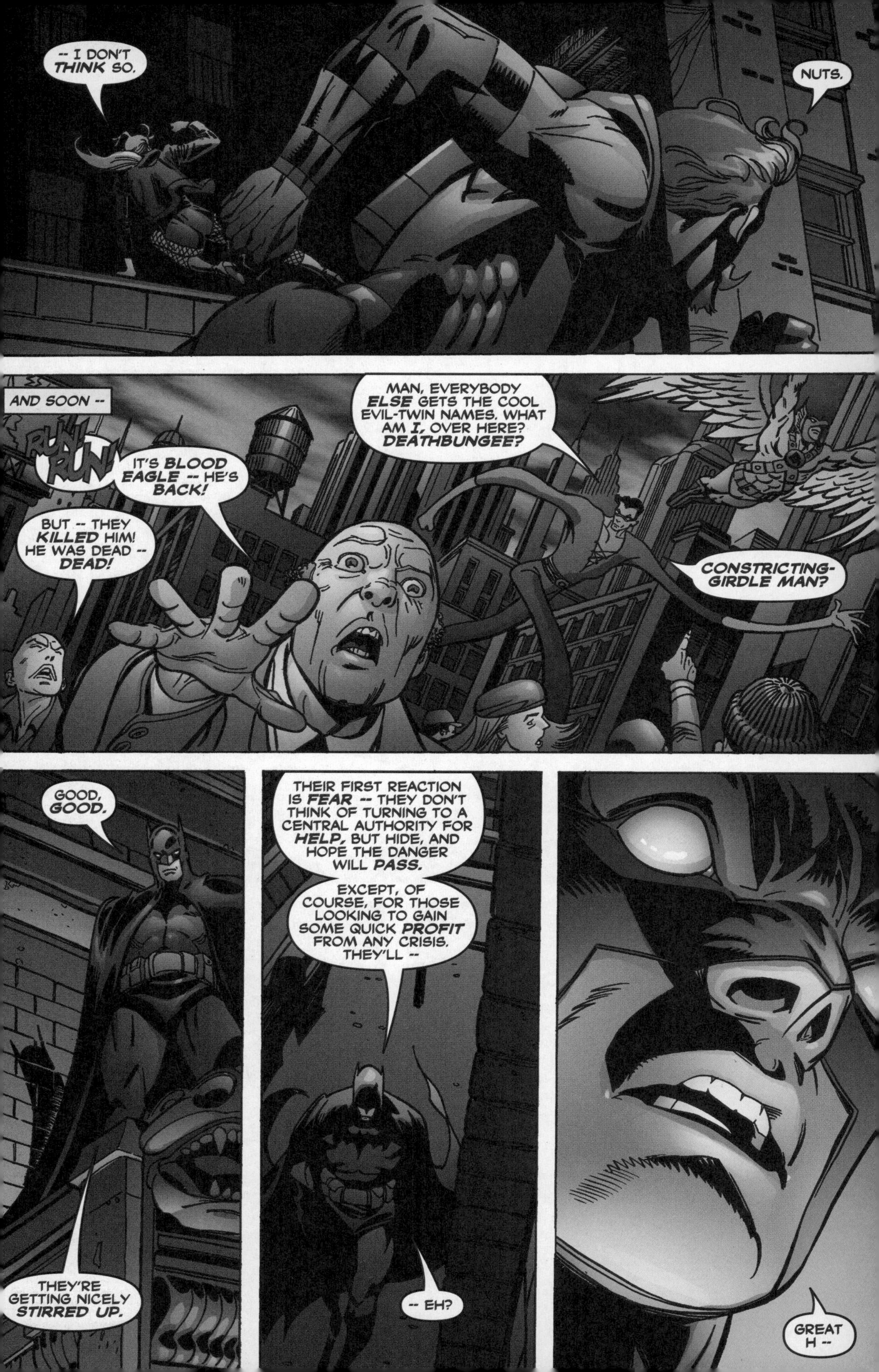
-- I DON'T THINK SO.
NUTS.
AND SOON --
RUN! RUN!
IT'S BLOOD EAGLE -- HE'S BACK!
BUT -- THEY KILLED HIM! HE WAS DEAD -- DEAD!
MAN, EVERYBODY ELSE GETS THE COOL EVIL-TWIN NAMES. WHAT AM I, OVER HERE? DEATHBUNGEE?
CONSTRICTING-GIRDLE MAN?
GOOD, GOOD.
THEY'RE GETTING NICELY STIRRED UP.
THEIR FIRST REACTION IS FEAR -- THEY DON'T THINK OF TURNING TO A CENTRAL AUTHORITY FOR HELP, BUT HIDE, AND HOPE THE DANGER WILL PASS.
EXCEPT, OF COURSE, FOR THOSE LOOKING TO GAIN SOME QUICK PROFIT FROM ANY CRISIS. THEY'LL --
-- EH?
GREAT H --

-- AT'S RIGHT, SYNDICATE-WATCHERS, IT'S ACTION TIME!

THE POSITIVES CALL IT "HONG KONG" -- TO US, IT'S PART OF THE GREATER CHINA CO-PROSPERITY SPHERE!

THE SYNDICATE'S DONE WITH THE FOUNDATIONS FOR THEIR CITADEL AND WANTS A FEW SLAVES FOR CONSTRUCTION --

-- BUT THE JUSTICE LEAGUE -- IF THAT'S REALLY SOM OF THE LEAGUE -- SAYS NO!

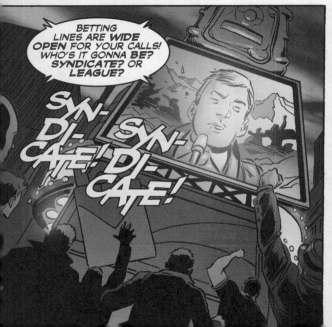

BETTING LINES ARE WIDE OPEN FOR YOUR CALLS! WHO'S IT GONNA BE? SYNDICATE? OR LEAGUE?

SYN-DI-CATE! SYN-DI-CATE!

THEY LIVE IN TERROR THEM, AND YET -- THEY CHEER THEM ON.

FIGHT WELL, LEAGUE. SHOW THEM WHAT POSITIVE WORLD CAN DO.

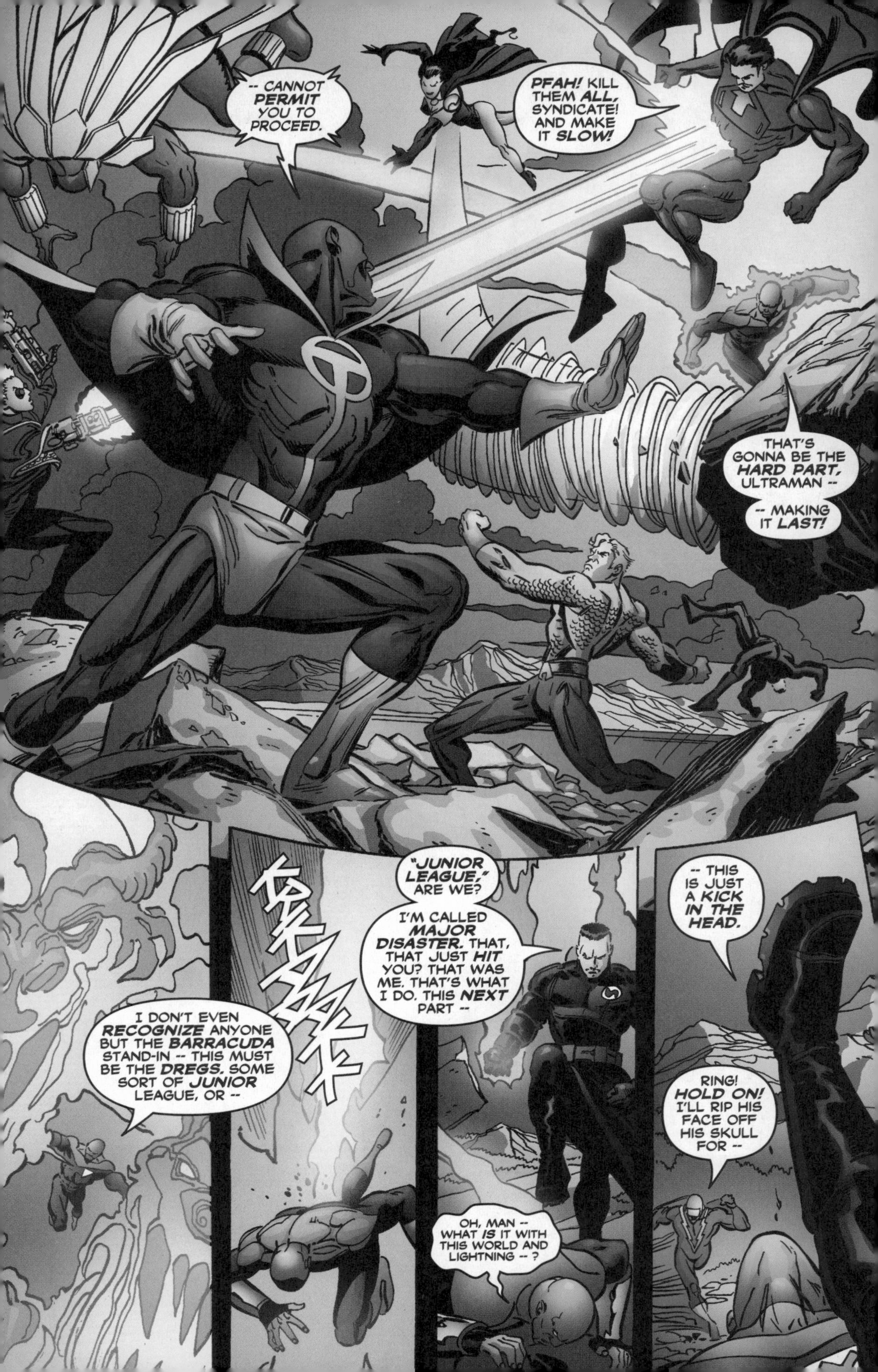
-- CANNOT PERMIT YOU TO PROCEED.
PFAH! KILL THEM ALL, SYNDICATE! AND MAKE IT SLOW!
THAT'S GONNA BE THE HARD PART, ULTRAMAN --
-- MAKING IT LAST!
I DON'T EVEN RECOGNIZE ANYONE BUT THE BARRACUDA STAND-IN -- THIS MUST BE THE DREGS. SOME SORT OF JUNIOR LEAGUE, OR --
KRAKAKAKK
"JUNIOR LEAGUE," ARE WE?
I'M CALLED MAJOR DISASTER. THAT, THAT JUST HIT YOU? THAT WAS ME. THAT'S WHAT I DO. THIS NEXT PART --
-- THIS IS JUST A KICK IN THE HEAD.
OH, MAN -- WHAT IS IT WITH THIS WORLD AND LIGHTNING -- ?
RING! HOLD ON! I'LL RIP HIS FACE OFF HIS SKULL FOR --

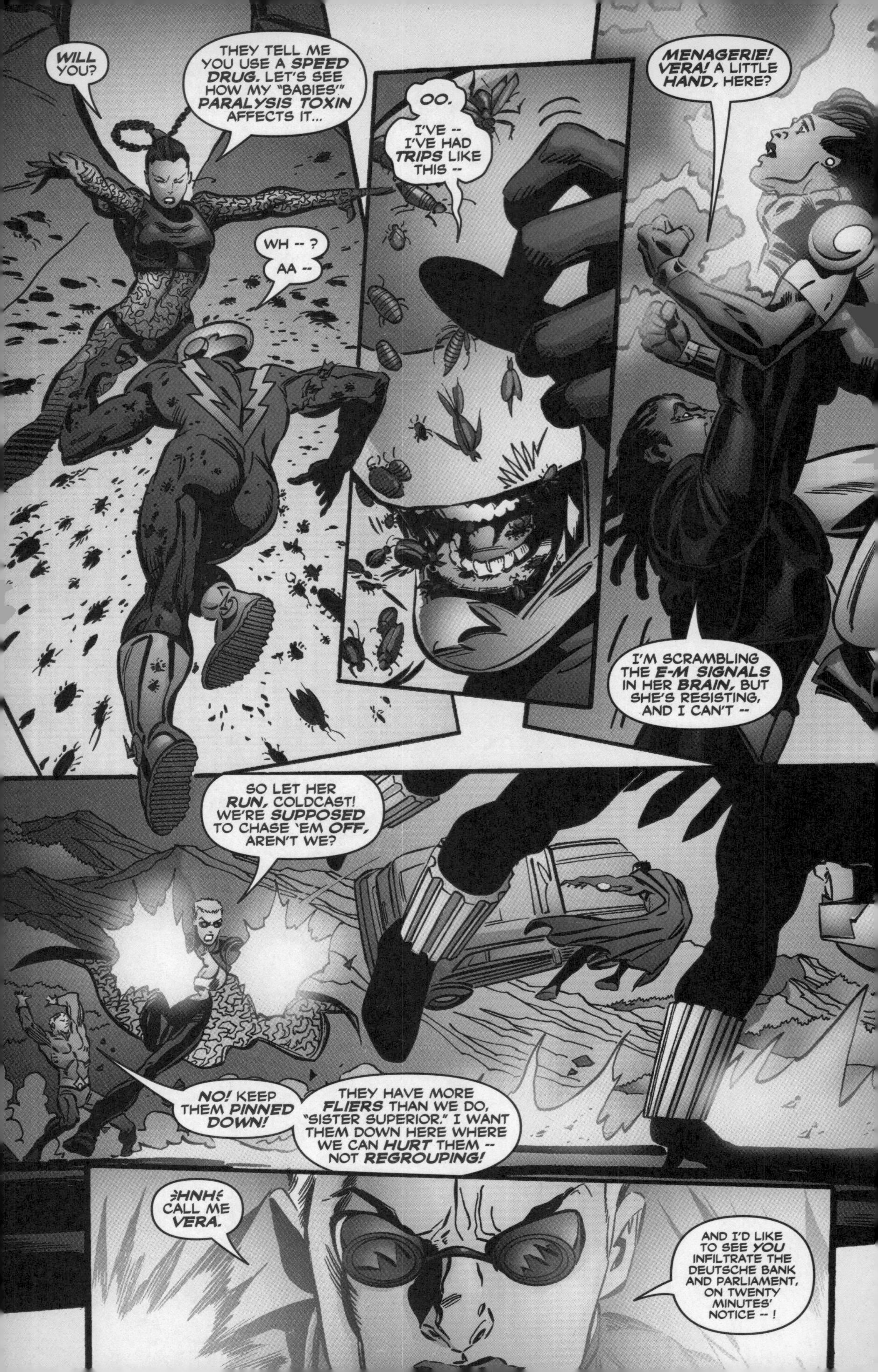

WILL YOU?
THEY TELL ME YOU USE A SPEED DRUG. LET'S SEE HOW MY "BABIES'" PARALYSIS TOXIN AFFECTS IT...
WH -- ?
AA --
OO.
I'VE -- I'VE HAD TRIPS LIKE THIS --
MENAGERIE! VERA! A LITTLE HAND, HERE?
I'M SCRAMBLING THE E-M SIGNALS IN HER BRAIN, BUT SHE'S RESISTING, AND I CAN'T --
SO LET HER RUN, COLDCAST! WE'RE SUPPOSED TO CHASE 'EM OFF, AREN'T WE?
NO! KEEP THEM PINNED DOWN!
THEY HAVE MORE FLIERS THAN WE DO, "SISTER SUPERIOR." I WANT THEM DOWN HERE WHERE WE CAN HURT THEM -- NOT REGROUPING!
HNH CALL ME VERA.
AND I'D LIKE TO SEE YOU INFILTRATE THE DEUTSCHE BANK AND PARLIAMENT, ON TWENTY MINUTES' NOTICE -- !

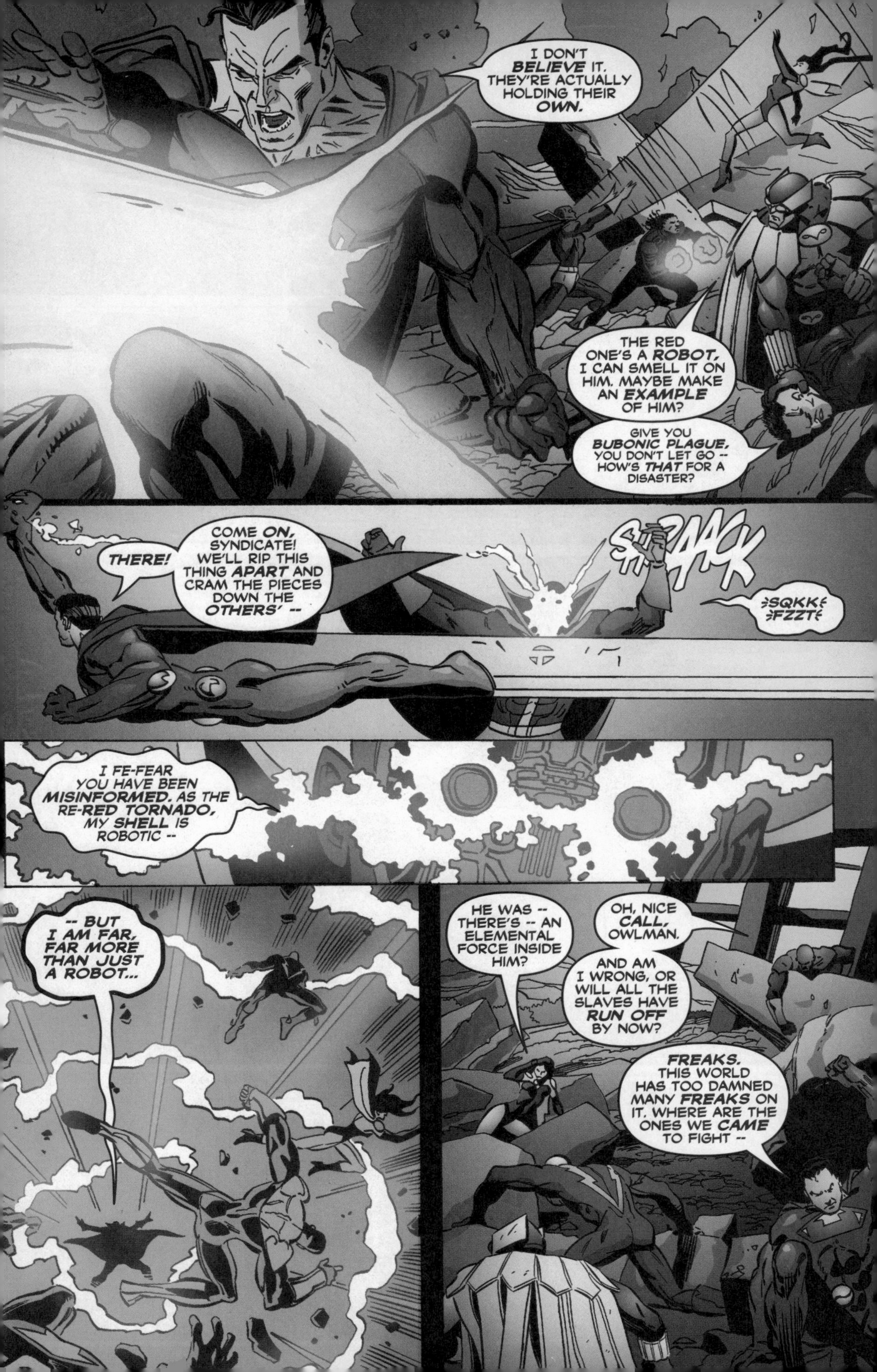
I DON'T BELIEVE IT. THEY'RE ACTUALLY HOLDING THEIR OWN.
THE RED ONE'S A ROBOT, I CAN SMELL IT ON HIM. MAYBE MAKE AN EXAMPLE OF HIM?
GIVE YOU BUBONIC PLAGUE, YOU DON'T LET GO -- HOW'S THAT FOR A DISASTER?
THERE!
COME ON, SYNDICATE! WE'LL RIP THIS THING APART AND CRAM THE PIECES DOWN THE OTHERS' --
SKRAACK
SQKK FZZT
I FE-FEAR YOU HAVE BEEN MISINFORMED. AS THE RE-RED TORNADO, MY SHELL IS ROBOTIC --
-- BUT I AM FAR, FAR MORE THAN JUST A ROBOT...
HE WAS -- THERE'S -- AN ELEMENTAL FORCE INSIDE HIM?
OH, NICE CALL, OWLMAN.
AND AM I WRONG, OR WILL ALL THE SLAVES HAVE RUN OFF BY NOW?
FREAKS. THIS WORLD HAS TOO DAMNED MANY FREAKS ON IT. WHERE ARE THE ONES WE CAME TO FIGHT --

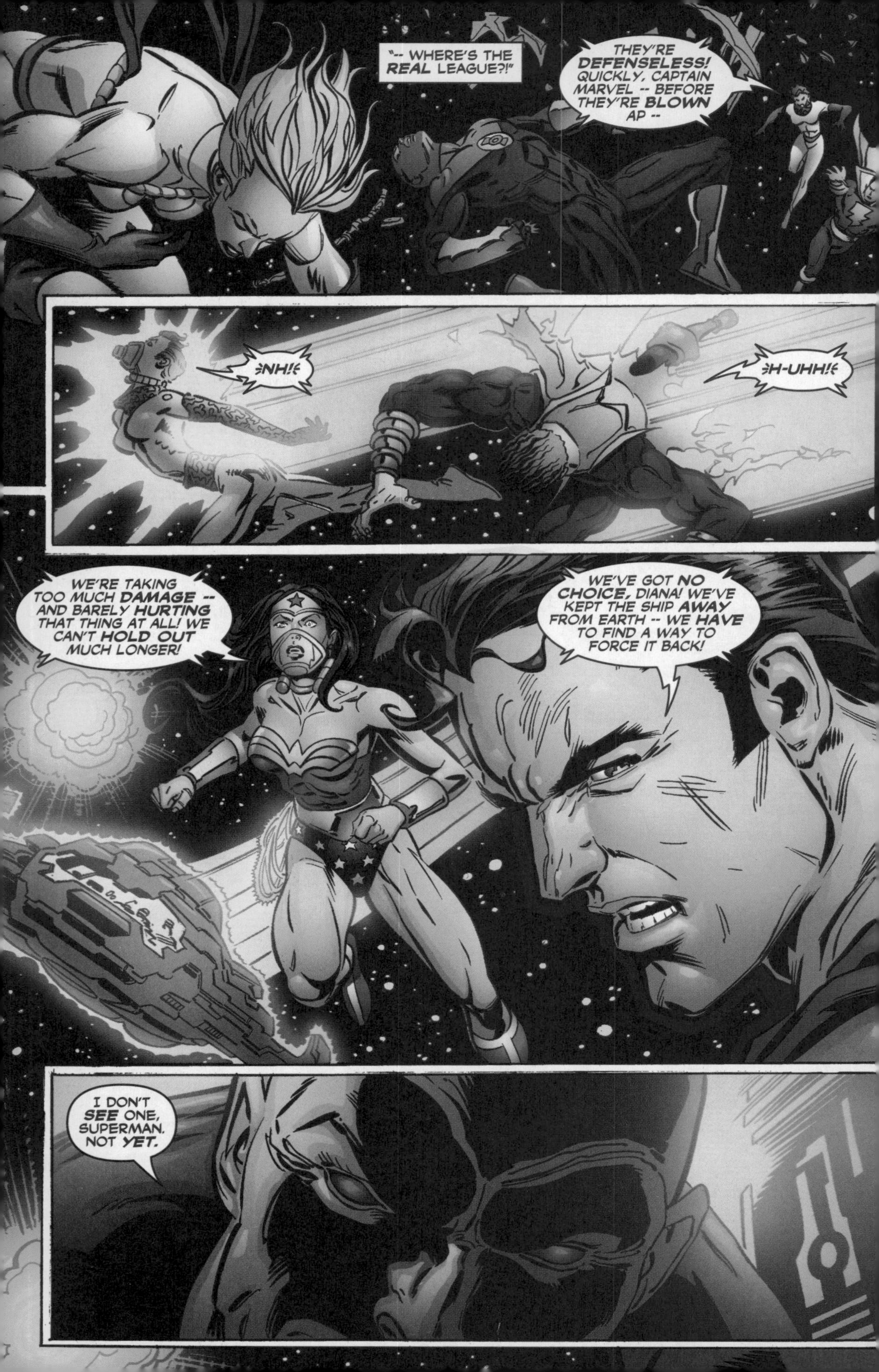
"-- WHERE'S THE REAL LEAGUE?!"
THEY'RE DEFENSELESS! QUICKLY, CAPTAIN MARVEL -- BEFORE THEY'RE BLOWN AP --
NH!
H-UHH!
WE'RE TAKING TOO MUCH DAMAGE -- AND BARELY HURTING THAT THING AT ALL! WE CAN'T HOLD OUT MUCH LONGER!
WE'VE GOT NO CHOICE, DIANA! WE'VE KEPT THE SHIP AWAY FROM EARTH -- WE HAVE TO FIND A WAY TO FORCE IT BACK!
I DON'T SEE ONE, SUPERMAN. NOT YET.

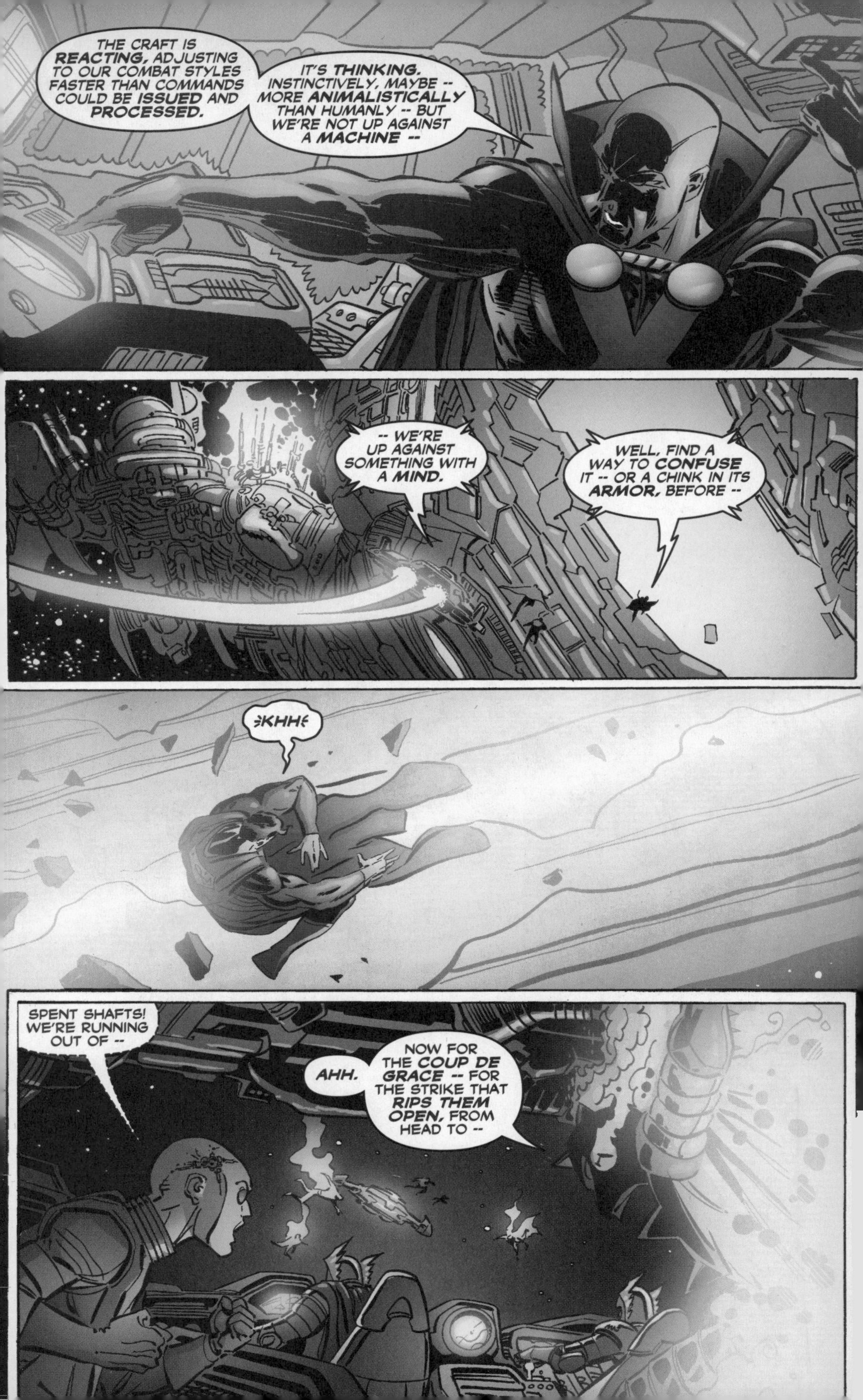
THE CRAFT IS REACTING, ADJUSTING TO OUR COMBAT STYLES FASTER THAN COMMANDS COULD BE ISSUED AND PROCESSED.
IT'S THINKING. INSTINCTIVELY, MAYBE -- MORE ANIMALISTICALLY THAN HUMANLY -- BUT WE'RE NOT UP AGAINST A MACHINE --
-- WE'RE UP AGAINST SOMETHING WITH A MIND.
WELL, FIND A WAY TO CONFUSE IT -- OR A CHINK IN ITS ARMOR, BEFORE --
KHH
SPENT SHAFTS! WE'RE RUNNING OUT OF --
AHH.
NOW FOR THE COUP DE GRACE -- FOR THE STRIKE THAT RIPS THEM OPEN, FROM HEAD TO --

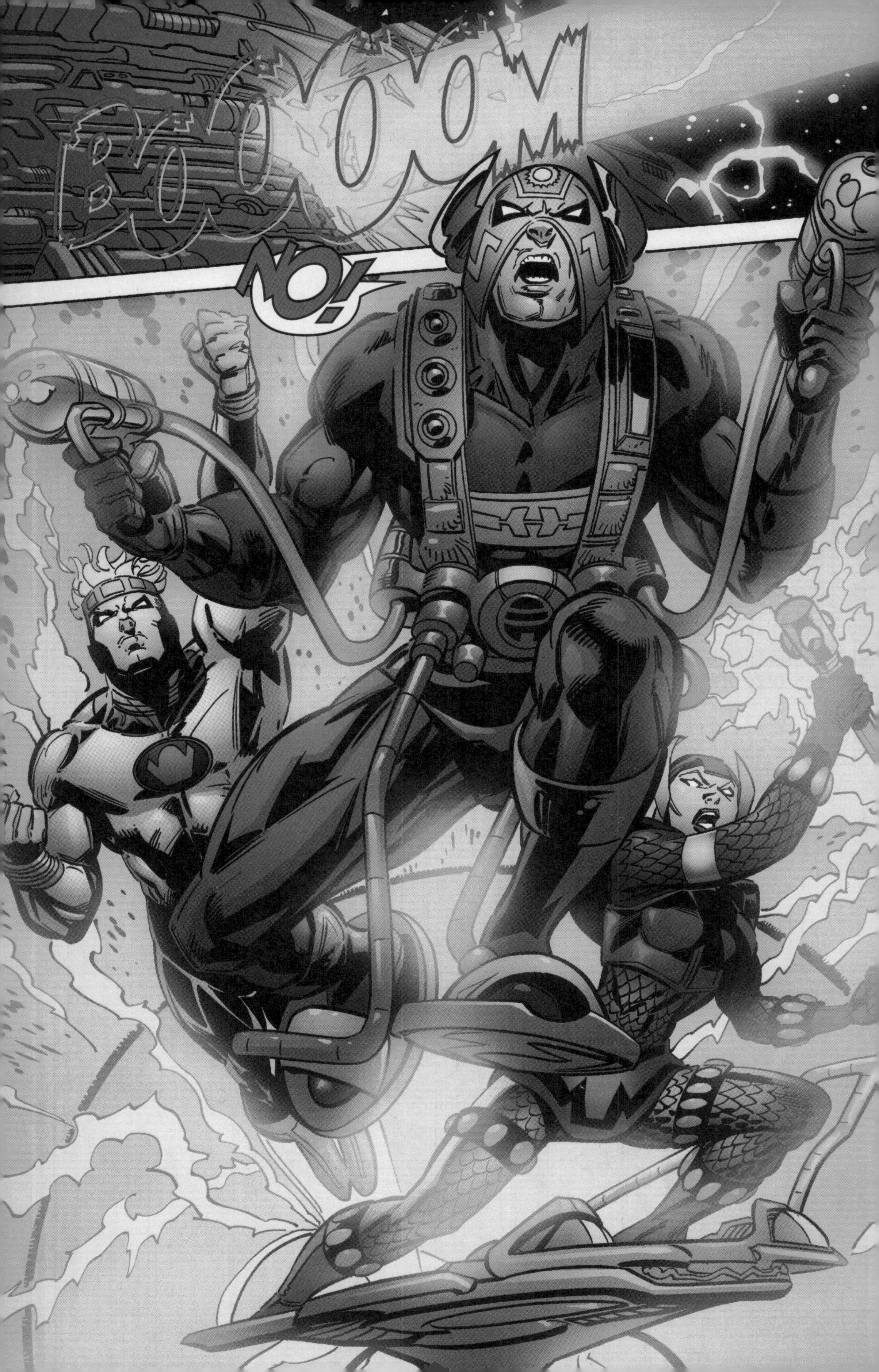
BOOOOOOM
NO!

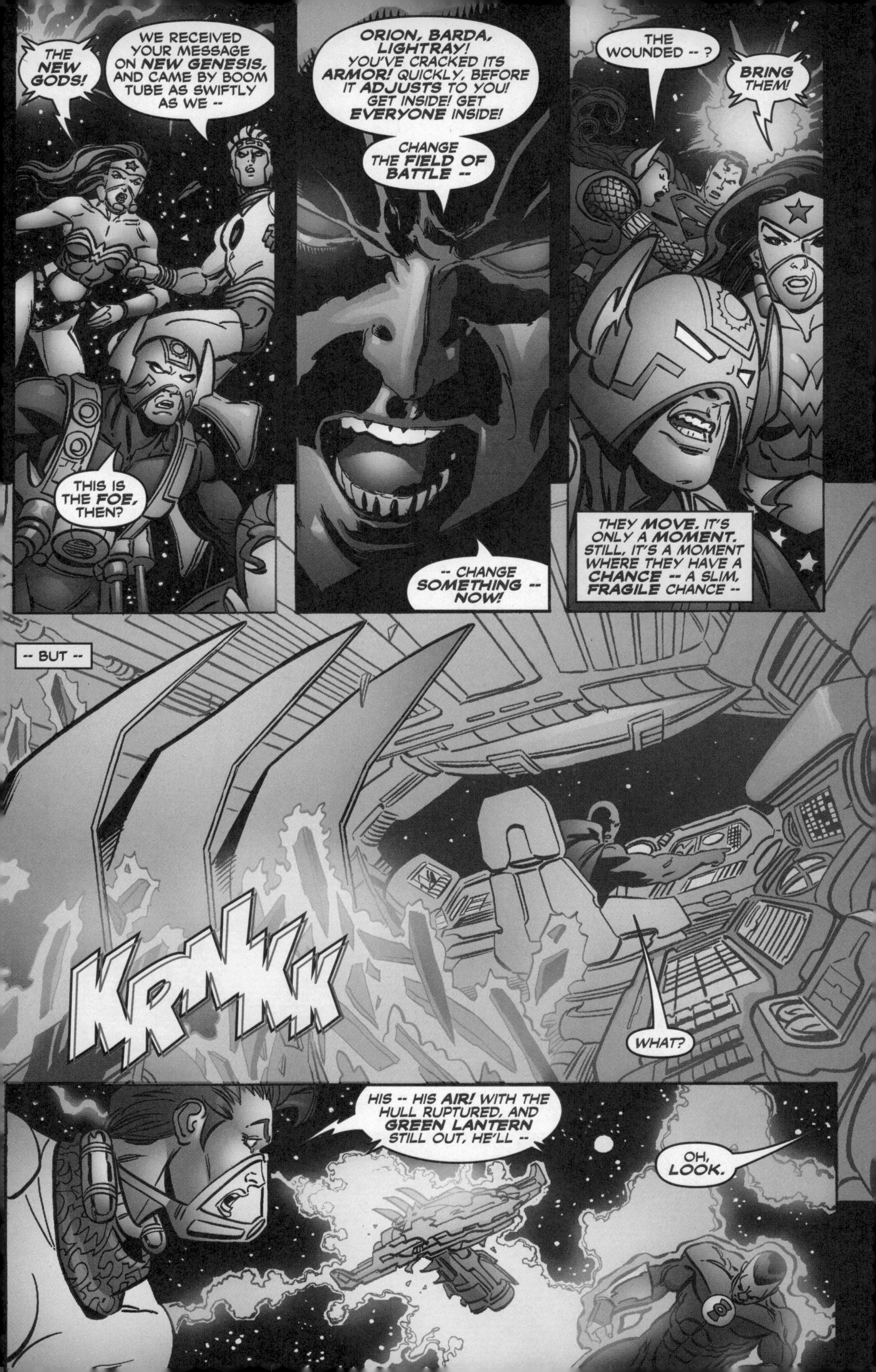
THE NEW GODS!
WE RECEIVED YOUR MESSAGE ON NEW GENESIS, AND CAME BY BOOM TUBE AS SWIFTLY AS WE --
THIS IS THE FOE, THEN?
ORION, BARDA, LIGHTRAY! YOU'VE CRACKED ITS ARMOR! QUICKLY, BEFORE IT ADJUSTS TO YOU! GET INSIDE! GET EVERYONE INSIDE!
CHANGE THE FIELD OF BATTLE --
-- CHANGE SOMETHING -- NOW!
THE WOUNDED -- ?
BRING THEM!
THEY MOVE. IT'S ONLY A MOMENT. STILL, IT'S A MOMENT WHERE THEY HAVE A CHANCE -- A SLIM, FRAGILE CHANCE --
-- BUT --
KRAKK
WHAT?
HIS -- HIS AIR! WITH THE HULL RUPTURED, AND GREEN LANTERN STILL OUT, HE'LL --
OH, LOOK.

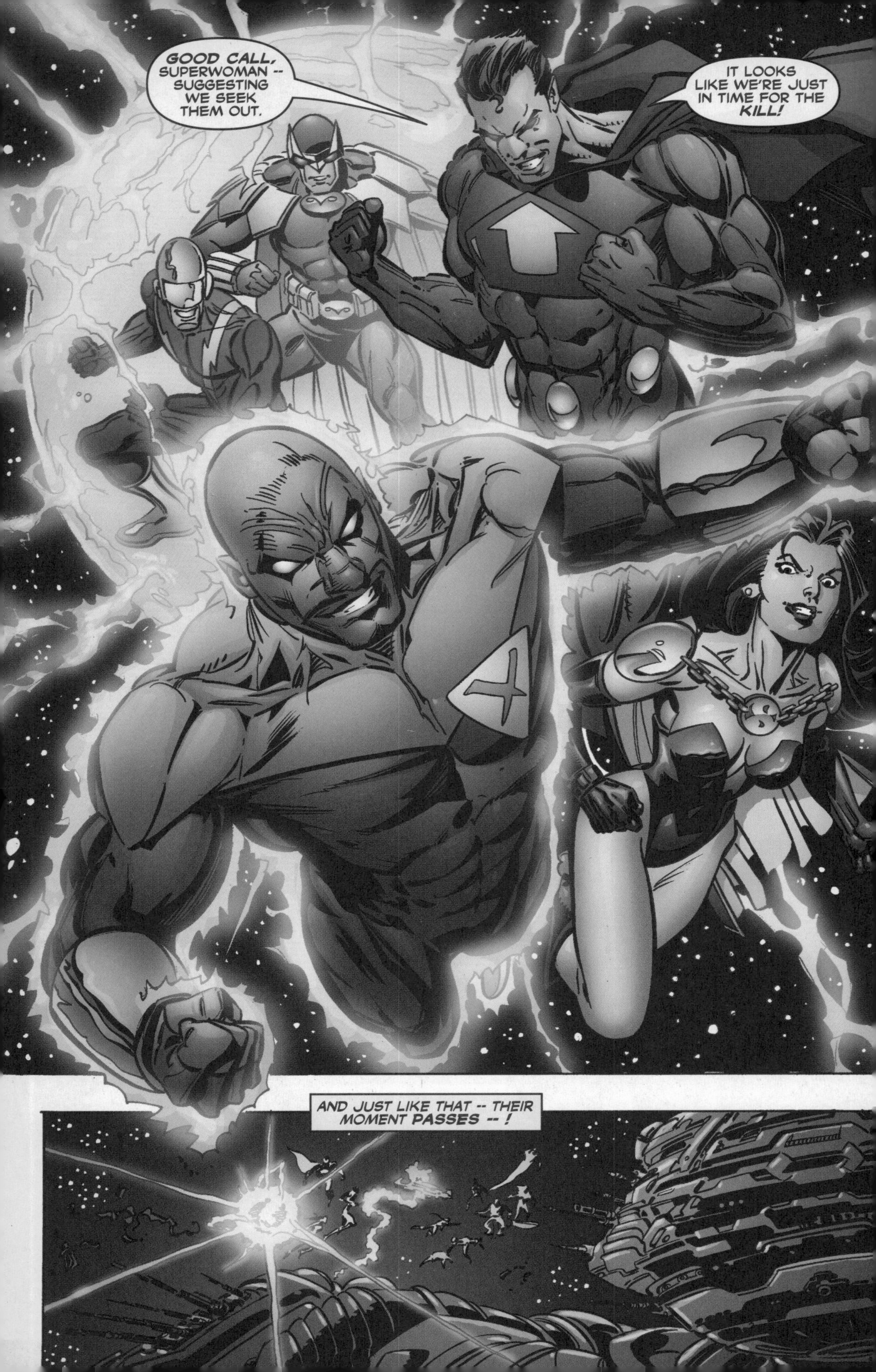
GOOD CALL, SUPERWOMAN -- SUGGESTING WE SEEK THEM OUT.
IT LOOKS LIKE WE'RE JUST IN TIME FOR THE KILL!
AND JUST LIKE THAT -- THEIR MOMENT PASSES -- !

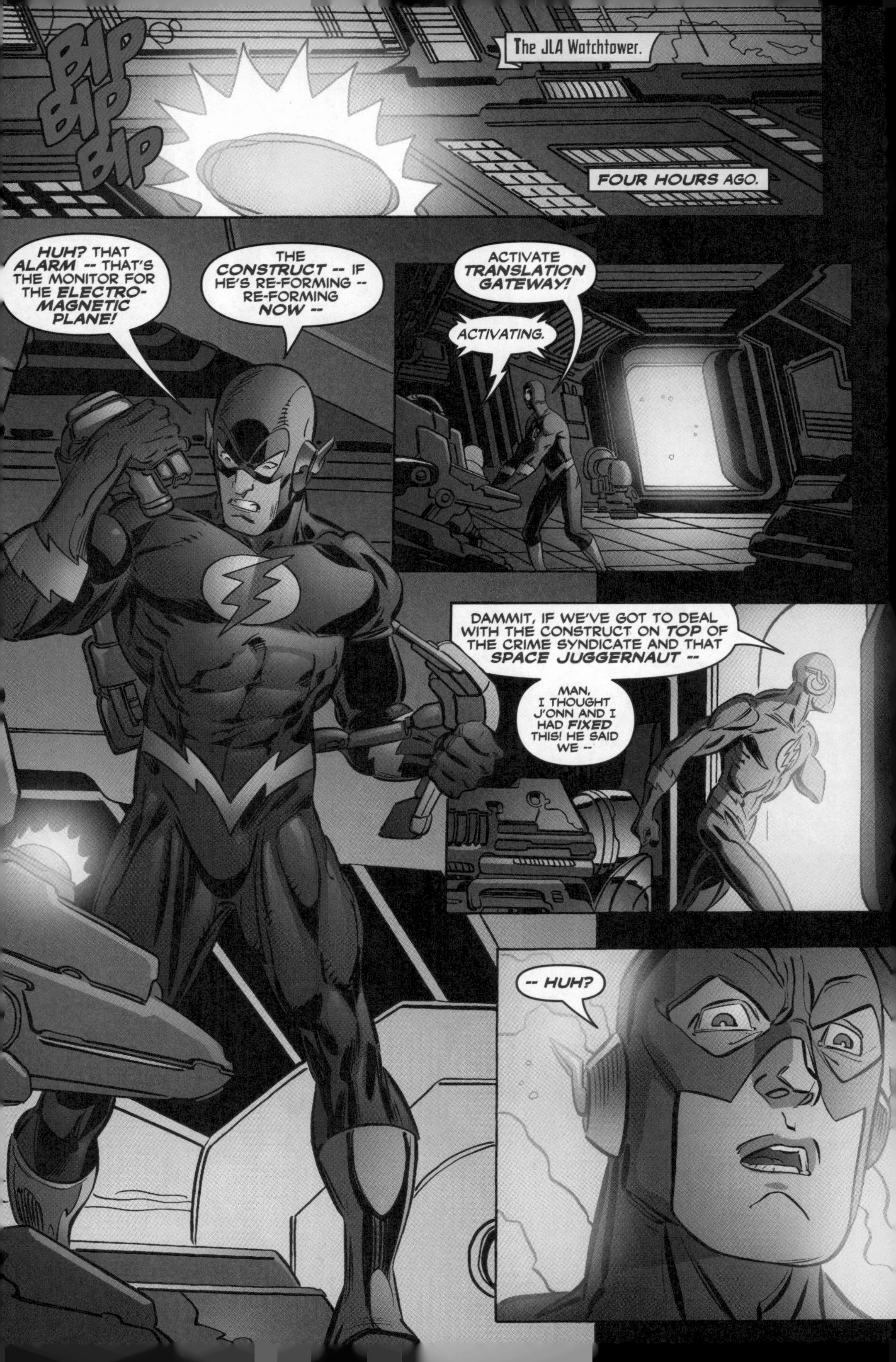
BIP BIP BIP
The JLA Watchtower.
FOUR HOURS AGO.
HUH? THAT ALARM -- THAT'S THE MONITOR FOR THE ELECTRO-MAGNETIC PLANE!
THE CONSTRUCT -- IF HE'S RE-FORMING -- RE-FORMING NOW --
ACTIVATE TRANSLATION GATEWAY!
ACTIVATING.
DAMMIT, IF WE'VE GOT TO DEAL WITH THE CONSTRUCT ON TOP OF THE CRIME SYNDICATE AND THAT SPACE JUGGERNAUT --
MAN, I THOUGHT J'ONN AND I HAD FIXED THIS! HE SAID WE --
-- HUH?

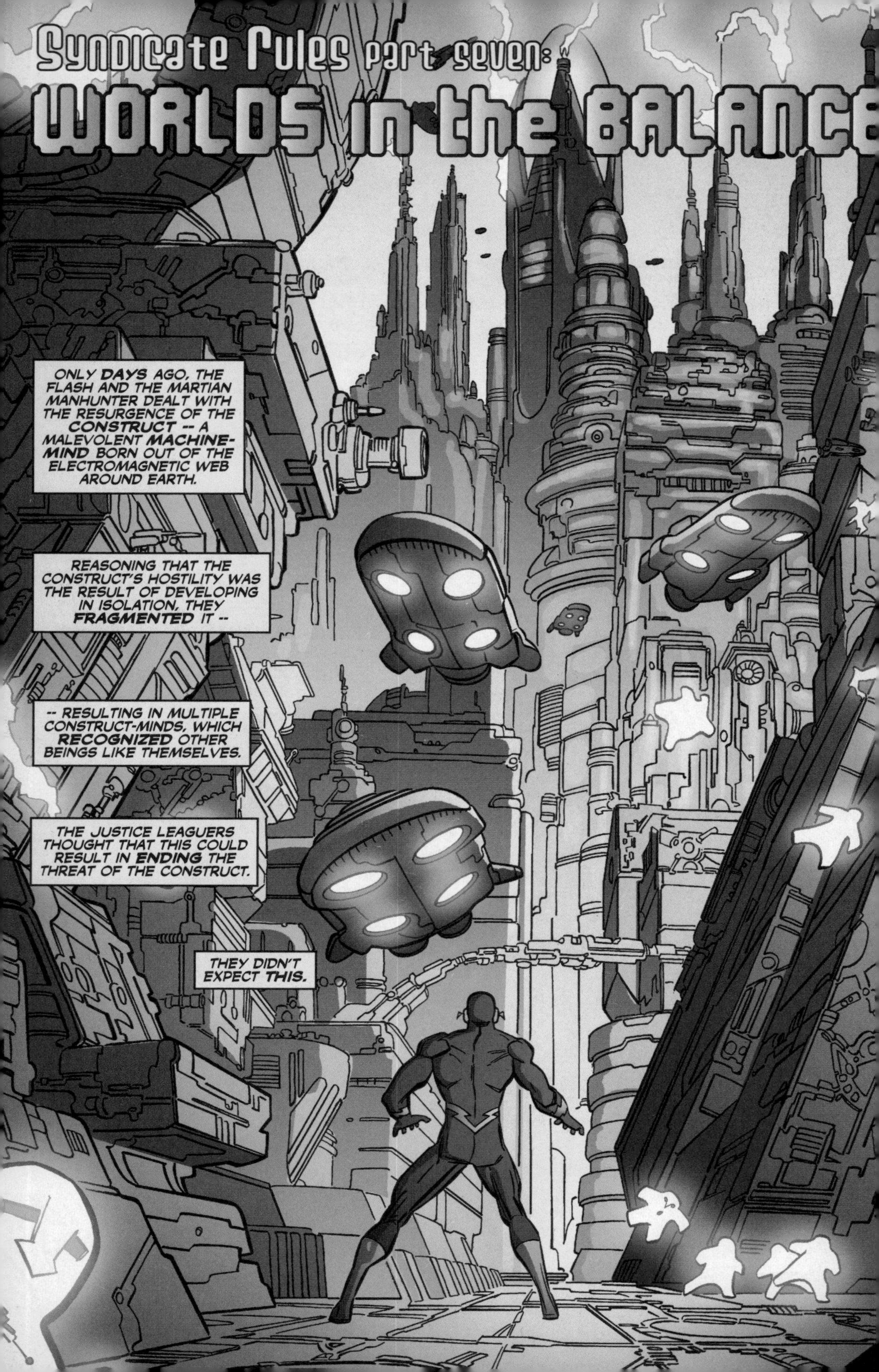
Syndicate Rules part seven:
WORLDS in the BALANCE
ONLY DAYS AGO, THE FLASH AND THE MARTIAN MANHUNTER DEALT WITH THE RESURGENCE OF THE CONSTRUCT -- A MALEVOLENT MACHINE-MIND BORN OUT OF THE ELECTROMAGNETIC WEB AROUND EARTH.
REASONING THAT THE CONSTRUCT'S HOSTILITY WAS THE RESULT OF DEVELOPING IN ISOLATION, THEY FRAGMENTED IT --
-- RESULTING IN MULTIPLE CONSTRUCT-MINDS, WHICH RECOGNIZED OTHER BEINGS LIKE THEMSELVES.
THE JUSTICE LEAGUERS THOUGHT THAT THIS COULD RESULT IN ENDING THE THREAT OF THE CONSTRUCT.
THEY DIDN'T EXPECT THIS.

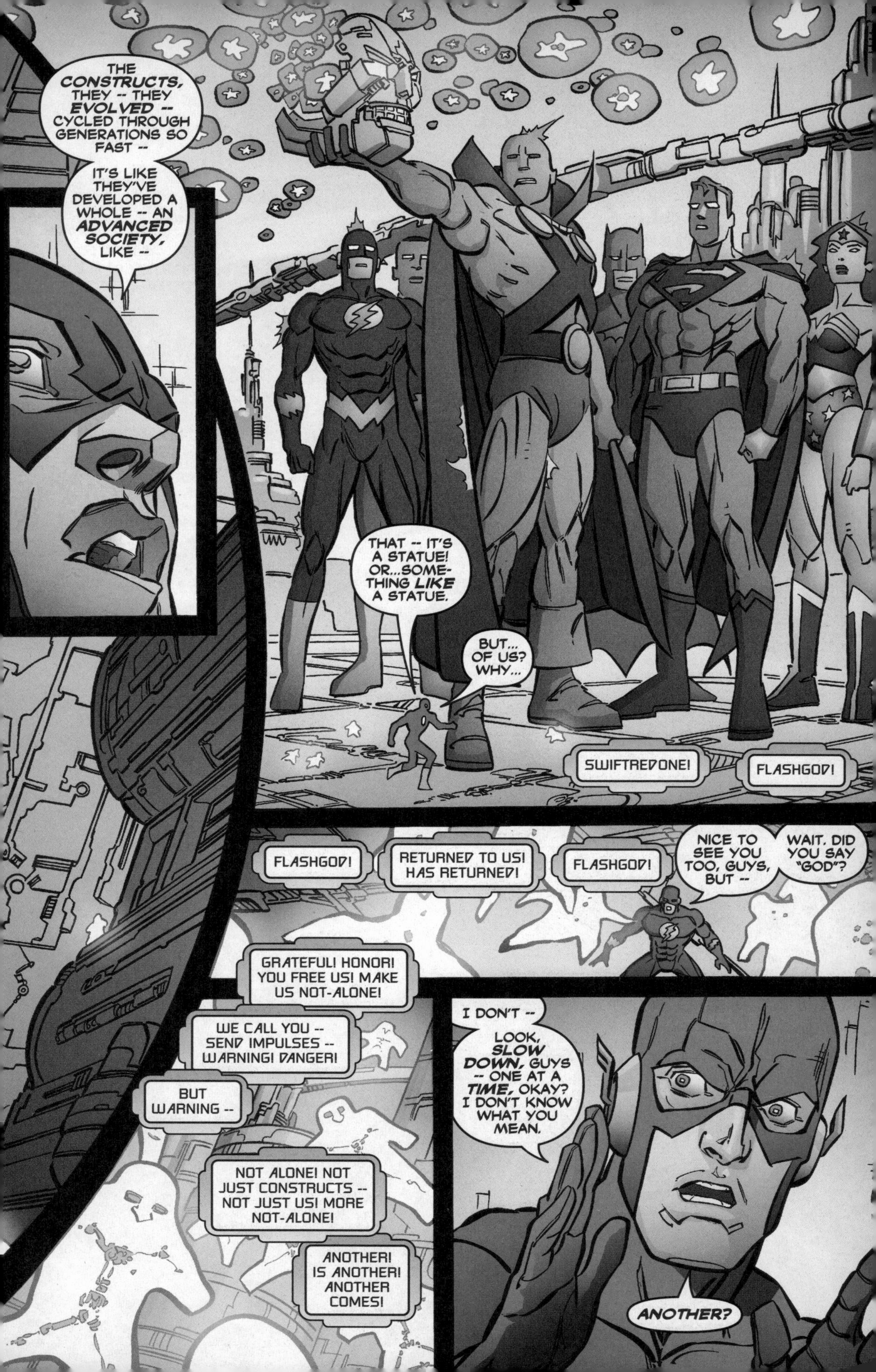
THE CONSTRUCTS, THEY -- THEY EVOLVED -- CYCLED THROUGH GENERATIONS SO FAST --
IT'S LIKE THEY'VE DEVELOPED A WHOLE -- AN ADVANCED SOCIETY, LIKE --
THAT -- IT'S A STATUE! OR...SOMETHING LIKE A STATUE.
BUT... OF US? WHY...
SWIFTREDONE!
FLASHGOD!
FLASHGOD!
RETURNED TO US! HAS RETURNED!
FLASHGOD!
NICE TO SEE YOU TOO, GUYS, BUT --
WAIT. DID YOU SAY "GOD"?
GRATEFUL! HONOR! YOU FREE US! MAKE US NOT-ALONE!
WE CALL YOU -- SEND IMPULSES -- WARNING! DANGER!
BUT WARNING --
NOT ALONE! NOT JUST CONSTRUCTS -- NOT JUST US! MORE NOT-ALONE!
ANOTHER! IS ANOTHER! ANOTHER COMES!
I DON'T --
LOOK, SLOW DOWN, GUYS -- ONE AT A TIME, OKAY? I DON'T KNOW WHAT YOU MEAN.
ANOTHER?

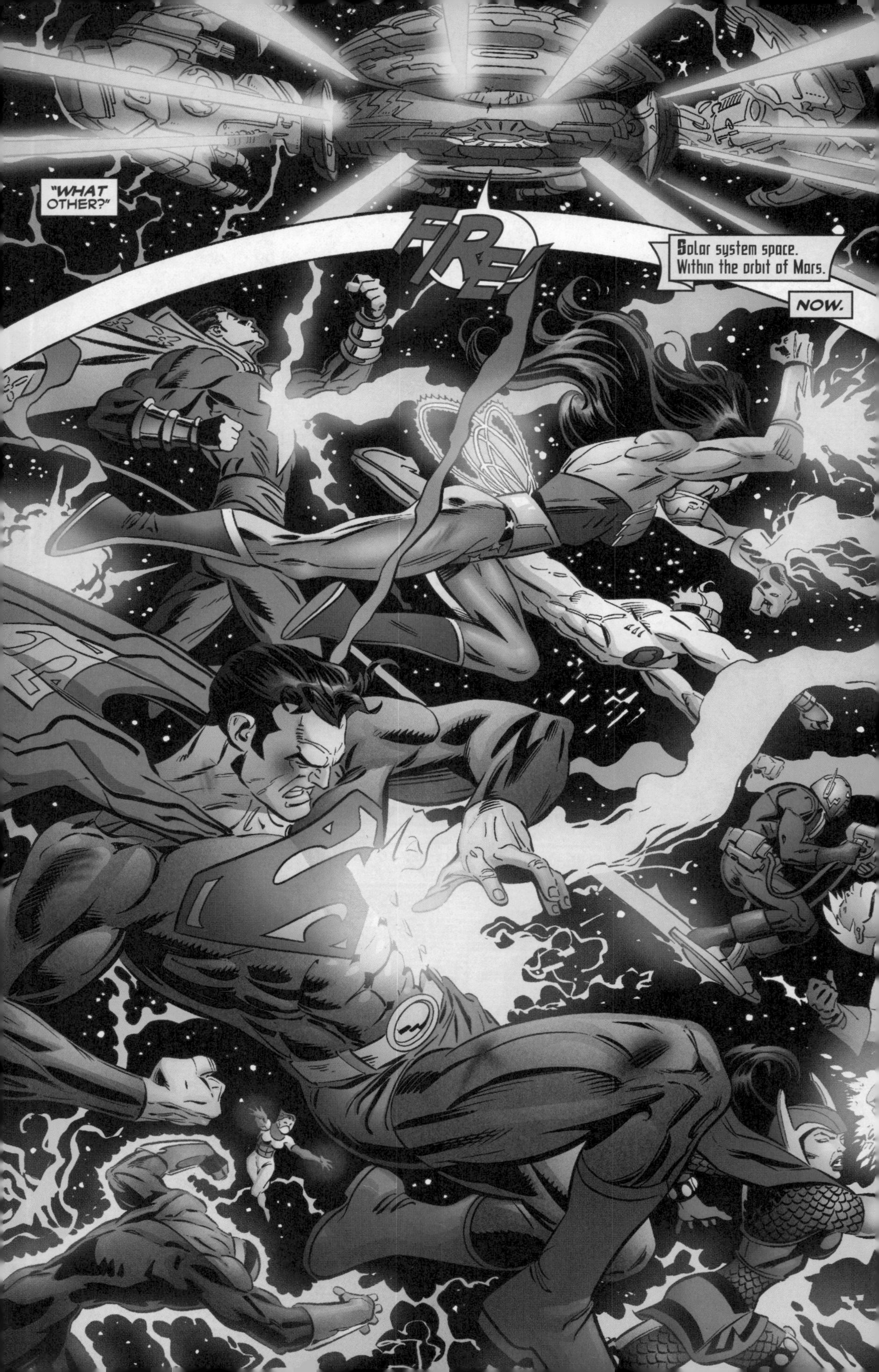
"WHAT OTHER?"
FIRE!
Solar system space. Within the orbit of Mars.
NOW.

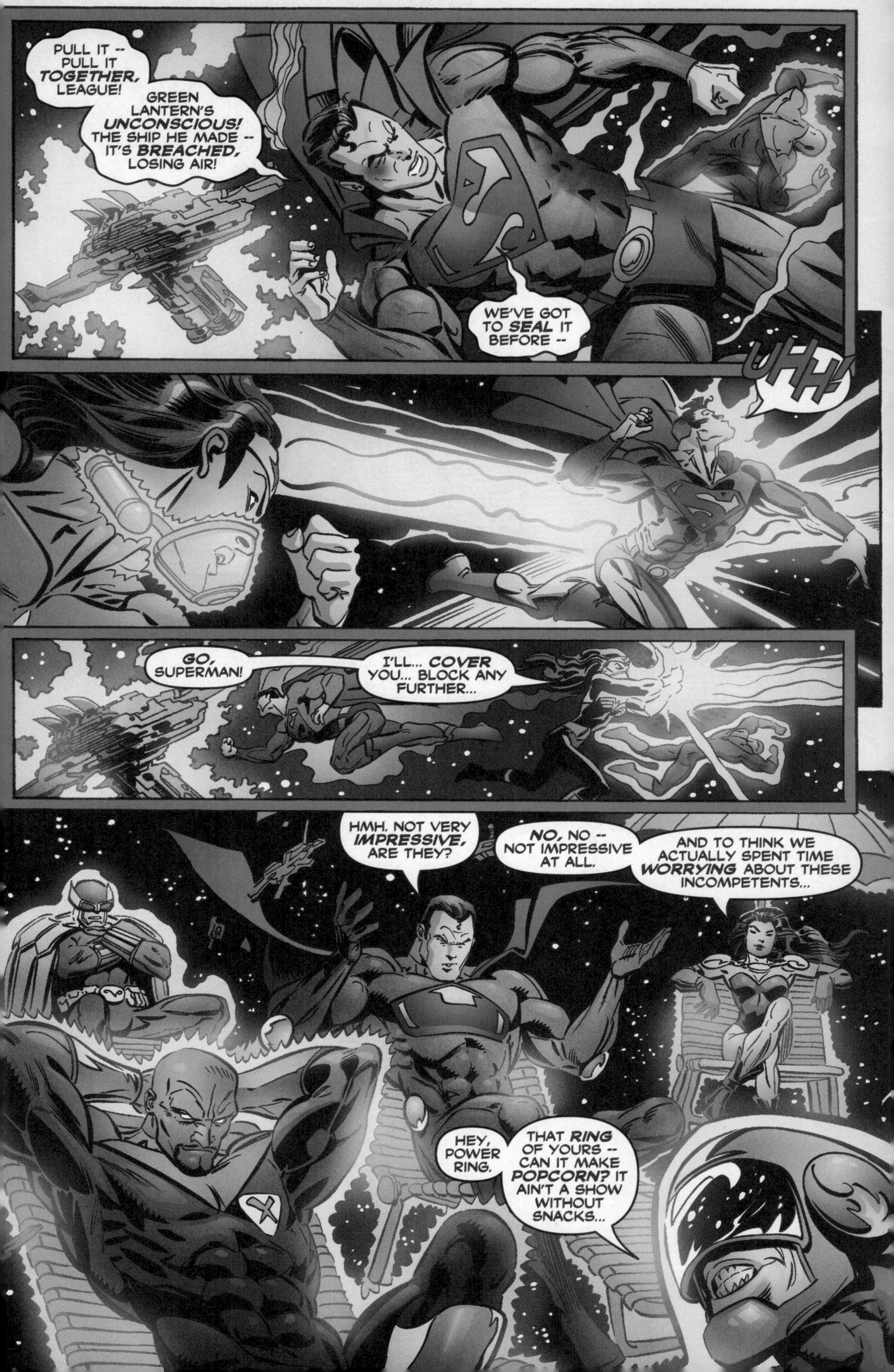
PULL IT -- PULL IT TOGETHER, LEAGUE!
GREEN LANTERN'S UNCONSCIOUS! THE SHIP HE MADE -- IT'S BREACHED, LOSING AIR!
WE'VE GOT TO SEAL IT BEFORE --
UHH!
GO, SUPERMAN!
I'LL... COVER YOU... BLOCK ANY FURTHER...
HMH. NOT VERY IMPRESSIVE, ARE THEY?
NO, NO -- NOT IMPRESSIVE AT ALL.
AND TO THINK WE ACTUALLY SPENT TIME WORRYING ABOUT THESE INCOMPETENTS...
HEY, POWER RING.
THAT RING OF YOURS -- CAN IT MAKE POPCORN? IT AIN'T A SHOW WITHOUT SNACKS...

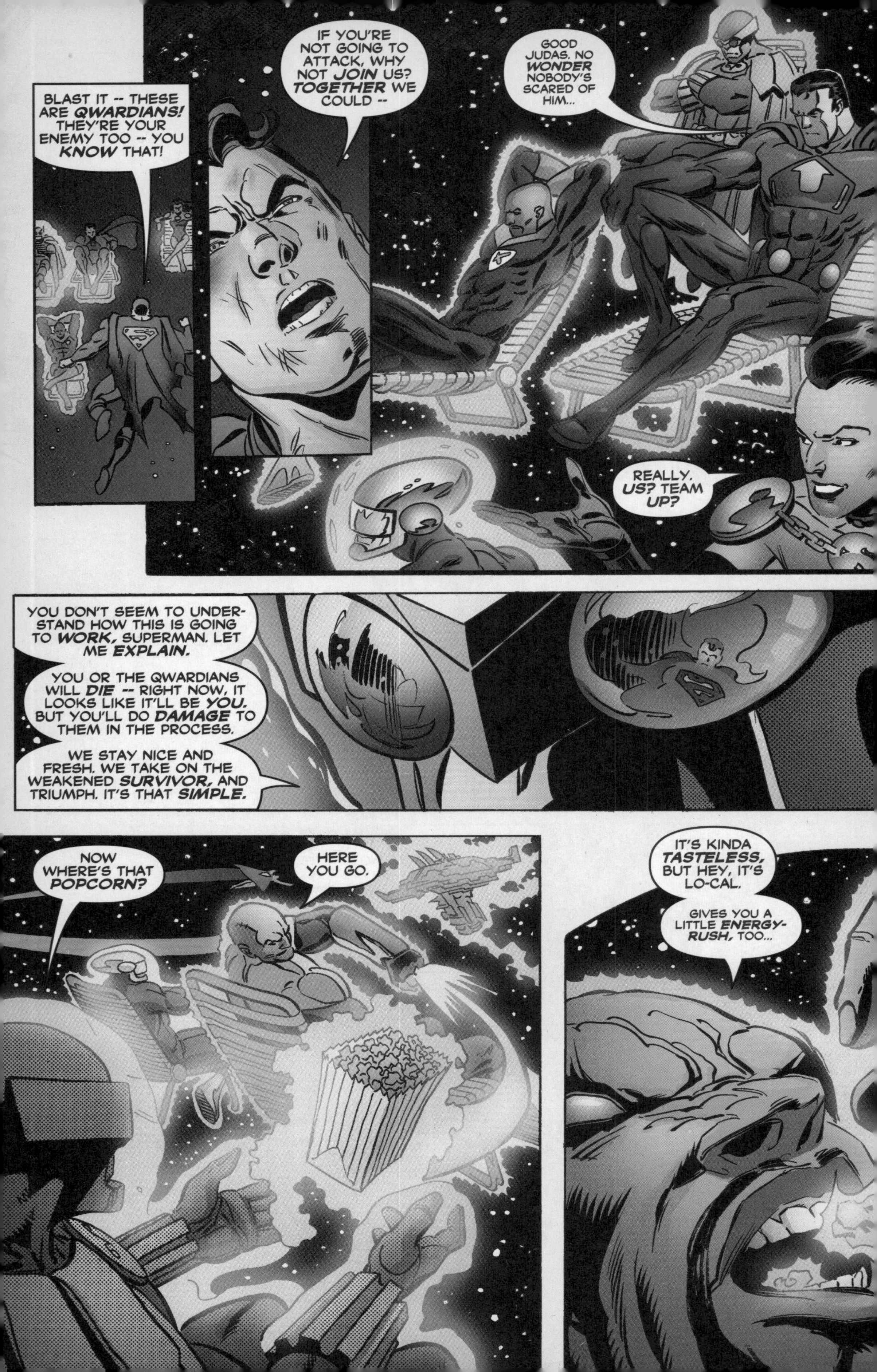
BLAST IT -- THESE ARE QWARDIANS! THEY'RE YOUR ENEMY TOO -- YOU KNOW THAT!
IF YOU'RE NOT GOING TO ATTACK, WHY NOT JOIN US? TOGETHER WE COULD --
GOOD JUDAS. NO WONDER NOBODY'S SCARED OF HIM...
REALLY. US? TEAM UP?
YOU DON'T SEEM TO UNDERSTAND HOW THIS IS GOING TO WORK, SUPERMAN. LET ME EXPLAIN.
YOU OR THE QWARDIANS WILL DIE -- RIGHT NOW, IT LOOKS LIKE IT'LL BE YOU. BUT YOU'LL DO DAMAGE TO THEM IN THE PROCESS.
WE STAY NICE AND FRESH. WE TAKE ON THE WEAKENED SURVIVOR, AND TRIUMPH. IT'S THAT SIMPLE.
NOW WHERE'S THAT POPCORN?
HERE YOU GO.
IT'S KINDA TASTELESS, BUT HEY, IT'S LO-CAL.
GIVES YOU A LITTLE ENERGY-RUSH, TOO...

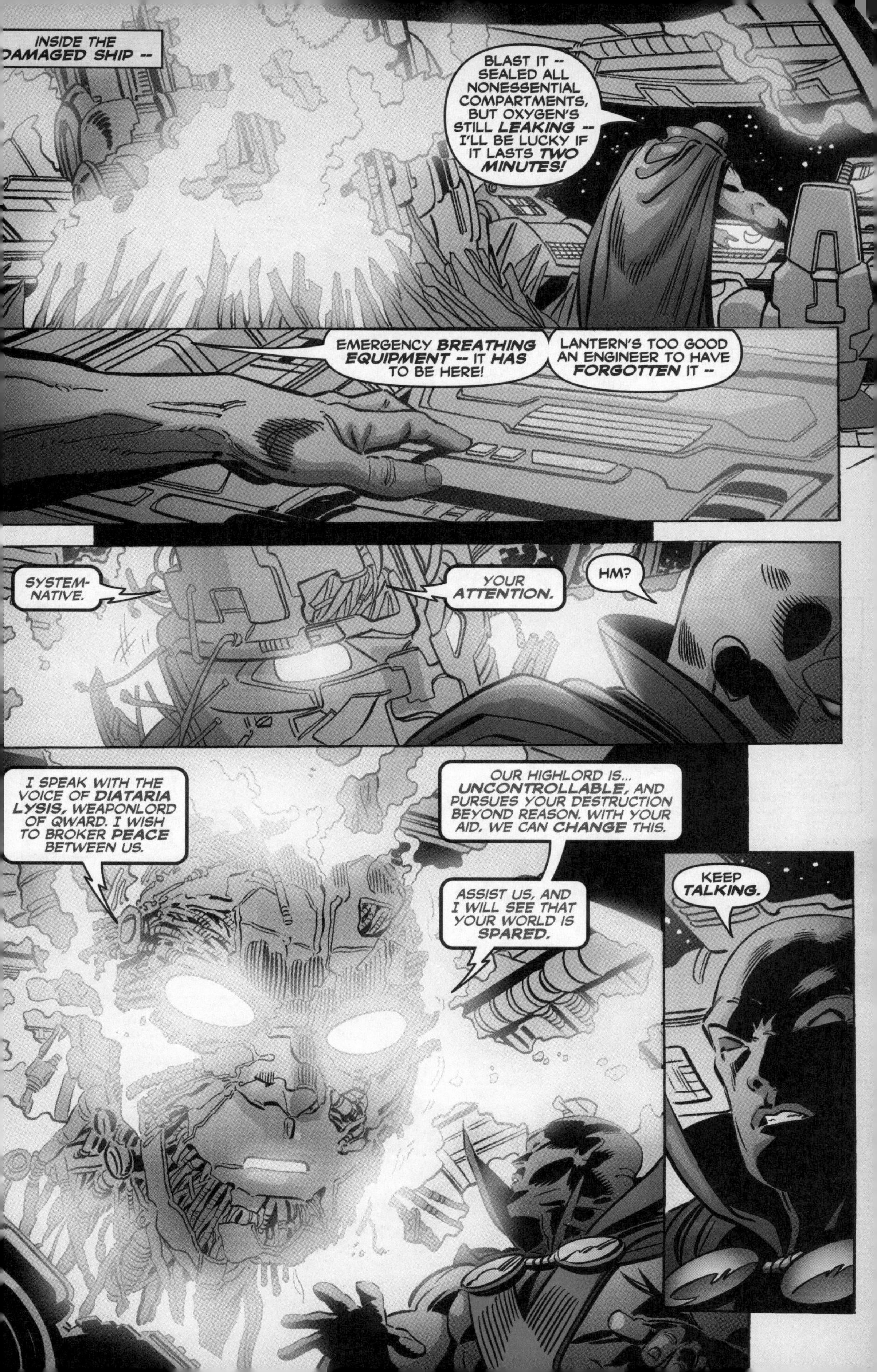
INSIDE THE DAMAGED SHIP --
BLAST IT -- SEALED ALL NONESSENTIAL COMPARTMENTS, BUT OXYGEN'S STILL LEAKING -- I'LL BE LUCKY IF IT LASTS TWO MINUTES!
EMERGENCY BREATHING EQUIPMENT -- IT HAS TO BE HERE!
LANTERN'S TOO GOOD AN ENGINEER TO HAVE FORGOTTEN IT --
SYSTEM-NATIVE.
YOUR ATTENTION.
HM?
I SPEAK WITH THE VOICE OF DIATARIA LYSIS, WEAPONLORD OF QWARD. I WISH TO BROKER PEACE BETWEEN US.
OUR HIGHLORD IS... UNCONTROLLABLE, AND PURSUES YOUR DESTRUCTION BEYOND REASON. WITH YOUR AID, WE CAN CHANGE THIS.
ASSIST US, AND I WILL SEE THAT YOUR WORLD IS SPARED.
KEEP TALKING.

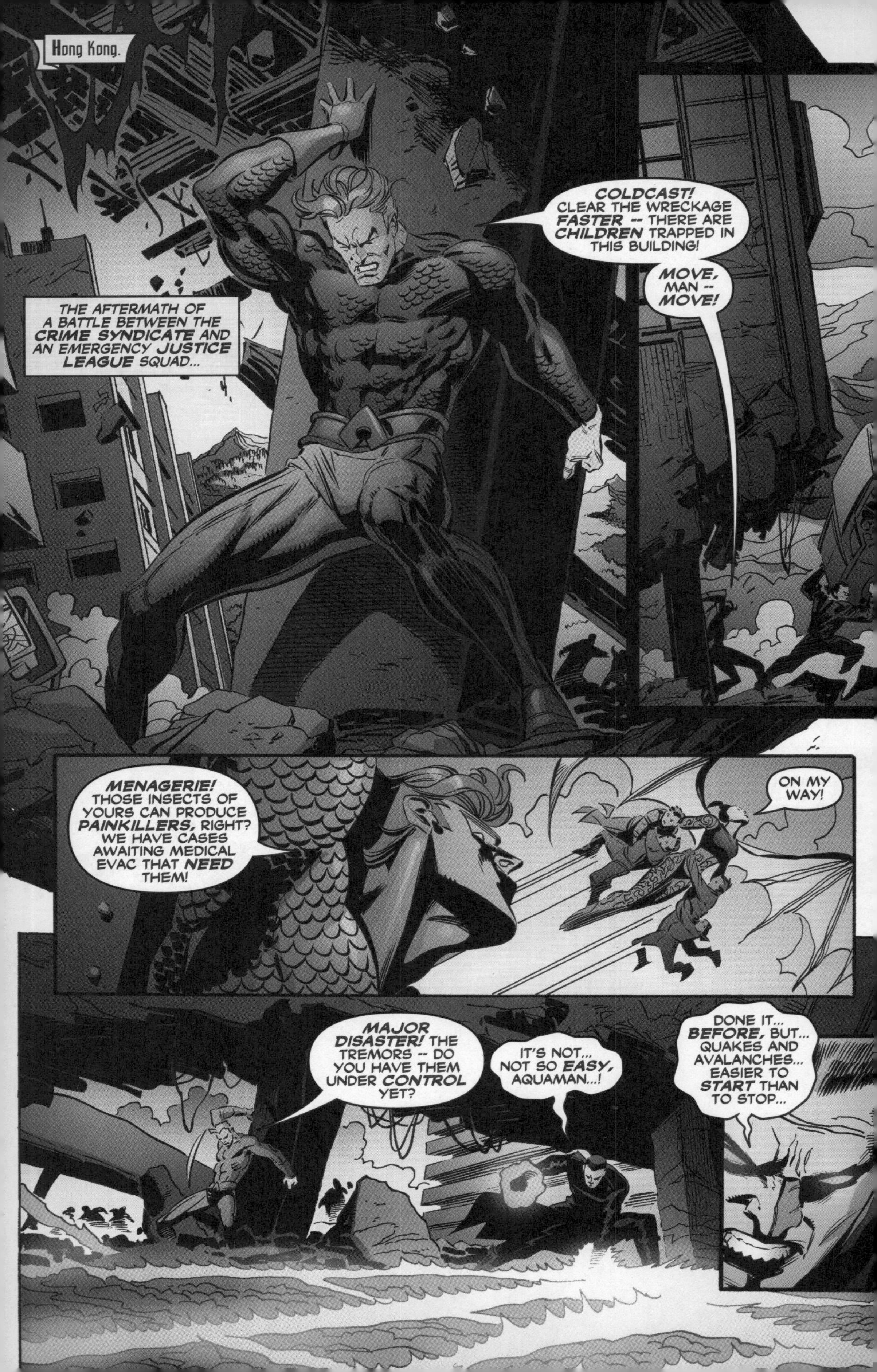
Hong Kong.
THE AFTERMATH OF A BATTLE BETWEEN THE CRIME SYNDICATE AND AN EMERGENCY JUSTICE LEAGUE SQUAD...
COLDCAST! CLEAR THE WRECKAGE FASTER -- THERE ARE CHILDREN TRAPPED IN THIS BUILDING!
MOVE, MAN -- MOVE!
MENAGERIE! THOSE INSECTS OF YOURS CAN PRODUCE PAINKILLERS, RIGHT? WE HAVE CASES AWAITING MEDICAL EVAC THAT NEED THEM!
ON MY WAY!
MAJOR DISASTER! THE TREMORS -- DO YOU HAVE THEM UNDER CONTROL YET?
IT'S NOT... NOT SO EASY, AQUAMAN...!
DONE IT... BEFORE, BUT... QUAKES AND AVALANCHES... EASIER TO START THAN TO STOP...

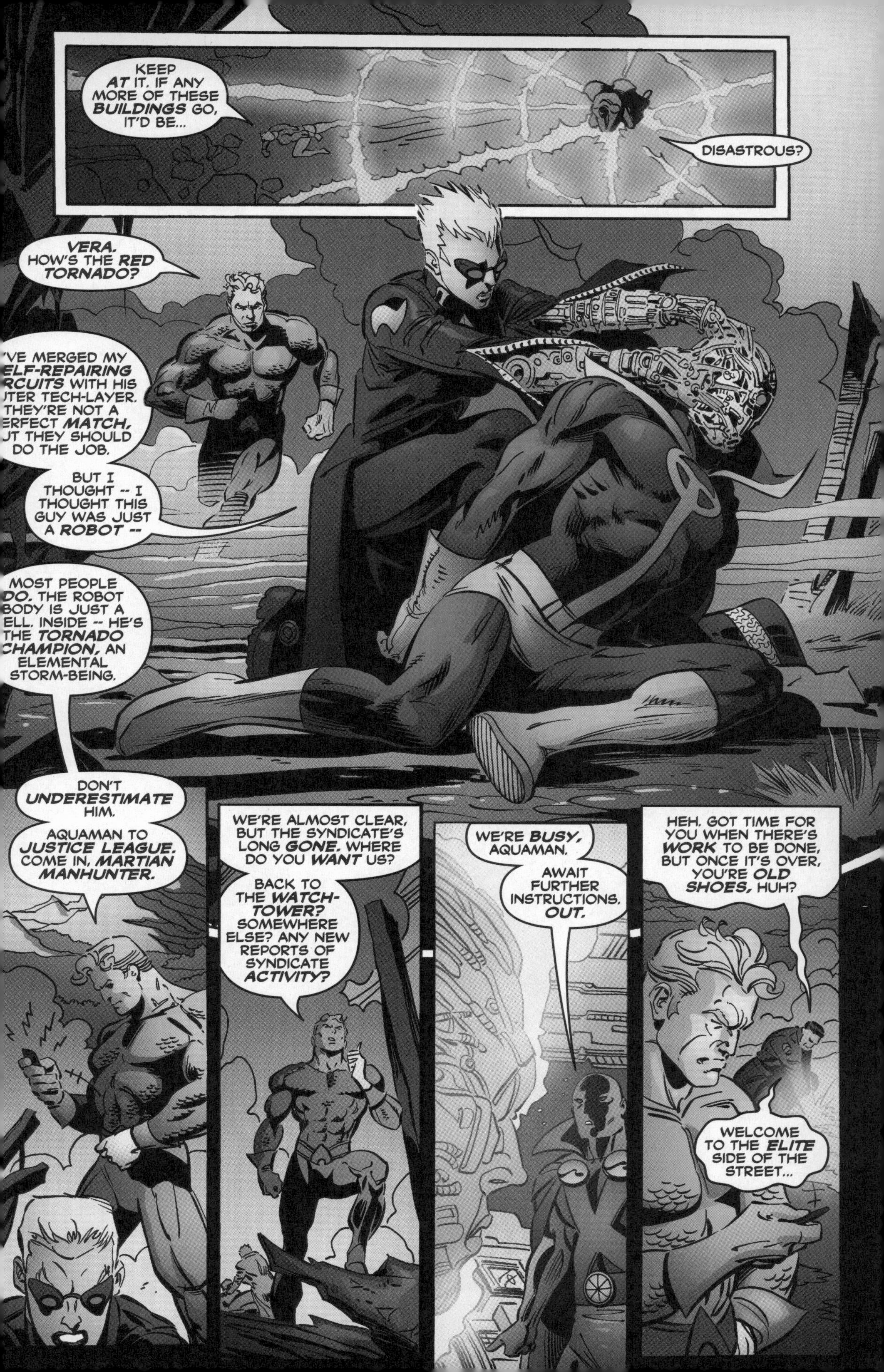
KEEP AT IT. IF ANY MORE OF THESE BUILDINGS GO, IT'D BE...
DISASTROUS?
VERA. HOW'S THE RED TORNADO?
'VE MERGED MY ELF-REPAIRING RCUITS WITH HIS UTER TECH-LAYER. THEY'RE NOT A ERFECT MATCH, UT THEY SHOULD DO THE JOB.
BUT I THOUGHT -- I THOUGHT THIS GUY WAS JUST A ROBOT --
MOST PEOPLE DO. THE ROBOT BODY IS JUST A ELL. INSIDE -- HE'S THE TORNADO CHAMPION, AN ELEMENTAL STORM-BEING.
DON'T UNDERESTIMATE HIM.
AQUAMAN TO JUSTICE LEAGUE. COME IN, MARTIAN MANHUNTER.
WE'RE ALMOST CLEAR, BUT THE SYNDICATE'S LONG GONE. WHERE DO YOU WANT US?
BACK TO THE WATCH-TOWER? SOMEWHERE ELSE? ANY NEW REPORTS OF SYNDICATE ACTIVITY?
WE'RE BUSY, AQUAMAN.
AWAIT FURTHER INSTRUCTIONS. OUT.
HEH. GOT TIME FOR YOU WHEN THERE'S WORK TO BE DONE, BUT ONCE IT'S OVER, YOU'RE OLD SHOES, HUH?
WELCOME TO THE ELITE SIDE OF THE STREET...

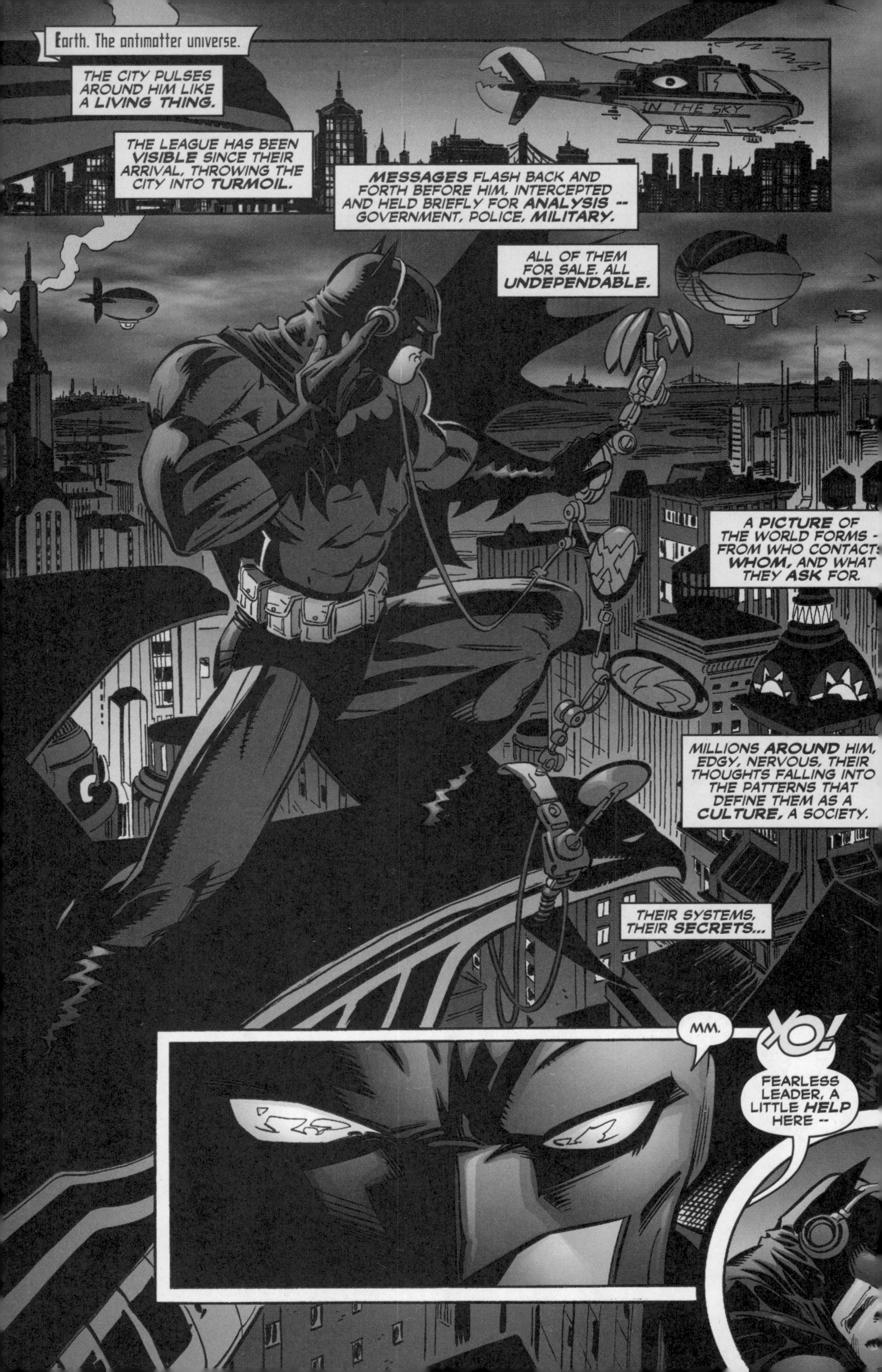
Earth. The antimatter universe.
THE CITY PULSES AROUND HIM LIKE A LIVING THING.
THE LEAGUE HAS BEEN VISIBLE SINCE THEIR ARRIVAL, THROWING THE CITY INTO TURMOIL.
IN THE SKY
MESSAGES FLASH BACK AND FORTH BEFORE HIM, INTERCEPTED AND HELD BRIEFLY FOR ANALYSIS -- GOVERNMENT, POLICE, MILITARY.
ALL OF THEM FOR SALE. ALL UNDEPENDABLE.
A PICTURE OF THE WORLD FORMS - FROM WHO CONTACTS WHOM, AND WHAT THEY ASK FOR.
MILLIONS AROUND HIM, EDGY, NERVOUS, THEIR THOUGHTS FALLING INTO THE PATTERNS THAT DEFINE THEM AS A CULTURE, A SOCIETY.
THEIR SYSTEMS, THEIR SECRETS...
MM.
YO!
FEARLESS LEADER, A LITTLE HELP HERE --

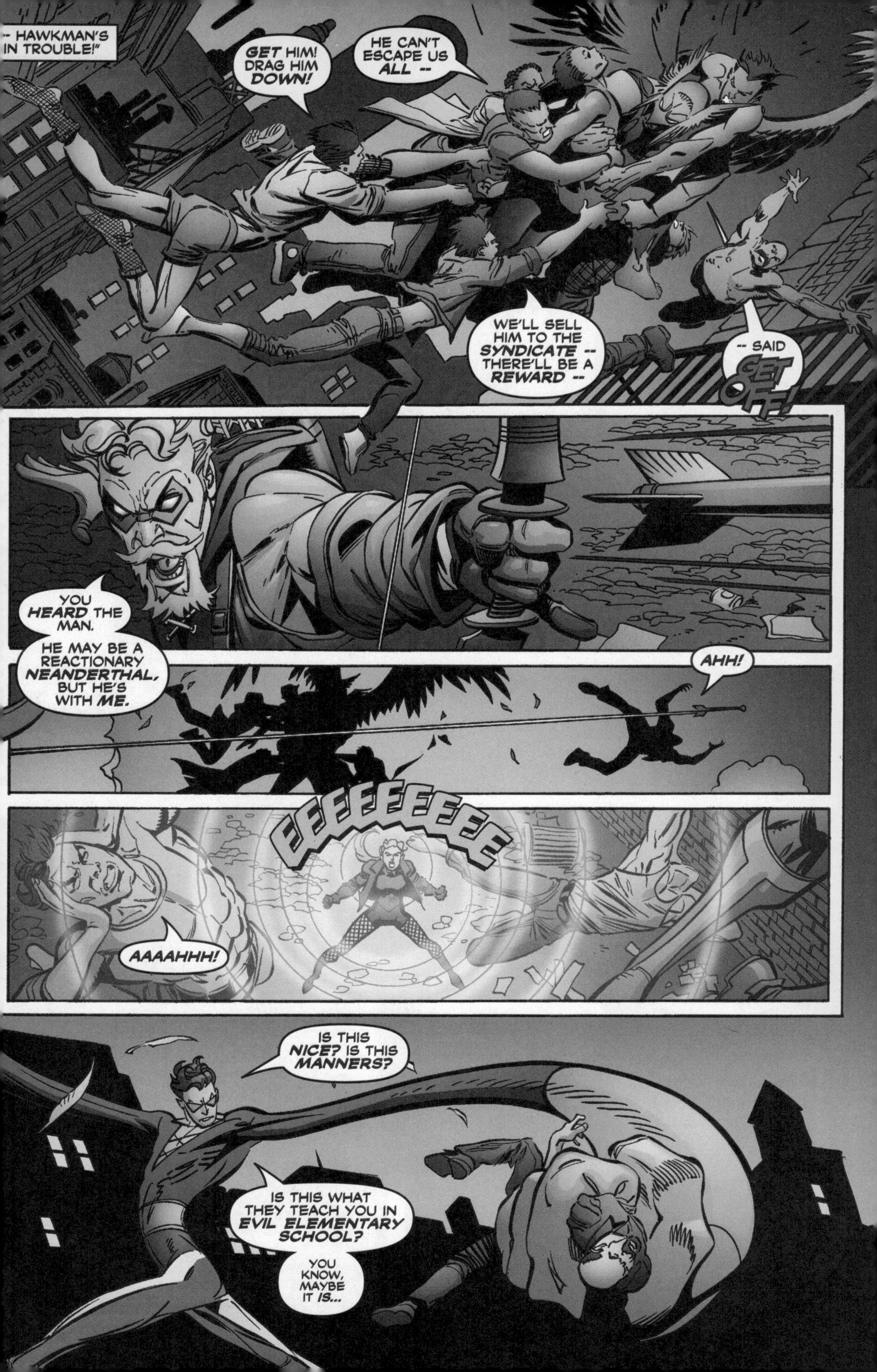
-- HAWKMAN'S IN TROUBLE!"
GET HIM! DRAG HIM DOWN!
HE CAN'T ESCAPE US ALL --
WE'LL SELL HIM TO THE SYNDICATE -- THERE'LL BE A REWARD --
-- SAID GET OFF!
YOU HEARD THE MAN.
HE MAY BE A REACTIONARY NEANDERTHAL, BUT HE'S WITH ME.
AHH!
EEEEEEEEE
AAAAHHH!
IS THIS NICE? IS THIS MANNERS?
IS THIS WHAT THEY TEACH YOU IN EVIL ELEMENTARY SCHOOL?
YOU KNOW, MAYBE IT IS...

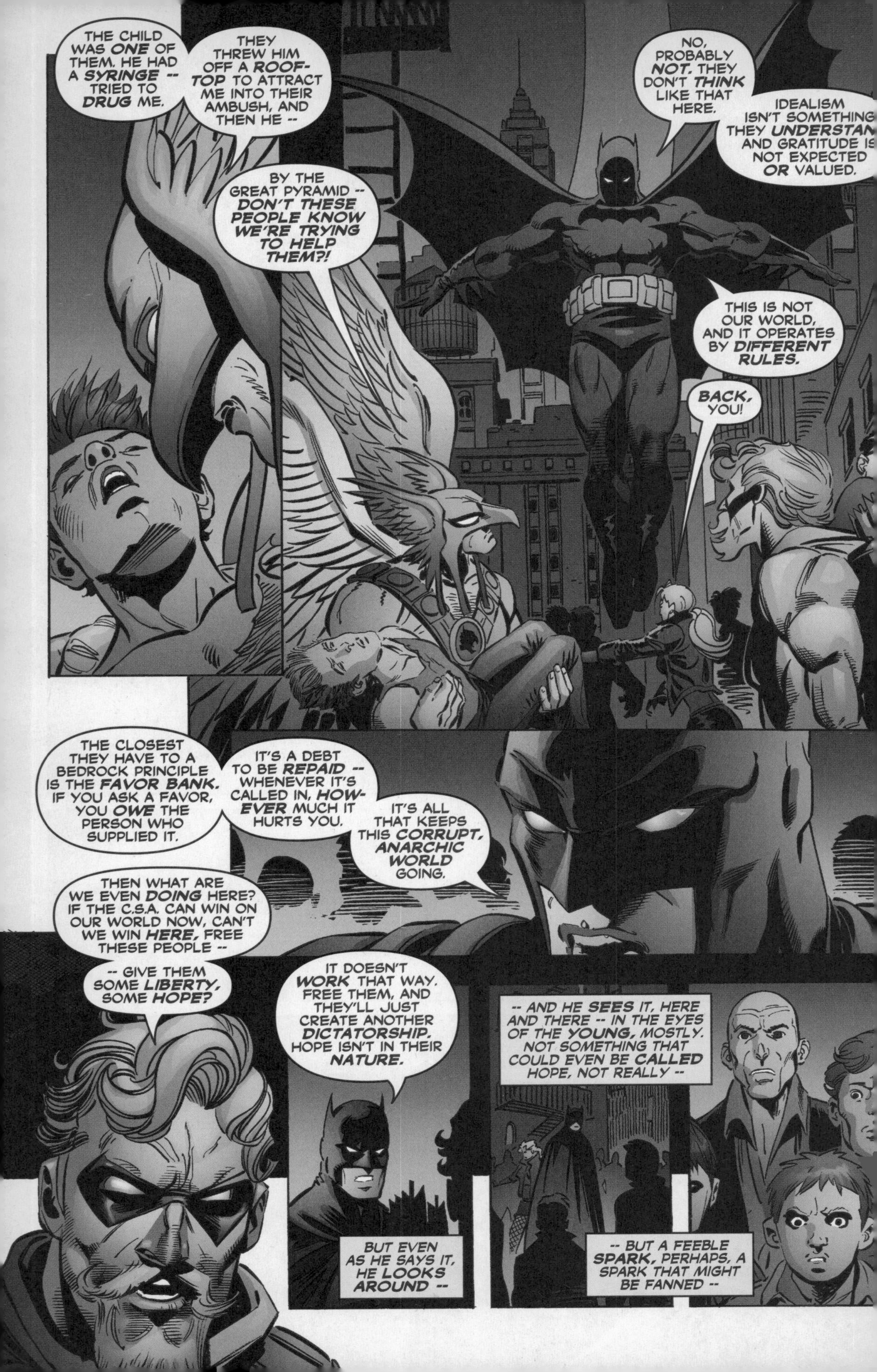
THE CHILD WAS ONE OF THEM. HE HAD A SYRINGE -- TRIED TO DRUG ME.
THEY THREW HIM OFF A ROOF-TOP TO ATTRACT ME INTO THEIR AMBUSH, AND THEN HE --
BY THE GREAT PYRAMID -- DON'T THESE PEOPLE KNOW WE'RE TRYING TO HELP THEM?!
NO, PROBABLY NOT. THEY DON'T THINK LIKE THAT HERE.
IDEALISM ISN'T SOMETHING THEY UNDERSTAN AND GRATITUDE IS NOT EXPECTED OR VALUED.
THIS IS NOT OUR WORLD, AND IT OPERATES BY DIFFERENT RULES.
BACK, YOU!
THE CLOSEST THEY HAVE TO A BEDROCK PRINCIPLE IS THE FAVOR BANK. IF YOU ASK A FAVOR, YOU OWE THE PERSON WHO SUPPLIED IT.
IT'S A DEBT TO BE REPAID -- WHENEVER IT'S CALLED IN, HOW-EVER MUCH IT HURTS YOU.
IT'S ALL THAT KEEPS THIS CORRUPT, ANARCHIC WORLD GOING.
THEN WHAT ARE WE EVEN DOING HERE? IF THE C.S.A. CAN WIN ON OUR WORLD NOW, CAN'T WE WIN HERE, FREE THESE PEOPLE --
-- GIVE THEM SOME LIBERTY, SOME HOPE?
IT DOESN'T WORK THAT WAY. FREE THEM, AND THEY'LL JUST CREATE ANOTHER DICTATORSHIP. HOPE ISN'T IN THEIR NATURE.
BUT EVEN AS HE SAYS IT, HE LOOKS AROUND --
-- AND HE SEES IT, HERE AND THERE -- IN THE EYES OF THE YOUNG, MOSTLY. NOT SOMETHING THAT COULD EVEN BE CALLED HOPE, NOT REALLY --
-- BUT A FEEBLE SPARK, PERHAPS, A SPARK THAT MIGHT BE FANNED --

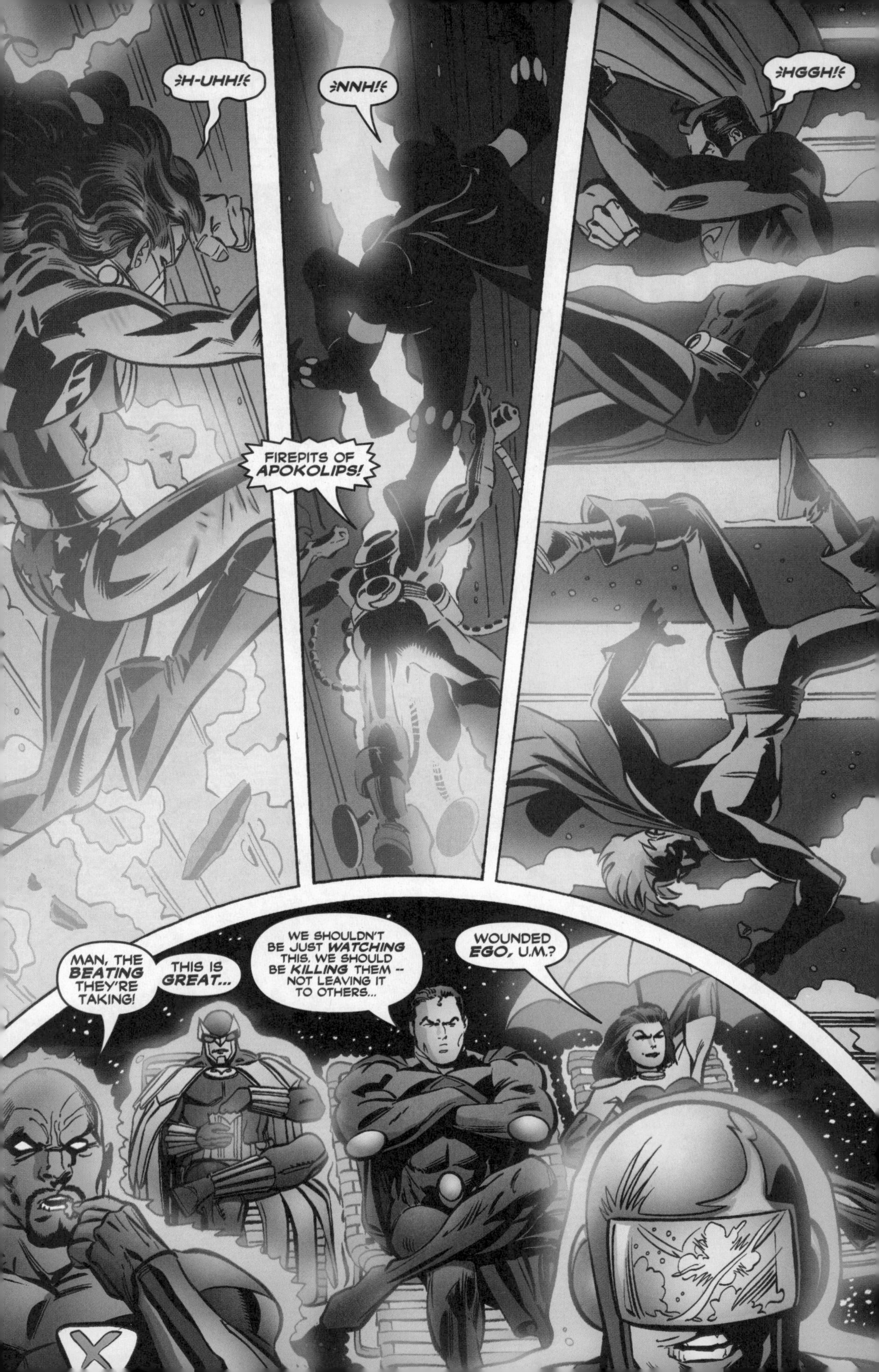
H-UHH!
NNH!
HGGH!
FIREPITS OF APOKOLIPS!
MAN, THE BEATING THEY'RE TAKING!
THIS IS GREAT...
WE SHOULDN'T BE JUST WATCHING THIS. WE SHOULD BE KILLING THEM -- NOT LEAVING IT TO OTHERS...
WOUNDED EGO, U.M.?

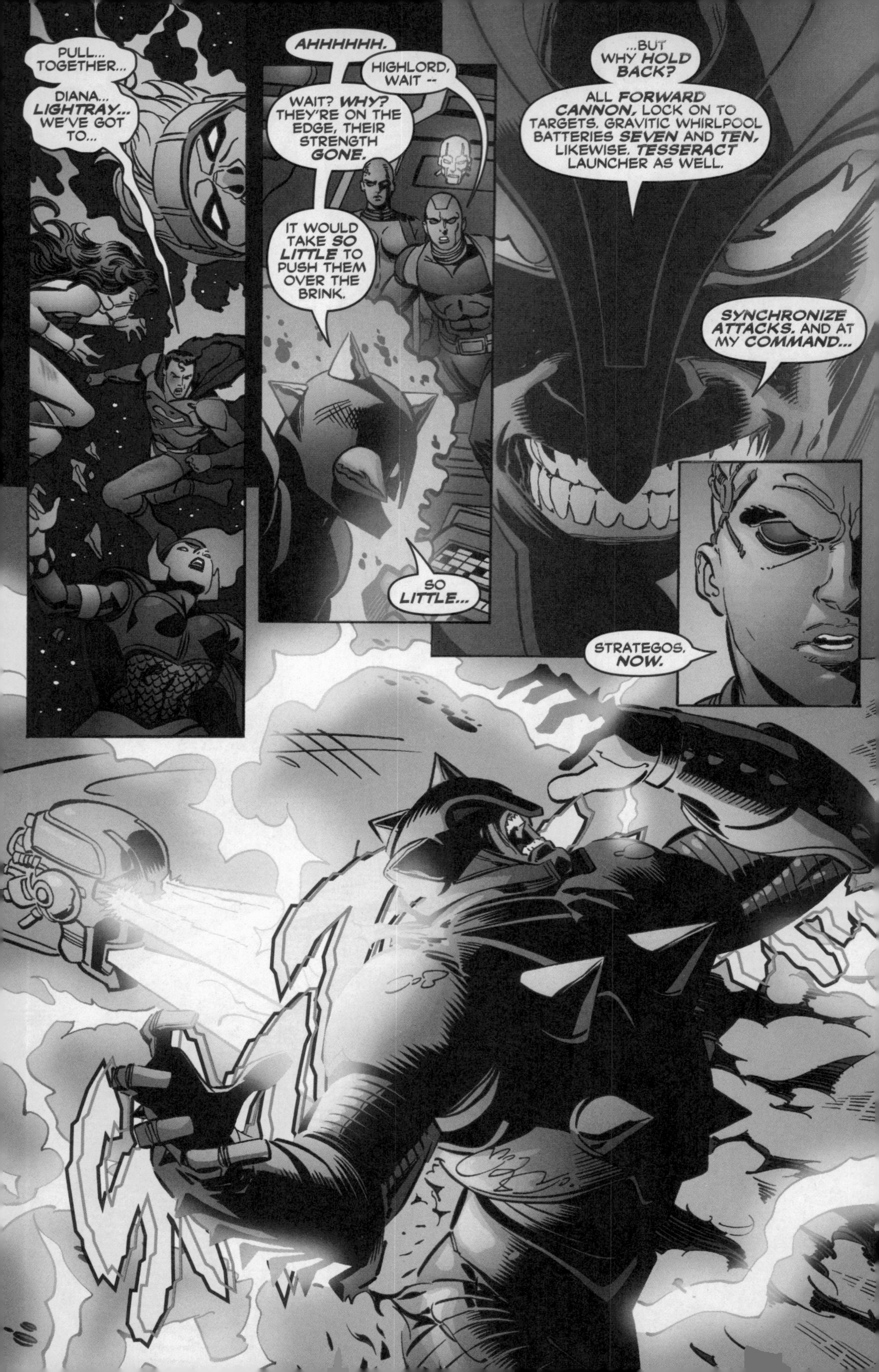
PULL... TOGETHER...
DIANA... LIGHTRAY... WE'VE GOT TO...
AHHHHHH.
HIGHLORD, WAIT --
WAIT? WHY? THEY'RE ON THE EDGE, THEIR STRENGTH GONE.
IT WOULD TAKE SO LITTLE TO PUSH THEM OVER THE BRINK.
SO LITTLE...
...BUT WHY HOLD BACK?
ALL FORWARD CANNON, LOCK ON TO TARGETS. GRAVITIC WHIRLPOOL BATTERIES SEVEN AND TEN, LIKEWISE. TESSERACT LAUNCHER AS WELL.
SYNCHRONIZE ATTACKS. AND AT MY COMMAND...
STRATEGOS. NOW.

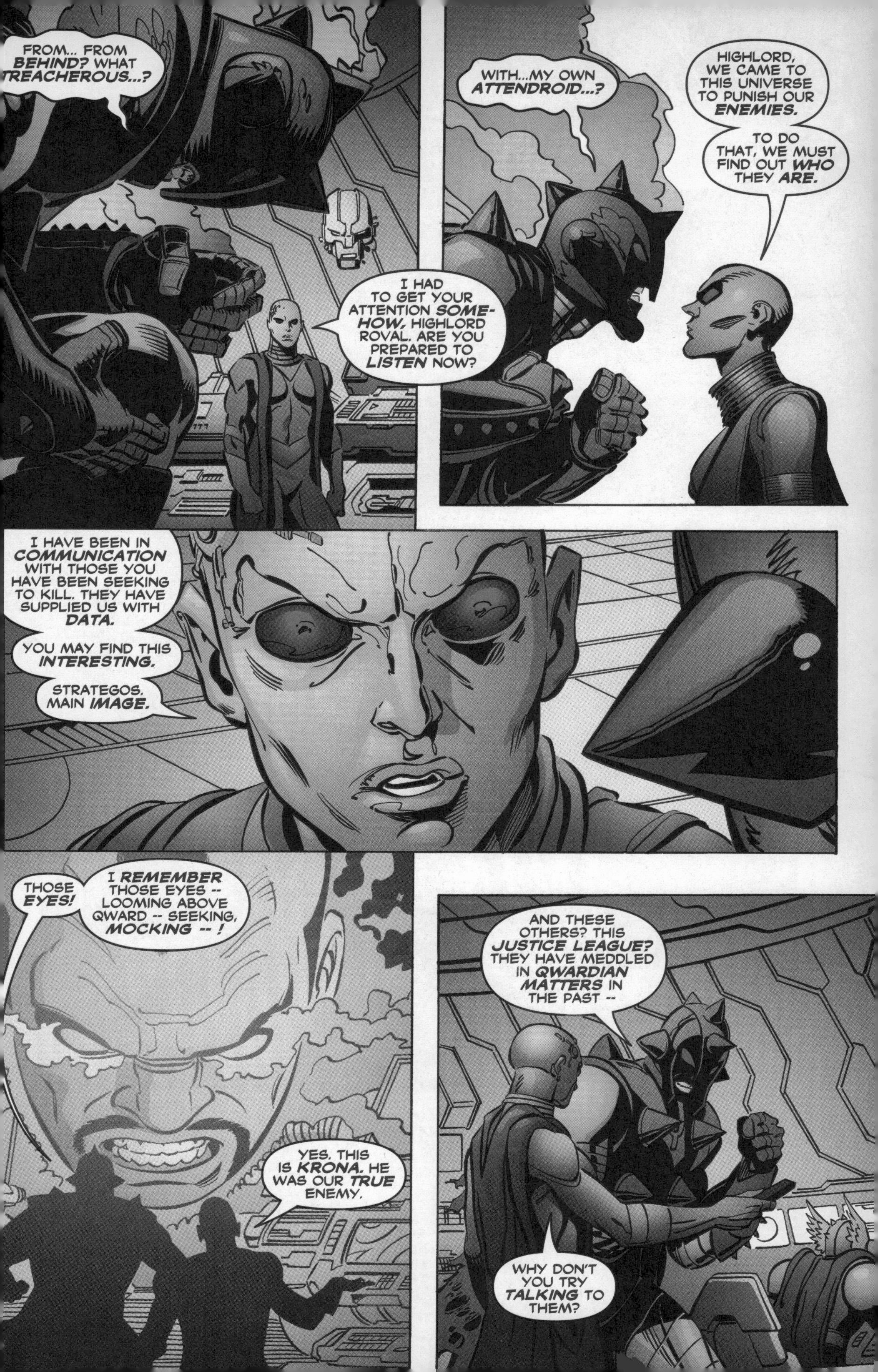
FROM... FROM BEHIND? WHAT TREACHEROUS...?
I HAD TO GET YOUR ATTENTION SOME-HOW, HIGHLORD ROVAL. ARE YOU PREPARED TO LISTEN NOW?
WITH...MY OWN ATTENDROID...?
HIGHLORD, WE CAME TO THIS UNIVERSE TO PUNISH OUR ENEMIES.
TO DO THAT, WE MUST FIND OUT WHO THEY ARE.
I HAVE BEEN IN COMMUNICATION WITH THOSE YOU HAVE BEEN SEEKING TO KILL. THEY HAVE SUPPLIED US WITH DATA.
YOU MAY FIND THIS INTERESTING.
STRATEGOS. MAIN IMAGE.
THOSE EYES!
I REMEMBER THOSE EYES -- LOOMING ABOVE QWARD -- SEEKING, MOCKING -- !
YES. THIS IS KRONA. HE WAS OUR TRUE ENEMY.
AND THESE OTHERS? THIS JUSTICE LEAGUE? THEY HAVE MEDDLED IN QWARDIAN MATTERS IN THE PAST --
WHY DON'T YOU TRY TALKING TO THEM?

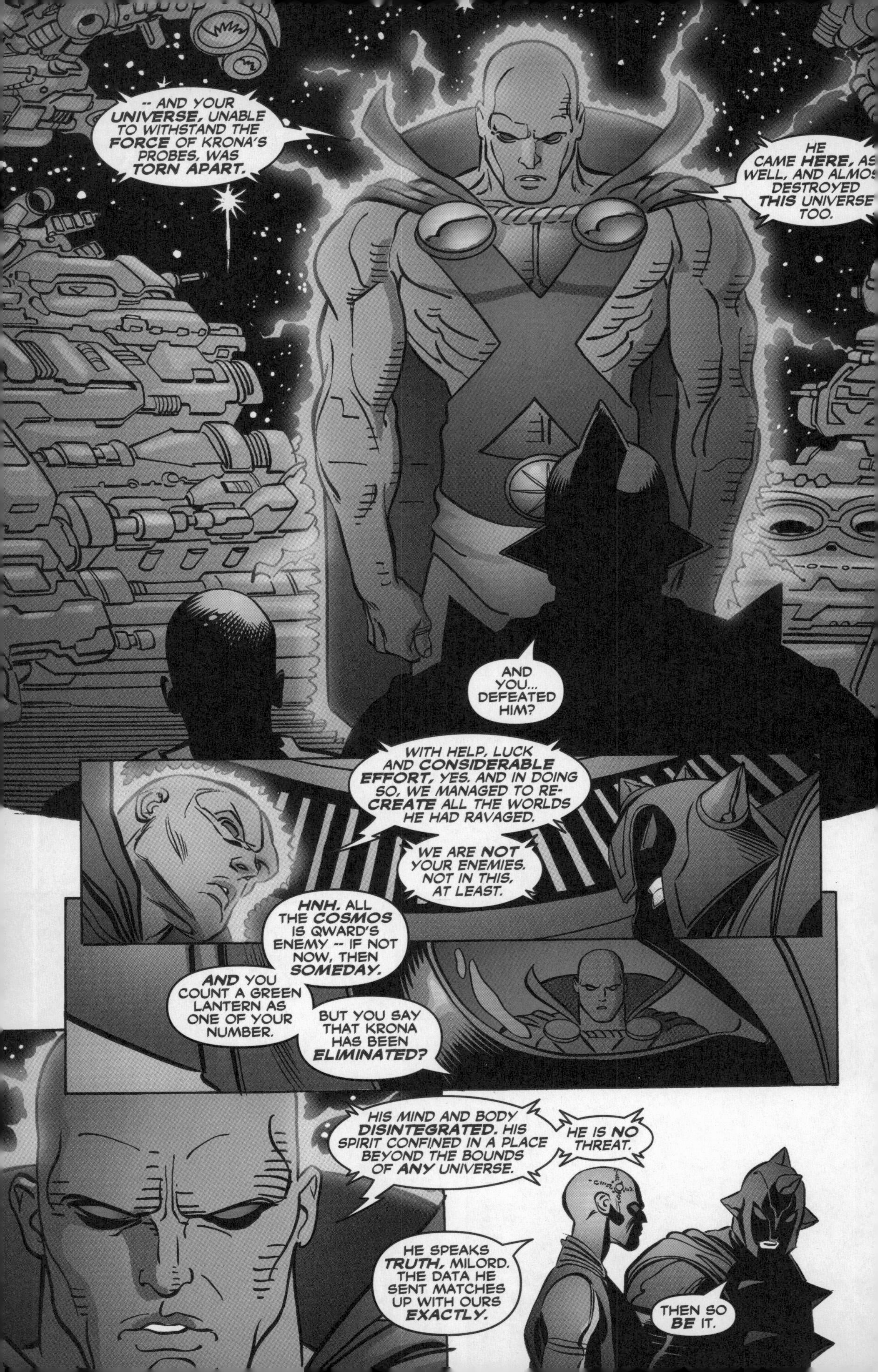
-- AND YOUR UNIVERSE, UNABLE TO WITHSTAND THE FORCE OF KRONA'S PROBES, WAS TORN APART.
HE CAME HERE, AS WELL, AND ALMOS DESTROYED THIS UNIVERSE TOO.
AND YOU... DEFEATED HIM?
WITH HELP, LUCK AND CONSIDERABLE EFFORT, YES. AND IN DOING SO, WE MANAGED TO RE-CREATE ALL THE WORLDS HE HAD RAVAGED.
WE ARE NOT YOUR ENEMIES. NOT IN THIS, AT LEAST.
HNH. ALL THE COSMOS IS QWARD'S ENEMY -- IF NOT NOW, THEN SOMEDAY.
AND YOU COUNT A GREEN LANTERN AS ONE OF YOUR NUMBER.
BUT YOU SAY THAT KRONA HAS BEEN ELIMINATED?
HIS MIND AND BODY DISINTEGRATED. HIS SPIRIT CONFINED IN A PLACE BEYOND THE BOUNDS OF ANY UNIVERSE.
HE IS NO THREAT.
HE SPEAKS TRUTH, MILORD. THE DATA HE SENT MATCHES UP WITH OURS EXACTLY.
THEN SO BE IT.

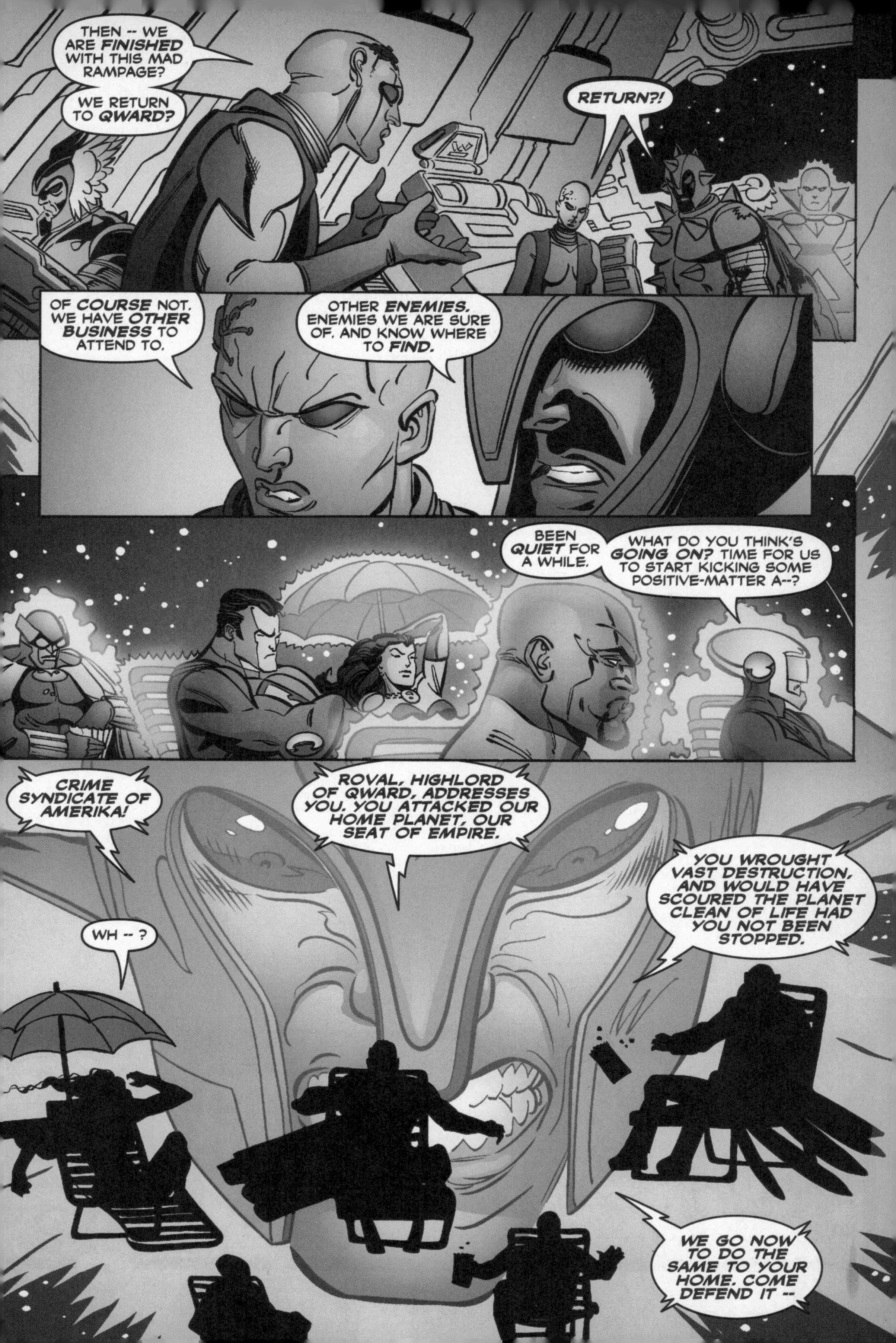
THEN -- WE ARE FINISHED WITH THIS MAD RAMPAGE?
WE RETURN TO QWARD?
RETURN?!
OF COURSE NOT. WE HAVE OTHER BUSINESS TO ATTEND TO.
OTHER ENEMIES. ENEMIES WE ARE SURE OF, AND KNOW WHERE TO FIND.
BEEN QUIET FOR A WHILE.
WHAT DO YOU THINK'S GOING ON? TIME FOR US TO START KICKING SOME POSITIVE-MATTER A--?
CRIME SYNDICATE OF AMERIKA!
ROVAL, HIGHLORD OF QWARD, ADDRESSES YOU. YOU ATTACKED OUR HOME PLANET, OUR SEAT OF EMPIRE.
YOU WROUGHT VAST DESTRUCTION, AND WOULD HAVE SCOURED THE PLANET CLEAN OF LIFE HAD YOU NOT BEEN STOPPED.
WH -- ?
WE GO NOW TO DO THE SAME TO YOUR HOME. COME DEFEND IT --

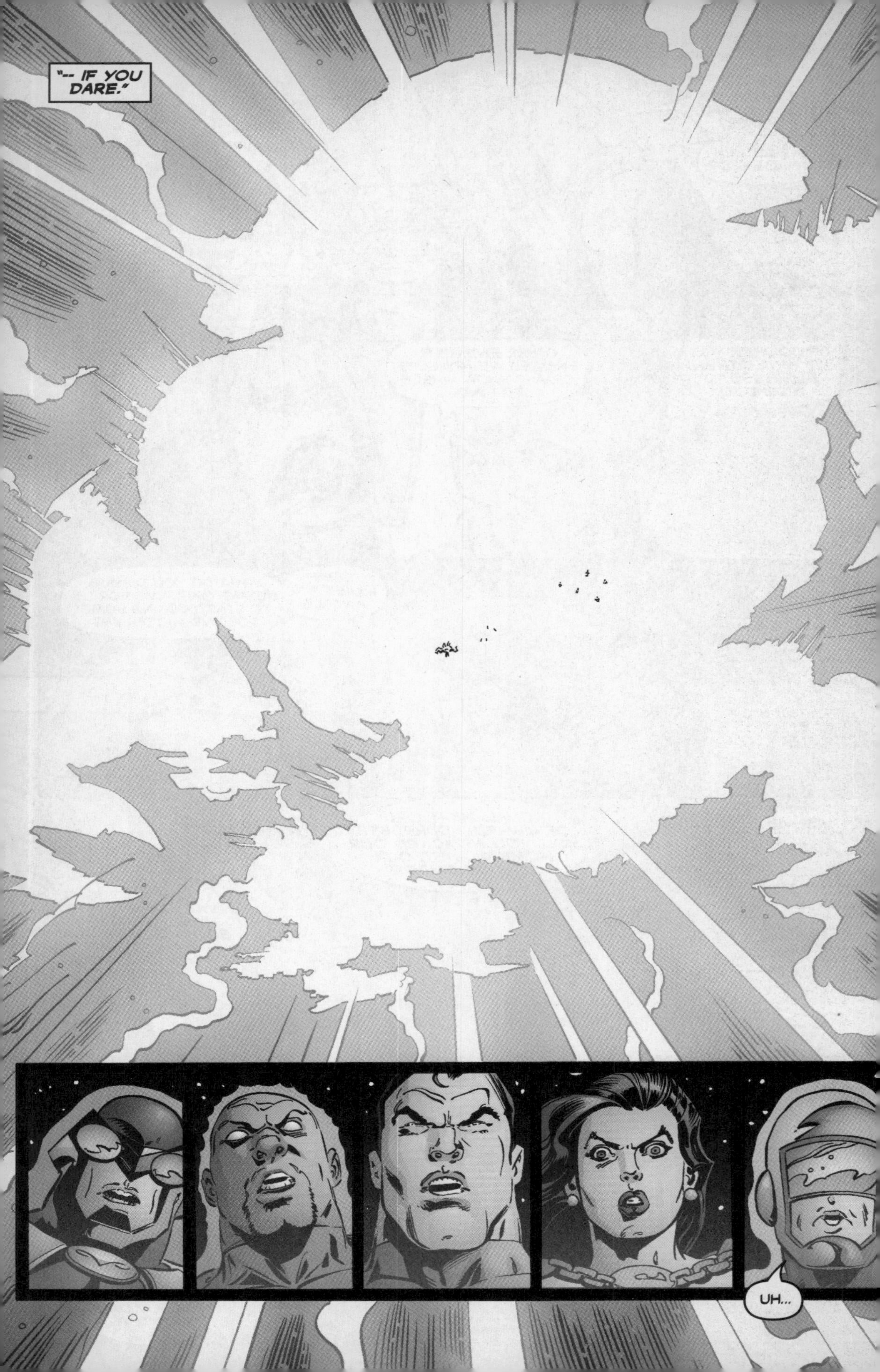
"-- IF YOU DARE."
UH...

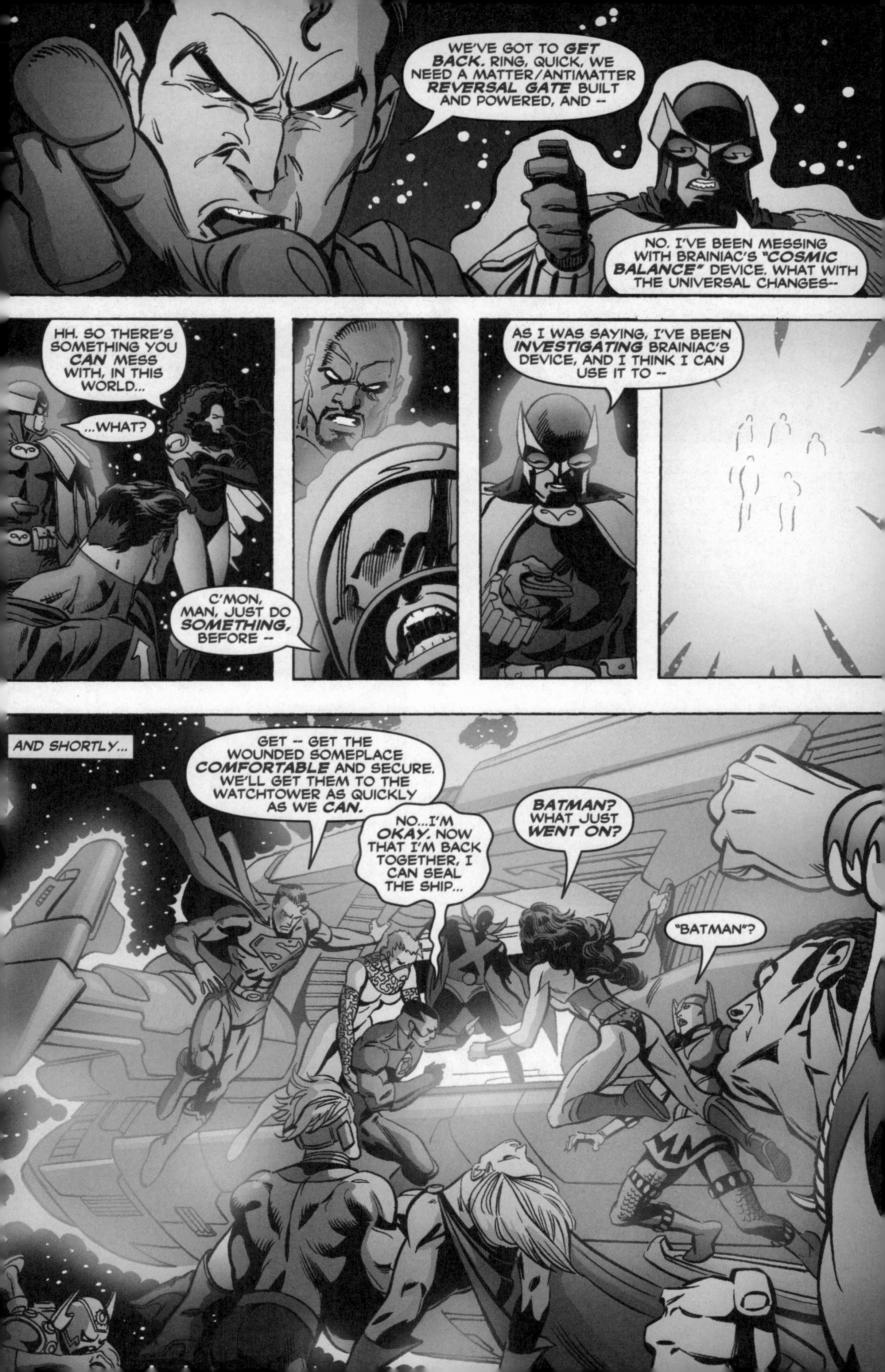
WE'VE GOT TO GET BACK. RING, QUICK, WE NEED A MATTER/ANTIMATTER REVERSAL GATE BUILT AND POWERED, AND --
NO. I'VE BEEN MESSING WITH BRAINIAC'S "COSMIC BALANCE" DEVICE. WHAT WITH THE UNIVERSAL CHANGES--
HH. SO THERE'S SOMETHING YOU CAN MESS WITH, IN THIS WORLD...
...WHAT?
C'MON, MAN, JUST DO SOMETHING, BEFORE --
AS I WAS SAYING, I'VE BEEN INVESTIGATING BRAINIAC'S DEVICE, AND I THINK I CAN USE IT TO --
AND SHORTLY...
GET -- GET THE WOUNDED SOMEPLACE COMFORTABLE AND SECURE. WE'LL GET THEM TO THE WATCHTOWER AS QUICKLY AS WE CAN.
NO...I'M OKAY. NOW THAT I'M BACK TOGETHER, I CAN SEAL THE SHIP...
BATMAN? WHAT JUST WENT ON?
"BATMAN"?

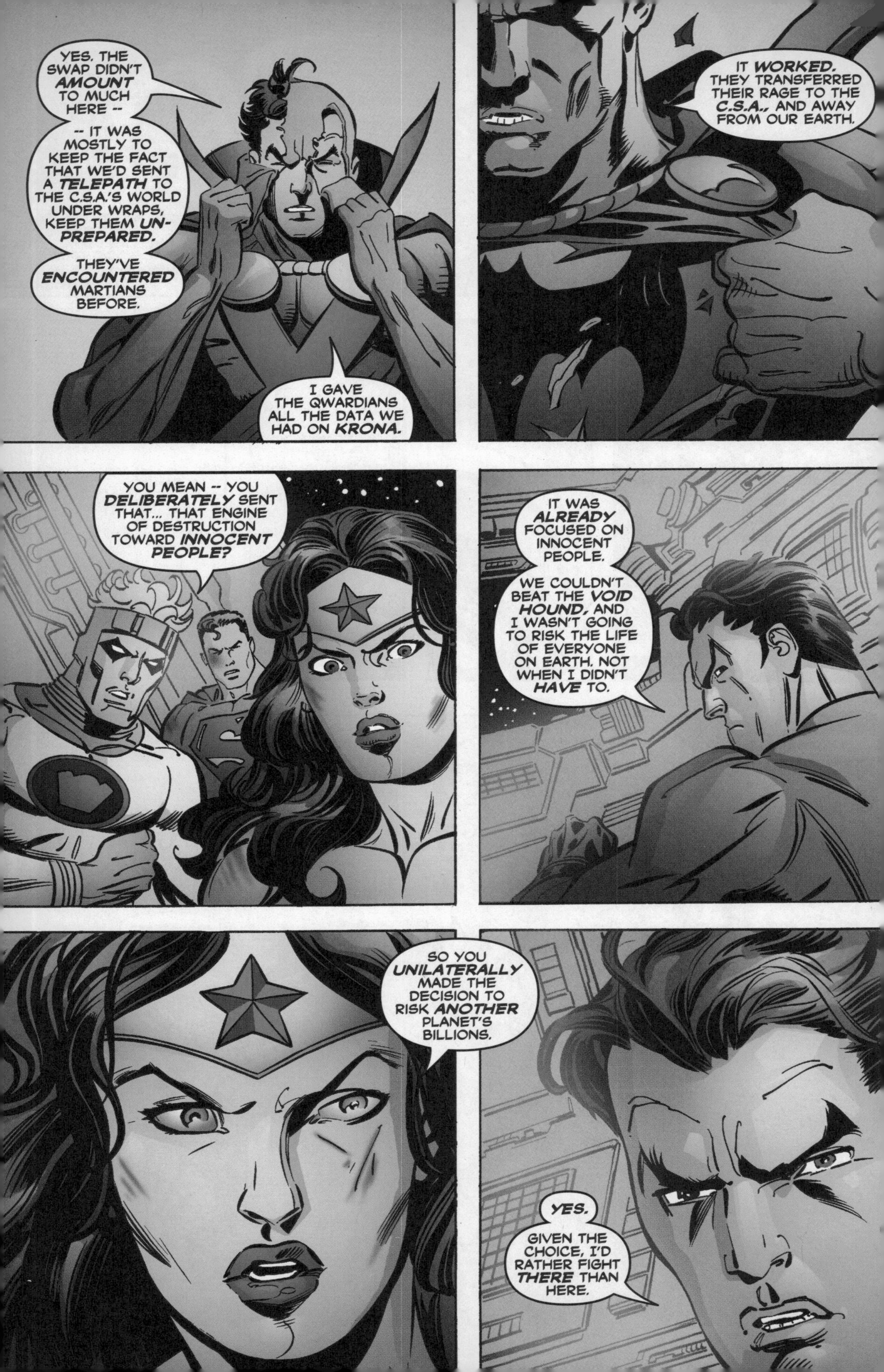
YES. THE SWAP DIDN'T AMOUNT TO MUCH HERE --
-- IT WAS MOSTLY TO KEEP THE FACT THAT WE'D SENT A TELEPATH TO THE C.S.A.'S WORLD UNDER WRAPS, KEEP THEM UN-PREPARED.
THEY'VE ENCOUNTERED MARTIANS BEFORE.
I GAVE THE QWARDIANS ALL THE DATA WE HAD ON KRONA.
IT WORKED. THEY TRANSFERRED THEIR RAGE TO THE C.S.A., AND AWAY FROM OUR EARTH.
YOU MEAN -- YOU DELIBERATELY SENT THAT... THAT ENGINE OF DESTRUCTION TOWARD INNOCENT PEOPLE?
IT WAS ALREADY FOCUSED ON INNOCENT PEOPLE.
WE COULDN'T BEAT THE VOID HOUND, AND I WASN'T GOING TO RISK THE LIFE OF EVERYONE ON EARTH. NOT WHEN I DIDN'T HAVE TO.
SO YOU UNILATERALLY MADE THE DECISION TO RISK ANOTHER PLANET'S BILLIONS.
YES.
GIVEN THE CHOICE, I'D RATHER FIGHT THERE THAN HERE.

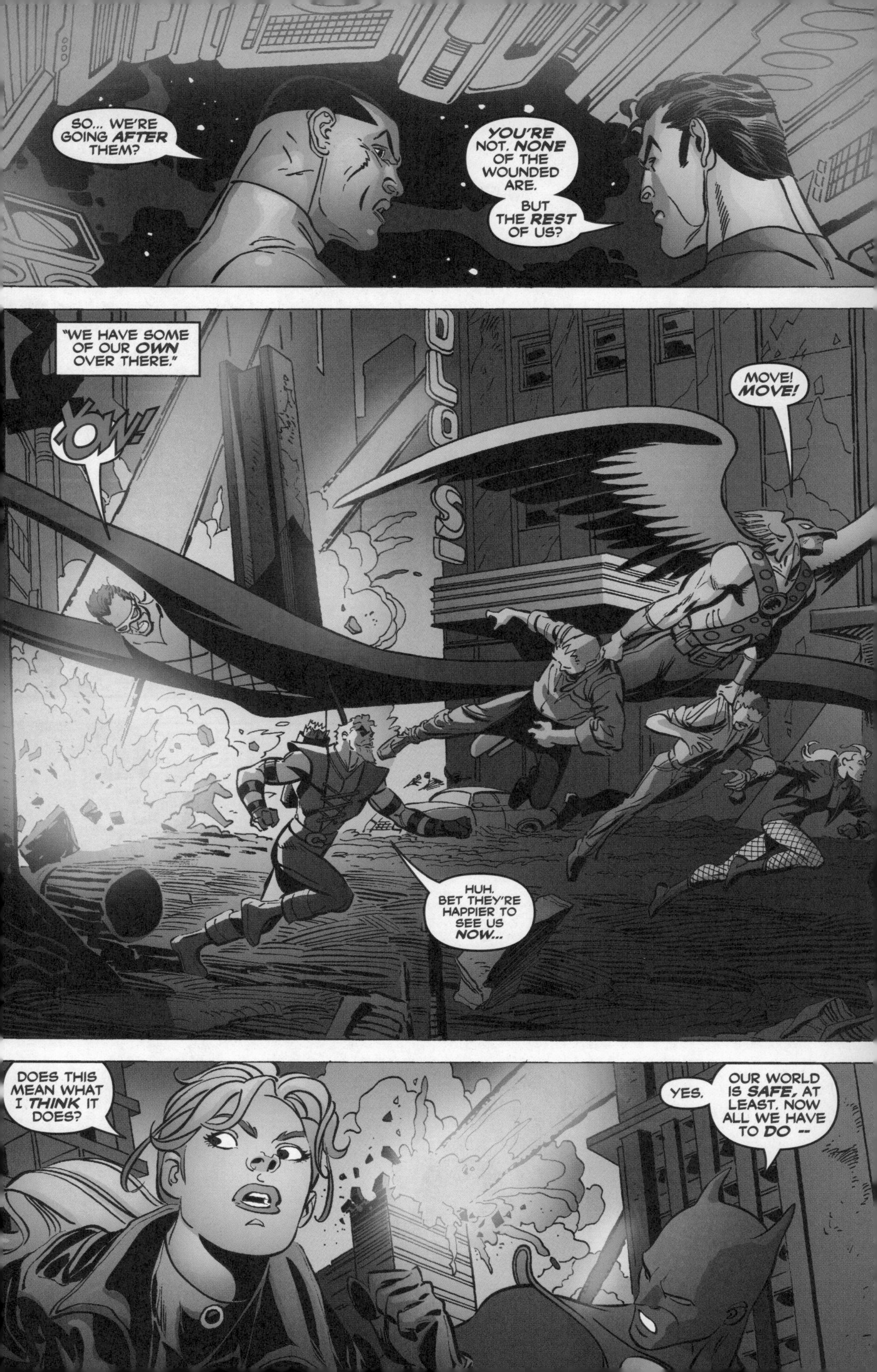
SO... WE'RE GOING AFTER THEM?
YOU'RE NOT. NONE OF THE WOUNDED ARE.
BUT THE REST OF US?
"WE HAVE SOME OF OUR OWN OVER THERE."
YOW!
MOVE! MOVE!
HUH. BET THEY'RE HAPPIER TO SEE US NOW...
DOES THIS MEAN WHAT I THINK IT DOES?
YES.
OUR WORLD IS SAFE, AT LEAST. NOW ALL WE HAVE TO DO --

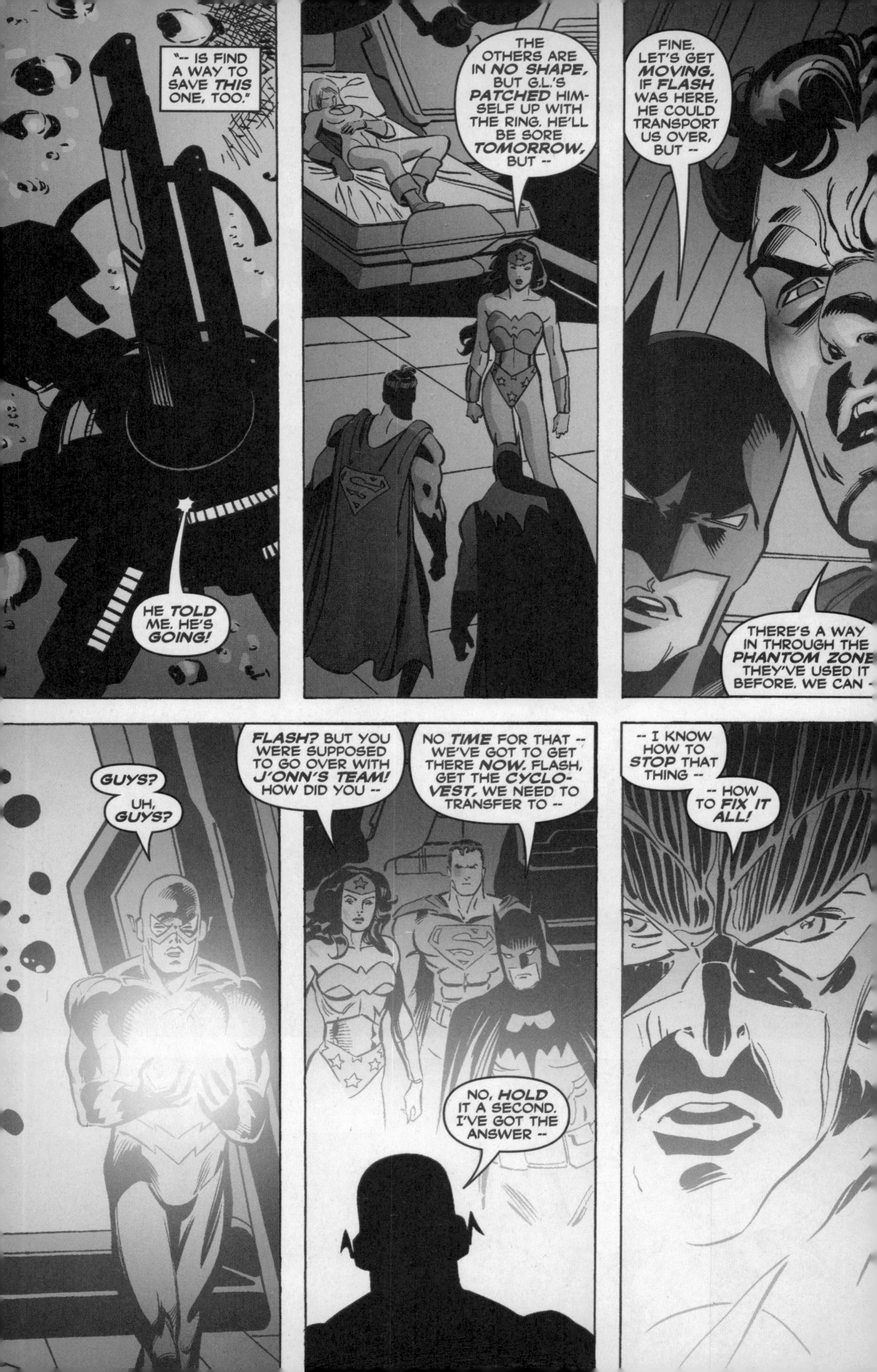
"-- IS FIND A WAY TO SAVE THIS ONE, TOO."
HE TOLD ME. HE'S GOING!
THE OTHERS ARE IN NO SHAPE, BUT G.L.'S PATCHED HIMSELF UP WITH THE RING. HE'LL BE SORE TOMORROW, BUT --
FINE. LET'S GET MOVING. IF FLASH WAS HERE, HE COULD TRANSPORT US OVER, BUT --
THERE'S A WAY IN THROUGH THE PHANTOM ZONE THEY'VE USED IT BEFORE. WE CAN -
GUYS? UH, GUYS?
FLASH? BUT YOU WERE SUPPOSED TO GO OVER WITH J'ONN'S TEAM! HOW DID YOU --
NO TIME FOR THAT -- WE'VE GOT TO GET THERE NOW. FLASH, GET THE CYCLO-VEST, WE NEED TO TRANSFER TO --
NO, HOLD IT A SECOND. I'VE GOT THE ANSWER --
-- I KNOW HOW TO STOP THAT THING --
-- HOW TO FIX IT ALL!

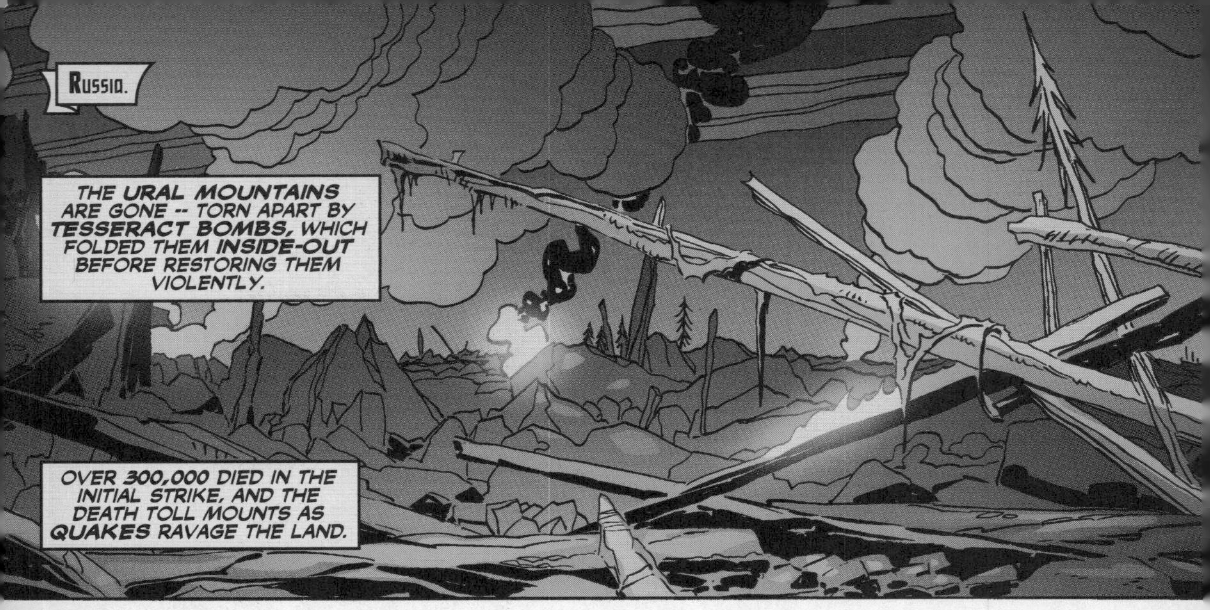
Russia.
THE URAL MOUNTAINS ARE GONE -- TORN APART BY TESSERACT BOMBS, WHICH FOLDED THEM INSIDE-OUT BEFORE RESTORING THEM VIOLENTLY.
OVER 300,000 DIED IN THE INITIAL STRIKE, AND THE DEATH TOLL MOUNTS AS QUAKES RAVAGE THE LAND.

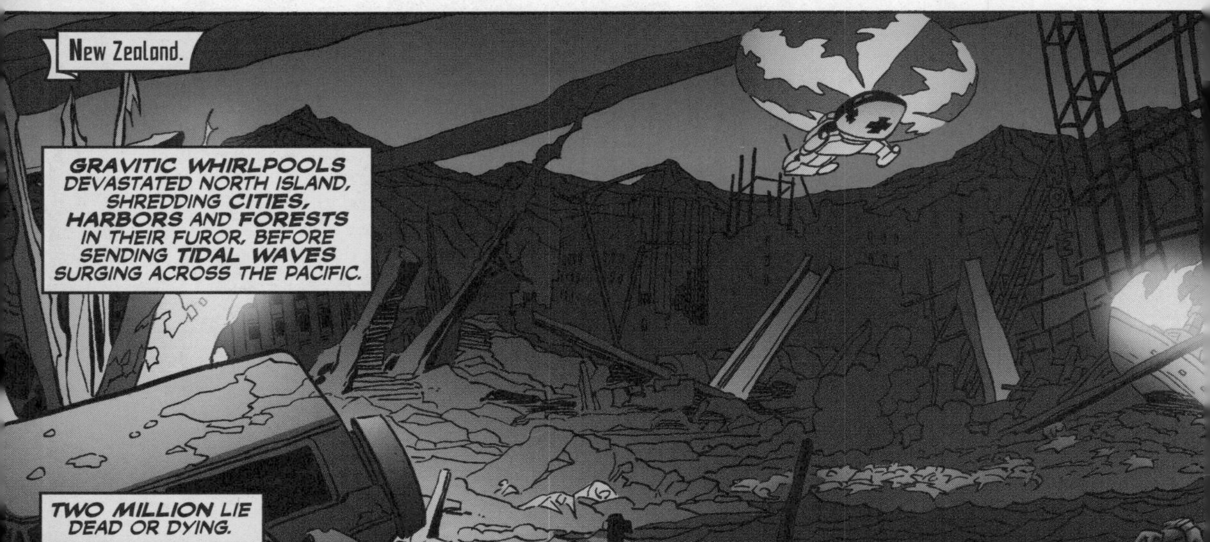
New Zealand.
GRAVITIC WHIRLPOOLS DEVASTATED NORTH ISLAND, SHREDDING CITIES, HARBORS AND FORESTS IN THEIR FUROR, BEFORE SENDING TIDAL WAVES SURGING ACROSS THE PACIFIC.
TWO MILLION LIE DEAD OR DYING.

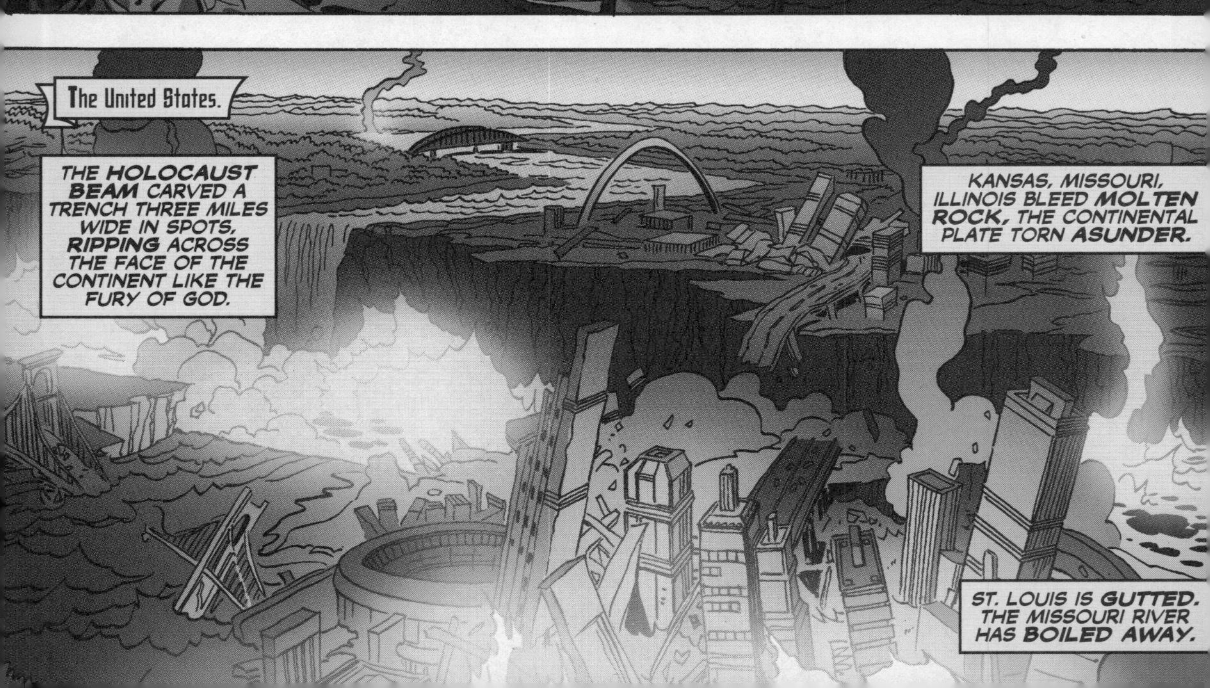
The United States.
THE HOLOCAUST BEAM CARVED A TRENCH THREE MILES WIDE IN SPOTS, RIPPING ACROSS THE FACE OF THE CONTINENT LIKE THE FURY OF GOD.
KANSAS, MISSOURI, ILLINOIS BLEED MOLTEN ROCK, THE CONTINENTAL PLATE TORN ASUNDER.
ST. LOUIS IS GUTTED. THE MISSOURI RIVER HAS BOILED AWAY.

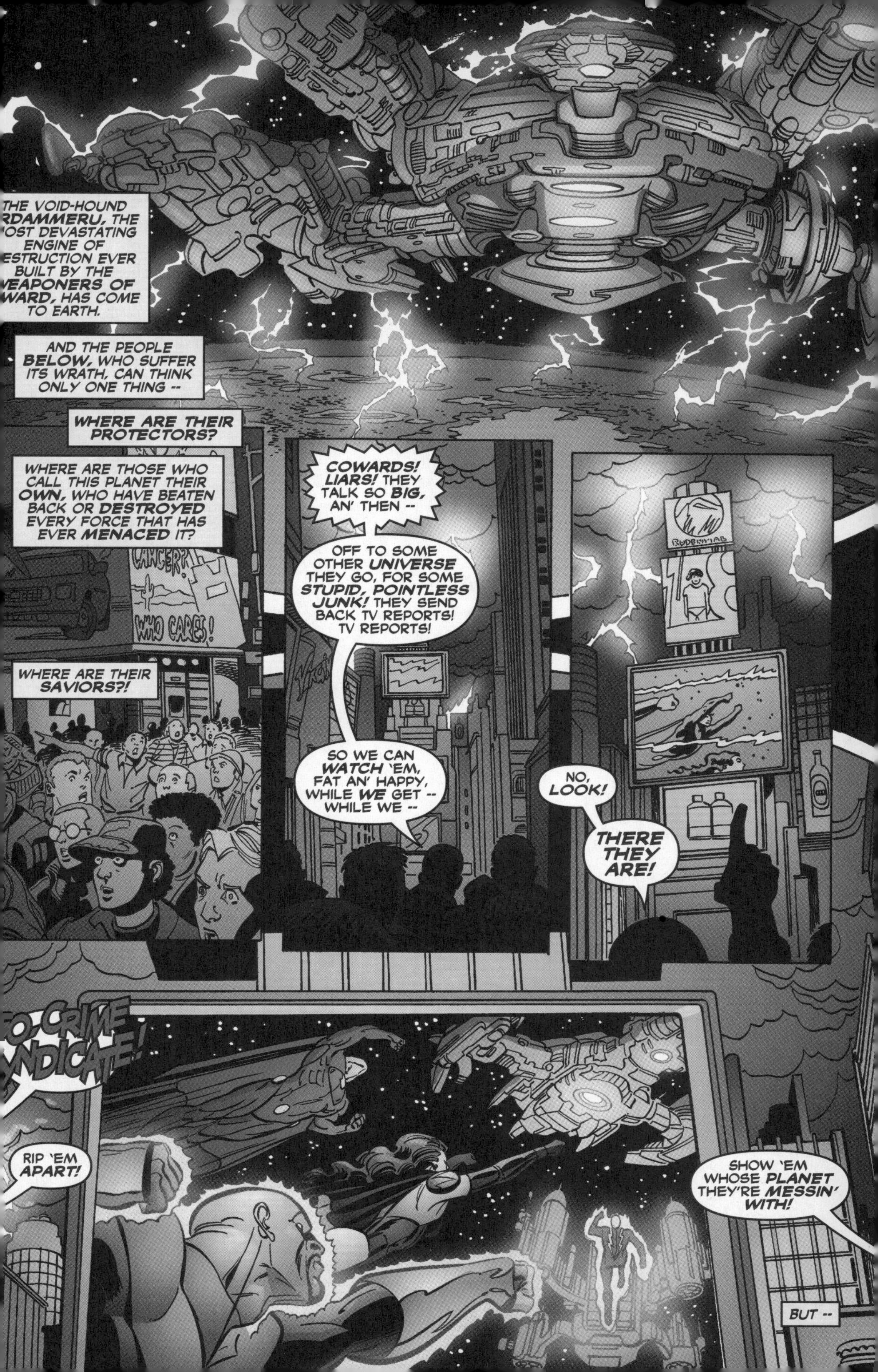
THE VOID-HOUND RDAMMERU, THE OST DEVASTATING ENGINE OF ESTRUCTION EVER BUILT BY THE WEAPONERS OF WARD, HAS COME TO EARTH.
AND THE PEOPLE BELOW, WHO SUFFER ITS WRATH, CAN THINK ONLY ONE THING --
WHERE ARE THEIR PROTECTORS?
WHERE ARE THOSE WHO CALL THIS PLANET THEIR OWN, WHO HAVE BEATEN BACK OR DESTROYED EVERY FORCE THAT HAS EVER MENACED IT?
CANCER?
WHO CARES!
WHERE ARE THEIR SAVIORS?!
COWARDS! LIARS! THEY TALK SO BIG, AN' THEN --
OFF TO SOME OTHER UNIVERSE THEY GO, FOR SOME STUPID, POINTLESS JUNK! THEY SEND BACK TV REPORTS! TV REPORTS!
SO WE CAN WATCH 'EM, FAT AN' HAPPY, WHILE WE GET -- WHILE WE --
NO, LOOK!
THERE THEY ARE!
NDICATE!
RIP 'EM APART!
SHOW 'EM WHOSE PLANET THEY'RE MESSIN' WITH!
BUT --

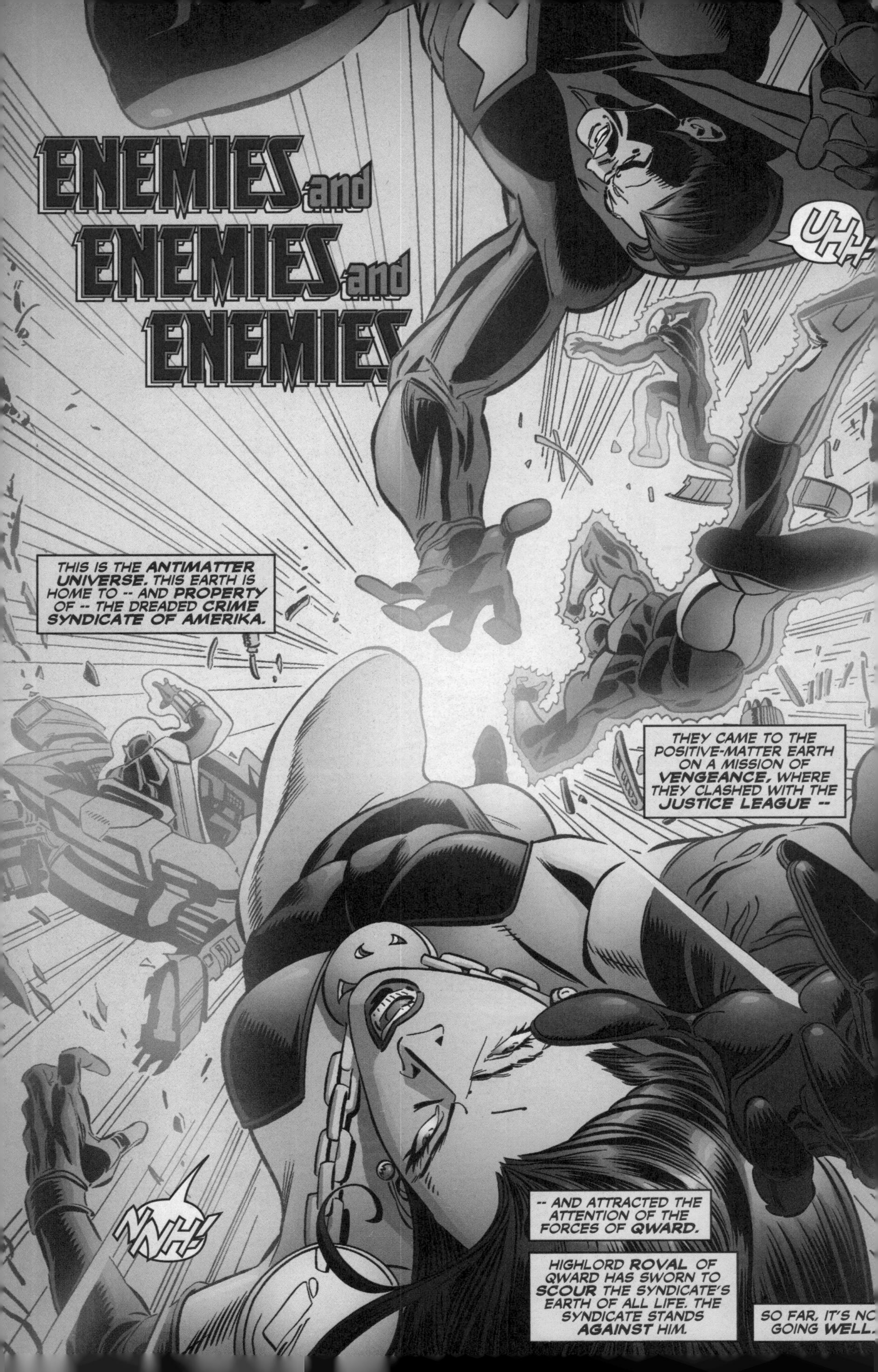

ENEMIES and ENEMIES and ENEMIES
UHH-
THIS IS THE ANTIMATTER UNIVERSE. THIS EARTH IS HOME TO -- AND PROPERTY OF -- THE DREADED CRIME SYNDICATE OF AMERIKA.
THEY CAME TO THE POSITIVE-MATTER EARTH ON A MISSION OF VENGEANCE, WHERE THEY CLASHED WITH THE JUSTICE LEAGUE --
-- AND ATTRACTED THE ATTENTION OF THE FORCES OF QWARD.
HIGHLORD ROVAL OF QWARD HAS SWORN TO SCOUR THE SYNDICATE'S EARTH OF ALL LIFE. THE SYNDICATE STANDS AGAINST HIM.
NNH!
SO FAR, IT'S NO
GOING WELL.

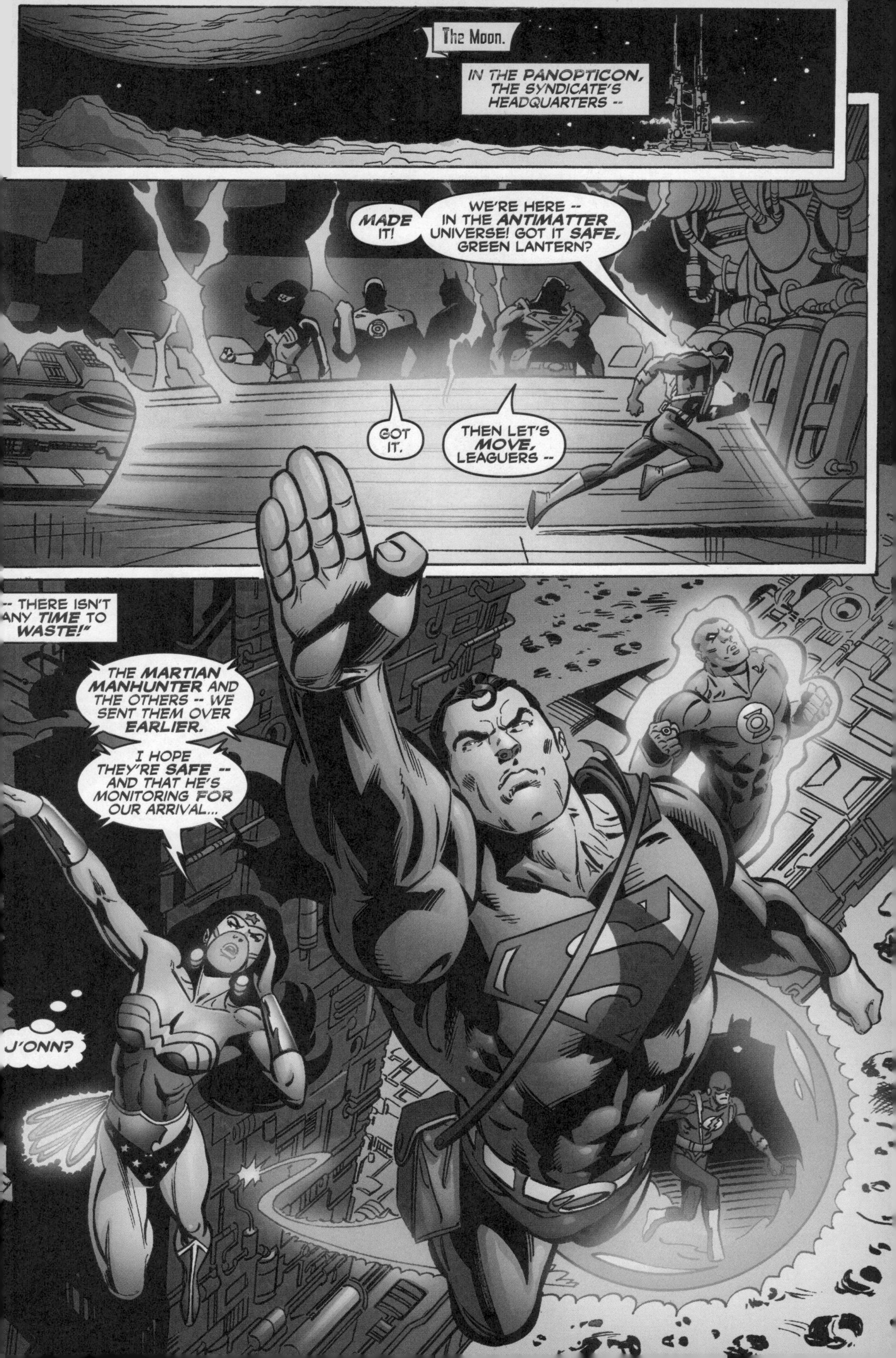

The Moon.
IN THE PANOPTICON, THE SYNDICATE'S HEADQUARTERS --
MADE IT!
WE'RE HERE -- IN THE ANTIMATTER UNIVERSE! GOT IT SAFE, GREEN LANTERN?
GOT IT.
THEN LET'S MOVE, LEAGUERS --
-- THERE ISN'T ANY TIME TO WASTE!"
THE MARTIAN MANHUNTER AND THE OTHERS -- WE SENT THEM OVER EARLIER.
I HOPE THEY'RE SAFE -- AND THAT HE'S MONITORING FOR OUR ARRIVAL...
J'ONN?

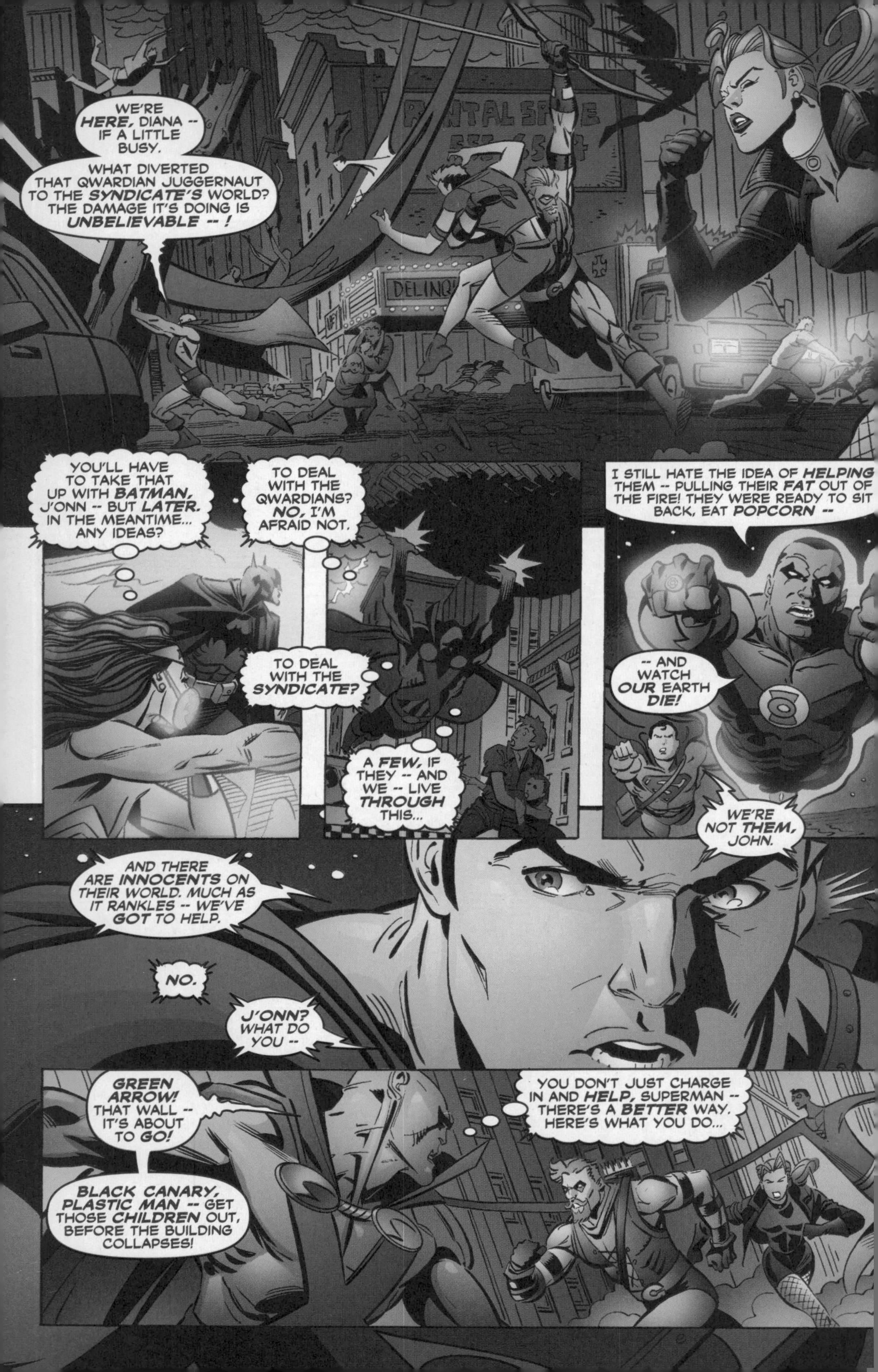

RENTAL SPACE
DELINQ
WE'RE HERE, DIANA -- IF A LITTLE BUSY.
WHAT DIVERTED THAT QWARDIAN JUGGERNAUT TO THE SYNDICATE'S WORLD? THE DAMAGE IT'S DOING IS UNBELIEVABLE -- !
YOU'LL HAVE TO TAKE THAT UP WITH BATMAN, J'ONN -- BUT LATER. IN THE MEANTIME... ANY IDEAS?
TO DEAL WITH THE QWARDIANS? NO, I'M AFRAID NOT.
TO DEAL WITH THE SYNDICATE?
A FEW, IF THEY -- AND WE -- LIVE THROUGH THIS...
I STILL HATE THE IDEA OF HELPING THEM -- PULLING THEIR FAT OUT OF THE FIRE! THEY WERE READY TO SIT BACK, EAT POPCORN --
-- AND WATCH OUR EARTH DIE!
WE'RE NOT THEM, JOHN.
AND THERE ARE INNOCENTS ON THEIR WORLD. MUCH AS IT RANKLES -- WE'VE GOT TO HELP.
NO.
J'ONN? WHAT DO YOU --
GREEN ARROW! THAT WALL -- IT'S ABOUT TO GO!
BLACK CANARY, PLASTIC MAN -- GET THOSE CHILDREN OUT, BEFORE THE BUILDING COLLAPSES!
YOU DON'T JUST CHARGE IN AND HELP, SUPERMAN -- THERE'S A BETTER WAY. HERE'S WHAT YOU DO...

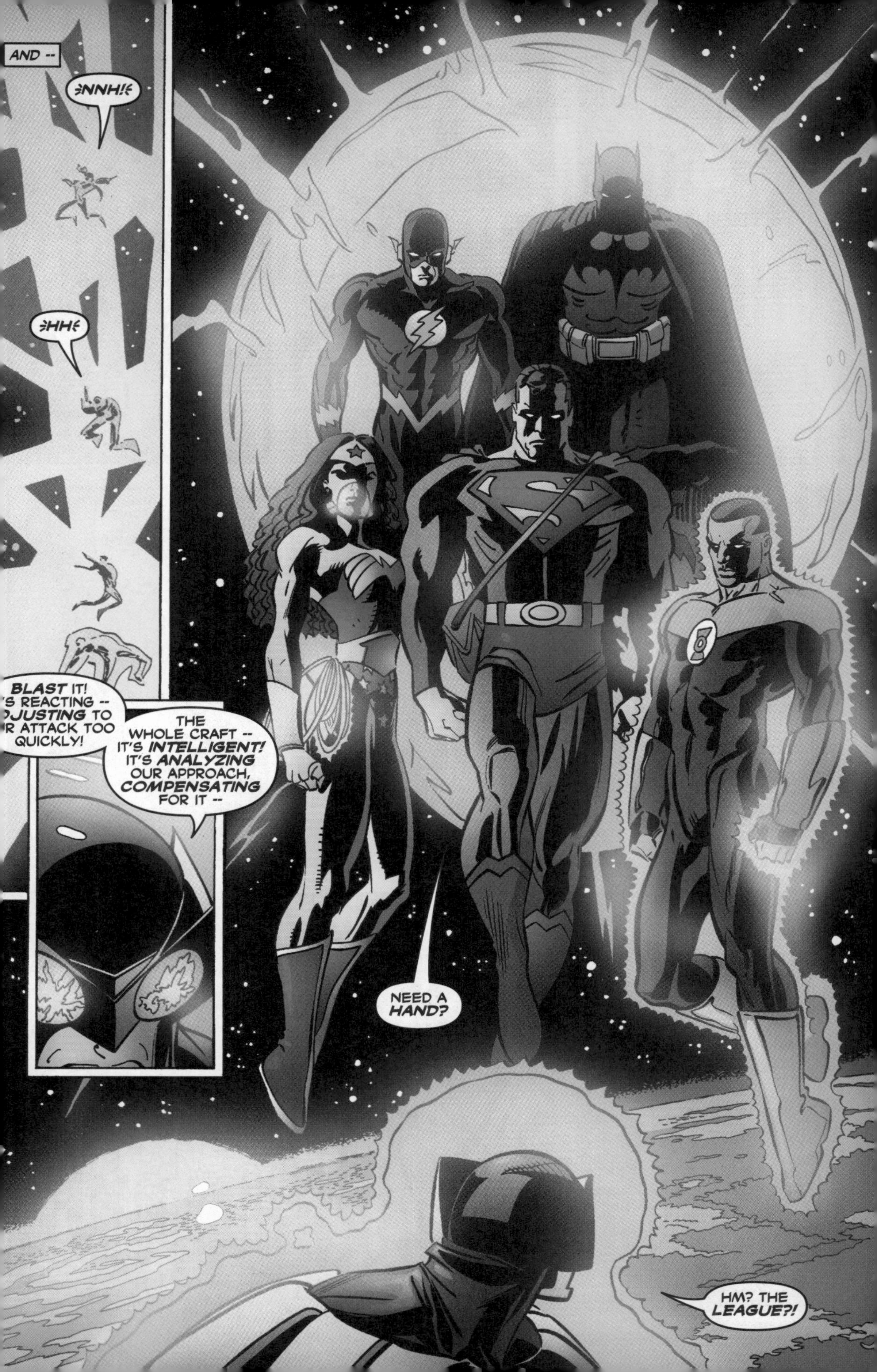
AND --
NNH!
HH
BLAST IT! 'S REACTING -- DJUSTING TO R ATTACK TOO QUICKLY!
THE WHOLE CRAFT -- IT'S INTELLIGENT! IT'S ANALYZING OUR APPROACH, COMPENSATING FOR IT --
NEED A HAND?
HM? THE LEAGUE?!

WELL, AS LONG AS YOU'RE *HERE*, FEEL FREE TO PITCH IN ANY TIME.

NO.

ASK US.

WHAT?

YOU HAVE TO ASK US TO HELP, OWLMAN, AS A *FAVOR*.

BUT YOU --

DON'T! I'LL SEE THE WORLD DIE BEFORE I ASK *THEM* FOR --

MOLOCH BELOW, ARE YOU *INSANE*?

YES, SUPERMAN -- I ASK FOR THE JUSTICE LEAGUE'S *ASSISTANCE*. I ASK IN THE NAME OF THE *ENTIRE* CRIME SYNDICATE.

IDIOT! IF WE'D REFUSED TO ASK, THEY'D HAVE HELPED *ANYWAY*.

AND THIS -- YOU JUST *BROADCAST* THIS TO THE SHEEP BELOW -- !

IT WON'T WORK.

THAT THING HAS ALREADY *FOUGHT* YOU -- IT KNOWS HOW TO *DEAL* WITH YOU, THERE'S NO WAY TO SURPRISE IT.

DON'T BE SO *SURE*.

SUPERMAN?

GOOD. THEY'VE ASKED A *FAVOR* -- THE ONLY *INVIOLABLE* BOND OF THIS WARPED WORLD.

GREAT, *GREAT*, WE GOT 'EM RIGHT WHERE WE *WANT* 'EM! NOT MUCH GOOD IF AN ENTIRE *STATE* FALLS IN ON US, THOUGH, IS IT?

PLASTIC MAN'S GOT A *POINT*, J'ONN -- NOT THAT I EVER THOUGHT I'D *SAY* THAT.

DO WE JUST TWIDDLE OUR THUMBS AND *PRAY* FROM HERE ON OUT, OR -- ?

WE'RE TOO FAR AWAY AND TOO *UNDERPOWERED* SQUAD TO BE MUCH HELP AGAINST THE *VOID HOUND*. BUT COME --

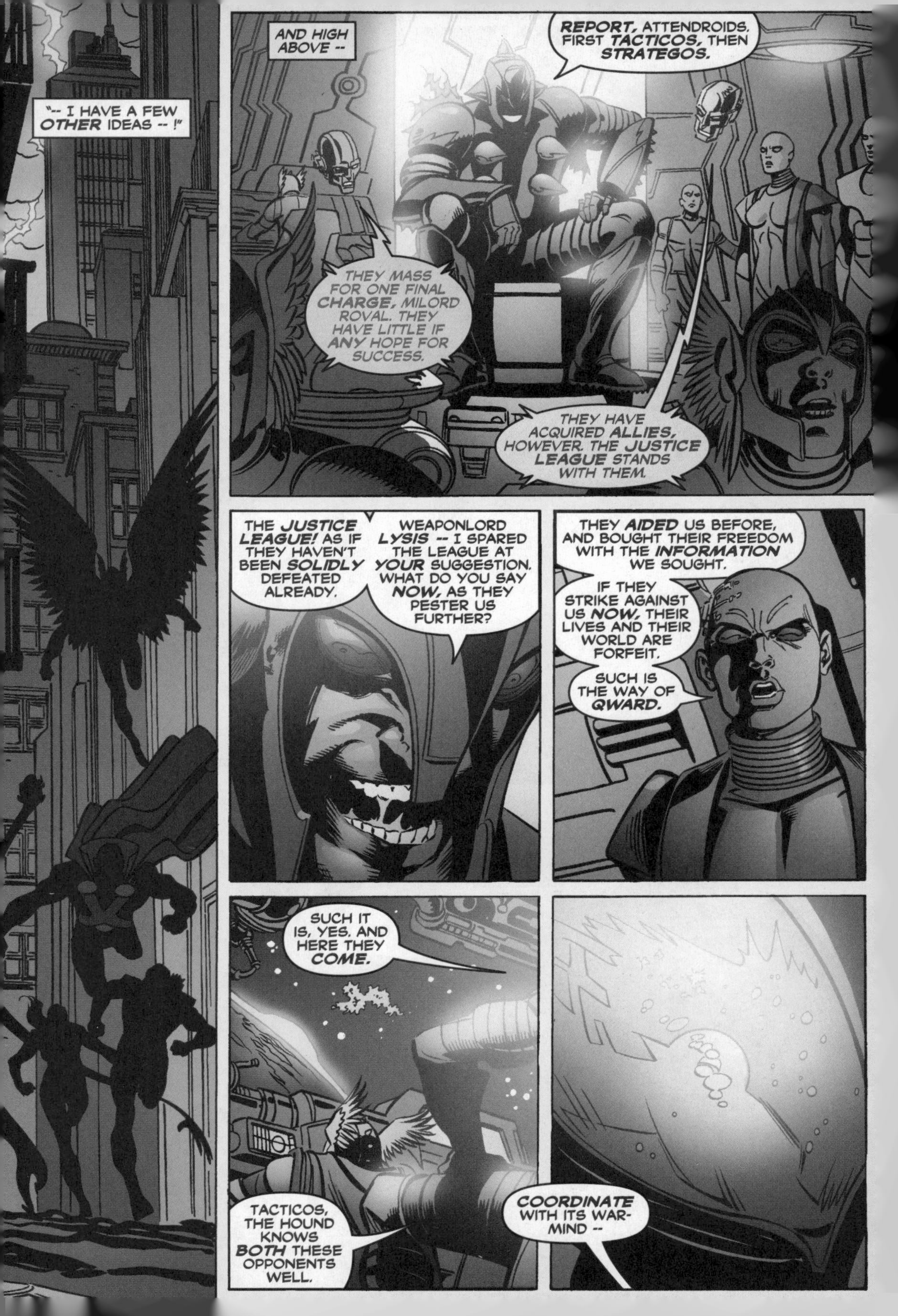
"-- I HAVE A FEW OTHER IDEAS -- !"
AND HIGH ABOVE --
REPORT, ATTENDROIDS. FIRST TACTICOS, THEN STRATEGOS.
THEY MASS FOR ONE FINAL CHARGE, MILORD ROVAL. THEY HAVE LITTLE IF ANY HOPE FOR SUCCESS.
THEY HAVE ACQUIRED ALLIES, HOWEVER. THE JUSTICE LEAGUE STANDS WITH THEM.
THE JUSTICE LEAGUE! AS IF THEY HAVEN'T BEEN SOLIDLY DEFEATED ALREADY.
WEAPONLORD LYSIS -- I SPARED THE LEAGUE AT YOUR SUGGESTION. WHAT DO YOU SAY NOW, AS THEY PESTER US FURTHER?
THEY AIDED US BEFORE, AND BOUGHT THEIR FREEDOM WITH THE INFORMATION WE SOUGHT.
IF THEY STRIKE AGAINST US NOW, THEIR LIVES AND THEIR WORLD ARE FORFEIT.
SUCH IS THE WAY OF QWARD.
SUCH IT IS, YES. AND HERE THEY COME.
TACTICOS, THE HOUND KNOWS BOTH THESE OPPONENTS WELL.
COORDINATE WITH ITS WAR-MIND --

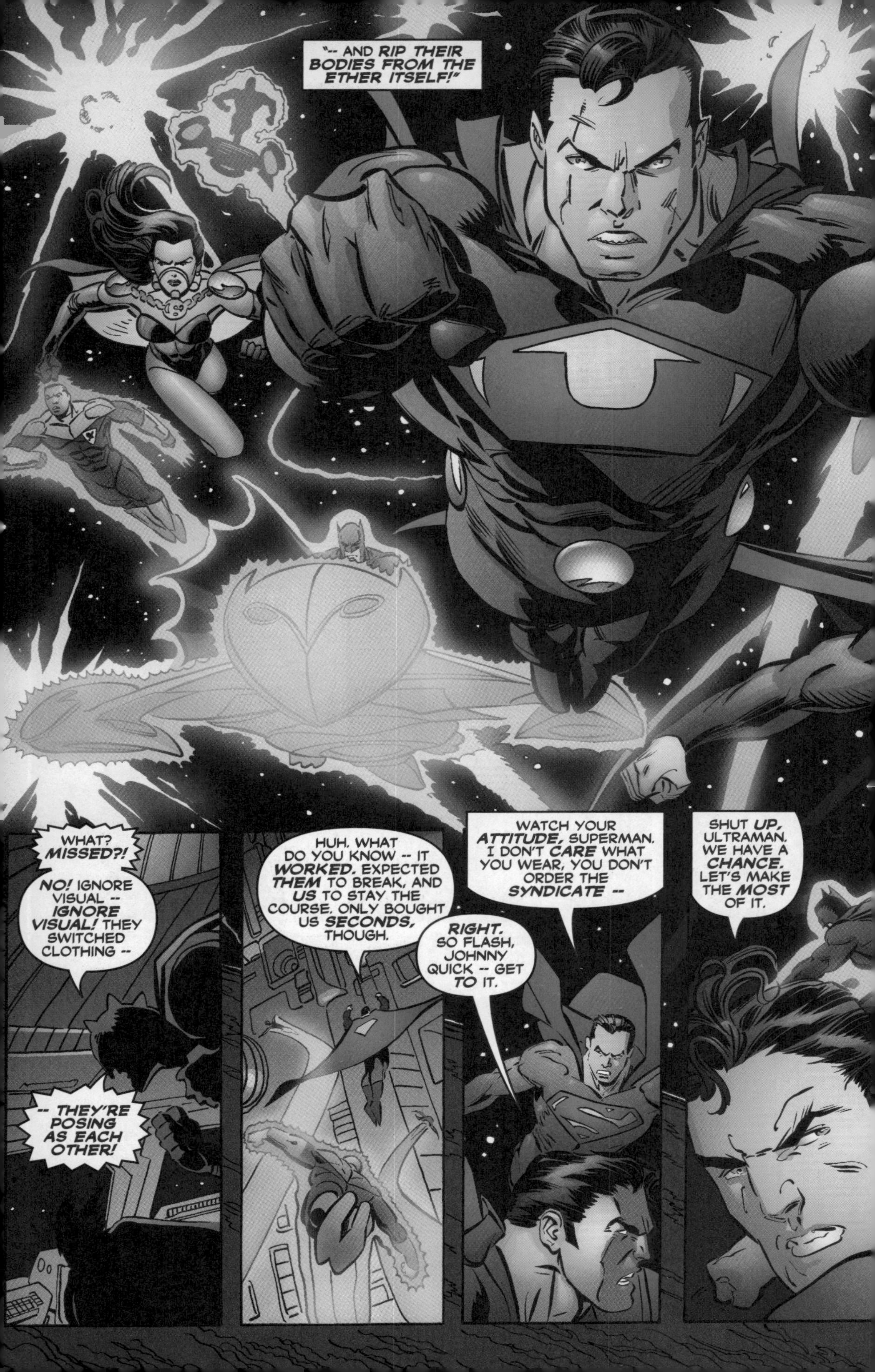
"-- AND RIP THEIR BODIES FROM THE ETHER ITSELF!"
WHAT? MISSED?!
NO! IGNORE VISUAL -- IGNORE VISUAL! THEY SWITCHED CLOTHING --
-- THEY'RE POSING AS EACH OTHER!
HUH. WHAT DO YOU KNOW -- IT WORKED. EXPECTED THEM TO BREAK, AND US TO STAY THE COURSE. ONLY BOUGHT US SECONDS, THOUGH.
RIGHT. SO FLASH, JOHNNY QUICK -- GET TO IT.
WATCH YOUR ATTITUDE, SUPERMAN. I DON'T CARE WHAT YOU WEAR, YOU DON'T ORDER THE SYNDICATE --
SHUT UP, ULTRAMAN. WE HAVE A CHANCE. LET'S MAKE THE MOST OF IT.

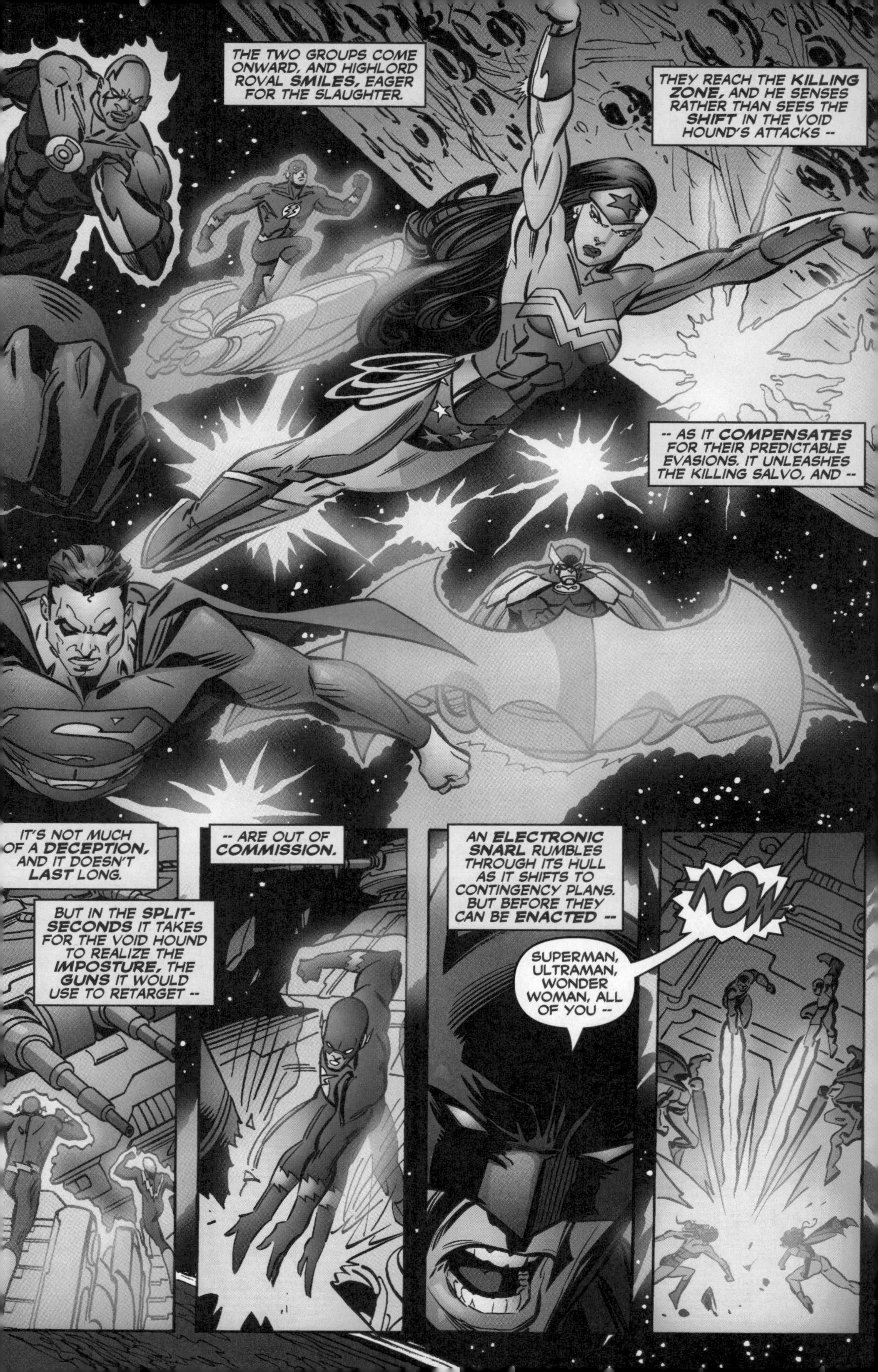
THE TWO GROUPS COME ONWARD, AND HIGHLORD ROVAL SMILES, EAGER FOR THE SLAUGHTER.
THEY REACH THE KILLING ZONE, AND HE SENSES RATHER THAN SEES THE SHIFT IN THE VOID HOUND'S ATTACKS --
-- AS IT COMPENSATES FOR THEIR PREDICTABLE EVASIONS. IT UNLEASHES THE KILLING SALVO, AND --
IT'S NOT MUCH OF A DECEPTION, AND IT DOESN'T LAST LONG.
BUT IN THE SPLIT-SECONDS IT TAKES FOR THE VOID HOUND TO REALIZE THE IMPOSTURE, THE GUNS IT WOULD USE TO RETARGET --
-- ARE OUT OF COMMISSION.
AN ELECTRONIC SNARL RUMBLES THROUGH ITS HULL AS IT SHIFTS TO CONTINGENCY PLANS. BUT BEFORE THEY CAN BE ENACTED --
SUPERMAN, ULTRAMAN, WONDER WOMAN, ALL OF YOU --
NOW!

AUTOMATIC **ENERGY-FIELDS** SPRING UP, TO PREVENT AIR LOSS, AND --

CUT THEM DOWN

THE **THUNDERERS** -- QWARD'S ELITE SHOCKTROOPS.

SHOULD HAVE GUESSED THEY'D BE **WAITING** FOR US.

LET THEM **COME,** POSITIVE-EARTHER.

NOW THAT WE'RE UP AGAINST **LIVING, BREATHING FOES,** FOR A CHANGE --

-- I'M ITCHING TO **GET MY FISTS BLOODY!**

FUNNY, ISN'T IT?

WE PUT ON **THEIR** OUTFITS TO GET BY ON THEIR EARTH --

-- AND THEY HAD TO PULL THE **SAME TRICK** TO PULL THE WOOL OVER THE **QWARDIANS'** EYES!

FUNNY TO **YOU,** QUICK, MAYBE --

-- BUT THERE ISN' A SHRED C THIS THAT' FUNNY TO ME!

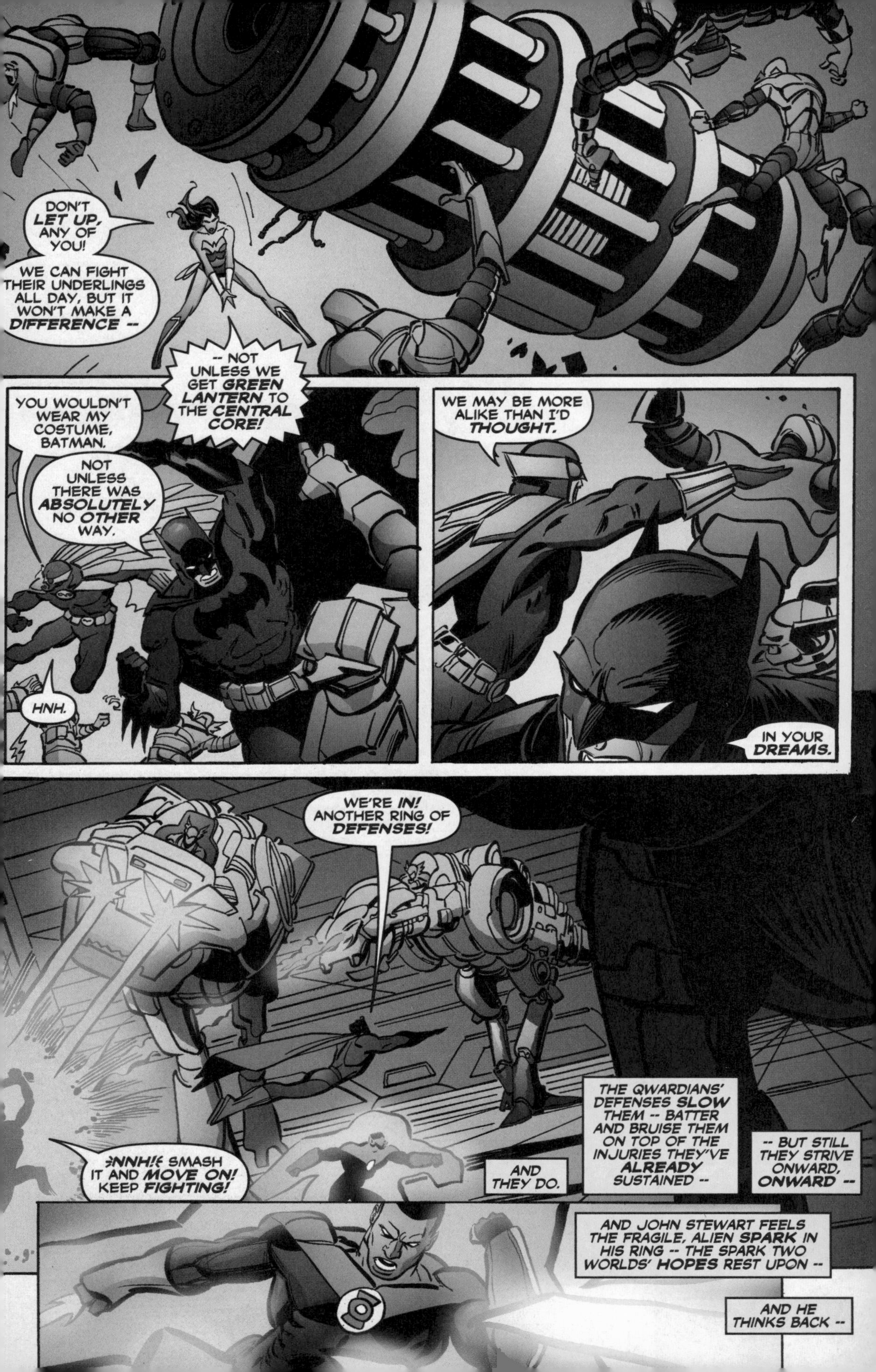
DON'T LET UP, ANY OF YOU!
WE CAN FIGHT THEIR UNDERLINGS ALL DAY, BUT IT WON'T MAKE A DIFFERENCE --
-- NOT UNLESS WE GET GREEN LANTERN TO THE CENTRAL CORE!
YOU WOULDN'T WEAR MY COSTUME, BATMAN.
NOT UNLESS THERE WAS ABSOLUTELY NO OTHER WAY.
HNH.
WE MAY BE MORE ALIKE THAN I'D THOUGHT.
IN YOUR DREAMS.
WE'RE IN! ANOTHER RING OF DEFENSES!
ƎNNH!ʕ SMASH IT AND MOVE ON! KEEP FIGHTING!
AND THEY DO.
THE QWARDIANS' DEFENSES SLOW THEM -- BATTER AND BRUISE THEM ON TOP OF THE INJURIES THEY'VE ALREADY SUSTAINED --
-- BUT STILL THEY STRIVE ONWARD, ONWARD --
AND JOHN STEWART FEELS THE FRAGILE, ALIEN SPARK IN HIS RING -- THE SPARK TWO WORLDS' HOPES REST UPON --
AND HE THINKS BACK --

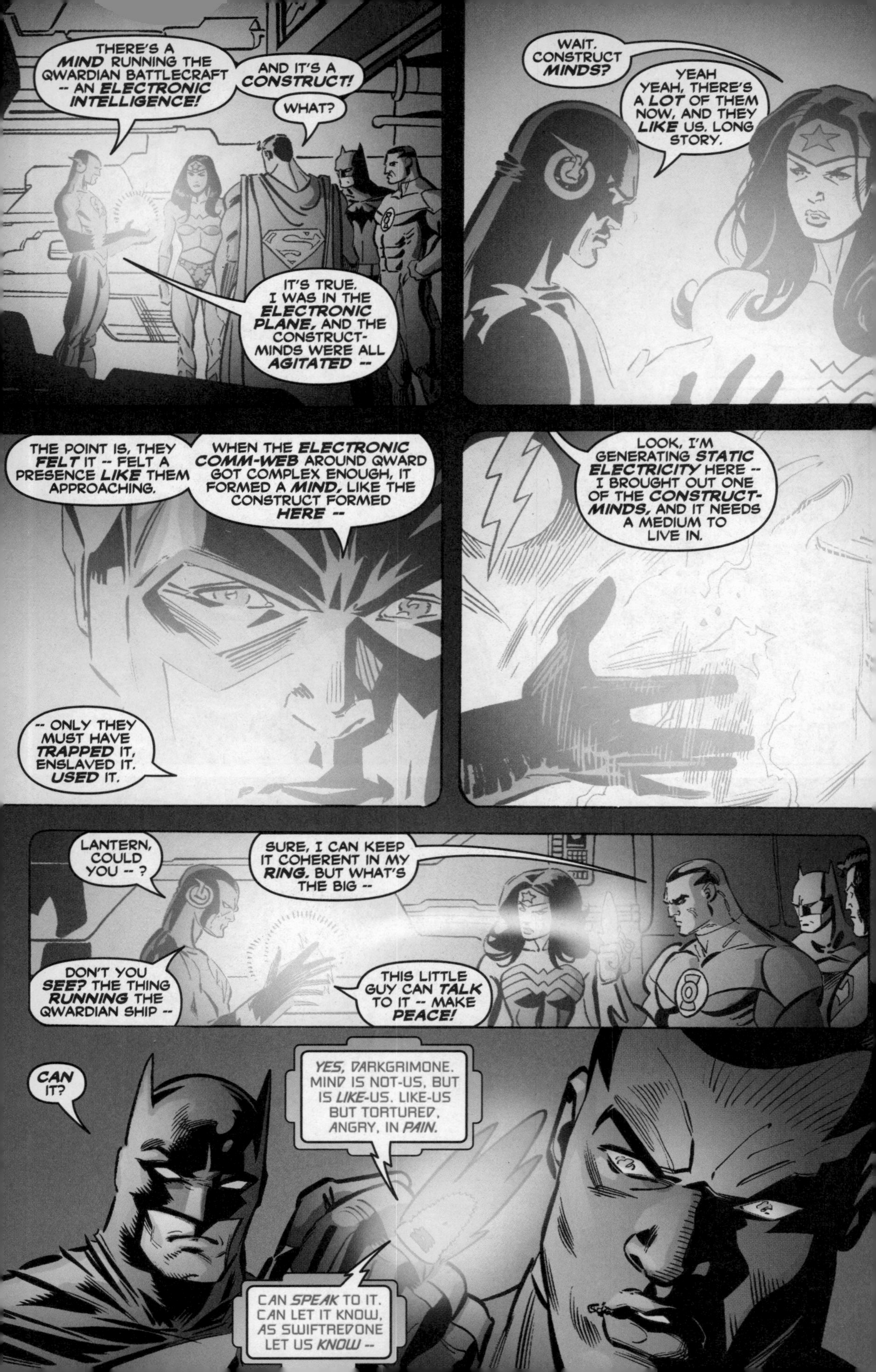
THERE'S A MIND RUNNING THE QWARDIAN BATTLECRAFT -- AN ELECTRONIC INTELLIGENCE!
AND IT'S A CONSTRUCT!
WHAT?
IT'S TRUE. I WAS IN THE ELECTRONIC PLANE, AND THE CONSTRUCT-MINDS WERE ALL AGITATED --
WAIT. CONSTRUCT MINDS?
YEAH YEAH, THERE'S A LOT OF THEM NOW, AND THEY LIKE US. LONG STORY.
THE POINT IS, THEY FELT IT -- FELT A PRESENCE LIKE THEM APPROACHING.
WHEN THE ELECTRONIC COMM-WEB AROUND QWARD GOT COMPLEX ENOUGH, IT FORMED A MIND, LIKE THE CONSTRUCT FORMED HERE --
-- ONLY THEY MUST HAVE TRAPPED IT, ENSLAVED IT. USED IT.
LOOK, I'M GENERATING STATIC ELECTRICITY HERE -- I BROUGHT OUT ONE OF THE CONSTRUCT-MINDS, AND IT NEEDS A MEDIUM TO LIVE IN.
LANTERN, COULD YOU -- ?
SURE, I CAN KEEP IT COHERENT IN MY RING. BUT WHAT'S THE BIG --
DON'T YOU SEE? THE THING RUNNING THE QWARDIAN SHIP --
THIS LITTLE GUY CAN TALK TO IT -- MAKE PEACE!
CAN IT?
YES, DARKGRIMONE. MIND IS NOT-US, BUT IS LIKE-US. LIKE-US BUT TORTURED, ANGRY, IN PAIN.
CAN SPEAK TO IT. CAN LET IT KNOW, AS SWIFTREDONE LET US KNOW --

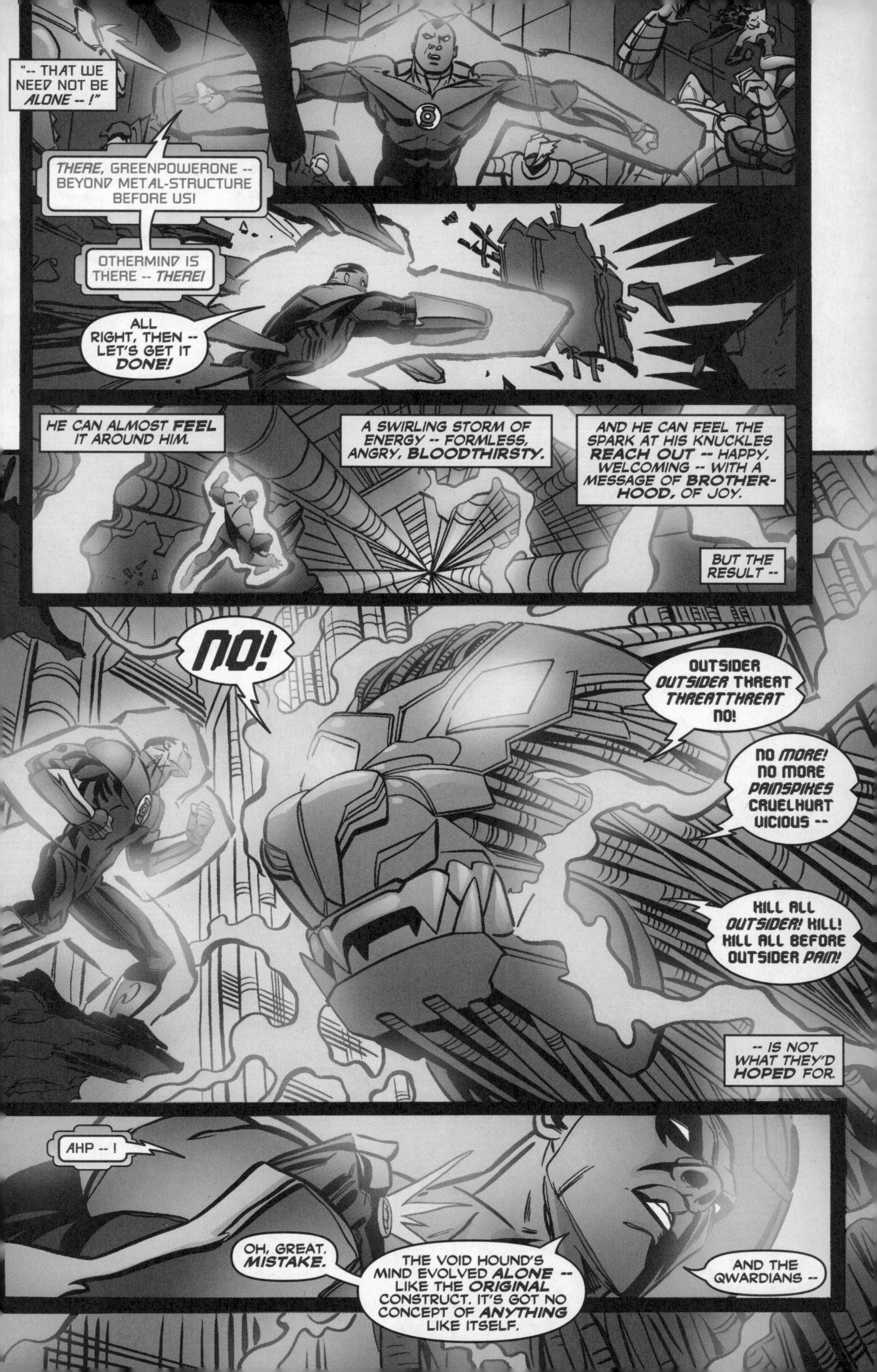
"-- THAT WE NEED NOT BE ALONE -- !"
THERE, GREENPOWERONE -- BEYOND METAL-STRUCTURE BEFORE US!
OTHERMIND IS THERE -- THERE!
ALL RIGHT, THEN -- LET'S GET IT DONE!
HE CAN ALMOST FEEL IT AROUND HIM.
A SWIRLING STORM OF ENERGY -- FORMLESS, ANGRY, BLOODTHIRSTY.
AND HE CAN FEEL THE SPARK AT HIS KNUCKLES REACH OUT -- HAPPY, WELCOMING -- WITH A MESSAGE OF BROTHER-HOOD, OF JOY.
BUT THE RESULT --
NO!
OUTSIDER OUTSIDER THREAT THREATTHREAT NO!
NO MORE! NO MORE PAINSPIKES CRUELHURT VICIOUS --
KILL ALL OUTSIDER! KILL! KILL ALL BEFORE OUTSIDER PAIN!
-- IS NOT WHAT THEY'D HOPED FOR.
AHP -- !
OH, GREAT. MISTAKE.
THE VOID HOUND'S MIND EVOLVED ALONE -- LIKE THE ORIGINAL CONSTRUCT. IT'S GOT NO CONCEPT OF ANYTHING LIKE ITSELF.
AND THE QWARDIANS --

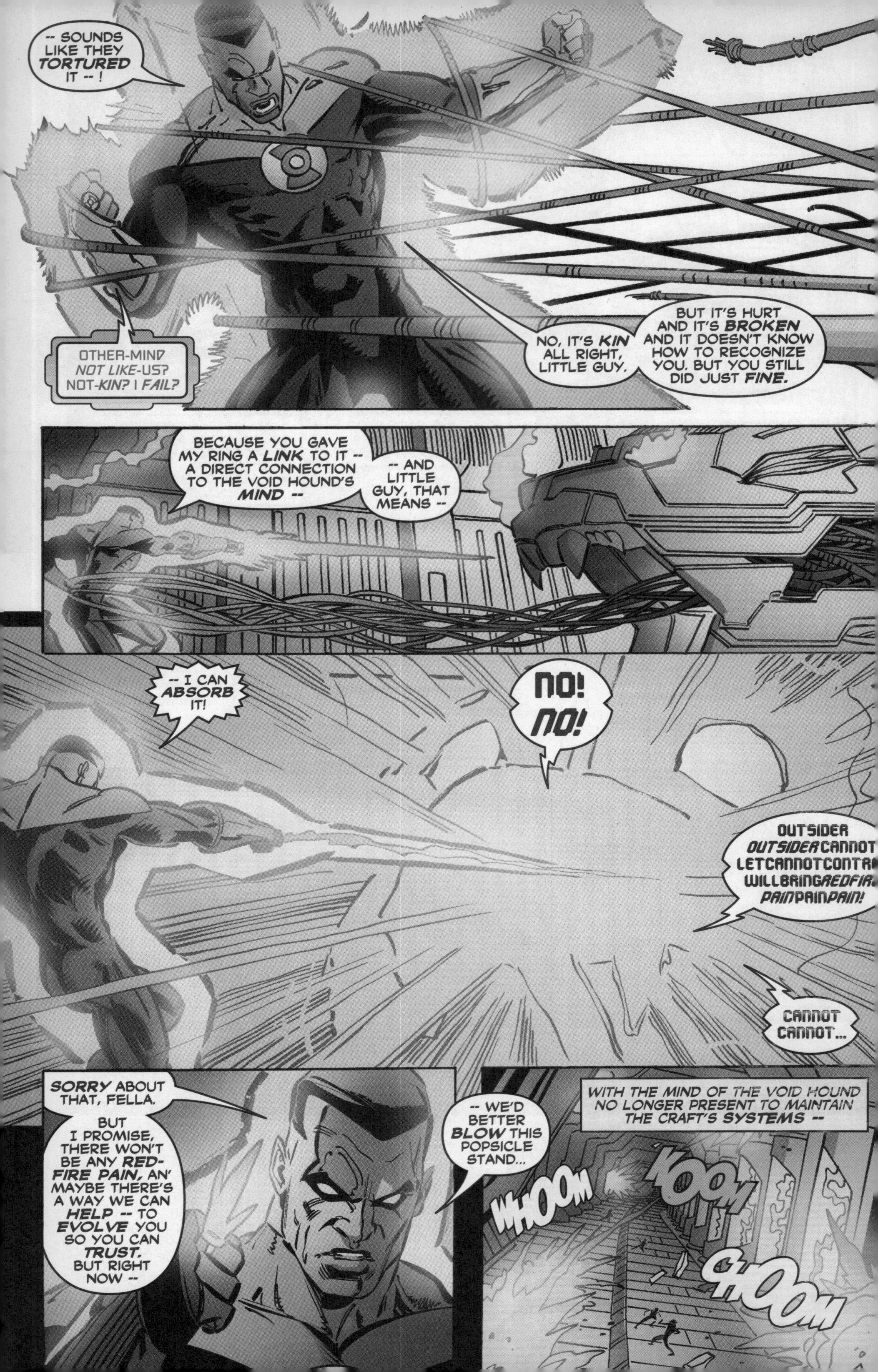

-- SOUNDS LIKE THEY TORTURED IT -- !
OTHER-MIND NOT LIKE-US? NOT-KIN? I FAIL?
NO, IT'S KIN ALL RIGHT, LITTLE GUY.
BUT IT'S HURT AND IT'S BROKEN AND IT DOESN'T KNOW HOW TO RECOGNIZE YOU. BUT YOU STILL DID JUST FINE.
BECAUSE YOU GAVE MY RING A LINK TO IT -- A DIRECT CONNECTION TO THE VOID HOUND'S MIND --
-- AND LITTLE GUY, THAT MEANS --
-- I CAN ABSORB IT!
NO! NO!
OUTSIDER OUTSIDERCANNOT LETCANNOTCONTR WILLBRINGREDFIR PAINPAINPAIN!
CANNOT CANNOT...
SORRY ABOUT THAT, FELLA.
BUT I PROMISE, THERE WON'T BE ANY RED-FIRE PAIN, AN' MAYBE THERE'S A WAY WE CAN HELP -- TO EVOLVE YOU SO YOU CAN TRUST. BUT RIGHT NOW --
-- WE'D BETTER BLOW THIS POPSICLE STAND...
WITH THE MIND OF THE VOID HOUND NO LONGER PRESENT TO MAINTAIN THE CRAFT'S SYSTEMS --
WHOOM
KOOM
CHOOM

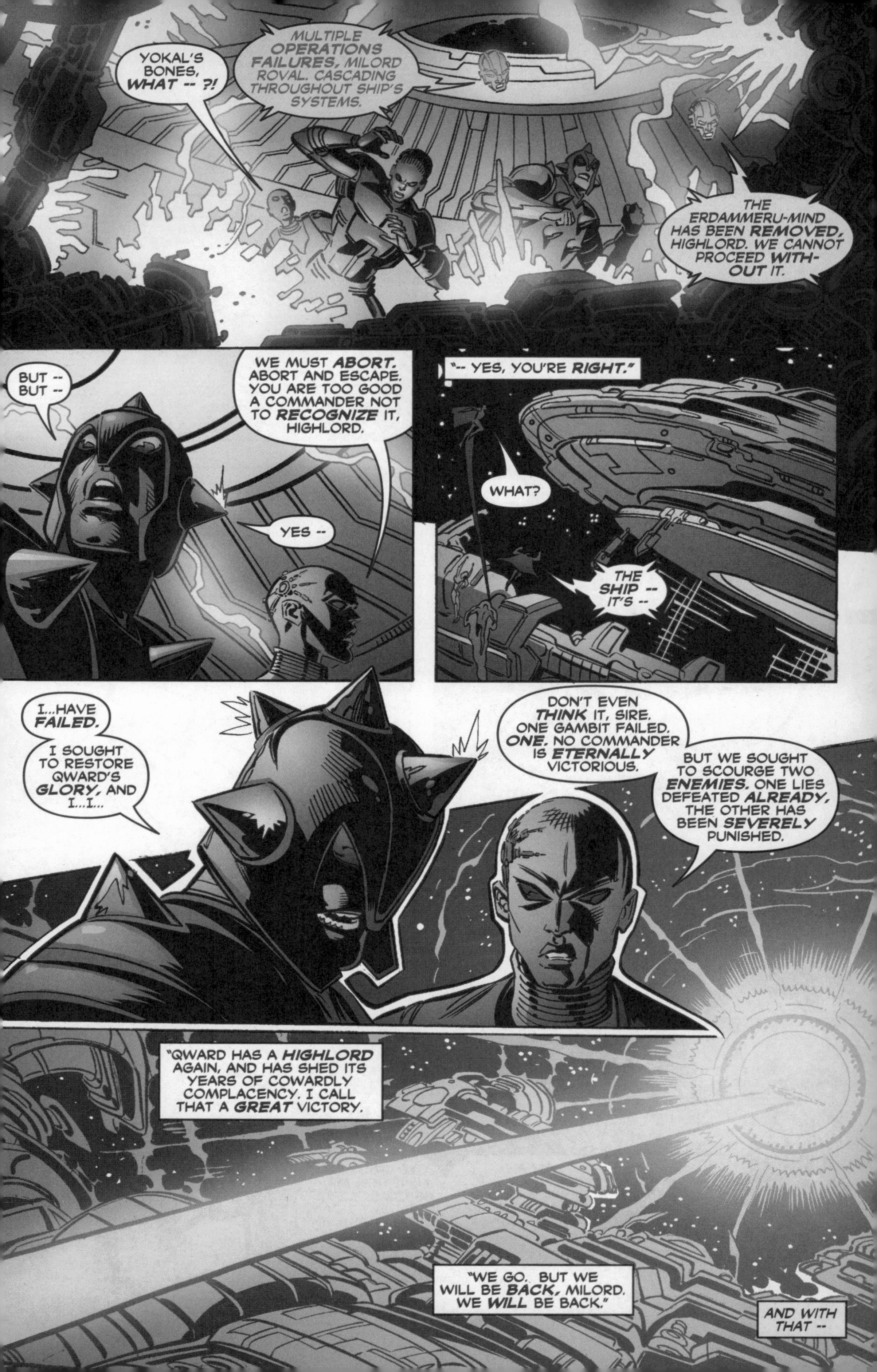
YOKAL'S BONES, WHAT -- ?!
MULTIPLE OPERATIONS FAILURES, MILORD ROVAL. CASCADING THROUGHOUT SHIP'S SYSTEMS.
THE ERDAMMERU-MIND HAS BEEN REMOVED, HIGHLORD. WE CANNOT PROCEED WITHOUT IT.
BUT -- BUT --
WE MUST ABORT. ABORT AND ESCAPE. YOU ARE TOO GOOD A COMMANDER NOT TO RECOGNIZE IT, HIGHLORD.
YES --
"-- YES, YOU'RE RIGHT."
WHAT?
THE SHIP -- IT'S --
I...HAVE FAILED.
I SOUGHT TO RESTORE QWARD'S GLORY, AND I...I...
DON'T EVEN THINK IT, SIRE. ONE GAMBIT FAILED. ONE. NO COMMANDER IS ETERNALLY VICTORIOUS.
BUT WE SOUGHT TO SCOURGE TWO ENEMIES. ONE LIES DEFEATED ALREADY, THE OTHER HAS BEEN SEVERELY PUNISHED.
"QWARD HAS A HIGHLORD AGAIN, AND HAS SHED ITS YEARS OF COWARDLY COMPLACENCY. I CALL THAT A GREAT VICTORY.
"WE GO. BUT WE WILL BE BACK, MILORD. WE WILL BE BACK."
AND WITH THAT --

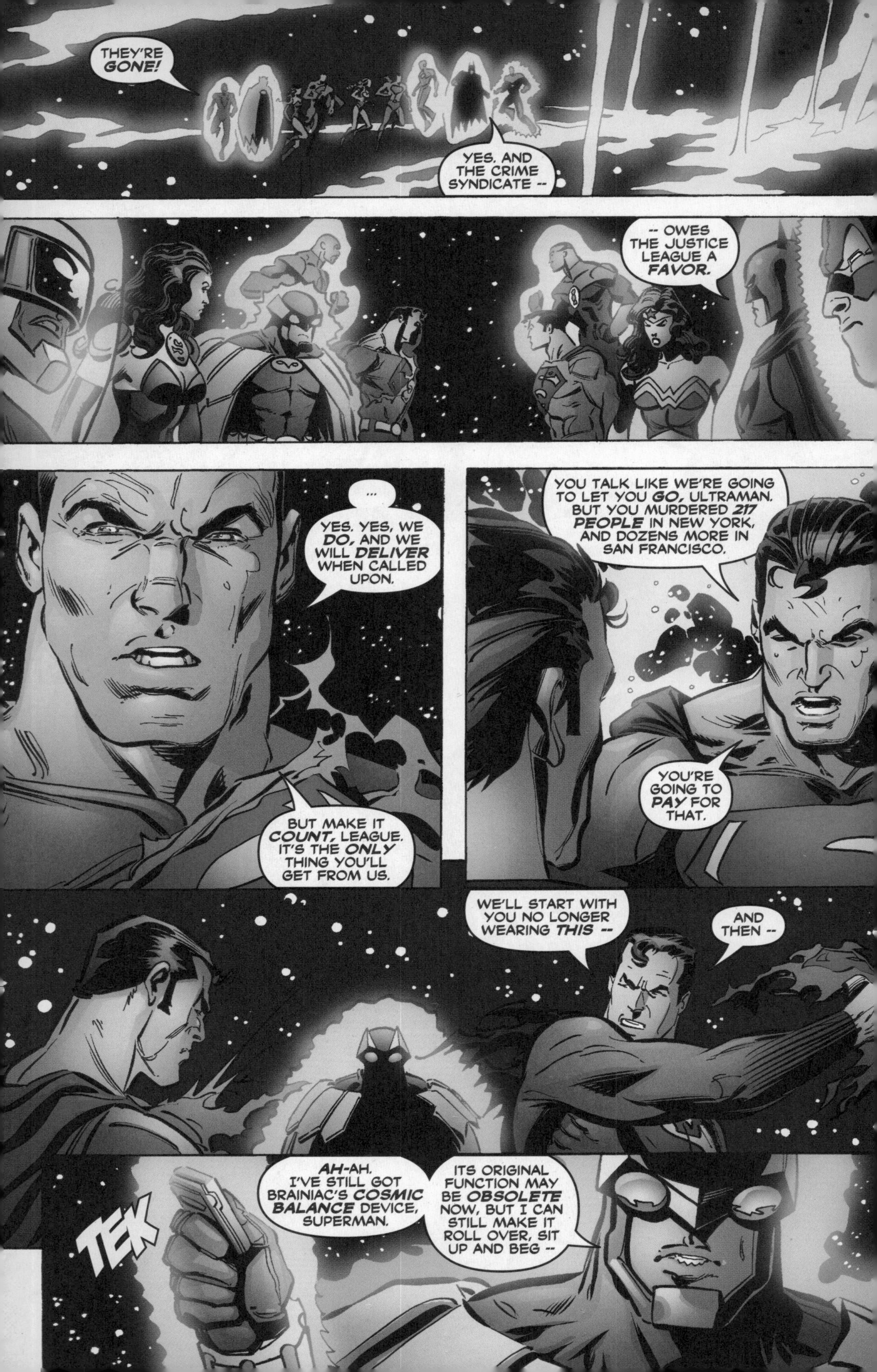
THEY'RE GONE!
YES. AND THE CRIME SYNDICATE --
-- OWES THE JUSTICE LEAGUE A FAVOR.
...
YES. YES, WE DO, AND WE WILL DELIVER WHEN CALLED UPON.
BUT MAKE IT COUNT, LEAGUE. IT'S THE ONLY THING YOU'LL GET FROM US.
YOU TALK LIKE WE'RE GOING TO LET YOU GO, ULTRAMAN. BUT YOU MURDERED 217 PEOPLE IN NEW YORK, AND DOZENS MORE IN SAN FRANCISCO.
YOU'RE GOING TO PAY FOR THAT.
WE'LL START WITH YOU NO LONGER WEARING THIS --
AND THEN --
TEK
AH-AH. I'VE STILL GOT BRAINIAC'S COSMIC BALANCE DEVICE, SUPERMAN.
ITS ORIGINAL FUNCTION MAY BE OBSOLETE NOW, BUT I CAN STILL MAKE IT ROLL OVER, SIT UP AND BEG --

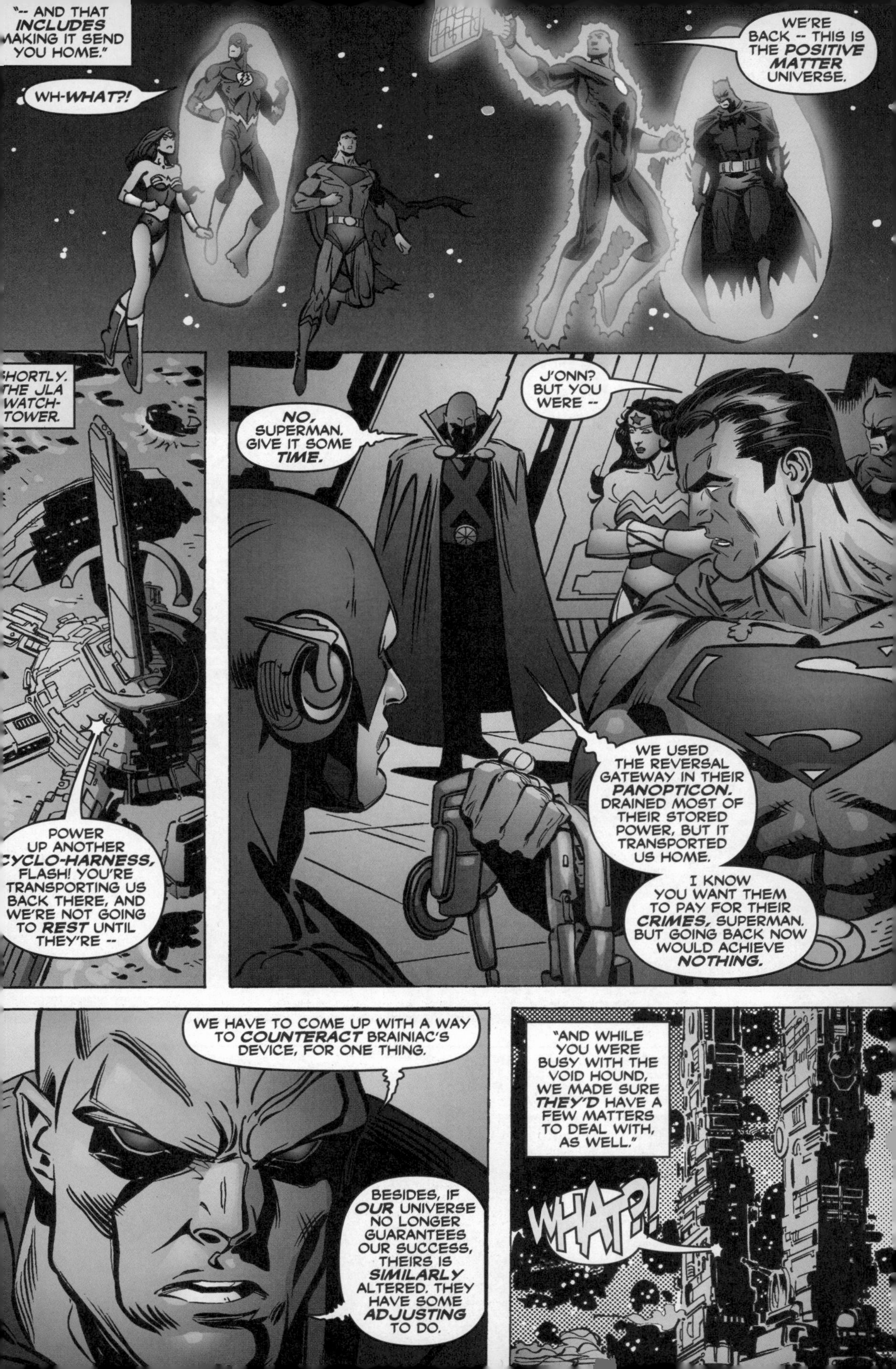
"-- AND THAT INCLUDES MAKING IT SEND YOU HOME."
WH-WHAT?!
WE'RE BACK -- THIS IS THE POSITIVE MATTER UNIVERSE.
SHORTLY. THE JLA WATCH-TOWER.
POWER UP ANOTHER CYCLO-HARNESS, FLASH! YOU'RE TRANSPORTING US BACK THERE, AND WE'RE NOT GOING TO REST UNTIL THEY'RE --
NO, SUPERMAN. GIVE IT SOME TIME.
J'ONN? BUT YOU WERE --
WE USED THE REVERSAL GATEWAY IN THEIR PANOPTICON. DRAINED MOST OF THEIR STORED POWER, BUT IT TRANSPORTED US HOME.
I KNOW YOU WANT THEM TO PAY FOR THEIR CRIMES, SUPERMAN. BUT GOING BACK NOW WOULD ACHIEVE NOTHING.
WE HAVE TO COME UP WITH A WAY TO COUNTERACT BRAINIAC'S DEVICE, FOR ONE THING.
BESIDES, IF OUR UNIVERSE NO LONGER GUARANTEES OUR SUCCESS, THEIRS IS SIMILARLY ALTERED. THEY HAVE SOME ADJUSTING TO DO.
"AND WHILE YOU WERE BUSY WITH THE VOID HOUND, WE MADE SURE THEY'D HAVE A FEW MATTERS TO DEAL WITH, AS WELL."
WHAT?!

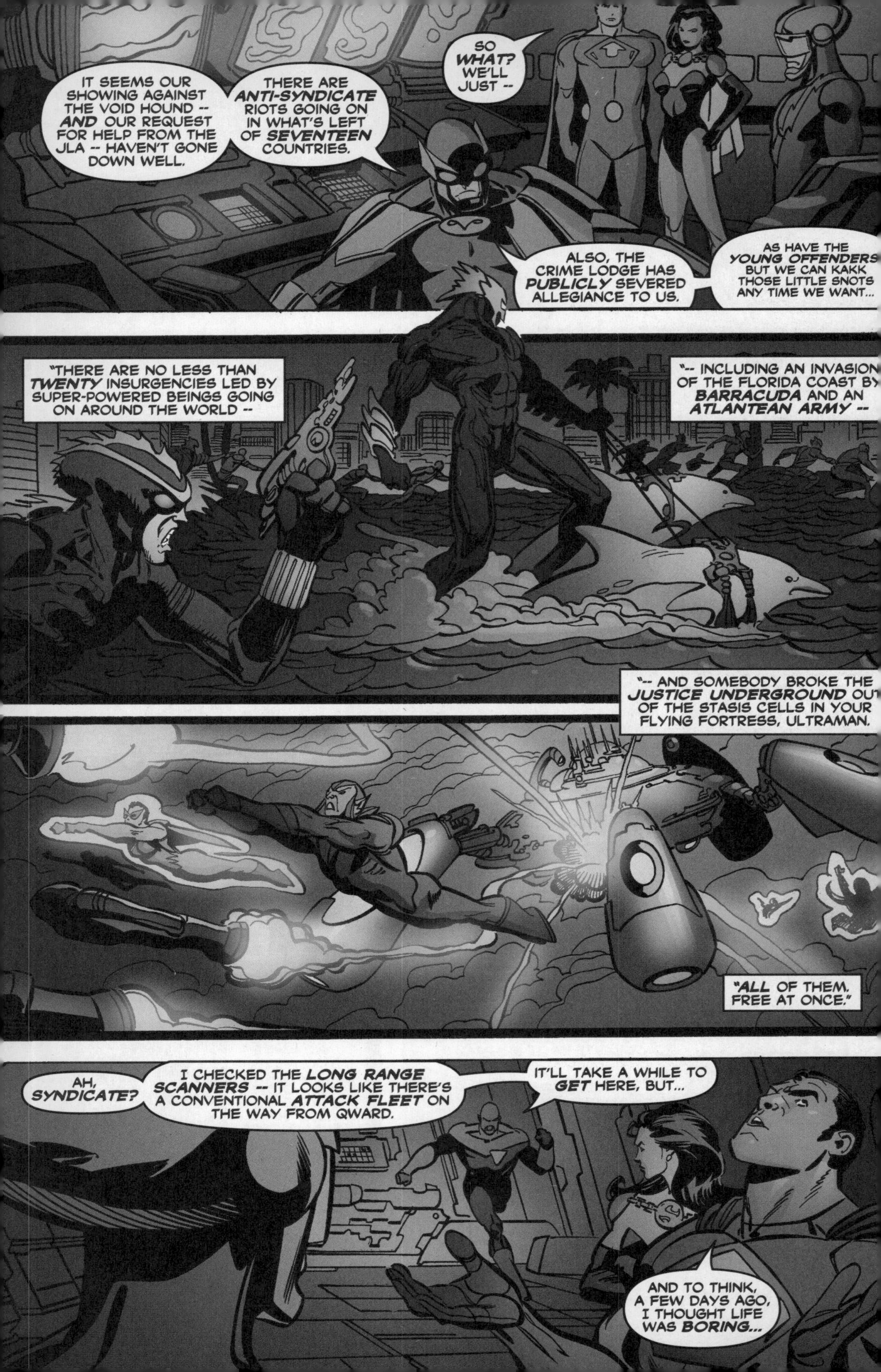
IT SEEMS OUR SHOWING AGAINST THE VOID HOUND -- AND OUR REQUEST FOR HELP FROM THE JLA -- HAVEN'T GONE DOWN WELL.
THERE ARE ANTI-SYNDICATE RIOTS GOING ON IN WHAT'S LEFT OF SEVENTEEN COUNTRIES.
SO WHAT? WE'LL JUST --
ALSO, THE CRIME LODGE HAS PUBLICLY SEVERED ALLEGIANCE TO US.
AS HAVE THE YOUNG OFFENDERS BUT WE CAN KAKK THOSE LITTLE SNOTS ANY TIME WE WANT...
"THERE ARE NO LESS THAN TWENTY INSURGENCIES LED BY SUPER-POWERED BEINGS GOING ON AROUND THE WORLD --
"-- INCLUDING AN INVASION OF THE FLORIDA COAST BY BARRACUDA AND AN ATLANTEAN ARMY --
"-- AND SOMEBODY BROKE THE JUSTICE UNDERGROUND OUT OF THE STASIS CELLS IN YOUR FLYING FORTRESS, ULTRAMAN.
"ALL OF THEM. FREE AT ONCE."
AH, SYNDICATE?
I CHECKED THE LONG RANGE SCANNERS -- IT LOOKS LIKE THERE'S A CONVENTIONAL ATTACK FLEET ON THE WAY FROM QWARD.
IT'LL TAKE A WHILE TO GET HERE, BUT...
AND TO THINK, A FEW DAYS AGO, I THOUGHT LIFE WAS BORING...

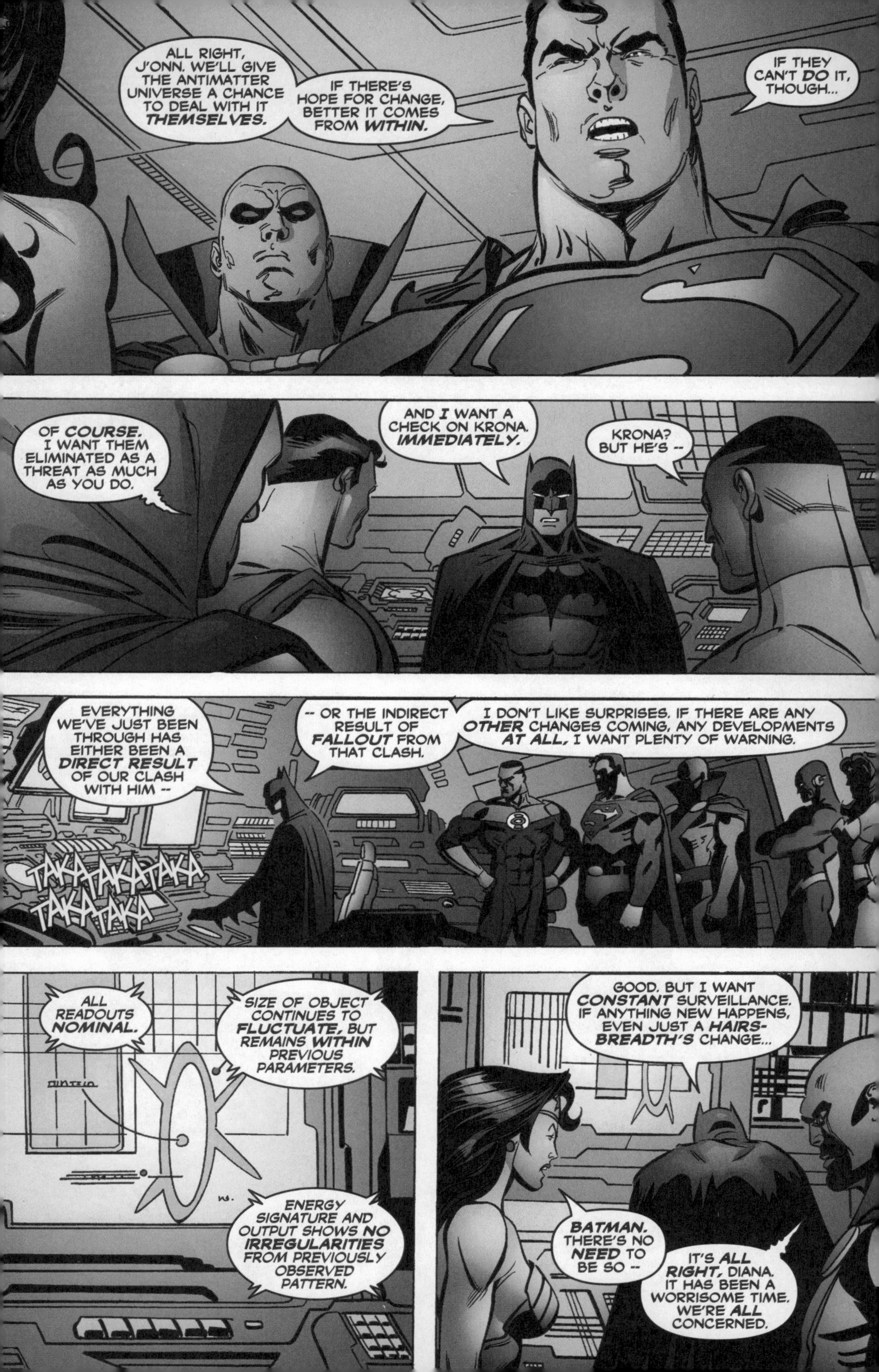
ALL RIGHT, J'ONN. WE'LL GIVE THE ANTIMATTER UNIVERSE A CHANCE TO DEAL WITH IT THEMSELVES.
IF THERE'S HOPE FOR CHANGE, BETTER IT COMES FROM WITHIN.
IF THEY CAN'T DO IT, THOUGH...
OF COURSE. I WANT THEM ELIMINATED AS A THREAT AS MUCH AS YOU DO.
AND I WANT A CHECK ON KRONA. IMMEDIATELY.
KRONA? BUT HE'S --
EVERYTHING WE'VE JUST BEEN THROUGH HAS EITHER BEEN A DIRECT RESULT OF OUR CLASH WITH HIM --
-- OR THE INDIRECT RESULT OF FALLOUT FROM THAT CLASH.
I DON'T LIKE SURPRISES. IF THERE ARE ANY OTHER CHANGES COMING, ANY DEVELOPMENTS AT ALL, I WANT PLENTY OF WARNING.
TAKATAKATAKA TAKATAKA
ALL READOUTS NOMINAL.
SIZE OF OBJECT CONTINUES TO FLUCTUATE, BUT REMAINS WITHIN PREVIOUS PARAMETERS.
ENERGY SIGNATURE AND OUTPUT SHOWS NO IRREGULARITIES FROM PREVIOUSLY OBSERVED PATTERN.
GOOD, BUT I WANT CONSTANT SURVEILLANCE. IF ANYTHING NEW HAPPENS, EVEN JUST A HAIRS-BREADTH'S CHANGE...
BATMAN. THERE'S NO NEED TO BE SO --
IT'S ALL RIGHT, DIANA. IT HAS BEEN A WORRISOME TIME. WE'RE ALL CONCERNED.

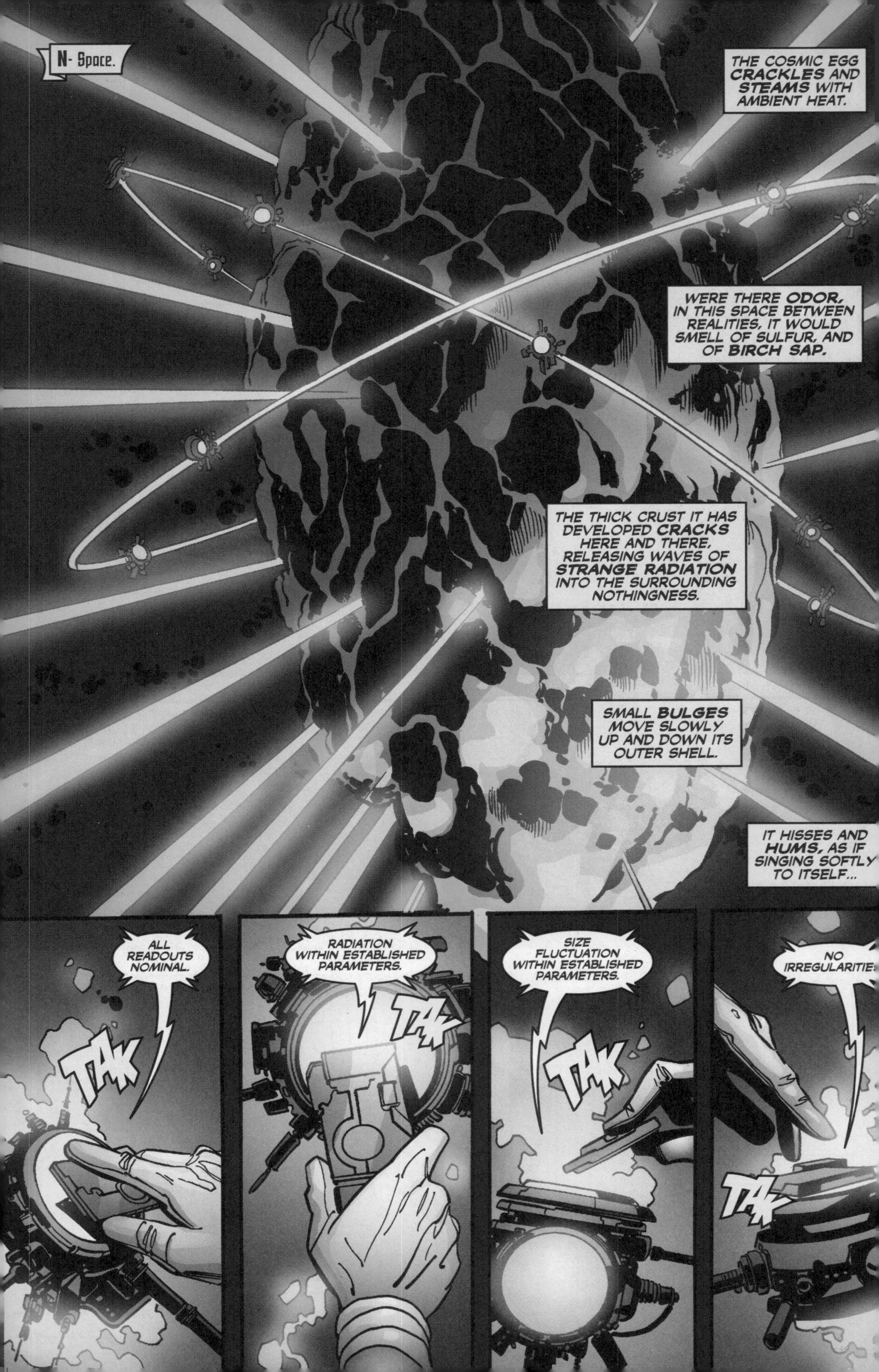
N- Space.
THE COSMIC EGG CRACKLES AND STEAMS WITH AMBIENT HEAT.
WERE THERE ODOR, IN THIS SPACE BETWEEN REALITIES, IT WOULD SMELL OF SULFUR, AND OF BIRCH SAP.
THE THICK CRUST IT HAS DEVELOPED CRACKS HERE AND THERE, RELEASING WAVES OF STRANGE RADIATION INTO THE SURROUNDING NOTHINGNESS.
SMALL BULGES MOVE SLOWLY UP AND DOWN ITS OUTER SHELL.
IT HISSES AND HUMS, AS IF SINGING SOFTLY TO ITSELF...
ALL READOUTS NOMINAL.
TAK
RADIATION WITHIN ESTABLISHED PARAMETERS.
TAK
SIZE FLUCTUATION WITHIN ESTABLISHED PARAMETERS.
TAK
NO IRREGULARITIES
TAK

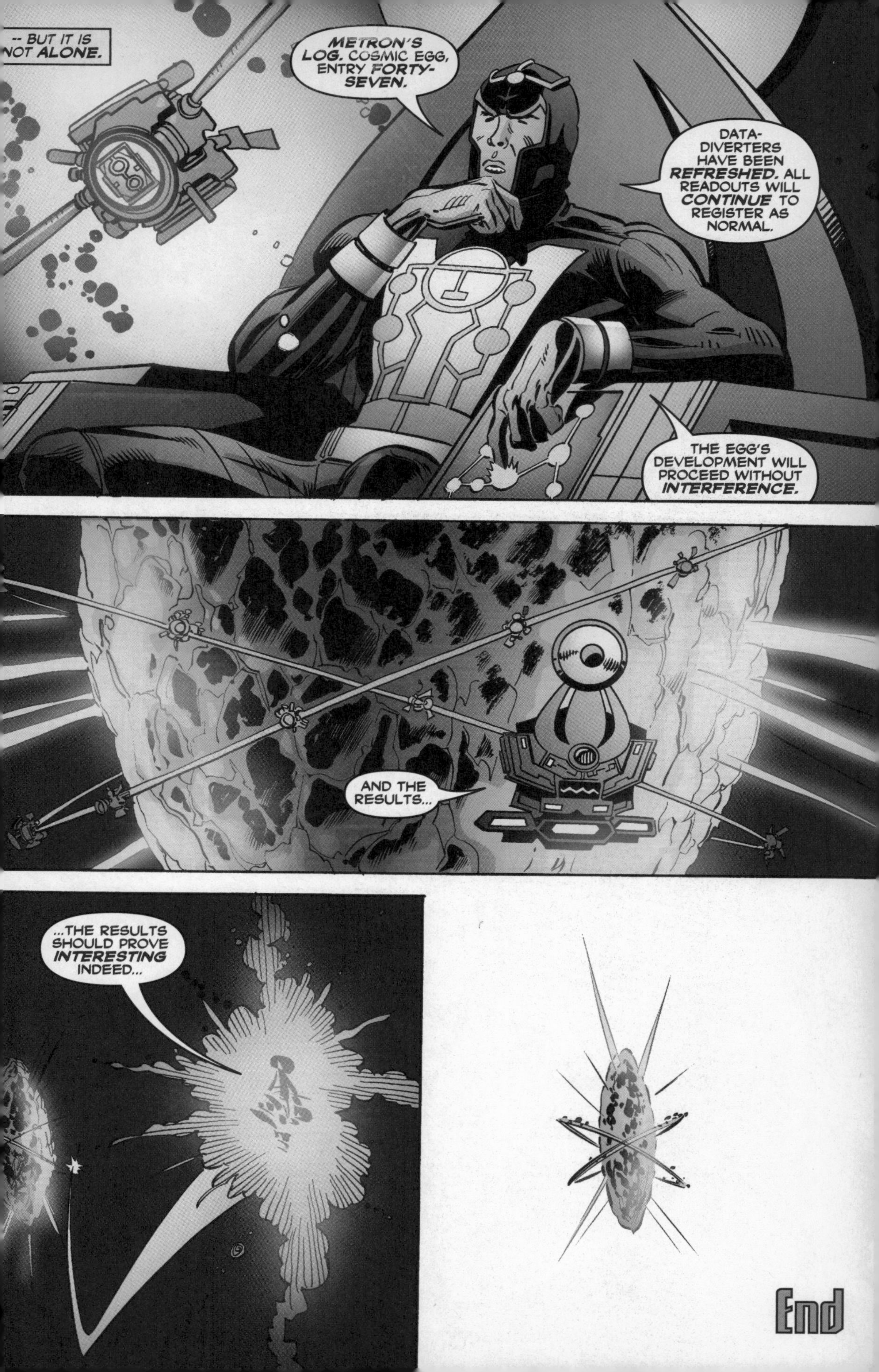
-- BUT IT IS NOT ALONE.
METRON'S LOG. COSMIC EGG, ENTRY FORTY-SEVEN.
DATA-DIVERTERS HAVE BEEN REFRESHED. ALL READOUTS WILL CONTINUE TO REGISTER AS NORMAL.
THE EGG'S DEVELOPMENT WILL PROCEED WITHOUT INTERFERENCE.
AND THE RESULTS...
...THE RESULTS SHOULD PROVE INTERESTING INDEED...
End

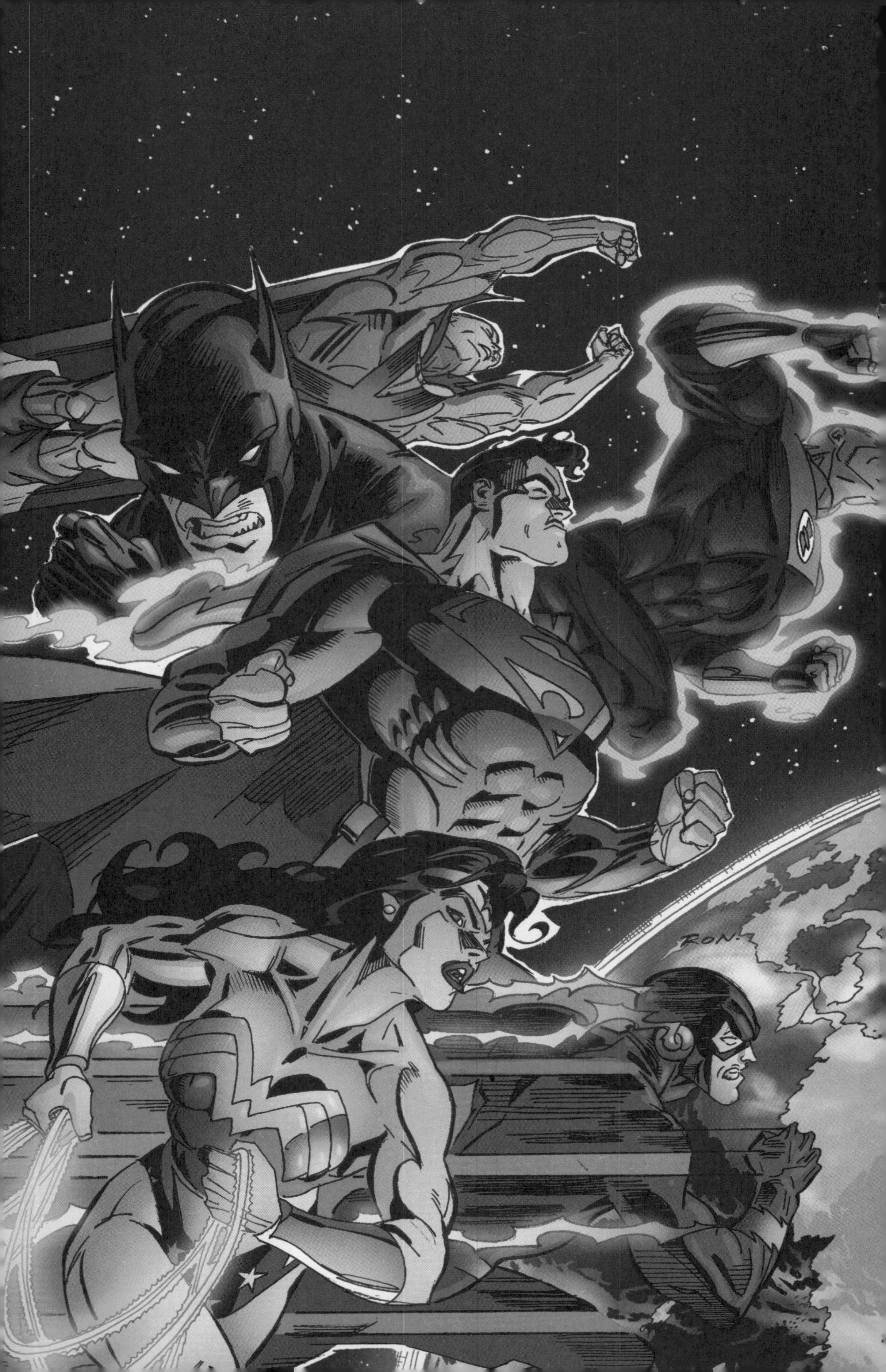
RON.

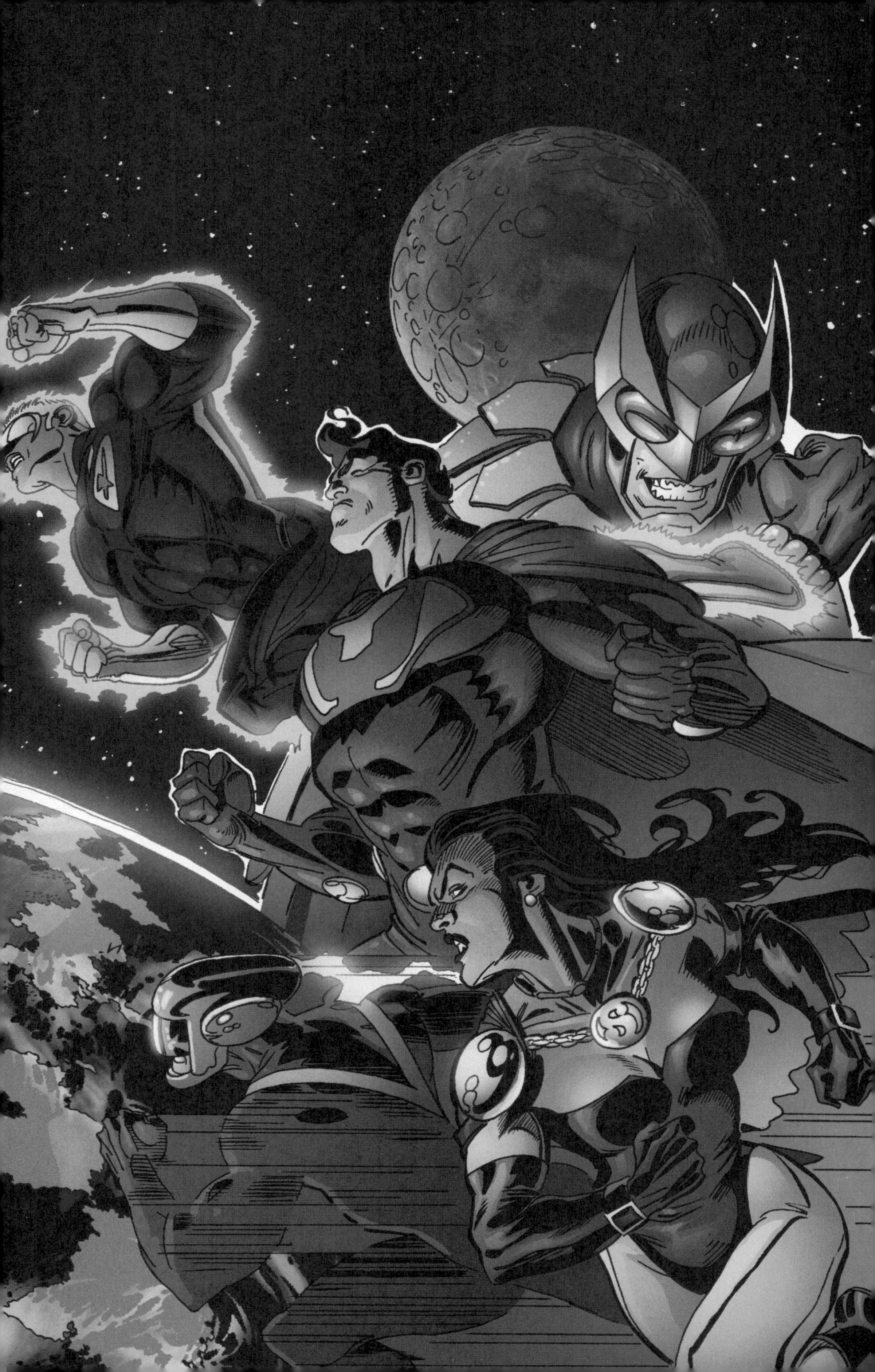

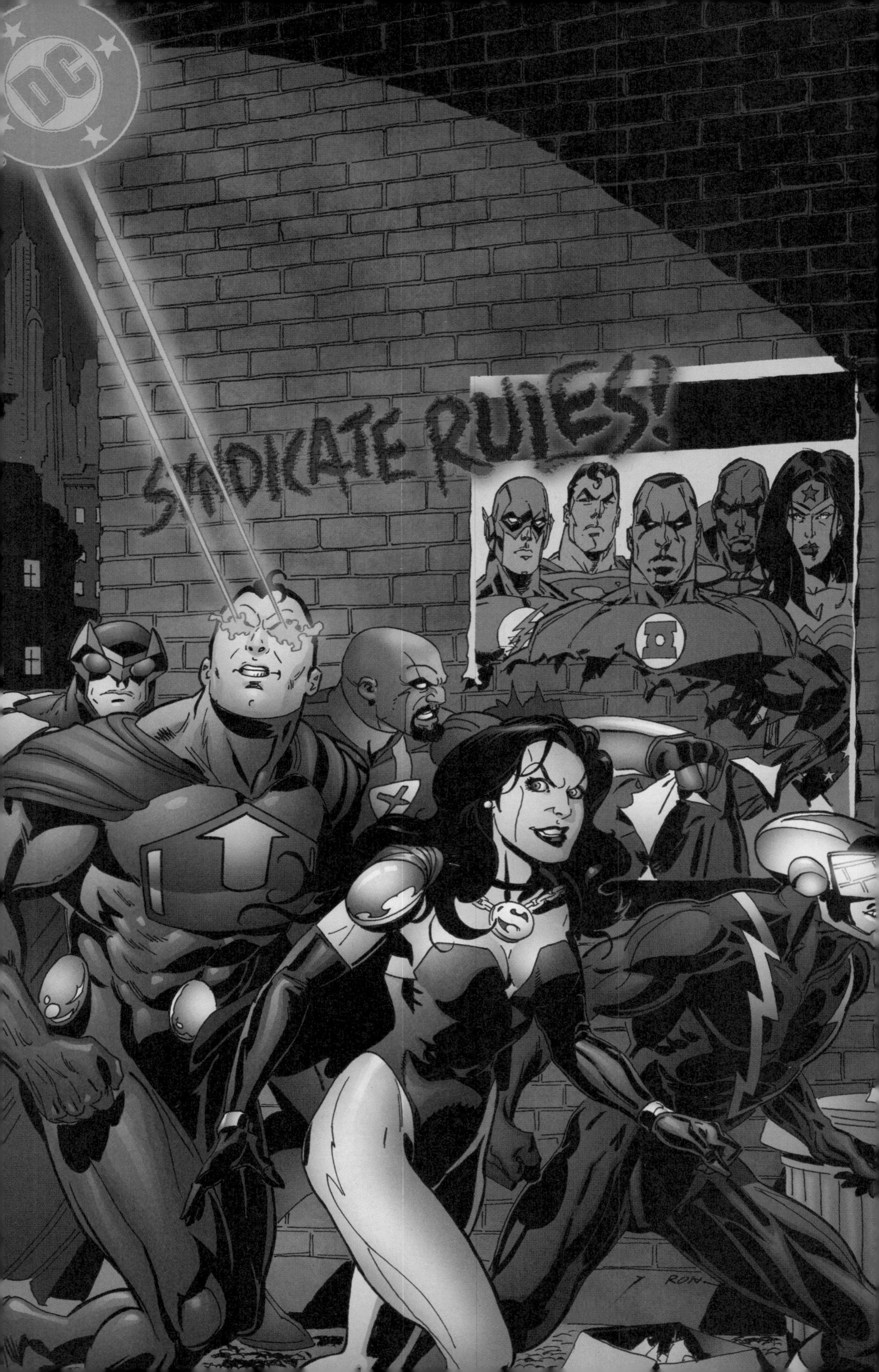
SYNDICATE RULES!
RON

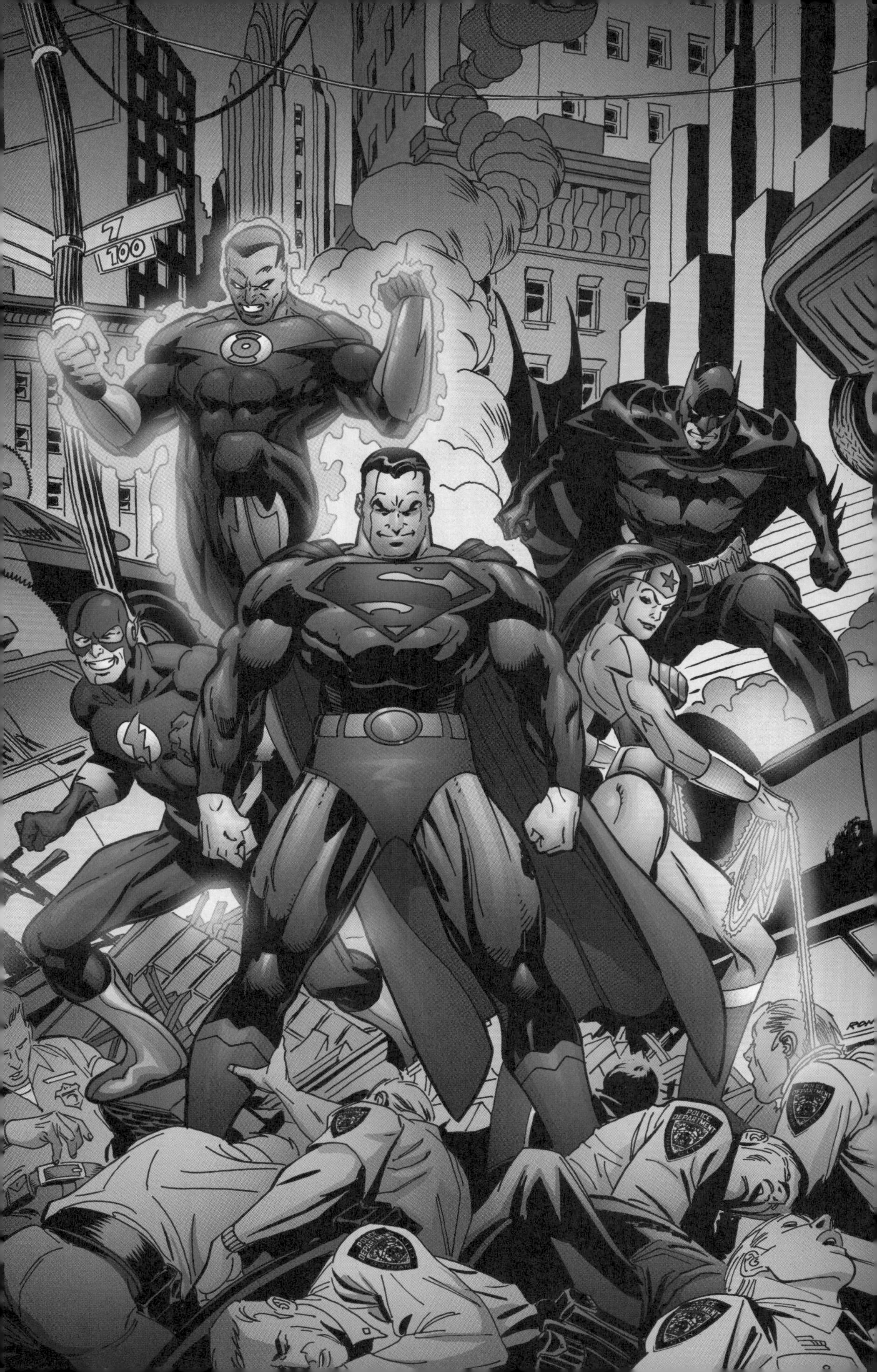
7
100
POLICE DEPARTMENT

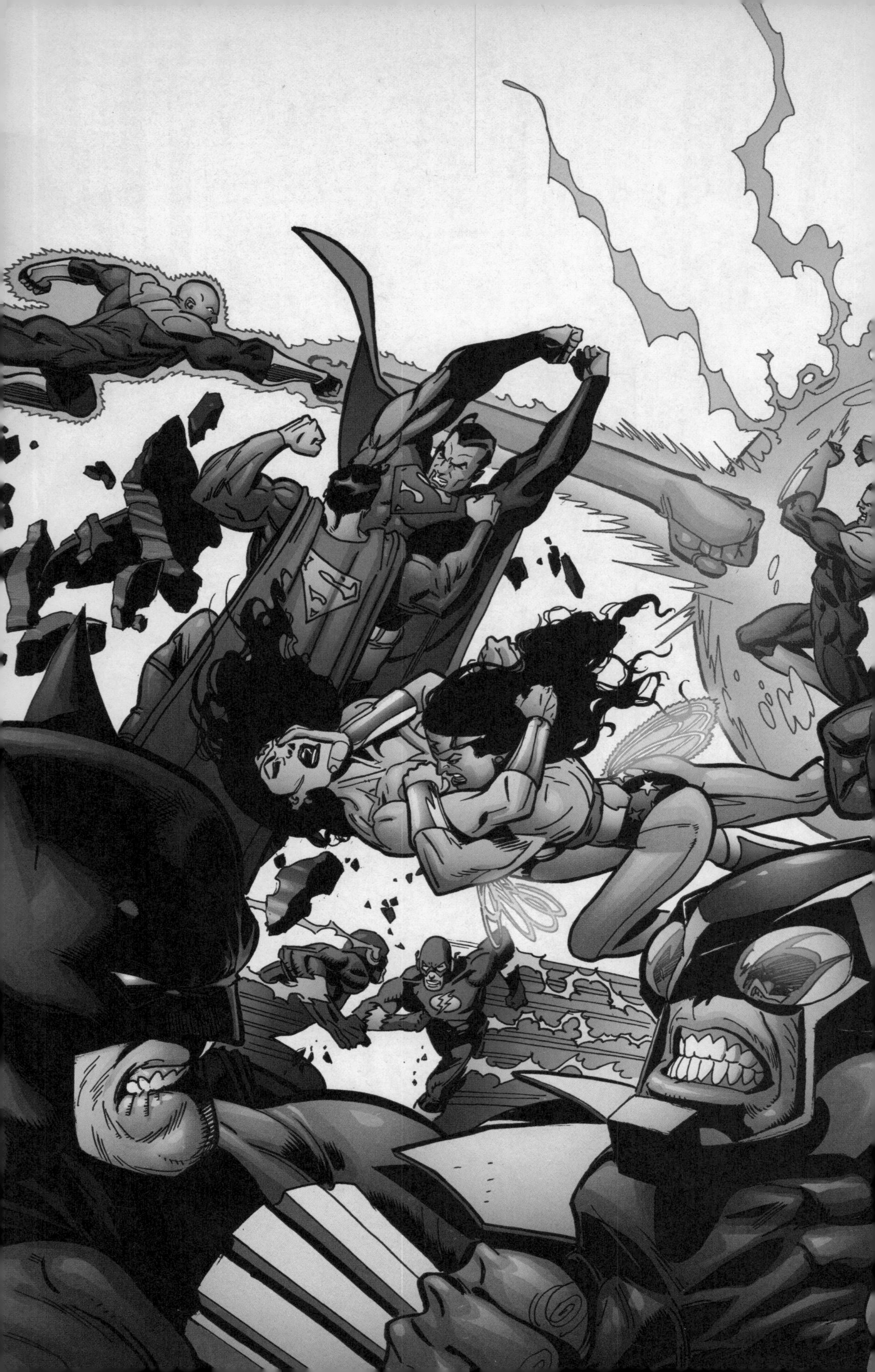

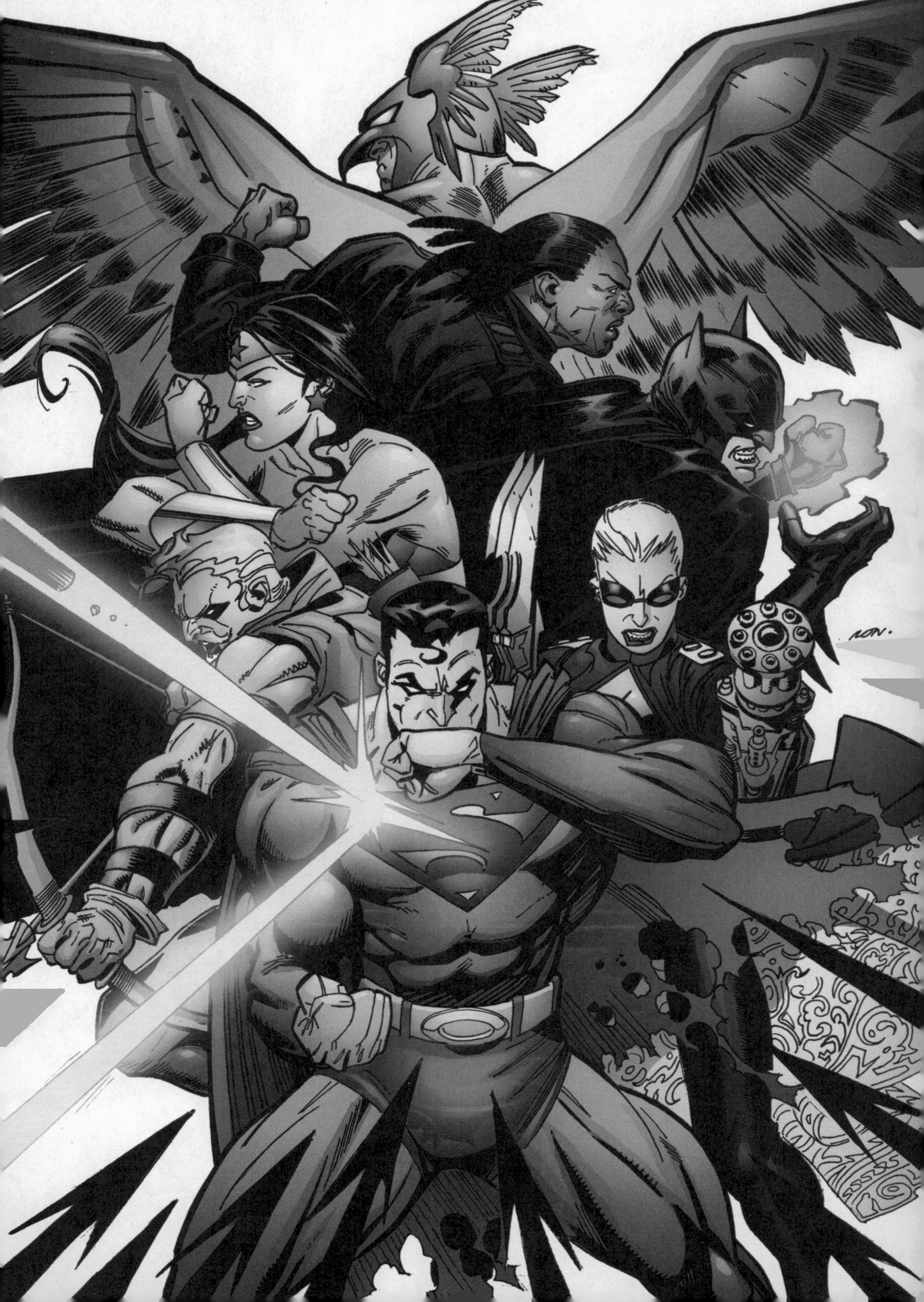
RON.

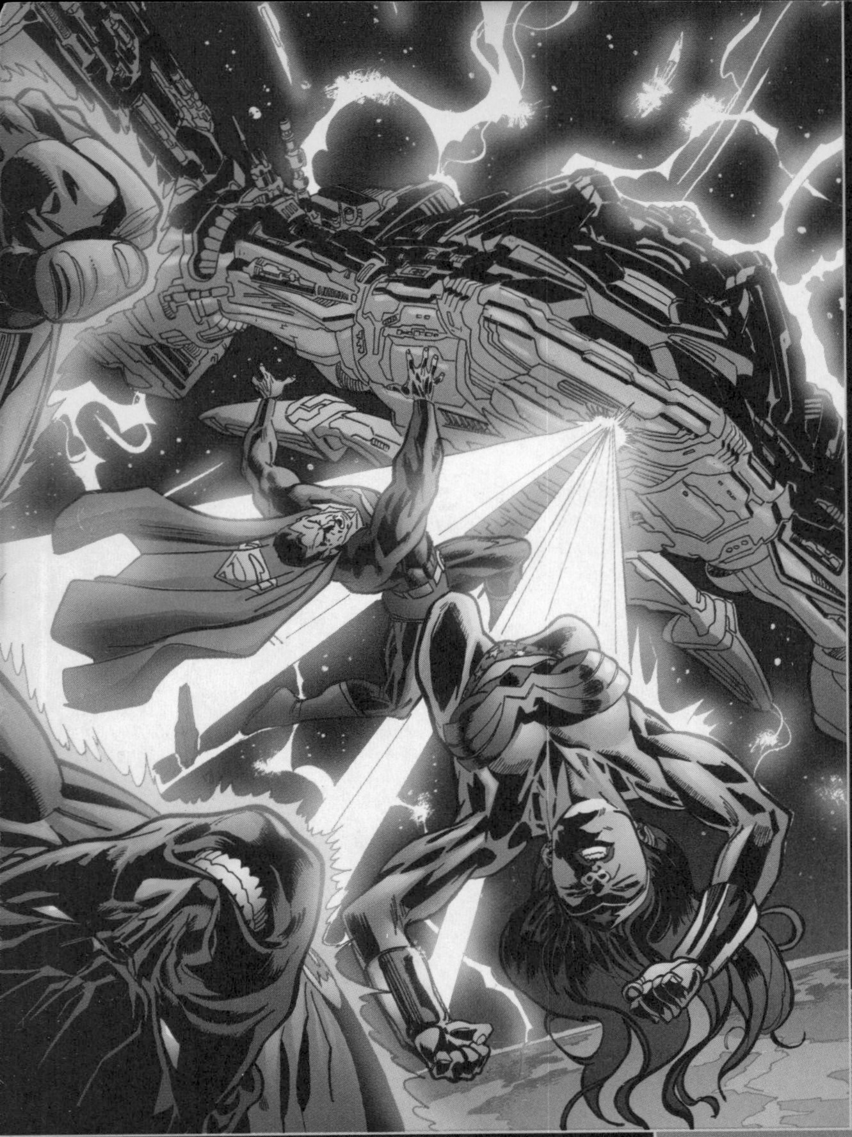

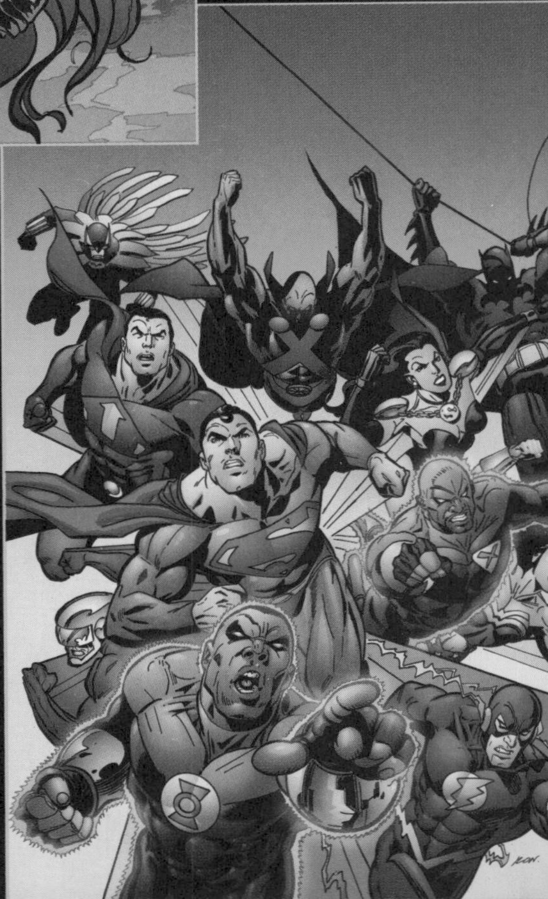

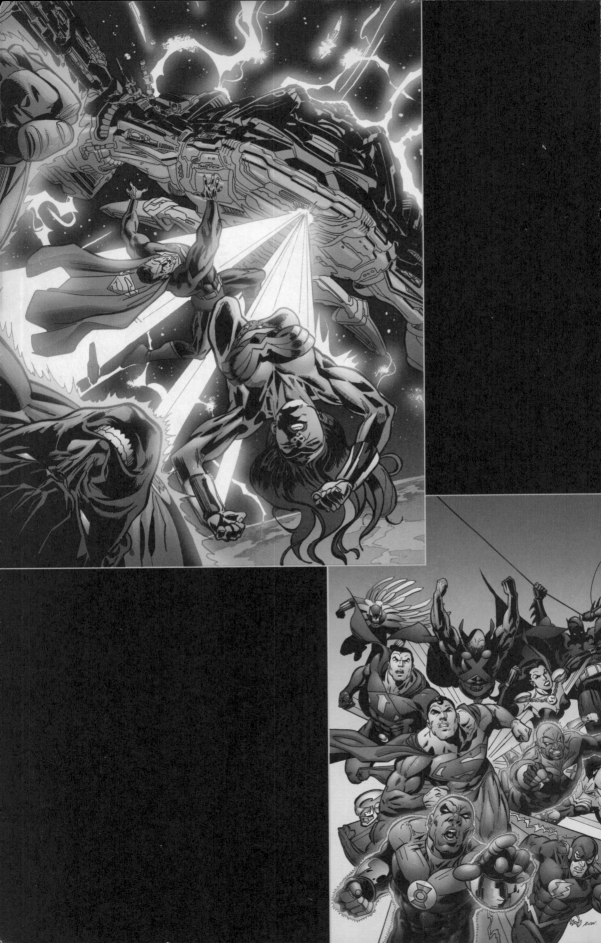